Reports of the Research Committee

of the

Society of Antiquaries of London

No. XXXI

The Excavation of the Roman Villa in Gadebridge Park Hemel Hempstead

1963–8

By

David S. Neal, F.S.A.

With sections by
S. A. Butcher, Dorothy Charlesworth, P. E. Curnow, G. Dannell, R. Goodburn,
R. A. Harcourt, B. R. Hartley, Katharine F. Hartley, J. Liversidge, W. H. Manning,
Stephen Moorhouse, G. C. Morgan, Jocelyn Toynbee, and R. P. Wright.

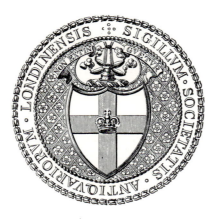

Published by
The Society of Antiquaries of London
Distributed by
Thames and Hudson Ltd
1974

ISBN 0 500 77023 9

PRINTED IN GREAT BRITAIN BY
W. S. MANEY AND SON LIMITED, LEEDS LS9 7DL

CONTENTS

PART I

THE EXCAVATIONS

PART II

THE FINDS

CONTENTS

ILLUSTRATIONS

LIST OF PLATES

LIST OF FIGURES IN THE TEXT

THE FINDS

REFERENCES AND ABBREVIATIONS

Antiq. J.	*Antiquaries Journal.*
Antiq.	*Antiquity.*
Arch.	*Archaeologia.*
A.A.	*Archaeologia Aeliana.*
Arch. Camb.	*Archaeologia Cambrensis.*
Arch. Cant.	*Archaeologia Cantiana.*
Arch. J.	*Archaeological Journal.*
Beds. Arch. J.	*Bedfordshire Archaeological Journal.*
B.R.G.K.	*Bericht der Römisch-Germanischen Kommission.*
Besançon	L. Lerat, 'Catalogue des collections archéologiques de Besançon, ii: les fibules gallo-romaines', *Annales Littéraires de l'Université de Besançon*, iii (1956).
Blackburn Mill	S. Piggott, 'Three Metalwork Hoards of the Roman Period from Southern Scotland', *P.S.A.S.*, LXXXVII (1953), 1 ff.
Bokerly Dyke	A. H. L. Pitt-Rivers, *Excavations in Cranborne Chase*, III (1892).
Brading Villa	H. F. Cleere, 'Roman Domestic Ironwork as illustrated by the Brading Isle of Wight Villa', *B.I.A.* (1958), 55 ff.
Brampton	W. H. Manning, 'A Hoard of Romano-British Ironwork from Brampton, Cumberland', *C. & W.*, LXVI (1966), 1 ff.
Brit.	*Britannia.*
B.M. Guide	British Museum *Guide to the Antiquities of Roman Britain* (1922).
B.M.Q.	*British Museum Quarterly.*
Brough	J. S. Wacher, *Excavations at Brough-on-Humber 1958–1961*, Society of Antiquaries Research Report, XXV (1969).
Brooke	G. C. Brooke, *English Coins* (1932).
B.I.A.	*Bulletin of the Institute of Archaeology.*
Caerleon Amphitheatre	R. E. M. and T. V. Wheeler, 'The Roman Amphitheatre at Caerleon, Monmouthshire', *Arch.*, LXXVIII (1928), 111 ff.
Camerton	W. J. Wedlake, *Excavations at Camerton, Somerset*, Camerton Excavation Club (1958).
Camulodunum	C. F. C. Hawkes and M. R. Hull, *Camulodunum*, Society of Antiquaries Research Report, XIV (1947).
Carlingwark Loch	S. Piggott, 'Three Metalwork Hoards of the Roman Period in Southern Scotland', *P.S.A.S.*, LXXXVII (1953), 1 ff.
C.G.	Central Gaulish *or* Gaul.
C.G.P.	J. A. Stanfield and J. Simpson, *Central Gaulish Potters* (1958).
Colchester	M. R. Hull, *Roman Colchester*, Society of Antiquaries Research Report, XX (1958).
Colchester Kilns	M. R. Hull, *The Roman Potters' Kilns of Colchester*, Society of Antiquaries Research Report, XXI (1963).
Collingwood	R. G. Collingwood and Ian Richmond, *The Archaeology of Roman Britain* (1969).
C & W	*Transactions of the Cumberland and Westmorland Archaeological and Antiquarian Society.*

D.	J. Déchelette, *Les vases céramiques ornés de la Gaule romaine*, II (1904).
Devizes	M. E. Cunnington and E. H. Goddard, *Catalogue of the Antiquities in the Museum . . . at Devizes*, II (1934).
Eckford	S. Piggott, 'Three Metalwork Hoards of the Roman Period from Southern Scotland', *P.S.A.S.*, LXXXVII (1953), 1 ff.
Exner	E. G. Exner, 'Die provinzial römischen Emailfibeln der Rheinlande', *B.R.G.K.*, XXIX (1939), 31 ff.
Faversham	B. Philp, *Excavations at Faversham, 1965* (1968).
Fishbourne, I, II	B. Cunliffe, *Excavations at Fishbourne 1961–1969*: I, *The Site;* II, *The Finds.* Society of Antiquaries Research Reports, XXVI and XXVII (1971).
Glastonbury, I, II	A. Bulleid and H. St. G. Gray, *The Glastonbury Lake Village*, I (1911); II (1917).
Gt. Chesterford	R. C. Neville, 'Descriptions of a Remarkable Deposit of Roman Antiquities of Iron discovered at Great Chesterford, Essex, in 1854', *Arch. J.*, XIII (1856), 1 ff.
G.H.	Guildhall Museum, London.
Hermet	F. Hermet, *La Graufesenque* (1934).
Hod Hill	J. W. Brailsford, *Antiquities from Hod Hill in the Durden Collection*, British Museum (1962).
Inchtuthil	N. S. Angus, G. T. Brown, and H. F. Cleere, 'The Iron Nails from the Roman Legionary Fortress at Inchtuthil, Perthshire', *Journal of the Iron and Steel Institute*, 200 (1962), 956 ff.
Isings	C. Isings, *Roman Glass from Dated Finds* (1957).
Jewry Wall	K. M. Kenyon, *Excavations at the Jewry Wall Site, Leicester*, Society of Antiquaries Research Report, XV (1948).
J.B.A.A.	*Journal of the British Archaeological Association.*
J.R.S.	*Journal of Roman Studies.*
Kingsholm	S. Lysons, *Reliquiae Britannico-Romanae*, II (1817).
Knorr 1912	R. Knorr, *Südgallische Terra Sigillata-Gefässe von Rothweil* (1912).
Knorr 1952	R. Knorr, *Terra-Sigillata-Gefässe des ersten Jahrhunderts mit Töpfernamen* (1952).
L.R.B.C.	R. A. G. Carson, P. Hill, and J. P. C. Kent, *Late Roman Bronze Coinage* (1965).
L	Layer.
London	R. E. M. Wheeler, *London in Roman Times*, L.M. Catalogue no. 3 (1930).
L.M.	London Museum.
Lowther	A. W. G. Lowther, *A Study of the Patterns on Roman Flue-Tiles and their Distribution*, Surrey Archaeological Society Research Paper, 1 (1948).
Lydney	R. E. M. and T. V. Wheeler, *Report on the Excavations of the Prehistoric, Roman and Post-Roman Site in Lydney Park, Gloucestershire*, Society of Antiquaries Research Report, IX (1932).
Lullingstone	G. W. Meates, *Lullingstone Roman Villa* (1955).
Maiden Castle	R. E. M. Wheeler, *Maiden Castle, Dorset*, Society of Antiquaries Research Report, XII (1943).
Mandeure	L. Lerat, 'Les fibules gallo-romaines de Mandeure', *Annales Littéraires de l'Université de Besançon*, XVI (1957).
Med. Arch.	*Medieval Archaeology.*

Newstead	J. Curle, *A Roman Frontier Post and its People: the Fort of Newstead in the Parish of Melrose* (1911).
Nornour	D. Dudley, 'Excavations on Nornour in the Isles of Scilly, 1962–6', *Arch. J.*, cxxiv (1967), 1 ff.
Num. Chron.	*Numismatic Chronicle.*
O.R.L.	*Der Obergermanisch-Rätische Limes des Römerreiches.*
O.	F. Oswald, *An Index of Figure Types on Terra Sigillata* (1937).
Oxon.	*Oxoniensia.*
P.C.A.S.	*Proceedings of the Cambridge Antiquarian Society.*
P. Leeds Phil. and Lit. Soc.	*Proceedings of the Leeds Philosophical and Literary Society.*
P.S.A.S.	*Proceedings of the Society of Antiquaries of Scotland.*
P.S.A.N.H.S.	*Proceedings of the Somerset Archaeological and Natural History Society.*
P.S.I.A.	*Proceedings of the Suffolk Institute of Archaeology.*
Records	*Records of Buckinghamshire.*
Richborough, I–IV	J. P. Bushe-Fox, *Excavations of the Roman Fort at Richborough, Kent*, Society of Antiquaries Research Reports vi (1926), vii (1928), x (1932), xvi (1949).
Richborough, V	B. W. Cunliffe (ed.), *Fifth Report on the Excavations of the Roman Fort at Richborough, Kent*, Society of Antiquaries Research Report, xxiii (1968).
Rivet	A. L. F. Rivet (ed.), *The Roman Villa in Britain* (1969).
R.I.C.	H. Mattingly and E. A. Sydenham, *The Roman Imperial Coinage* (1923).
R.R.C.	E. A. Sydenham, *The Roman Republican Coinage* (1952).
Rotherley	A. H. L. Pitt-Rivers, *Excavations in Cranbourne Chase*, ii (1888).
R.C.H.M.	Royal Commission on Historical Monuments (England).
S.J.	*Saalburg Jahrbuch.*
Sandy	W. H. Manning, 'A Roman Hoard of Iron-Work from Sandy, Beds.', *Beds. Arch. J.*, ii (1964), 50 ff.
Sellye	J. Sellye, 'Les bronzes émaillés de la Pannonie romaine', *Dissertationes Pannonicae*, Second series, 8 (1939).
S.A.C.	*Surrey Archaeological Collections.*
SF	Small find.
Thomas	S. Thomas, *Berliner Jahrbuch*, vi (1966).
T.B.G.A.S.	*Transactions of the Bristol and Gloucestershire Archaeological Society.*
T.S.A.H.A.A.S.	*Transactions of the St. Albans and Hertfordshire Architectural and Archaeological Society.*
V.C.H.	*Victoria County History.*
Verulamium 1936	R. E. M. and T. V. Wheeler, *Verulamium: a Belgic and Two Roman Cities*, Society of Antiquaries Research Report, xi (1936).
Verulamium 1972	S. S. Frere, *Verulamium Excavations*, i, Society of Antiquaries Research Report, xxviii (1972).
Viatores	The Viatores, *Roman Roads in the South-East Midlands* (1969).
W.A.M.	*Wiltshire Archaeological Magazine.*
Woodcuts	A. H. L. Pitt-Rivers, *Excavations in Cranborne Chase*, i (1887).
Woodyates	A. H. L. Pitt-Rivers, *Excavations in Cranborne Chase*, iii (1892).

Wroxeter, I-III   J. P. Bushe-Fox, *Excavations on the site of the Roman Town at Wroxeter, Shropshire*, Society of Antiquaries Research Reports, I (1913), II (1914), IV (1916).

Y.A.J.   *Yorkshire Archaeological Journal.*

Zugmantel   L. Jacobi, 'Kastell Zugmantel', *S.J.*, V for 1913 (1924).

ACKNOWLEDGEMENTS

The writer would like to acknowledge his debt to the Hemel Hempstead Borough Council for bearing the greater part of the cost of excavation, and for providing the Hemel Hempstead Excavation Society with every facility. This society would not have been formed had it not been for the enthusiasm of the Town Clerk, Mr C. W. G. T. Kirk, and the Borough Treasurer, Mr H. Aughton. As well as funds provided by the Borough Council, other donations were received from the general public, Ministry of Public Building and Works, Commission for New Towns, Haverfield Bequest, Society of Antiquaries of London, and the British Academy. Generous grants towards the publication of this report have also been received from the Department of the Environment and the Hemel Hempstead Borough Council.

The following industries in Hemel Hempstead also provided assistance in the form of machinery and printing services: Bernard Sunley, Atlas Copco, Easy Stages (Access Equipment), Masters Plant, and Addressograph Multigraph. But for the personal interest in the excavating of Mr Carpenter of Bernard Sunley, and Mr Ron Williams of Atlas Copco, who provided machinery, the excavation would have taken many more years to complete.

The author is indebted to many volunteers, but is particularly grateful to Mr John Collis, Miss M. Pearce, Mr M. Haynes, Miss Sara Slater, Miss Jane Wyborn, Mr John Bowring, Mr Roger Stangar, Mr A. Righini, Miss Sally Stewart, Miss Gillian Thomas, Mr Christopher White, Mr Jonathan Dunkley, Mr Malcolm Harrison, Mr Christopher Henderson, Mr Christopher C. Pratt, Mrs M. Cousins, Miss Katherine Ede, Miss Meg Amesden, and to his wife, Mrs Gillian Neal, for either supervising the work, or organizing the pottery shed. Mr James Brown of Verulamium Museum deserves special thanks for undertaking all the site photography, and his splendid photographs illustrate this report. He never declined the invitation to climb hair-raising heights to carry out his work.

The line illustrations are mainly the work of the author, but much help was given in the preparation of the pottery drawings by Mr Jonathan Dunkley. Many of the bronzes were drawn by Mr Peter Broxton. Miss G. D. Jones, Mrs C. Boddington, Mr James C. Thorn and Mr F. Gardiner have also provided illustrations.

The author would also like to express his gratitude to Mr P. Curnow for identifying the coins; Miss S. A. Butcher for the notes on the brooches and miscellaneous bronzes; Professor J. M. C. Toynbee for the note on the bronze head of Medusa; Dr W. H. Manning for the iron report; Dr G. J. Wainwright for comments on the flint artifacts; Miss D. Charlesworth for her contribution on the glass; Mr G. Dannell for his notes on the samian pottery; Mr B. R. Hartley for his notes on the samian potters' stamps; Mrs K. Hartley for the note on the mortaria; Mr R. Harcourt for his report on the animal bones; Mr G. C. Morgan for his identification of the charcoal and slag samples; Professor A. J. Cain and Mr A. Featherstone for the notes on the molluscs; Mr R. P. Wright for his identification of the graffiti; and Mr S. Moorhouse for his note on the medieval and post-medieval pottery.

The paper was read in typescript by Miss G. D. Jones, Mr R. B. Adams, Miss S. A. Butcher and Professor S. S. Frere, to all of whom I am grateful for making many valuable suggestions. Professor Frere has constantly guided the work, and gave many useful observations on the site. Thanks are offered to other contributors mentioned in the text.

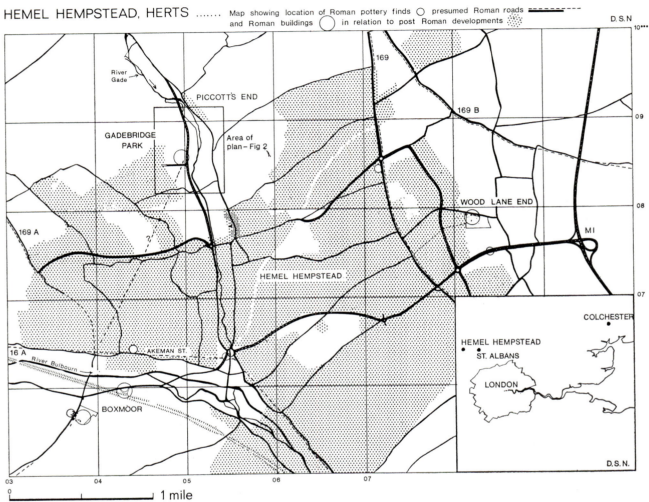

FIG. 1

INTRODUCTION

THE SITE

THE site is in the foothills of the Chilterns (fig. 1). It lies about half a mile to the north of Hemel Hempstead, and a quarter mile south-west of the village of Piccotts End (Grid Reference TL 051086) (fig. 2). The villa stands on the west bank of the River Gade, over-looking a wide floodplain, commanding a fine view up and down the valley (frontispiece, pl. I). The Gade itself rises as a spring three miles to the north, and flows past the site, through Hemel Hempstead, into the canalized Bulbourne stream at Two Waters. Standing at an ordnance datum (OD) level of 300 ft., the site is sheltered from westerly winds by a hill rising to a height of 380 ft. The subsoil is chalk, with areas of clay above, but near the river the clay is mixed with gravel. In areas away from the river, the clay and chalk are mixed to form marl.

Originally the Leighton Buzzard road ran north from Hemel Hempstead on the east bank of the river and passed through Piccotts End, but this route was superseded by a new road on the west bank in 1963, which unfortunately ran over part of the villa. Immediately to the south of the site is Galley Hill, which connects the Gadebridge Estate with the main road. This road is in a cutting, which when made destroyed a Roman gully and a trackway. Opportunity was provided during the 1966 season to observe work on a water catchment scheme east of the river but no finds were made.

The alignment of the Roman Road leading south from the villa (fig. 3) suggests that it connected with the estate at Boxmoor,[1] two miles to the south, either by a direct route, or a spur from route 169A.[2] It is also probable that the villa was linked with the Roman site at Wood Lane End,[3] two miles to the south-east, possibly by a trackway leading to route 169.[4] There may also have been a route running north, linking Gadebridge with the possible sites at Great Gaddesden,[5] Little Gaddesden,[6] and Ivinghoe.[7] It is also likely that the river was wider in Roman times, and that it ran much closer to the villa than it does today. An old water-leat bank lined with trees runs to, and away from, the Roman baths.

No trace of Roman buildings was found in the upper Gade valley until 1962, but a coin-hoard was found on the site in the 1840s and was published by Sir John Evans in his account of the excavations on the Roman Villas at Boxmoor.[8] This coin-hoard is discussed by Mr P. Curnow in an appendix to this report (p. 120).

---

[1] This villa was excavated by Sir John Evans in the 1850s. (*Arch.*, XXXV (1853), 56), and re-excavated by the author 1966–70 (interim report, *Brit.*, I (1970), 156.)

[2] Viatores.

[3] N.G.R., TL 083078. Trial excavations directed by the author (unpublished).

[4] Viatores.

[5] N.G.R., TL 028113. R.C.H.M. *Herts.*, p. 100.

[6] N.G.R., SP 995139. *Arch. J.*, CXXIV (1967), 154.

[7] N.G.R., SP 966171. *Records*, XVII (1961–5), 440.

[8] *Arch.*, XXXV (1853), 56.

GADEBRIDGE PARK, HEMEL HEMPSTEAD

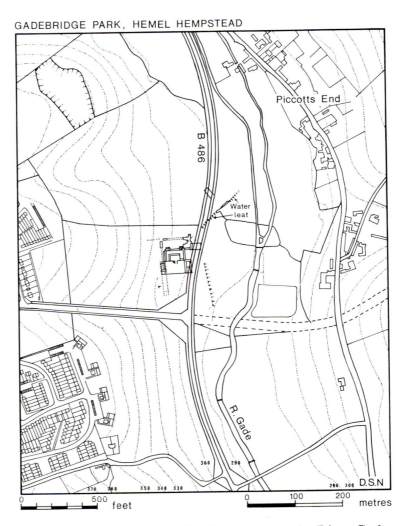

FIG. 2. Situation of the villa in relation to the River Gade
and modern buildings

METHOD OF EXCAVATION

Trial excavations began in the Easter of 1963 to determine the extent of the site and, as a result of these, work started on the baths. Three concrete bench points were set in the field to form the basis of the excavation grid, which was originally based on units of 50 ft., divided into four trenches, each 10 ft. wide, with intervening baulks 2 ft. 6 in. wide. Over the six-year period of excavation this grid-pattern was discarded in favour of larger trenches, although the trench alignment remained the same (fig. 3).

The whole operation was highly mechanized, being aided by dumper trucks, air compressors, bulldozers, and other mechanical diggers. Earth-moving machines were used to

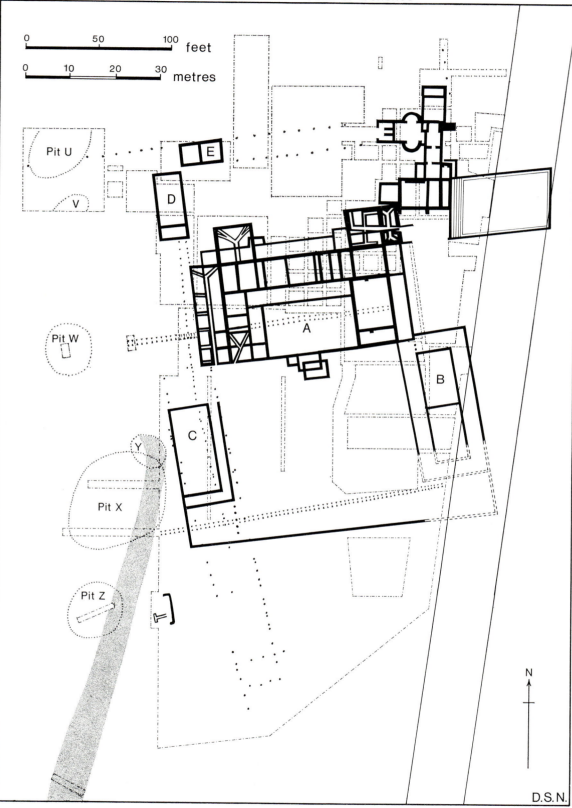

FIG. 3

remove over-burden covering the courtyards, the chalk quarries, and the outer wings. The area of the baths and Building A was dug by hand.

Throughout the excavation, future preservation of the villa had to be borne in mind; therefore many of the solid floors were not cut through. Sufficient dating evidence was obtained from below floors that had been removed by the plough. The site was backfilled after every excavation. The finds are in the possession of the Hemel Hempstead Borough Council (from 1974 the Dacorum District Council).

SUMMARY (fig. 4)

PERIOD 1.　The earliest buildings on the site were probably a timber house dated c. A.D. 75, with an isolated three-roomed bath-house. An area of farmland immediately to the south of the villa was bordered by ditches.

PERIOD 2.　No structural changes have been detected in the Period 1 villa, but additional services were added to the bath-house (date not known).

PERIOD 3.　In the Antonine period, Building A was constructed in stone over the site of the Period 1 occupation. The building was of the winged-corridor type with corridors all the way around. The south-east wing was of two storeys, the lower level being a semi-basement. A new wing was constructed on the west side of the bath-house.

PERIOD 4.　In the late second or early third century additional wings were constructed enclosing an outer courtyard (Buildings B and C). The bath-house was also enlarged.

PERIOD 5.　Building C was demolished and by c. A.D. 300 Building A had undergone major alterations. The wings were extended and extra rooms added to the north side of the building. Buildings D, E and F were also constructed. The outer courtyard was transferred to the north side of the villa.

PERIOD 6.　By c. A.D. 325 a large bathing pool was built on to the bath-house, and a massive heated room built on to the west side of Building A. The scale of rebuilding on the bath-house suggests the possibility that the bathing establishment now became the primary attraction of the settlement.

PERIOD 7.　In the mid-fourth century the baths and villa appear to have been deliberately demolished. Stockades or cattle pens were built into the northern courtyard and over Building A and the earlier site of Building C. Occupation continued in Building E until the late fourth century, and may have extended into the early fifth century.

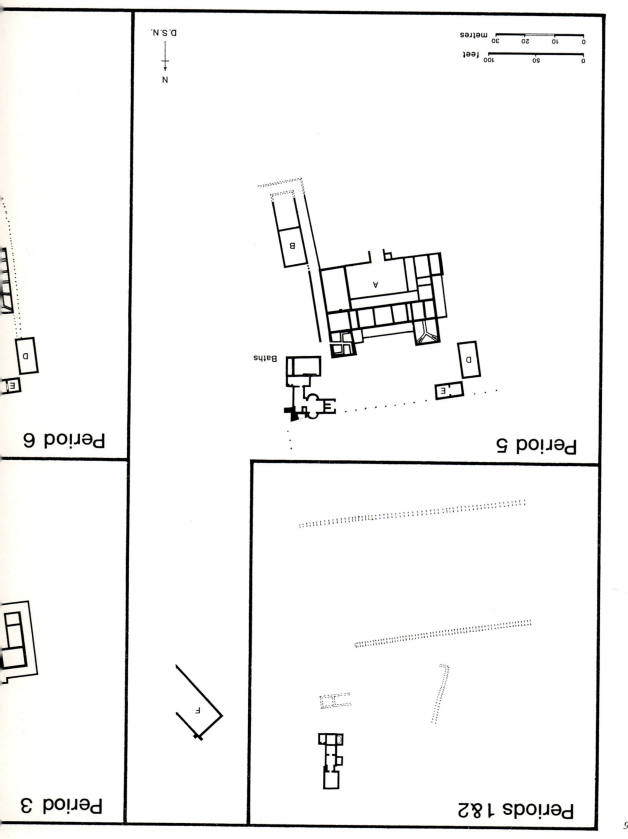

Period 6

Period 5

D.S.N.

N

Baths

B

A

D

E

metres
30 20 10 0

feet
100 50 0

Period 3

Periods 1&2

F

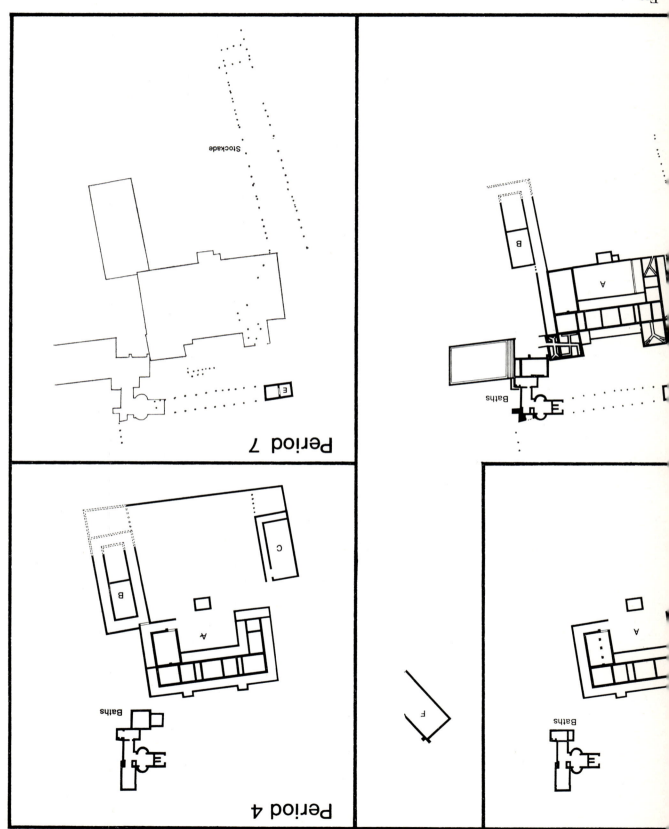

Fig. 4

PART I

The Excavations

PERIOD 1

PRE-MASONRY BUILDING (fig. 9)

A small three-roomed bath-house was found which must have been associated with a dwelling-house. Only slight traces of this house survived.

TRACES of occupation earlier than the Antonine house were found over most of the northern area of the site, but the greatest concentration was beneath Building A (fig. 5). Beneath Room 20, the inner courtyard, Room 29 and Room 34 was a V-shaped ditch, Ditch 1; this continued west beyond the villa where it was cut by a chalk quarry, Pit W. Its western limit was not found, but its eastern extent was beneath the east wall of Room 20. The ditch (Section N–O, fig. 6) was 6 ft. (1.83 m.) wide and 3 ft. 6 in. (1.07 m.) deep. Amongst the filling were large quantities of pottery ranging over a wide period, but this may be explained by the ditch having been open for a long time. Fragments of worn pottery in the Belgic tradition were found together with poppy-head beakers, and samian sherds of late Antonine date (Pottery nos. 1–140, figs. 95–9).

125 ft. (38.10 m.) to the south of Ditch 1 was another smaller V-shaped ditch, Ditch 2 (fig. 3), which ran parallel to it and measured 4 ft. (1.22 m.) in width by 2 ft. 9 in. (.84 m.) in depth (Section EE–FF, fig. 7). To the west it petered out just short of the incoming Roman trackway but the eastern limit was not found as it continued up to, and under, the modern road. Much of the pottery in the southern ditch is later in date than that in the northern, but this may be explained by the fact that the ditch was too far south of the occupation area to have been used as a convenient rubbish dump, and the pottery found in it (Pottery nos. 230–57, fig. 104) is associated with the occupation of the earlier phases of the outer wings (Buildings B and C). The whole length was excavated and the only sections to yield significant quantities of pottery were those adjacent to these buildings. Here the pottery was not found at the bottom of the ditch (as was the pottery in the ditch beneath Building A) but above a thick layer of silting (L4). This would suggest that the ditch had been open for some time before any refuse was thrown into it. The primary silting (L4) was chalky clay covered by a layer of sandy clay (L3) with the refuse layer (L2) containing pottery, bone and oyster shells above. Oyster shells were not common on the site, and the only places where they occurred in quantity were this layer, and the well (see p. 27 below).

It is probable that both ditches indicate a division of farmland, since ancient plough-furrow marks were found within the area. It is unlikely that they formed a boundary to a cattle enclosure, as they were not linked.

B2

Beneath Rooms 25 and 26 in Building A (fig. 5) was a gully running on a north-east/ south-west alignment, which also contained pottery similar to that in the adjacent Ditch 1. The gully turned beneath Rooms 25 and 26 towards the east, but no trace of it was found in Room 24. Northwards it extended for 60 ft. (18.30 m.), beyond which it had been eroded. Its purpose is uncertain, but it could have been a gully around the corner of a building, because the angle of turn at its southern end was almost 90°.

Cut into the southern side of the Ditch 1, east of Room 29, was an oven constructed in roofing tiles (fig. 5), circular in plan. Another oven was found further north (east of Room 29, fig. 16). It was oval in plan and 4 ft. (1.22 m.) long by 18 in. (.45 m.) wide by 9 in. (.23 m.) deep. It was constructed in chalk and clay reinforced with tiles and was sealed by the clay make-up for the later corridor. Pottery forms similar to 14, 60, 62, 95 and 142 were found in the filling of this oven.

Cut by the eastern wall of Room 28, and by a Period 5 division wall in the corridor, was an area of crushed-tile mortar (fig. 16), approximately 2 ft. (.61 m.) long by 1 ft. (.31 m.) wide. One side of it was curved. The building materials would suggest it to have been the base of a circular water tank or possibly a lower foundation requiring waterproofing.

East of Building A (fig. 5) was an area of occupation associated with the flint foundations of a structure, Room 17 (pl. IIa), approximately 32 ft. (9.75 m.) long by 12 ft. (3.65 m.) wide, with a partition wall dividing the area into two. The structure was extremely eroded, and had been partially cut by the later Period 4 plunge-bath, Room 13, and used as a foundation for the Period 6 screen or corridor walls linking Room 18 with the bathing pool.

South of this structure was a quern of Hertfordshire Puddingstone (SF 697, fig. 84) and an oven or hearth associated with a chalk floor (Section S–T, fig. 6). The floor extended 17 ft. (5.18 m.) south of the building, but no post-holes or sleeper beams were found associated with it. This floor was sealed by a layer of clay (L12) which was either put down prior to the construction of Building A or was collapsed wall-daub. As some of the surviving fragments are on the same alignment as the later building A, it is possible that the dwelling-house of Period 1 lay on the same site.

THE BATHS (fig. 8)

Though little structural evidence for the early villa was found, the original three-roomed bath-house (pl. IIb) was probably associated with it. The bath-house lay on a north/south axis, approximately 30 ft. (9.15 m.) from the occupation just described. The building was 41 ft. (12.50 m.) long by 12 ft. 6 in. (3.81 m.) wide, but was reduced to 11 ft. 6 in. (3.50 m.) wide by a 'dog leg' in Room 2. Room 1 was the *caldarium*, Room 2 the *tepidarium*, and Room 3 the *frigidarium*; the stoke-hole was situated in the north wall of Room 1. The walls were 2 ft. (.61 m.) wide and survived in places to a height of 3 ft. 6 in. (1.07 m.); they were constructed in flint and hard white mortar, with a double bonding course of roofing tiles. The walls close to the stoke-hole, forming the reduced area of Room 1, were faced throughout with roofing tiles except for a foundation of flints rising 9 in. (.23 m.) above the floor. All the tiles had been burnt.

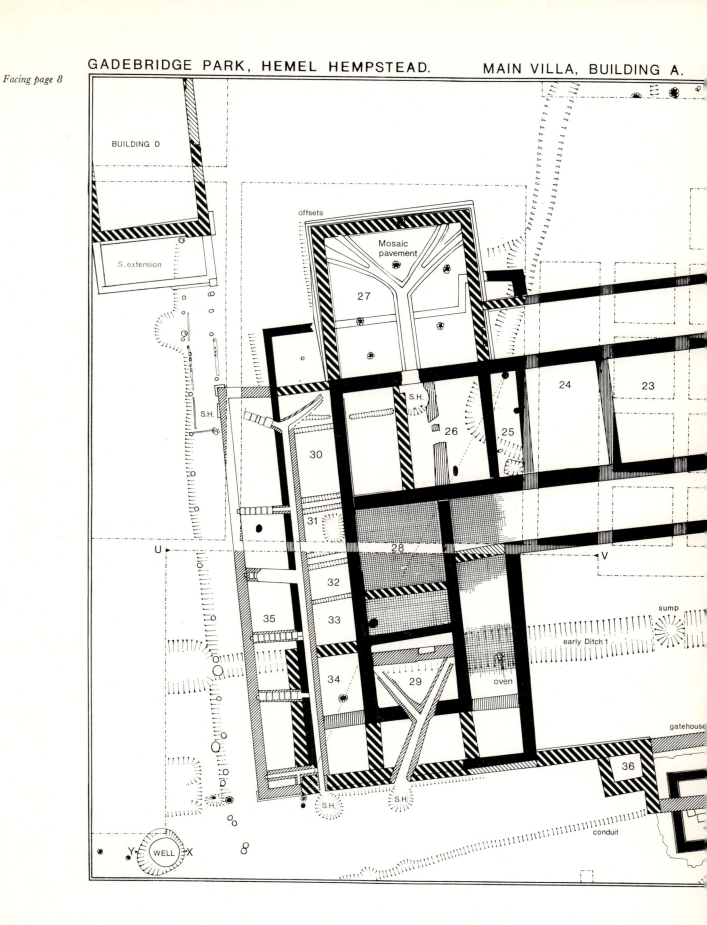

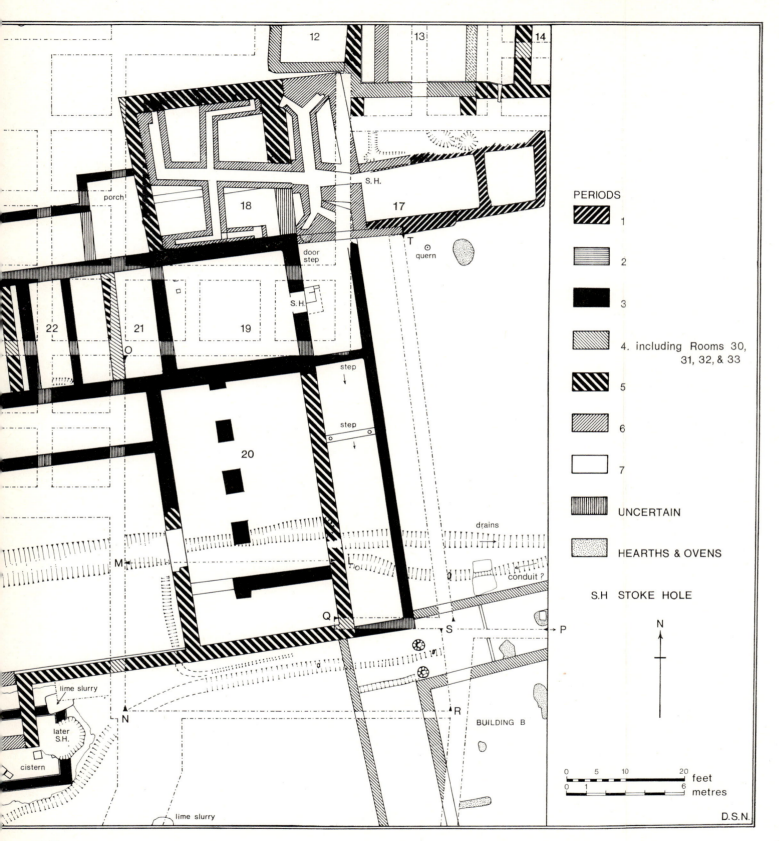

PERIODS

▨	1
▤	2
■	3
▨	4. including Rooms 30, 31, 32, & 33
▨	5
▨	6
☐	7
▥	UNCERTAIN
▦	HEARTHS & OVENS

S.H STOKE HOLE

N

0   5   10   20 feet
0   1   6 metres

D.S.N.

porch

12   13   14

S.H.

18   17

door step   T   quern

S.H.

22   21   19

O

step

step

20

M   L

drains

Q   conduit ?

S   P

R   BUILDING B

lime slurry

later S.H.

cistern

lime slurry

FIG. 5

Section L –M, Room 20.   Section N-O, Courtyard and Southern Corridor, Building A.

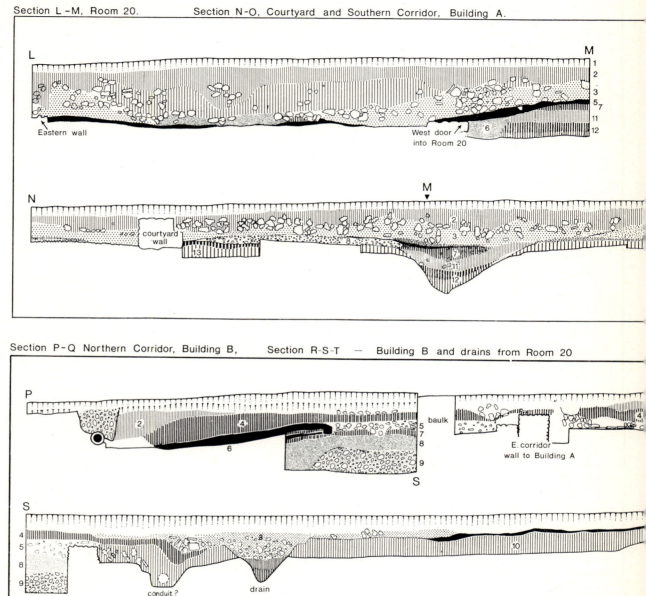

Section P–Q Northern Corridor, Building B,   Section R-S-T — Building B and drains from Room 20

FIG. 6

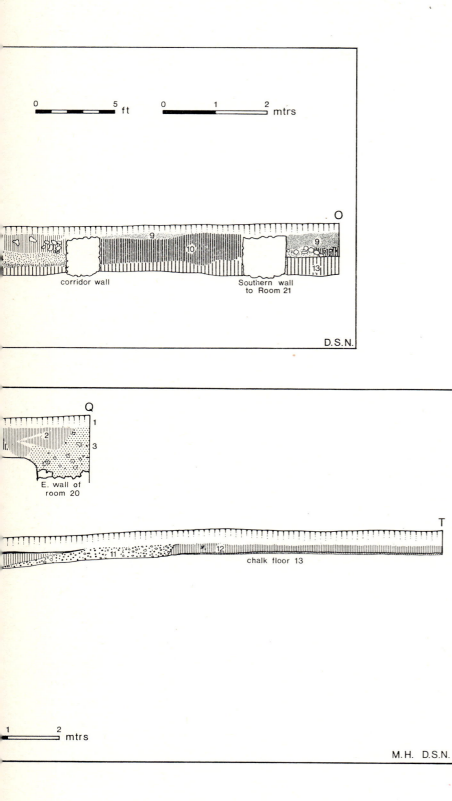

Layer No.	Description of layer	Pottery Nos. illustrated
1	Ploughsoil	—
2	Brown earth mixed with flints and small building rubble	—
3	Destruction level, with heavy flints and yellow mortar	—
4	Collapsed red painted *opus signinum* wall rendering	—
5	Silty black soil mixed with charcoal and occupational rubbish	259–323
6	Fine dark grey silt filling hollow dug to stop water entering Room 20	—
7	Clay and stone filling of Ditch 1	—
8	Stony surface of courtyard	—
9	Chalk build-up for floors	—
10	Clay build-up for southern corridor	—
11	Earth brown clay filling of Ditch 1	—
12	Lower filling of Ditch 1, comprising grey silt and pebbles	1–140
13	Disturbed brown clay	—

Layer No.	Description of layer
1	Ploughsoil
2	Brown earth mixed with small flints and building rubble
3	Destruction rubble over robbed wall of Room 20
4	Clay spread over northern corridor of Building B
5	Chalk and flint rubble
6	Thick layer of burning over ovens in northern corridor, Building B
7	Clay
8	Black silty clay with small stones. Geological feature possibly associated with the river
9	Dark brown clay with many flints. Geological feature as 8 above
10	Dark grey clay soil with black occupation, and cobbled layer above
11	Tile chippings and mortar
12	Clay covering chalk floor 13
13	Chalk floor

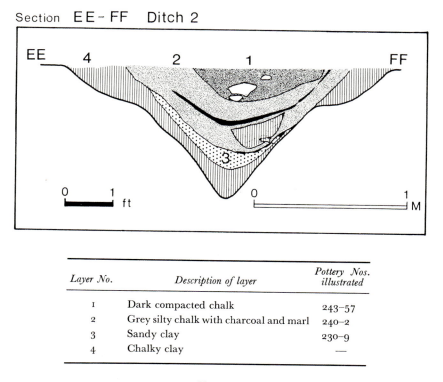

Section E E - F F   Ditch 2

Layer No.	Description of layer	Pottery Nos. illustrated
1	Dark compacted chalk	243–57
2	Grey silty chalk with charcoal and marl	240–2
3	Sandy clay	230–9
4	Chalky clay	—

FIG. 7

Room 1 was divided from Room 2 by a cross wall, with a centrally positioned space 2 ft. 6 in. (.76 m.) wide. In the east wall of Room 2 was a drain for condensation or for any water that might have flooded into the lower hypocaust; the drain appeared to have been a secondary feature as it was cut through the wall and left unpatched. If the hypocaust was being flooded, this would explain the presence of a V-shaped ditch on the west side of Rooms 1 and 2. The ditch was 4 ft. (1.22 m.) wide by 3 ft. (.91 m.) deep, and appears to have been confined to the length of the bath-suite. An *opus signinum* door-step 2 ft. 6 in. (.76 m.) wide survived in the wall between Rooms 2 and 3. It was 3 ft. 6 in. (1.07 m.) above the lower hypocaust floor in Room 2: presumably the upper floor of Room 2 must have been about level with the door-step. No evidence was found for the position of flues or *pilae*, but this may be explained by the reconstruction-work in Period 3 when the original baths were gutted of useful building materials.

Immediately to the south of the Period 6 bathing pool was a gully (Section E–F, fig. 40) which, when found, was believed to be an overflow for the pool. This assumption was probably correct, but it is also possible that it was a leat from the river, and was originally associated with the early bath-suite. Pottery in the gully was contemporary with the pottery in the ditch below Building A. It was approximately 8 ft. (2.44 m.) wide and 2 ft. 6 in. (.76 m.) deep and was filled with river-gravels.

PERIOD 2

The bath-house was enlarged by the addition of hot and cold plunge-baths, an apodyterium and a praefurnium.

THE BATHS (figs. 8 and 9)

Period 2 rebuilding was confined to the baths, where a hot douche, Room 4, was added against the west side of Room 1, and another room, Room 5, containing a cold plunge-bath, was built against the west wall of Room 3. An *apodyterium* (Room 6) was built against the eastern side of Room 3, and a *praefurnium* (Room 7) built on to the northern end of the baths. The Period 2 additions are likely to be earlier than Building A because pottery again identical to that found in Ditch 1 below Building A was found in the *praefurnium* (fig. 10, Pottery nos. 141–3, fig. 99) sealed by a later Period 3 floor (L 3, Section A–B, fig. 11).

Room 4

Room 4 measured 6 ft. 6 in. (1.98 m.) by 4 ft. (1.22 m.) with walls 1 ft. 9 in. (.53 m.) wide built in flint and hard white mortar. The room may have contained a hot douche similar to the Purbeck marble basin found to the east of Building A (SF 706, fig. 85). Where the room had cut through the western wall of Room 1 the original wall was repaired with bonding tiles. The floor was of *opus signinum*, identical in colour and texture to the lower hypocaust floor in Room 1, and was confined to this room. With the construction of the new floor it is evident that the *pilae* and consequently the upper hypocaust floor were removed and rebuilt. At this time, the division-walls between Room 1 and 2 had holes cut through them, possibly to improve the circulation of hot air.

Room 5

Room 5 measured 8 ft. 6 in. (2.59 m.) by 4 ft. (1.22 m.) and had walls 1 ft. 9 in. (.53 m.) wide, and the remains of an apsidal cold plunge-bath. When the large plunge-bath (Room 13) was constructed to the south of the baths in Period 4 the wall separating the bath from Room 3 was demolished and the foundation covered with a mortar floor.

Room 6

Room 6 measured 7 ft. 6 in. (2.29 m.) by 5 ft. (1.53 m.) and had walls 2 ft. (.61 m.) wide. The walls were a little irregular in plan, and thicker than those in Rooms 4 and 5, but this was probably because the foundations had to be deeper and stronger than those in the opposite rooms since the ground east of the bath-suite sloped down into the leat. In the north wall was a small niche measuring 2 ft. (.61 m.) by 1 ft. (.30 m.), the purpose of which was not determined, but the room was considerably altered in later periods, so much so that total dissection of the wall would have been necessary to unravel it. This was not done. The room, situated on the south side of the bath-suite, and approached in Period 5 by a corridor, was either part of the *frigidarium* or possibly an *apodyterium*.

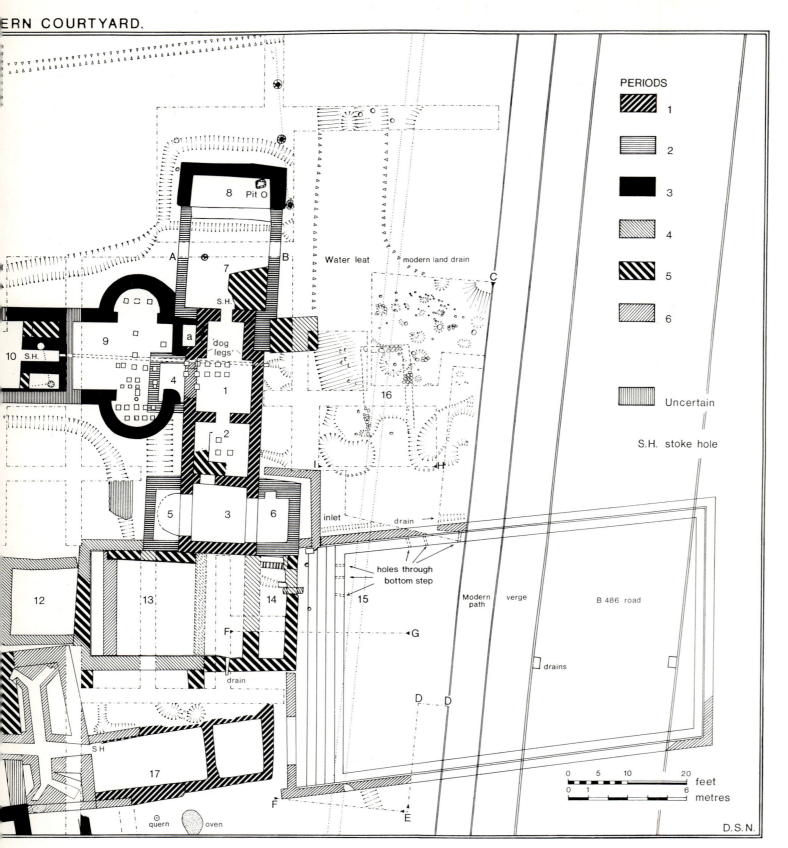

PERIODS

1

2

3

4

5

6

Uncertain

S.H. stoke hole

FIG. 8

D.S.N.

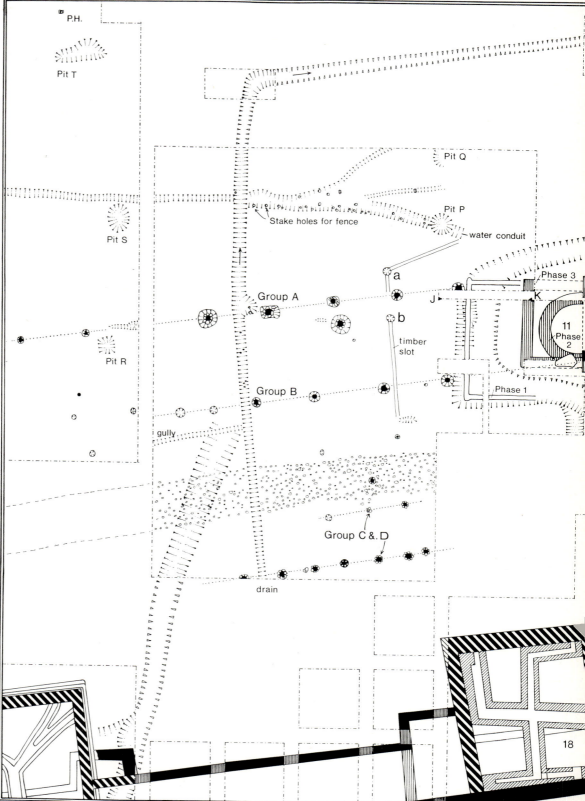

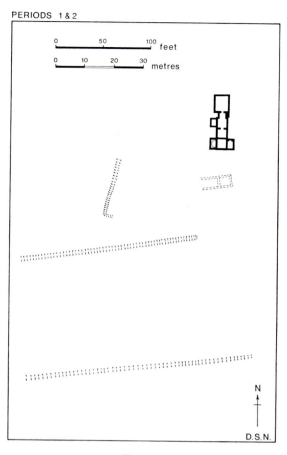

PERIODS 1 & 2

Fig. 9

Room 7 (fig. 10; Section A–B, fig. 11)

Room 7 measured 13 ft. 6 in. (4.11 m.) by 15 ft. (4.58 m.) and butted against the north side of Room 1. The walls, 1 ft. 9 in. (.53 m.) wide, were constructed in very large flint nodules and white mortar and survived in places to a height of 2 ft. 6 in. (.76 m.). The floor was level with the lower floor of the hypocaust in Room 1, and was 2 ft. 6 in. (.76 m.) below the outside ground level. As the room was built adjacent to the stoke-hole, it was probably a *praefurnium*. Unfortunately the levels in the stoke-hole could not be related to Room 1 as a Period 5 masonry feature and a robber trench cut through them. The room also appeared to have been used for other purposes, as follows.

The lowest level in the *praefurnium* was a natural clay floor covered by a charcoal spread (L 8). Above this was a layer composed of tile chippings, tile dust, *tesserae*, and a thin layer of lime mortar (L 7). This could have been a floor, but as the surface was irregular and thickened towards the east, where larger fragments of tile predominated, it is possible that the level represents the waste created from the crushing of tiles used to prepare *opus signinum* floors.

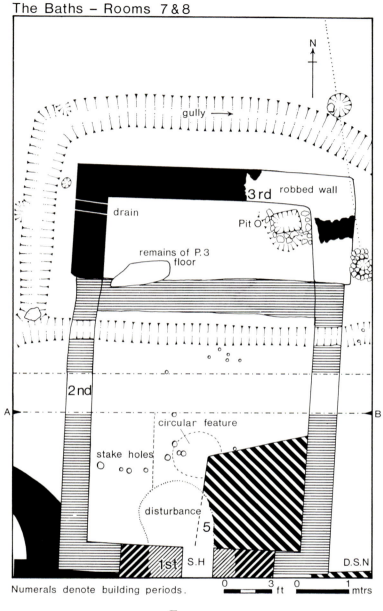

The Baths – Rooms 7 & 8

Numerals denote building periods.

F IG. 10

On the west side of the room was a layer of clay which extended 4 ft. (1.22 m.) east of the wall. Above this was a layer of fine grey wood ash (L 6) believed to have been raked from the furnace. The eastern edge of the clay ran parallel to the wall so it is possible that a sleeper beam existed here. There was also a circular feature, 3 in. (.08 m.) deep, filled with fine wood ash; no post-holes or nails were found associated with it and its purpose is doubtful.

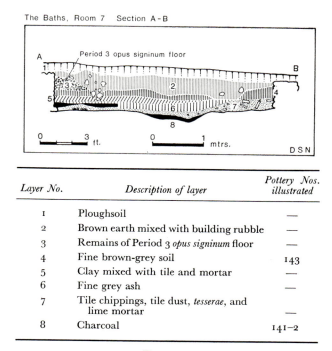

The Baths, Room 7   Section A – B

Layer No.	Description of layer	Pottery Nos. illustrated
1	Ploughsoil	—
2	Brown earth mixed with building rubble	—
3	Remains of Period 3 *opus signinum* floor	—
4	Fine brown-grey soil	143
5	Clay mixed with tile and mortar	—
6	Fine grey ash	—
7	Tile chippings, tile dust, *tesserae*, and lime mortar	—
8	Charcoal	141–2

FIG. 11

Cut through the ash (L 6) were a number of stake-holes which formed a circle and which are believed to have formed a receptacle for ash. When the western wing was built in Period 3 the room was sealed by an *opus signinum* floor (L 3).

During the construction of the *praefurnium* the 'dog-leg' in the east wall of Room 1 (fig. 8) was filled by a clasping wall.

PERIOD 3 (fig. 12)

In the late Antonine period the earlier dwelling-house of Period 1 was demolished and a new masonry house was constructed. It was of winged-corridor type, with a corridor around all sides of the building. The south-east wing was of two storeys, the lower level (Room 20) being a semi-basement. In front, and partially enclosing the courtyard, was a water cistern, served by a well. The baths were also extensively modernized and enlarged by the addition of a new wing.

THE BATHS

Rooms 9 and 10 (fig. 8)

With the construction of a new villa, in the late Antonine period, the existing bath-buildings were enlarged. The rebuilding resulted in almost total reconstruction of the existing structure, as the level of the hypocaust floors was raised by approximately 3 ft. (.91 m.). This was probably an attempt to protect the new wing from flooding, which appears to have affected the baths of Periods 1 and 2.

The new wing (pl. III*a*) was 32 ft. (9.76 m.) long and was constructed against the western side of Room 1. It had apses, presumably to contain hot plunge-baths, in the north and south walls and a stoke-hole on its western side. With the transfer of the stoke-hole, the function of the individual rooms was altered. The new wing became the *caldarium* and the original *praefurnium* (pl. III*b*), now extended towards the north, and the *caldarium* (Rooms 7 and 1) became the *tepidarium*. The plunge-bath (5), and Rooms 3 and 6 remained unaltered. The hot plunge-bath or douche (4) was transferred to the apses in the new wing.

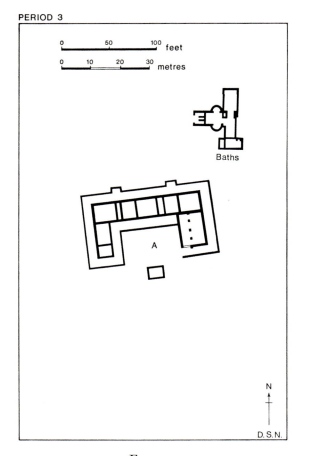

FIG. 12

A drain (pl. IV*a*), made from re-used relief-patterned flue-tiles (pl. IV*b*), was constructed beneath the lower hypocaust floor to take water from the stoke-hole to the eastern side of the building (pl. IV*c*). In addition to the flue-tiles many shaped fragments of tile had also been re-used in the construction of the southern apse, and of the flue channels or *testudo* supports in the stoke-hole (fig. 43, pl. V*a*). These tiles varied in type, semi-circular, triangular and rectangular examples being present — their odd shapes suggest that this material also came from the earlier bath-house. All the flue-tiles in the drain were burnt; some were decorated with the 'W'-Chevron roller-stamp design (SF 714, fig. 86 and pl. IVb),[1] and others had comb-patterns. A single example was decorated with a 'diamond and lattice' pattern (SF 716, fig. 86); it was found at the easternmost point of the drain, outside the building, and may have been added at a later date. In the northern and southern apses square tiles supported circular *pilae*, yet no circular *pilae* were found *in situ* elsewhere. The variety of sizes and lack of arrangement among the other *pilae* suggest they were later than the wing, and were repairs. Frequent repairs to the upper floors and *pilae* were probably necessary, especially in the vicinity of the fire. The *pilae* on the floor of Rooms 1 and 2 belonged to Period 5.

A rectangular feature (*a*, fig. 8) measuring internally 2 ft. 3 in. (.69 m.) by 3 ft. 6 in. (1.07 m.) was constructed south-east of the northern apse, and occupied the space created by the 'dog-leg' in the western wall of the Period 1 baths. Its floor was level with the floor of the new wing and was lined with crushed-tile mortar, identical to the plaster lining the interior walls of the new extension. Its purpose is uncertain.

When the level of the hypocaust in Room 3 was raised, the door between Rooms 2 and 3 became obsolete and was blocked, although it is possible the door remained in the same relative position but was raised 3 ft. (.91 m.).

Owing to robbing and Period 7 disturbances the relationship and function of the features on the west side of the bath wing are uncertain, but they are later than the wing (with the exception of the gully which is probably contemporary) and construction can be placed in the following sequence:

Phase 1: room constructed over gully immediately west of Room 11 and possibly associated with a corridor paved with *opus signinum*.

Phase 2: apse constructed against west wall of *praefurnium*.

Phase 3: apse demolished and replaced by a square room.

Gully

The gully is believed to have served two purposes (a) as a surface water drain to prevent water from the uphill slope penetrating the hypocaust — a similar purpose to the V-shaped ditch west of Rooms 1 and 2; and (b) as an eaves-drip.[2] The gully did not drain the Period 4 plunge-bath (Room 13) because its original floor was slightly lower than the level of the gully, and in later periods the bath was drained from the south-east. Nor did the gully drain the Period 2 plunge-bath (Room 5) because its floor was also deeper than the level of the gully. The gully drained northwards, encircled the baths and flowed into the leat. In Period 5, Room 7 and its extension 8 were demolished and the gully diverted across the remains (pl. IIIb).

---

[1] For type series and distribution of decorated flue tiles see Lowther.

[2] From the large numbers of pieces of frost-fractured tile found in the gully, the baths would appear to have had a tiled roof, probably pitched.

PHASE 1

On the west side of the wing a room measuring 18 ft. (5.49 m.) by at least 12 ft. (3.65 m.), with a floor 2 ft. 6 in. (.76 m.) below the level of the outside surface, was built (Section J–K, fig. 13). The walls of the room were constructed in timber and wattle-and-daub supported on sleeper beams approximately 9 in. (.23 m.) wide (L 6, filling of) laid over the filling of the gully (L 10). The room was floored with a thin mortar skin laid on a bed of clay (L 9). No evidence was found to suggest its use, but its relationship to the stoke-hole indicates it to have been part of the *praefurnium*.

West of the west wall of the room, but on the surface level, was a timber slot which may have been the position of a north-south corridor wall. This feature was associated with two post-holes, *a* and *b* (fig. 8), which were probably the positions of vertical supports for a roof, and with the remains of an *opus signinum* floor much damaged by the plough. Slight traces of this floor were found just north of the swastika-shaped hypocaust, Room 18, making it possible that the corridor ran south to the east porch (later cut by the construction of Room 18) in the northern corridor of Building A. The alignment of post-holes *a* and *b* with others further south is a coincidence.

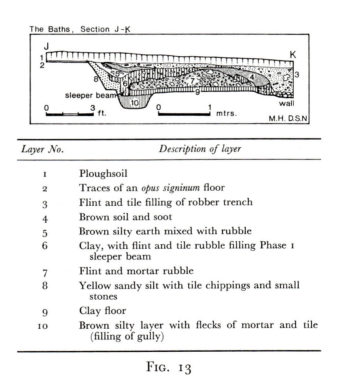

The Baths, Section J–K

Layer No.	Description of layer
1	Ploughsoil
2	Traces of an *opus signinum* floor
3	Flint and tile filling of robber trench
4	Brown soil and soot
5	Brown silty earth mixed with rubble
6	Clay, with flint and tile rubble filling Phase 1 sleeper beam
7	Flint and mortar rubble
8	Yellow sandy silt with tile chippings and small stones
9	Clay floor
10	Brown silty layer with flecks of mortar and tile (filling of gully)

FIG. 13

PHASE 2

The purpose of the apse on the western side of the baths is uncertain; possibly it was a water-tank supplying a *testudo* over the stoke-hole, since the water conduit north-west of the baths headed towards it. The apse is thought to be of a later build than the wing mainly because it was not placed symmetrically on the west side of the baths, and because the mortar used in its construction was a different colour, i.e. yellow and not white. The start of the conduit was not traced, but it was probably to the north of Building E, running from a well which may have been situated there. The conduit was similar to that running from the well to the water-cistern south of Building A, and may be contemporary with it. The conduit divided into three separate channels, two of which had iron pipe-collars *in situ*. The southernmost conduit ran towards the apse.

PHASE 3

The apse was demolished, and the area made into a square room measuring 8 ft. (2.44 m.) by 11 ft. (3.35 m.), open on the stoke-hole side. The Phase 1 timber-framed room to the west was no longer used; its floor was covered by a layer of rubble (L 7, Section J–K, fig. 13) which had been cut by the foundation-trench for the new wall (L 3).

DATING

No dating evidence was found for the construction of the features described although it is possible that Phase 2 or 3 correlates with the construction of the Period 4 plunge-bath, Room 13. However, no similarity of construction was noted.

BUILDING A (fig. 5)

A new masonry villa, Building A, was built on an east–west axis over the site of the earlier buildings. The villa measured 136 ft. (41.45 m.) by 79 ft. (24.09 m.), and was laid out as a central range of rooms with projecting wings, surrounded on all sides by a corridor. Two porches opened out of the northern corridor, one opposite a passage. At the south side of the villa was a water cistern which was supplied from a well further to the west.

The plan of the house was symmetrical. The wings projected equal distances from the main range and the water cistern outside the courtyard was equidistant between the wings. The porches in the north wall were set an equal distance from the sides of the house.

No evidence was found to suggest the villa was originally a single range of rooms, or that the wings and surrounding corridors were later features. All the walls in the building were identical in construction and materials. The building is dated by coarse pottery (Pottery nos. 1–140, figs. 95–9) and samian found in Ditch 1 below the building. The latest pottery belongs to the late Antonine period.

Prior to the construction of Building A, the site was cleared of existing buildings and levelled. It is curious that the same site was chosen for the new house; not only did the new construction involve the demolition of existing structures, but also the ditch and gully might be expected to have caused overlying buildings to subside. The reason why the old site was chosen, in preference to one further south, was probably that it was on higher ground, and safer from the river. To the south-east, under Building B, was a natural hollow, filled with dark earth and stones. This at one time may have been part of the river, and was shunned by the builders who thought it more likely to subside than the ditch and gully.

c

ROOM 20,   PERIOD 3.

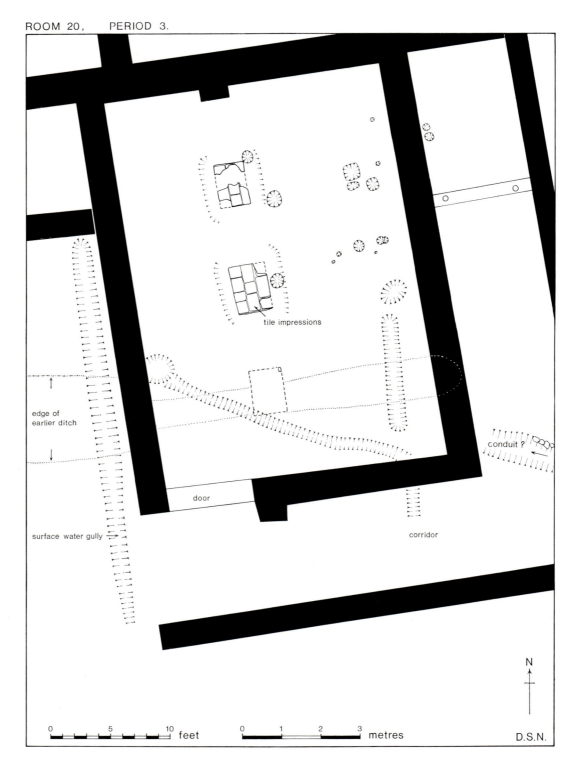

tile impressions

edge of
earlier ditch

surface water gully →

door

conduit ?

corridor

N

0   5   10 feet   0   1   2   3   metres

D.S.N.

FIG. 14

The villa respected existing alignments by running parallel to the Period 1 ditches, and to the slight foundations of Room 17.

The walls of the villa[1] were constructed on shallow flint footings set directly on to natural clay. Several of the walls had been rendered with mortar and scored to imitate ashlar blocks down to the footing level (pl. V*b*). Had the walls been constructed in foundation-trenches this rendering and subsequent decoration would not have been possible. The floor-levels in the main east–west range were destroyed by the plough, but were originally the same level as the floors in the western wing and the upper floor over Room 20. The level of the inner courtyard was 3 ft. (.91 m.) lower than that in the east–west range. The basement, Room 20, was terraced into the natural slope of the land, so that its floor was approximately 6 to 7 ft. (1.83–2.13 m.) below the level of the adjacent rooms, 3 to 4 ft. (.91–1.22 m.) below the level of the courtyard, and, on the south, 1 ft. (.31 m.) below the outside surface. To allow for the fall in levels the eastern corridor was ramped and provided with two steps.

The corridor bordering the east side of the west wing and the south side of the main range was level with the rooms, but the corridor walls rested on the lower courtyard surface. It is probable that these walls not only supported a corridor roof but also acted as a revetment to the corridor. This explains why they were 6 in. (.15 m.) thicker than the other corridor walls surrounding the villa.

Traces of red-painted tile mortar were found on the exterior southern corridor alongside the main rooms; probably other corridor walls were decorated in a similar way. No evidence was found to suggest that the outer walls of the rooms were also painted although they may well have been. From a distance the villa must have appeared garish; the roof was covered with red and yellow tiles.

Room 19

This room was in the north-east corner of the villa and was flanked on its north and east sides by corridors. The room measured 20 ft. by 17 ft. (6.10 by 5.18 m.). Little is known about this room in its early phases, because in Period 5 it was converted into a hypocaust.

Room 20 (fig. 14, pl. VI*a*)

This basement room was the largest room in the Period 3 building, measuring 23 ft. 9 in. by 33 ft. (7.24 by 10.6 m.); it occupied the whole of the eastern wing. Its floor was 5 ft. (1.52 m.) lower than the lower hypocaust floor in Room 19; assuming that the upper hypocaust floor in this room was between 2 ft. 6 in. (.76 m.) and 3 ft. (.91 m.) above the lower floor, the basement area may have had a ceiling height of between 7 and 8 ft. (2.13–2.44 m.).

[1] To avoid duplication the common measurements and details of the individual rooms in the villa will be given. Most of the walls in this period were 2 ft. 6 in. (.76 m.) wide and were constructed in flint and hard white mortar. Many of the walls survived just above floor level, but in some places the walls were robbed to their lowest footings. This robbing was never extensive, however, and is not shown on the plan, although its extent will be apparent from photographs and sections. All the measurements of the rooms will give east–west dimensions first, followed by north–south dimensions. Some of the rooms that have several periods of construction will be described in the same chapter so as to provide continuity. Rooms that have been added or enlarged will be described in their appropriate period chapter.

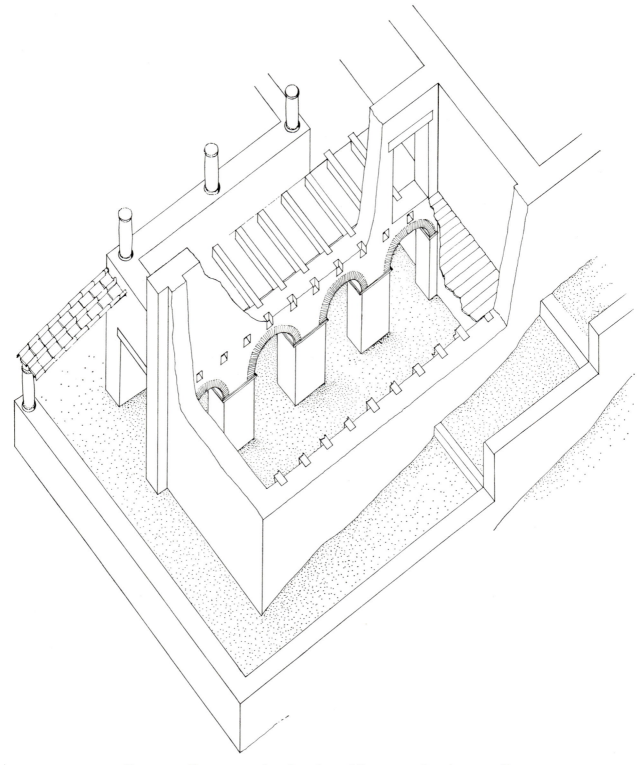

Fig. 15. Reconstruction drawing of Room 20 showing arcading
supporting walling in upper storey (scale 1 in. to 10 ft.)

The north wall had the same imitation ashlar rendering as the internal walls of the building, and was 6 in. (.15 m.) thicker than the other walls of the villa, probably because it had to revet Room 19. The doorway was at the western end of the south wall, and was 7 ft. (2.13 m.) wide. Adjacent to the doorway was an external buttress on the same alignment as one against the north wall; three bases measuring 2 ft. 6 in. by 3 ft. 6 in. (.76 by 1.07 m.) were located along the imaginary line joining the two buttresses. The bases were constructed of tiles set in pink tile mortar (pl. VIb) supported on shallow flint foundations spaced 5 ft. to 5 ft. 6 in. (1.52 to 1.68 m.) apart. The distance between the west wall and the bases was equal to the width of the opposite corridor (i.e. along the west wing). Considering that the villa had such a symmetrical plan, the suggestion that this space was a corridor or aisle would seem the most likely and, as there was no wall linking the bases, the room must have had an 'open plan'. The purpose of the bases is a major problem. The explanation that they were for industrial use, as suggested in interim reports,[1] is no longer believed to be correct; the idea that they were bases for presses is also not tenable. In view of the symmetry of the building, the corridor around two sides of the inner courtyard probably continued on the same level around the west side of the storey over Room 20 (fig. 15), and the stands therefore would seem to have been piers supporting arcading, which carried a wall that rose into the upper storey, there dividing the corridor from the rooms.

On the west side of the room was a shallow sump with a gully leading from it across the floor, and out through the south wall into the corridor. The southernmost pier appears to have been partially cut back as the line of the gully ran across its corner. The sump probably drained water from below the foundations. On the north-east side of the room were several post-holes varying in width from about 12 in. (.31 m.) to 6 in. (.15 m.), as well as stake-holes 4 in. (.10 m.) wide, the average depth of all being 6 in. (.15 m.).

At the south end of the room was a channel running north–south and a circular pit; the channel was 10 ft. by 1 ft. 6 in. (3.05 by .46 m.) and 9 in. (.23 m.) deep, the pit 2 ft. (.61 m.) wide and 1 ft. 3 in. (.38 m.) deep. The purpose of the channel is doubtful, but it could have been used for collecting horse or cattle dung.

A surface water gully and eaves-drip was also dug outside the west wall of the room in another attempt to prevent rainwater from running below the foundations of the wall. The gully was approximately 6 in. (.15 m.) deep and 2 ft. (.61 m.) wide, and drained south beyond the southern corridor. It may originally have been revetted — cf. SF 518 (fig. 74). Throughout the history of the room flooding was a major problem, mainly because the filled-in ditch running beneath acted as a land drain and the water that collected in it discharged into the room. Attempts were made to overcome this flooding in Period 5 by the addition of a timber conduit (fig. 31). To the south-east of the room was a V-shaped gully in which was an iron water-pipe collar (SF 375, fig. 70) with a diameter of 6 in. (.15 m.). This is very wide compared with other pipe collars found on the site, which would suggest that the pipe carried a large volume of water. It would appear to be unnecessary for waste water to be carried in a pipe rather than an open gully and therefore it would be more reasonable to assume that the pipe was bringing water from the river — presumably water for the animals.

[1] J.R.S., LVI (1966), 208.

The purpose of the room in this period is uncertain, but the relationships of the post-holes to the stands suggest that the eastern part of the room was divided into a stabling area for horses. Evidence was found that in Period 6 the room had also been partly used as a smithy. It may be that the room housed the owner's riding horses and that other livestock was kept in the barns of Buildings B and C. However, since there appears to have been a short time-gap between the construction of Building A and the outer wings, it is quite possible that cattle were housed in the room until alternative accommodation could be provided.

The basement at Park Street was considered by the late Sir Ian Richmond[1] to have also been used as a stable. Another cellar on the nearby villa at Gorhambury[2] must have been a little too small for stalling livestock and its ramp too steep for easy entry and exit. The basement room at Lullingstone[3] was constructed in a similar way to that of Gadebridge since it was also terraced into the slope of the land. Col. G. W. Meates considered the change of level was designed to enable water transport to unload close to the villa.

Room 21 (Section N–O, fig. 6)

Room 21 measured 13 ft. × 17 ft. 9 in. (3.96 × 5.41 m.). To make up its floor, earth tips were spread successively into the room from the southern side. A layer of builder's waste (over L 13) comprising flints and mortar was found immediately to the north of the south wall. Over this was a layer of clay and chalk (L 9). A similar layer also ran over the clay build-up (L 10) in the southern corridor. Therefore the floor-level in the southern corridor appears to have been made up before those in the rooms.

The only finds were a bronze pin (SF 222, fig. 64) and a quantity of iron slag, but they came from the upper levels of the final build-up, and were disturbed.

Room 22

Room 22 was presumably a passage linking the north and south corridors. Its dimensions were 5 ft. 6 in. × 17 ft. 9 in. (1.68 × 5.41 m.). It had a similar earth build-up to Room 21, although the chalk tip did not extend into the room. Both the east and west walls were bonded into the north and south walls and were identical in their construction and materials, but the eastern passage wall was 6 in. (.15 m.) narrower; the reason for this is not clear.

In Period 5, Rooms 21 and 22 were re-arranged when the passage was moved eastwards to the west side of Room 19, immediately opposite the porch in the northern corridor. After this re-arrangement Room 22 measured 15 ft. 3 in. by 17 ft. 9 in. (4.65 × 5.41 m.) and the new passage 6 ft. by 17 ft. 9 in. (1.83 × 5.41 m.).

Set over the south wall of the original passage (Room 22) were the remains of two timber slots about 3 ft. 6 in. (1.07 m.) long and 4 in. (.10 m.) wide, running over and parallel with the wall. They were set in a layer of yellow mortar and clay and lined on the south side with

[1] Rivet, p. 50.
[2] N.G.R., TL 117078. *St Albans Architectural and Archaeological Society Transactions*, 1961, 21 ff. A new series of excavations (directed by the author) began on this villa in 1972.
[3] *Lullingstone*, p. 64.

two rows of brick *tesserae*. Two feet (.61 m.) to the north of the wall was a gully, oval in plan and 12 in. (.31 m.) wide. It appeared to be confined to the width of the passage and to run beneath the south wall, although it is possible that it was a continuation of the gully beneath Room 25. The filling comprised brown silt, mixed with tile, chalk and yellow mortar. The yellow mortar belonged to either Period 5 or 6. Since the wall along this section was robbed, its relationship to the room-filling was not established. The timber slots were not door-steps because they were lower than the surface of the floor. It is possible therefore that the wall at this point was rebuilt in Period 5 or 6 (possibly because the wall had subsided into the filling of the gully) and that the timbers were laid to reinforce this section of the wall. The red brick *tesserae* in association with a layer of clay may have been an attempt at waterproofing. Similar layers of pure clay were found over the lower foundations on other sections of the walls and were presumably laid as a damp-course. This did not represent a separate phase of building.

Room 23

This room was almost identical in size to Room 19, measuring 20 ft. by 17 ft. 9 in. (6.10 × 5.41 m.). It was probably the principal living-room in Period 3, because it was placed centrally along the axis. The walls were decorated with lines scored in the mortar rendering to imitate ashlar blocks (pl. V*b*). Patches of white mortar were found in the room, level with the wall footings; this was probably builders' waste left after the wall was rendered. Above this level was a build-up of brown clay, covered by the remains of a yellow mortar floor and traces of a floor of *opus signinum*. This was used to pave Rooms 24, 25 and 26, so it would be reasonable to assume that the ploughed-out floors in Rooms 22 and 21 were similarly paved. In Period 5 the room was reduced in width when alterations were carried out in Rooms 22 and 21. A new wall was constructed on the eastern side, reducing it to 17 ft. by 17 ft. 9 in. (5.18 × 5.41 m.).

A very worn *dupondius* of Hadrian was found sealed in the mortar of the south wall; it presumably intruded into either the sand or lime during the construction of the house. An unstratified coin of the Fel Temp Reparatio series (A.D. 346–50) was found in the robber trench of the northern wall, and an uncertain AE 4 in the ploughsoil.

Room 24

Room 24 measured 12 ft. by 17 ft. 9 in. (3.65 × 5.41 m.). All that remained of the floor was a layer of make-up flints for an *opus signinum* pavement. This had been destroyed by ploughing and only slight traces of tile chippings remained.

Room 25

Room 25 measured 4 ft. 3 in. by 17 ft. 9 in. (1.30 × 5.41 m.) and was a passage linking the north and south corridors. Both its east and west walls were contemporary with the main walls of the villa although the east wall did not bond. The west wall bonded into the north wall and butted against the south wall. The room was originally paved with an *opus signinum* floor laid directly on to natural clay. North of the passage, outset from the north corridor wall, was a porch.

Main Villa – Building A. Detail. Numerals indicate room numbers

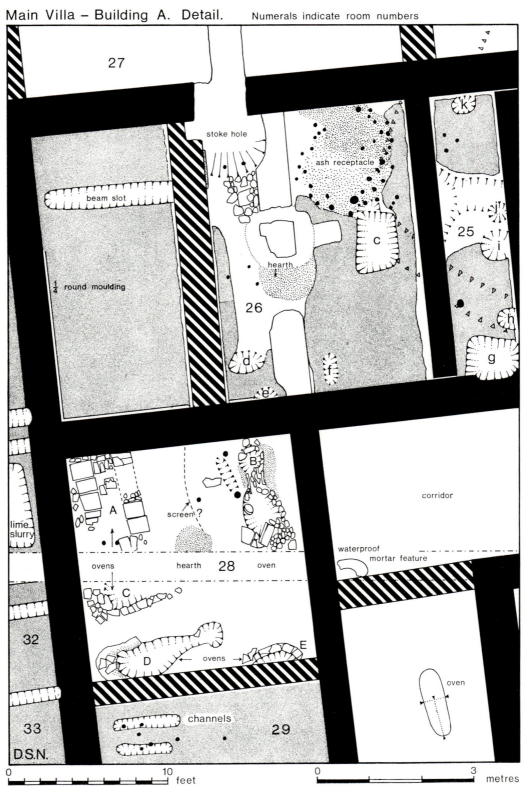

Fig. 16

Room 26

Room 26, together with Room 25, had many later alterations and these will be described in the chapter for Period 5 (p. 52).

WEST WING (Section U–V, fig. 36)

Two rooms occupied the west wing and it is possible there may have been a third, a sub-division of Room 28. The southern limit of Room 28 is uncertain. The two southernmost ovens in it (D and E) were cut by a Period 5 wall (fig. 16). South of this wall was an *opus signinum* floor covered with a tessellated pavement, also cut by the wall. These floors were removed and no evidence was found beneath them to suggest that the ovens continued southwards. It is possible therefore that the Period 5 wall may have been constructed over the alignment of an earlier partition.

Room 28 (fig. 16)

Five ovens occupied the room (pls. VII*a, b*); all were constructed against its sides. Oven A, built in the north-west corner had a channelled flue, 16 in. (.41 m.) wide, between two tile stands 5 ft. 3 in. (1.60 m.) long. Oven B was 1 ft. 6 in. (.46 m.) in diameter and 1 ft. 2 in. (.36 m.) deep; it was connected to a circular stoke-hole about 2 ft. 6 in. (.76 m.) in diameter and 9 in. (.23 m.) deep. The flue was lined with roofing tiles and the oven sides packed with chalk blocks. Amongst the collapsed superstructure in the stoking pit were roofing tiles, and in one instance a circular *pila* tile. This was identical with those found in the apses in the north and south walls of the Period 3 bath wing (see p. 15).

Immediately to the west of the oven was a shallow cutting: it measured 2 ft. 6 in. (.76 m.) long by 9 in. (.23 m.) wide and had stake-holes at its northern and southern ends. Its purpose is uncertain but it may have been the impression of a sleeper beam. Midway between ovens A and B was a colour and texture change; to the east was brown soil and to the west undisturbed brown clay. It is possible that some type of screen had been erected at this division. In the middle of the room was a hearth.

The southern area of the room had the remains of three ovens. Oven C was probably later than Oven A because the former was built in front of the stoke-hole of the latter. It was constructed in tile and lime mortar and originally measured about 3 ft. (.91 m.) in diameter. Oven D lay on an east–west axis, was oval in plan and 2 ft. (.61 m.) wide by 7 ft. (2.13 m.) long. The superstructure was made of tiles, some of which survived on its western side. On its southern side it had been partially cut by the Period 5 wall which also cut Oven E further to the east. All that remained of the latter was a semi-circular area of tiles that formed its northern wall. In Period 5 the ovens were sealed by a tessellated pavement, which sealed two coins, one of Postumus and another of Claudius II.

Subdivision of Room 28

Immediately south of the south wall was an *opus signinum* floor which was later paved in red-brick *tesserae* and paved again in brick *tesserae* in Period 5. The first tessellated pavement had a hearth and two parallel channels cut through it. The latter features ran on an east–west alignment: the northern channel was 4 ft. 3 in. (1.30 m.) long and the southern 3 ft. 6 in. (1.07 m.) long — both were about 9 in. (.23 m.) wide and 2 in. (.05 m.) deep. Their purpose is doubtful as they were both filled with burnt clay, but since quantities of iron slag were found close by, it is possible that they were associated with iron working. At a later date seven stakes were driven through the floor.

The corridor on the eastern side of the wing was paved with a red brick tessellated floor, identical with the first tessellated pavement over Room 29: it sealed pottery forms similar to 21, 220 and 237.

Room 29

The southernmost room (Room 29) measured 14 ft. by 10 ft. 6 in. (4.27 × 3.20 m.) and was also paved with an *opus signinum* floor, but in Period 5 the rooms in the wing were re-arranged and the original north wall robbed for flint. These alterations will be discussed in the chapter for Period 5 (p. 44).

The Water Cistern (fig. 5, pl. VIIIa)

In front of the villa, midway between the two wings and beneath the Period 5 gatehouse was a rectangular structure. It measured 18 ft. by 13 ft. 6 in. (5.48 × 4.11 m.), with walls 18 in. (.46 m.) thick. The building was probably contemporary with the Period 3 villa because it was constructed in similar materials — blue flints and white mortar — and because it appears to have been an integral part of the villa plan. The floor was laid in tile mortar, which was also used to render both the interior and exterior walls. Quarter-round moulding skirted the interior walls, although little survived. Most of the exterior rendering had fallen from the wall in slabs.

The building seems to have been a water cistern, its water source being a well south-west of the villa. The cistern and the well were linked by a conduit constructed from bored tree trunks; these were joined with iron collars set about 8 ft. (2.44 m.) apart. At a later date the cistern went out of use, and consequently another conduit was built which ran south of the former and around the south-east corner of the cistern. The exterior rendering had collapsed by this date because the new conduit cut through the debris. The start of the conduit was south of the well — it did not continue further west — and, apart from iron collars, was identifiable by a U-shaped trough filled with an accumulation of gravel. This had either been deposited as packing for the pipe, or was a result of the pipe leaking and washing out the loose earth.

The association of a building rendered throughout in waterproof cement with a well and conduits implies that water from the well was hoisted into a catchment at the head of the pipe and then flowed downhill into the cistern. It is reasonable to assume that the cistern was gravity-fed since its floor was 5 to 6 ft. (1.52 to 1.83 m.) lower than the ground level at the head of the pipe. After the cistern went out of use it was adapted as a hypocaust or furnace, because five *pila* tiles, which presumably supported a floor, were set into it. The east wall was breached by a stoking pit which also cut the collapsed rendering. However, no traces of charcoal or ash were found, although the floor and the *pilae* did show signs of burning: the floor close to the stoke-hole had been burnt through to reveal its flint make-up.

The purpose of the building in this phase is uncertain. The presence of a lime slurry over its north-west corner and others to the south-east and south-west may possibly indicate that the cistern was converted into a temporary furnace or kiln for burning lime[1] for use in the Period 5 rebuilding.

The Well (Section X–Y, fig. 17)

The well was situated to the south-west of the villa, about 14 ft. (4.25 m.) away from the walls. It had been cut through marl and chalk and was 17 ft. 5 in. (5.30 m.) deep. The width would have been about 4 ft. (1.22 m.) but this measurement is uncertain as the well was bottle-shaped, due primarily to erosion of the sides by water. There was no evidence on the surrounding surface or in the chalk-silt filling to show the nature of the well-head construction, and the well was not lined. A bucket (SF 673, fig. 79) was found in the silt at a depth of about 16 ft. (4.88 m.), complete with hoops, handle and rope ring. Also found in the silt was an iron lamp (SF 346, fig. 69).

As the section across the well (fig. 17) runs east–west, it does not show a fall in the filling levels from the south to the north. The lowest filling was chalk silt (L 13) — this contained the bucket and lamp, and pottery of the late second century. In the upper levels of the silt were traces of clay, followed by a deposit (L 12) of red wall-plaster, oyster shells, pottery and the skeletons of possibly a Maltese terrier and a Pomeranian dog.[2] Layer 9 was a thick deposit of pure sand (it contained a single *imbrex*) which in turn was covered by a deposit of rubble (L 8) and a layer of charcoal (L 7), sealed by a further collapse of the sides (L 6). Layer 5 comprised brown clay mixed with large quantities of painted ceiling-plaster decorated with imitation coffering formed by a grid of guilloche (pl. XXVIIa, fig. 89b). All the plaster was painted on a rendering of yellow mortar, 2½ inches (0.5 m.) thick: none of this type of plaster was found in the lower levels. Layer 4 contained building rubble which included part of a column drum similar to SF 688, fig. 82. This layer covered the skeleton of an ox. Layer 3 was a chalk spread below the final filling (L 2) which comprised dark soil mixed with traces of burnt yellow mortar. Associated with this layer was a coin of Julia Domna and a coin dated A.D. 388.

The presence of building rubble indicates either that the villa was being demolished or that repairs were being carried out. Some of the mortar was slightly burnt, so it is possible one of the rooms has been damaged by fire. Where in the villa the plaster had come from is not known, but Dr Norman Davey[3] considered, on the evidence of another associated mortar-fragment, that it could possibly have come from a corridor ceiling. The associated fragment was moulded, suggesting that the surface of the ceiling angled upwards towards the eaves. However it is possible for the fragment to have come from the junction of the ceiling and a clerestorey window. The column drum, which may have originally come from a dwarf wall supporting a corridor roof, supports Dr Davey's view. Since the rubble with the wall-plaster was about 8 ft. (2.44 m.) from the floor of the well, it is clear that the well had

[1] I am grateful to Mr R. Goodburn for suggesting this interpretation.

[2] Mr R. Harcourt has kindly reported on the animal bones, and his report appears as an appendix, p. 256.

[3] The writer gratefully acknowledges the generous help given by Dr N. Davey, F.S.A., in reconstructing the ceiling plaster, and in discussing various features of the site. For a detailed description of the plaster see note by Miss J. Liversidge, F.S.A., p. 200.

Well Section X–Y

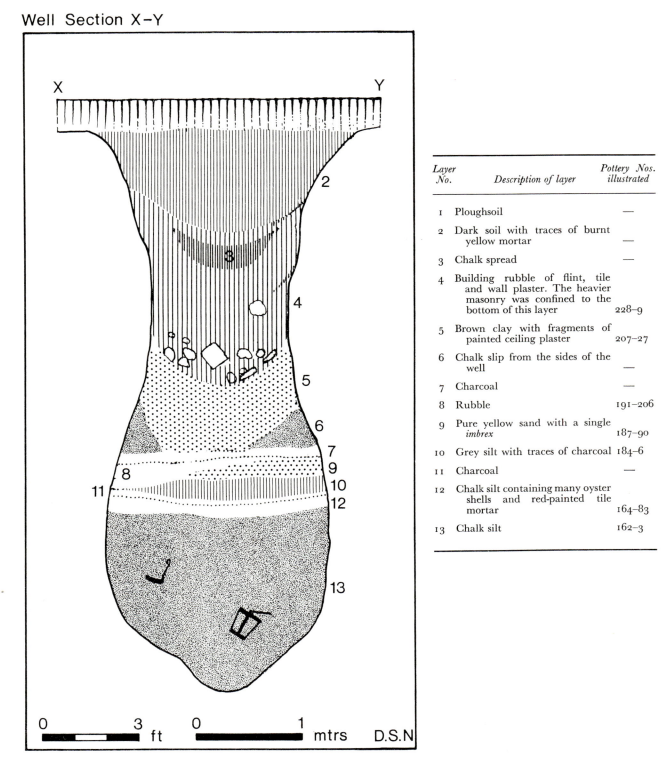

Layer No.	Description of layer	Pottery Nos. illustrated
1	Ploughsoil	—
2	Dark soil with traces of burnt yellow mortar	—
3	Chalk spread	—
4	Building rubble of flint, tile and wall plaster. The heavier masonry was confined to the bottom of this layer	228–9
5	Brown clay with fragments of painted ceiling plaster	207–27
6	Chalk slip from the sides of the well	—
7	Charcoal	—
8	Rubble	191–206
9	Pure yellow sand with a single *imbrex*	187–90
10	Grey silt with traces of charcoal	184–6
11	Charcoal	—
12	Chalk silt containing many oyster shells and red-painted tile mortar	164–83
13	Chalk silt	162–3

Fig. 17

already fallen into disuse. The latest pottery associated with this material is of early third-century date, but whether this represents an abandonment of parts of the villa in this period is far from certain.

The water source after this date is not known (perhaps it was the river), but it is possible that a well existed to the north-east of Building E, as another conduit was found there running east towards the Phase 2 apse on the western side of the bath wing (p. 17).

DISCUSSION

The Period 3 villa (reconstruction drawing, fig. 28) is typical of the winged-corridor type and compares in plan with other villas. The wings would appear to be further extended than most, and consequently the courtyard area between was more enclosed. This was emphasized still further by the siting of the water cistern. Corridors are not generally assumed to have been included in the original design and construction of a villa, but the evidence found at Gadebridge suggests that here the corridors were original.[1] However the different mortar in the eastern corridor did suggest that the wall was either added shortly afterwards or was repaired. The colour of the mortar varied in places, but this of course may only indicate a variety of sands used in the mix.

Parallels to Gadebridge are few, mainly because the corridors of other villas do not enclose the whole building. The closest plan is that of the Roman villa at Ditchley[2] which also had a corridor on all sides, although Mr Radford considered it to have been constructed later. The villa appears to have been divided into social areas. The main range of rooms presumably contained the living rooms of the family, but the siting of the kitchens in the south-west wing suggests that this area was the servants' quarters. The lower storey in the eastern wing (Room 20), used as a stable, appears to have been deliberately detached from the main living block since there was no direct access to the room from upstairs or from the courtyard. The only door (in this period) was in the south wall, out of view from the main range. The house, although well built and of a fine architectural plan, could boast of no luxuries other than the bath-house. Most of the rooms had only *opus signinum* floors and plain undecorated walls, but the evidence of the wall-plaster from the well would suggest that decorative improvements were not long in coming.

How much the villa was a self-supporting economic unit is uncertain: the occupants were doubtless dependent on farming, possibly both cereal and stock. From the minimum numbers of each domestic species determined from the animal bones, it appears that there was a greater variety of species in the first and second centuries. Although this may be merely chance, it is possible that in the early period the estate did not specialize in a particular product. From the discovery of slag,[3] it appears that iron working was also being practised, although the slag may only have been the waste from a smithy.

[1] The timber building at Boxmoor (*Brit.*, 1 (1970), 156) also had a surrounding corridor which appears to have been an integral concept of the overall design. For further discussion on this topic see p. 88.

[2] *Oxon.*, 1 (1936), 24.
[3] For report on the slag see p. 264.

PERIOD 4 (fig. 18)

Farm buildings were constructed on the south-east and south-west sides of the villa, thereby forming an outer courtyard. Several corridors in Building A were sub-divided into rooms.

The date of construction of the outer wings (Buildings B and C) is doubtful,[1] but they would appear to have been added shortly after Building A, towards the close of the second century. The eastern wing, Building B, comprised two large rooms bordered on the north, west and east sides by corridors. Severe erosion had occurred in the southern area and its extent was not determined, nor whether a corridor also ran round the south side. The wing probably continued south up to the line of the east–west outer courtyard wall.

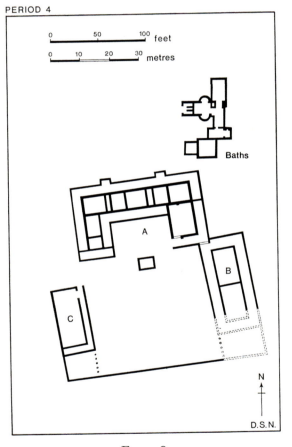

Fig. 18

---

[1] The bulk of the pottery from the filling of Ditch 2 to the south of the site is dated to the mid-second century and was mainly found in sections of the ditch adjacent to Buildings B and C. The possibility that (contrary to the structural evidence in the north-west corner of Building B) the wings pre-date Building A and were associated with an earlier building should not be dismissed.

Building C, which was of four phases A-D, was divided into three rooms, bordered on the east and south sides by corridors. Its plan was different from that of Building B, as it did not link with the main house, nor was it as long; however it was extended in Phase C as far south as the outer courtyard wall. Why the building did not abut the main house is uncertain. It may have been due to the position of the well, but it is also possible that the space between the buildings was used as an approach to the villa, since a Roman road ran towards this area from the south-west. No road, track or path led into the villa across the outer courtyard. It is unlikely that the villa was approached between the outer wings since no provision for an entrance or gatehouse was made in the southern courtyard enclosure.

Other building works attributed to this phase are the sub-division of the western corridor alongside Building A, and the construction of Rooms 12 and 13 on the south side of the baths.

BUILDING A (fig. 5)

The western corridor in Building A was subdivided into rooms by the construction of wattle-and-daub walls set on sleeper beams (pl. IX*b*). The rooms were each paved with an *opus signinum* floor, laid up to the sleeper beams. The corridor appears to have been divided into at least four rooms, 30, 31, 32 and 33. These varied in size from 9 ft. by 5 ft. 6 in. (2.75 × 1.68 m.) to 9 ft. by 13 ft. (2.75 × 3.96 m.). The existing foundation of the outer corridor wall became the foundation for the western walls of the rooms. There may also have been another room north of Room 30 since a sleeper beam was laid on top of the corridor wall foundation (pl. XI*a*) on both its north and west sides. However the area was never paved.

At a later date, possibly in Period 5, the rooms were rearranged. New sleeper beams were put down, cutting through the existing *opus signinum* floor, and the western face of the villa wall. This re-arrangement occurred in Rooms 30, 31 and 32, all of which have pairs of sleeper beams between them, the northernmost of which was the replacement. Other rooms may also have been built into the southern corridor because two flint walls, both extensions of the south wall of the villa, ran over the corridor.

THE BATHS (fig. 8)

Hitherto the bath-suite's only *frigidarium* (Room 3) had been small by comparison with the *caldarium* (Room 9) and the *tepidarium* (Rooms 1, 2, 7 and 8) and bathers wishing to have a cold plunge-bath were restricted to the small apsidal bath (Room 5) on the western side of the *frigidarium*. Consequently a larger plunge-bath (Room 13) was constructed on the south-west side of the bath-suite, together with a smaller room (Room 12) on its western side. Room 13 will be described first.

Room 13 (fig. 19, pl. X*a*)

The new bath measured 17 ft. 6 in. by 18 ft. (5.33 × 5.98 m.) with walls 2 ft. (.61 m.) wide and was constructed in flint and white mortar. Both the south wall of the original Period 2 plunge-bath (Room 5) and the Period 1 *frigidarium* (Room 3) were incorporated into

The Baths – Plunge Bath, Room 13

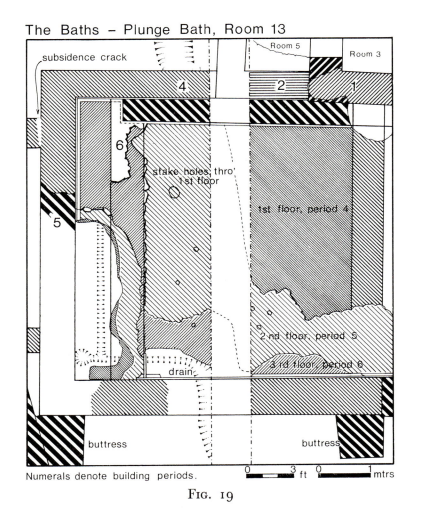

Numerals denote building periods.

FIG. 19

its north wall. The bath was terraced into the natural slope of the ground so that its floor on the west side was 2 ft. (.61 m.) below the outside natural clay surface. The bath was paved throughout with *opus signinum* and lined with red-painted tile-mortar. Much of the floor in the south-west corner was robbed, although walls survived in places to a height of 2 ft. (.61 m.). The water outlet was probably in the north-east corner, an existing drain which ran from the old plunge-bath (Room 5) being used (see Room 14, fig. 8).

The gully to the north was an earlier eaves-drip. The floor of the bath was re-laid twice (pl. X*b*) but beneath the original floor was a shallow drain 6 in. (.15 m.) wide which ran parallel to the west and south walls and out through the south wall into a sump. Tiles were used to cap the drain prior to laying the floor. The nature of repairs carried out in later periods suggest that the bath leaked. This may have been envisaged by the builders, who built the drain in order to get rid of water that would penetrate the floor and endanger the foundations. If this was the reason, they were unsuccessful, because the walls of Room 12 settled and cracked away from the plunge-bath (pl. XI*b*).

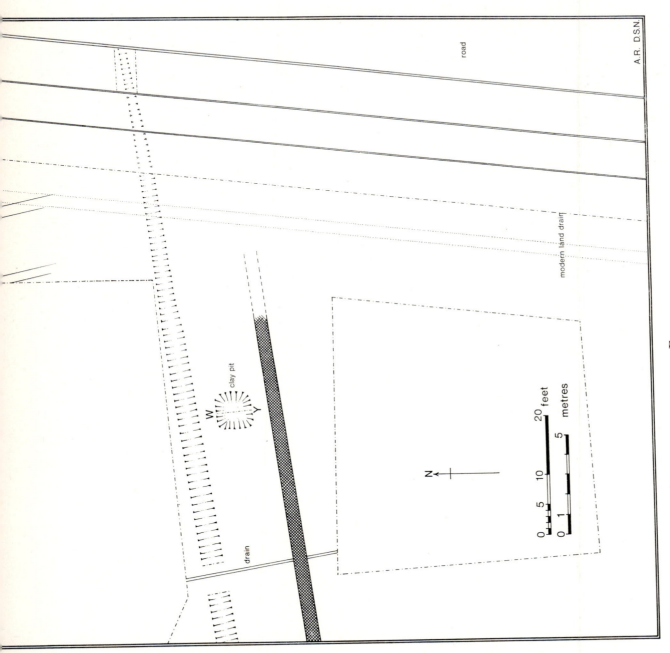

road

A.R. D.S.N

modern land drain

clay pit

W
Y

drain

N

20 feet
20 metres
10
5
5
5
0
0
1

Fig. 20

Facing page 32

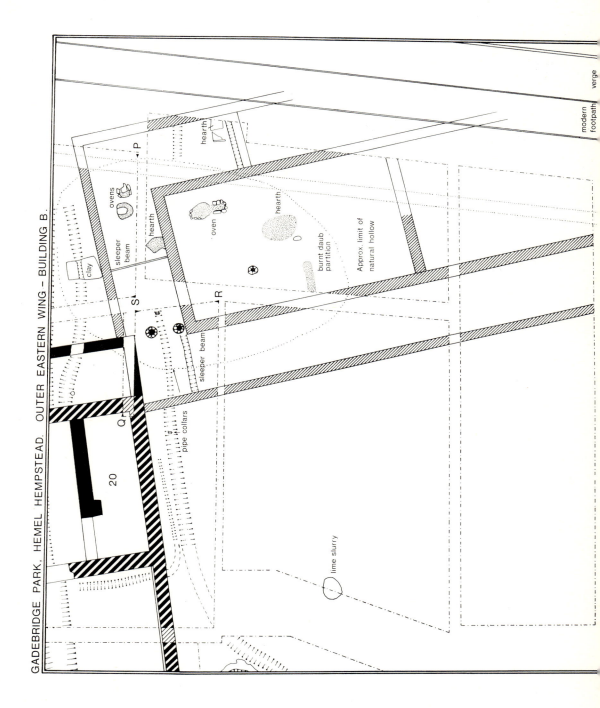

GADEBRIDGE PARK, HEMEL HEMPSTEAD. OUTER EASTERN WING – BUILDING B.

Room 12 (fig. 8)

This room had also been terraced into the slope of the ground so that its floor was 2 ft. 8 in. (.81 m.) below the natural clay surface. The floor, a very thin skim of pink tile-mortar, was about 8 in. (.20 m.) deeper than the floor of the plunge-bath, and had the remains of a rectangular hearth. The room was 11 ft. (3.35 m.) square with walls 2 ft. 6 in. (.76 m.) thick, constructed in flint and white mortar. Even though the north wall had subsided away from the bath, it was clear it was originally bonded into it and was not butt jointed. The sunken nature of its floor would suggest it to have been a hypocaust, but no *pilae* or stoke-hole were found. However, its southern wall was badly robbed, so the stoke-hole may have been situated there. If it contained a hypocaust it may have been a *sudatorium*.

The Period 5 and 6 enlargements and repairs to room 13 will be discussed in their appropriate chapters (pp. 55 and 60).

BUILDING B (fig. 20. Section S-R and Section P-Q, fig. 6)

Building B was 48 ft. (14.64 m.) wide, by at least 80 ft. (24.40 m.) long, and it probably extended as far south as the later outer courtyard wall, thus making its total length 122 ft. (37.21 m.). The only surviving room was at the north end, measuring 21 ft. 6 in. (6.55 m.) by 37 ft. 6 in. (11.43 m.); the walls were 2 ft. (.61 m.) wide and constructed in flint and pale yellow mortar. The corridors, which were 9 ft. 9 in. (2.97 m.) wide, ran around the north, east and west sides of the building, that on the west side being a direct continuation of the eastern corridor alongside Building A. To effect a direct route, the corridor wall turning south of Room 20 was breached.

It is probable that the western corridor wall was a later addition to the main building. A layer of chalk cobbles resting on a white mortar floor ran along the west side of the building. This surface was later cut by the construction of the outer corridor wall and sealed by a clay floor which also covered the northern room. No post-holes were found in the cobbled surface to suggest that a simple lean-to existed and therefore it would appear that the building had an open walk alongside it.

The northern room was probably servants' quarters or a kitchen; a hearth was found in the centre of the room and an oven in the north-east corner. It had a post-hole cutting its floor, and the remains of a burnt daub partition on its western side. No notable finds were made in the building, no doubt because of its eroded state. The clay floor (L 7) that covered the room and the western corridor also covered the northern corridor. At a later date the latter was divided into two rooms by a sleeper beam placed directly on to the clay floor.

The room on the eastern side was a kitchen. A hearth was built against the north face or the inner corridor wall and two ovens (pl. IXa) were built in the central area slightly further to the east. The two ovens were not contemporary: that to the east was later in date as if had been built on a layer of soot which covered the western oven. Both of them were constructed in tiles mortared with lime, and both had been severely burnt and cracked by heat. They appeared to have been in constant use, as a thick deposit of ash had accumulated. This level contained a samian sherd of Albucius of Antonine date. The purpose of the room at the west end of the northern corridor is not known.

D

The eastern corridor had an *opus signinum* floor and appears to have been divided into rooms. Little of the corridor was excavated because most of it lay beneath the modern footpath. The *opus signinum* floor was probably later than the main building and contemporary with the division of this corridor into small rooms. The floor was laid up against the sleeper beams and was not cut by them. The sleeper beams supported division walls constructed in wattle-and-daub and faced with decorated wall-plaster which had collapsed over the floor. In the south-east corner of the room were the remains of a small hearth, constructed in tiles. A gully or drain running east–west also cut the floor. Why the corridor should have been divided into small rooms is not clear; they appear to be very similar to the rooms dividing the western corridor, alongside Building A, also attributed to Period 4 (p. 31).

Clay Pit, Section W–X

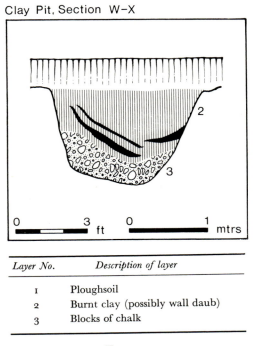

Layer No.	Description of layer
1	Ploughsoil
2	Burnt clay (possibly wall daub)
3	Blocks of chalk

Fig. 21

The siting of the building was unfortunate; it was constructed over a natural hollow filled with loose black earth (L 8) and stones (L 9) containing a fragment of Hadrianic pottery in the style of Geminus, which the builders of Building A were careful to avoid. Consequently the northern corridor wall collapsed. When this happened a layer of clay (L 4) was spread over its floor, the collapsed northern wall and the filling of the Period 3 conduit from Room 20. The corridor was also blocked by two large posts (pl. VIII*b*) built due north of the western wall of the room and by a sleeper beam laid across the western corridor at right-angles to the post-holes. Whether the sleeper beam indicates division into another room, or that this corridor was also blocked and the building abandoned, is uncertain. A water conduit also cut the western corridor. Since the northern room was not covered by the same clay (L 4) as was spread over the corridor, the principal rooms presumably remained in use.

As the southern extent of the wing was eroded, little can be said about it. If the building extended as far south as the courtyard boundary wall, then it would have sealed the V-shaped ditch (Ditch 2) that ran east–west across the site. However, the original Phase 1 outer western wing (Building C) did not extend as far south as this ditch, so likewise the eastern wing may also have stopped before it.

Close to the courtyard wall, further west than the wing, was a pit (Section W–X, fig. 21) filled with chalk blocks (L 3) and covered with a layer of burnt clay (L 2). The pit was roughly 6 ft. (1.83 m.) square and 4 ft. (1.22 m.) deep and is thought to have been originally dug for clay, used to prepare wall daub. It contained a latch-lifter (SF 396, fig. 71) and a bronze stud (SF 32, fig. 55).

Further west was a long narrow feature, 6 in. (.15 m.) wide and 6 in. (.15 m.) deep, running on a north–south axis. It was possibly a sleeper beam, but as no occupation was found associated with it, nor any right-angled turns, it is more probably a drain. Where it came from is uncertain, perhaps the water cistern in front of Building A. It was cut later by the outer courtyard wall.

BUILDING C (fig. 22, pl. XII*a*)

Building C was constructed 26 ft. (7.92 m.) south-west of Building A and had 4 phases of construction: (A) the construction of a rectangular building that lay on a north–south axis; (B) the addition of a corridor against the east and south walls; (C) the extension of the building south; and (D) the construction of the outer courtyard wall between Buildings B and C.

The building was constructed in flint and white mortar and slightly terraced into the hillside on its north and west sides so as to secure a level floor throughout the building. Unfortunately it had been severely robbed in Roman times and only the lowest foundation flints survived. The northernmost section of the eastern corridor remained a single course above foundation level. None of the walls were constructed in foundation trenches.

Phase A

The main building was 62 ft. 6 in. (19.0 m.) long by 29 ft. (8.84 m.) wide, with walls about 2 ft. (.61 m.) thick. The layout appeared to be that of a barn, with access possibly in the east and west walls although entrances probably existed elsewhere as well. A cobbled path ran from the road to a door in the west wall. Whether this door is contemporary with Phase A is uncertain, but it was later blocked, or partially so, by a sleeper beam. No internal features can be positively identified as belonging to the Phase A building, mainly due to the state of preservation, and what features there are will be described under Phase B.

Phase B

A corridor measuring 5 to 7 ft. (1.52 to 2.13 m.) wide was built against the east and south sides of the building. The corridor wall at its south-west return was thicker than the main wall of the building and the flints used in the construction were larger.

A length of the east wall of the building was demolished and replaced with three post supports set at 10 ft. (3.05 m.) intervals, with a smaller gap of 4 ft. (1.22 m.) between the northern post and the surviving piece of the wall. The two northern supports were heaps of flint, but the southern support was a large block of Hertfordshire Puddingstone. The post-bases were clearly later than the walls because the shallow robber trench of the wall ran beneath them. The builders removed all the foundation flints prior to their construction, presumably to provide access into the building.

It is possible therefore that the structure was altered in design from a simple rectangular barn to an aisled building, and that the corridor wall became the outer wall of the house. The roof of the original building was probably left intact, with the roof timbers over the demolished section supported by posts resting on the stone bases. The corridor roof was probably tied into the original wall, just below the eaves; as the room was only 25 ft. (7.62 m.) wide it was probably spanned in one. No post-bases or post-holes of this period were found within the building to suggest it had ridge supports. The western side of the building may also have been provided with an aisle. How the interior features relate to this theory will be discussed below, although it must be emphasized that none of them can be attributed with certainty to any one phase.

The northern area of the room was divided by a flint foundation running north–south, with a corridor on its western side, and a kitchen to the east. This foundation may have supported a partition wall which rested on a sleeper beam since the foundation had a groove running down the centre which may have been the matrix for such a beam. There could have been a door at the northern end of the wall, as it was narrower at this point. The southern area of the building was probably a barn. The destruction material in these rooms contained five coins, one of Gallienus, two of Tetricus I and two of Victorinus.

THE KITCHEN (fig. 23)

The kitchen had three ovens and a hearth; its southern limits were not definitely established because the southern tip of the western partition-wall ran beneath a later east–west wall. Whether the partition originally turned east at this point was not determined — if it had, the kitchen would have measured 16 ft. by 25 ft. (4.87 × 7.62 m.). Only the lower stoking areas of the ovens survived: the oven in the north-east corner of the room (Oven A) lay on a north–south axis and measured 2 ft. 9 in. (.84 m.) long by 12 in. (.31 m.) wide. It was constructed in tile resting on a row of chalk blocks and had a shallow stoke-hole on its southern end. This was cut by two Period 6 post-holes. The oven was filled with soot and burnt clay, the latter having been part of the superstructure. The oven in the north-west corner (Oven B) lay on an east–west axis and was 3 ft. 6 in. (1.07 m.) long by 1 ft. 6 in. (.46 m.) wide, being also constructed in tile. The stoke-hole was a shallow pit filled with soot and burnt clay. To the south was another tile oven (Oven C), considerably disturbed. A hearth (D) occupied the southern extent of the kitchen but only comprised an area of burnt clay. Against the north wall of the room was an irregular-shaped pit (E) cut into natural clay and into the foundations of the northern wall. It contained quantities of burnt clay and tile and at one time may have been an oven, but its shape was very irregular and none of the tiles or burnt clay was found *in situ*.

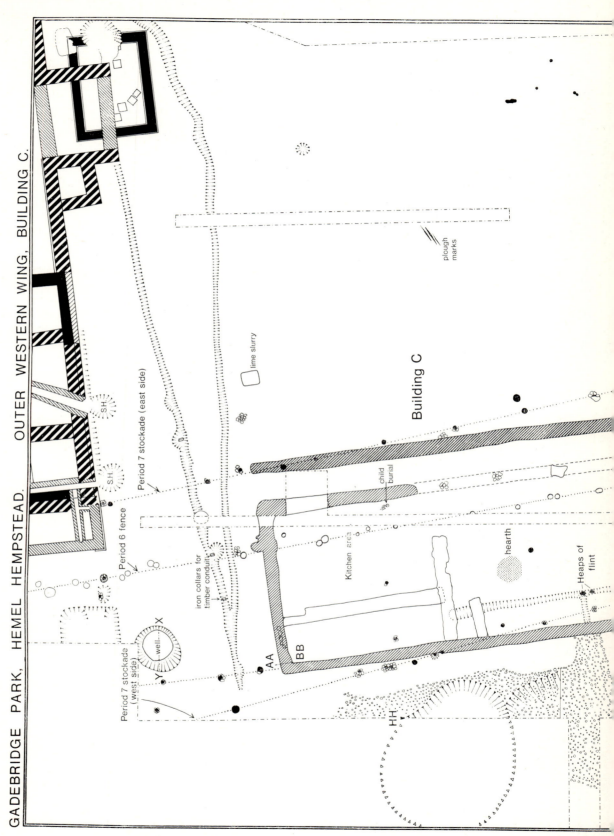

GADEBRIDGE PARK, HEMEL HEMPSTEAD. OUTER WESTERN WING, BUILDING C.

Building C

plough marks

lime slurry

S.H.

S.H.

Period 7 stockade (east side)

Period 6 fence

iron collars for timber conduit

Period 7 stockade (west side)

well—X

Y

AA

BB

HH

Kitchen area

child burial

hearth

Heaps of flint

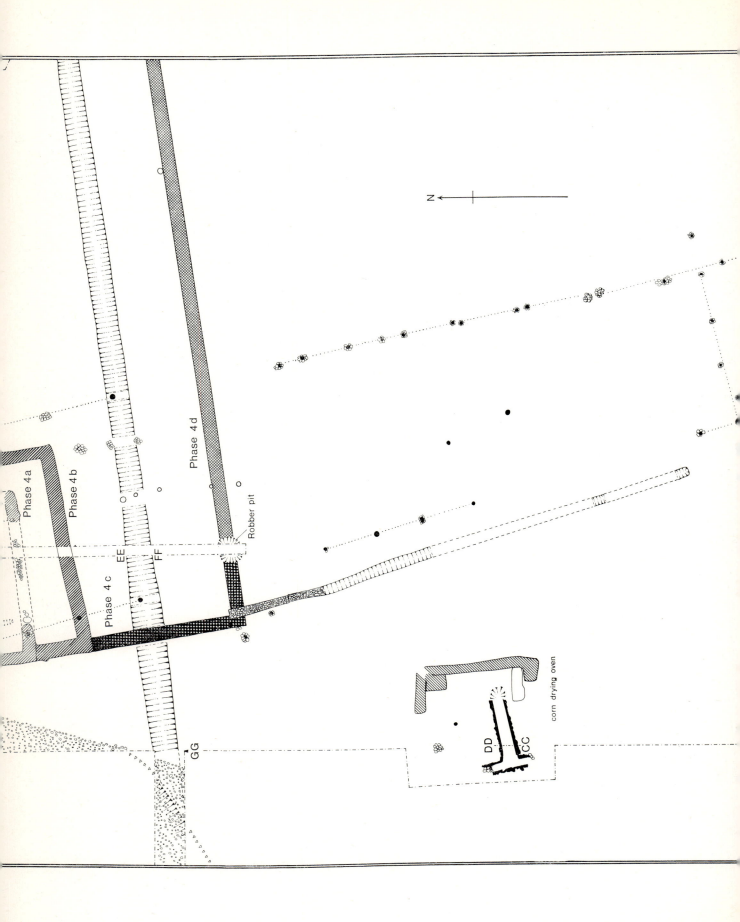

Phase 4a

Phase 4b

Phase 4c

Phase 4d

EE

FF

Robber pit

GG

DD

CC

corn drying oven

N

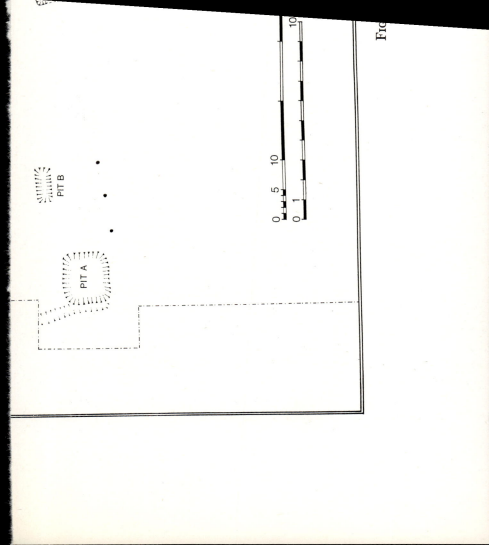

PIT B

PIT A

0   5   10

0 1   10

Fig

Outer Western Wing – Kitchen Area

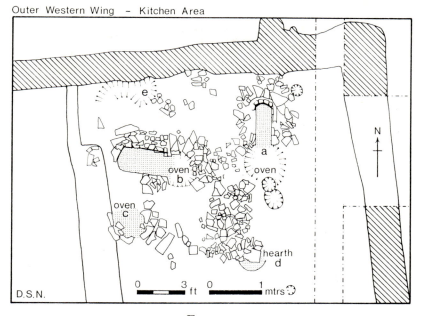

D.S.N.

FIG. 23

CHILD BURIAL

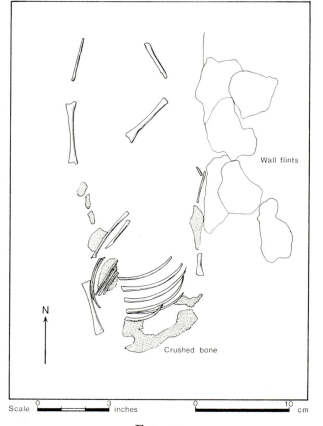

Wall flints

Crushed bone

Scale   0   3 inches   0   10 cm

FIG. 24

D1

A fragment of coal was found in the destruction level over the ovens which may indicate that this fuel was in use. Wood, however, appears to have been chiefly used, since large deposits of charcoal were found. Owing to disturbance the relationship of one oven to another was not established, but Oven B on the north-west side of the room seems to be later: it appeared to have been built over the stoke-hole of Oven C. Against the eastern face of the kitchen wall were the remains of an infant burial (fig. 24). Unfortunately the bones were in too poor a state of preservation for analysis.[1]

THE BARN (fig. 22)

On the south-west side of the barn was a sleeper beam which ran parallel to the west wall; it measured 1 ft. 6 in. (.46 m.) wide at the north, tapering to 9 in. (.23 m.) wide at the south and was 30 ft. (9.15 m.) long. The distance from wall to sleeper beam was 5 ft. (1.52 m.), the same width as the eastern corridor; it is reasonable to assume therefore that this space, too, was a corridor. However, another sleeper beam ran on an east–west axis from the first beam to the wall just at the point where the doorway is suggested, and may have been a partition for a small room in the south-west corner. Over the filling of the north–south beam slot were two small piles of flint which may have been all that remained of later post-supports, possibly replacing the decayed sleeper beam. A wall running east–west was constructed across the northern side of the barn over the southern extent of the west wall to the kitchen, and over the northern end of the sleeper beam. Whether it was constructed at the same time as the two post-supports mentioned above is uncertain. Since the wall did not extend as far as the east wall of the room, it is possible that a door existed here to enable access from the barn into the kitchen.

Immediately south of this wall on the western side of the room was a shallow flint- and chalk-lined slot or wall-footing running east–west: its relationship to the timber slot is uncertain because the filling of both was the same. The barn would appear therefore to have been bordered on both sides by corridors, although, admittedly, the west wall of the kitchen and the sleeper beam were not on the same alignment and any continuous corridor that existed on this side must later have been blocked by the construction of the east–west wall.

A raised floor would have been essential for storing hay or corn. Since apparently no such floor was provided, the building probably housed cattle. Fodder could have been stored in the loft. The kitchen may indicate that the building also provided living quarters for the servants or farm-labourers.

Phase C

In Phase C, the southern limit of the wing was extended 26 ft. (7.93 m.) over the line of the east–west ditch (Ditch 2, Section EE–FF, fig. 7). The extension wall butted against the western side of the south corridor, but no wall was constructed on the eastern side. It is

---

[1] The burial was submitted to Dr Srboljub Zivanovic of the Department of Anatomy, St Bartholomew's Hospital, for analysis. Unfortunately the bones were in too poor a state of preservation for useful comment.

probable therefore that the extension was open to the courtyard. A fence may also have been constructed in this phase to the north of the building; three post bases ran on the same alignment as its western wall. How far it extended was not determined.

Phase D

The courtyard wall between the east and west wings was built over the Phase C extension. The wall measured 2 ft. 3 in. (.69 m.) wide, and was constructed in flint and white mortar, and set in a foundation trench. None of the wall survived owing to robbing but its western limit ran to within 15 ft. (4.57 m.) of the west wall where it met existing masonry of the Phase C extension. Why it was not built up to the corner of the building is uncertain, possibly either to make use of an existing wall or because a door existed at this point. A pit, 4 ft.

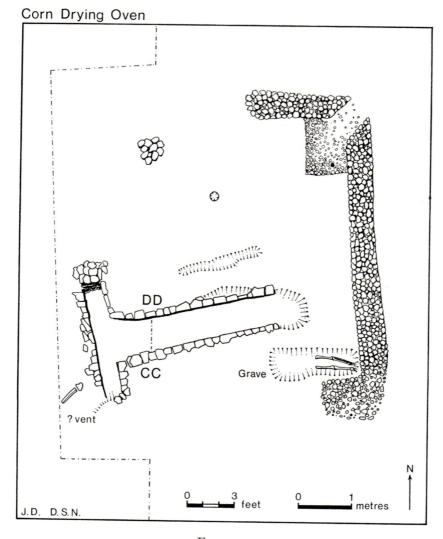

Fig. 25

3 in. (1.30 m.) in diameter, cut its western limit, possibly to rob any tiles that may have been present. The eastern extent of the wall was traced almost as far as Building B (fig. 19, p. 33) but it too had suffered severely from erosion and could not be traced any further. No evidence was found in the centre of the wall for a door or gatehouse leading into the courtyard.

T-SHAPED CORN-DRYING OVEN (fig. 25, pl. XII*b*)

The T-shaped corn-drying oven lay south-west of Building C on an east–west alignment with the stoke-hole on the eastern side. The main flue, which was 1 ft. 6 in. (.46 m.) below the natural clay surface level, measured 11 ft. 6 in. (3.50 m.) long by 2 ft. (.61 m.) wide: the bar of the T was 7 ft. (2.13 m.) long by 1 ft. 3 in. (.38 m.) wide. The structure was well preserved, surviving in places to a height of 1 ft. 7 in. (.48 m.), and was built mainly of *tegulae*. Generally the flanged side of the tiles formed the inside face of the wall which was mortared and rendered throughout with lime and clay (Section CC–DD, fig. 26).

Section **CC-DD**

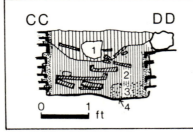

Layer No.	Description of layer
1	Brown clay with flint and tile
2	Chalk, clay and tile. Destruction material from oven
3	Marl with charcoal flecking
4	Charcoal on floor of oven

Fig. 26

Flint was used to construct the northern terminal wall of the bar, which was not built vertically, but at an angle. Flints were also used in the south wall of the main flue where they occurred in a single course — the only course to survive above ground level. No masonry was used in the southern terminal wall although the natural clay also sloped at an angle. The ground surface around this point was disturbed and had a tile standing on end sunken into the clay. It is possible, therefore, that the southern terminal was a vent.

The occurrence of flint in the upper course of the main channel might suggest that the oven was rebuilt; but this is unlikely, since no repairs were carried out in the stoke-hole, the area most subjected to heat, and because the tiles in the wall were built over the flints in the northern terminal. The filling of the oven consisted mainly of chalk and tile which had collapsed from the superstructure; but beneath this was a layer of charcoal[1] that extended from the stoke-hole to just before the 'bar'. This layer was treated by flotation, but no carbonized grain was found.

The only features associated with the oven were a shallow depression north of the flue which may have held a sleeper beam, a post-hole, and a number of compacted flints, which

[1] Mr G. Morgan identified the charcoal (sample 37) as from the *Populus* species; see p. 264.

may have been a post-base: none of these features could be interpreted as having formed part of the superstructure. The date of this structure is problematical. The majority of the pottery forms (p. 253) indicate an Antonine date, but the occurrence of a small sherd from a Castorware beaker may possibly advance the date into the third century. It also contained a samian stamp, CIRIVNA.

To the east of the oven was a wall on a north–south axis with short westerly return walls at either end. The structure was irregular in plan, for the northern return extended 6 ft. (1.83 m.) whereas the southern return extended only 2 ft. 6 in. (.76 m.). A gap of 1 ft. 9 in. (.53 m.) occurred in the north corner of the wall, which was associated with a square platform of small pebbles that were more compacted on the west side, but thinned towards the east.

A grave 5 ft. 6 in. (1.68 m.) long had been dug in the inside corner of the southern return-wall. Only the lower limb-bones of a male skeleton survived,[1] the *femora*, *tibiae*, *fibulae*, *tarsi*, *metatarsi* and *phalanges*: the *patellae* and the remainder of the skeleton were missing. The grave-filling was uniform throughout, but presumably since only half a skeleton was found in a full-length grave, the body must have been disturbed.

The purpose of the structure is most doubtful. Either it was a screen for sheltering the stoke-hole (unless it was the reverse and was designed to encourage a better draught) or the structure had no association with it at all. The presence of the grave may possibly indicate that it was a mausoleum, since a similar mausoleum, enclosing three graves, was discovered at Normangate Field, Castor, by G. Dannell[2] and J. P. Wild. Furthermore, south of the corn-drying oven were two pits (described below), one of which, Pit B, was roughly the same shape, and the correct orientation for a grave. Since the trackway leading to the villa was close by, it is possible that the structure and Pit B formed part of a mortuary alongside the road, and that with the extensions to the villa complex, or chalk-quarrying, and the apparent realignment of the road, the burials were transferred. At least this would explain why there was only part of the skeleton surviving in the main grave, and if Pit B had also been a grave, why no traces of bones were found.

Pit A (fig. 22)

Pit A measured 9 ft. by 8 ft. (2.75 × 2.44 m.) with a maximum depth of 1 ft. 6 in. (.46 m.). It was filled with dark earth, flecked with charcoal, and contained pottery, flints and fragments of a relief-patterned box tile with the W-Chevron roller-stamp decoration. It also contained a sherd of samian of the potter Iustus, A.D. 150–80. Surrounding the pit was a layer of cobbles, which appeared to run over the pit. Running into its north-west corner was an irregular gully, about 2–3 in. (.05–.08 m.) deep, containing a similar fill to that of the pit itself. Parallel with the south side were three post-holes set 6 ft. (1.83 m.) apart, each about 6 in. (.15 m.) in diameter and at least 1 ft. 11 in. (.59 m.) deep. They

---

[1] The author is particularly grateful to Dr Srboljub Zivanovic for the following information: an adult male skeleton, bearing no evidence of any disease. The height estimated from the length of the *tibia* was 176.16 cm. according to Trotter-Glesser formula. Cnemic index was 38.3 (*tibia* is mesocnemic). Platymeric index was 81.81 (femurs are platymeric). Post-mineralization of the bones is not very high.

[2] Mr G. Dannell kindly discussed this feature with the author.

were filled with brown clay, containing flecks of charcoal. Although their filling was different from that of the pit, they seem to have been associated since their alignment was similar. The post-holes did not continue further east or west. The purpose of the pit is uncertain. Its association with the post-holes may indicate that it was the sunken floor of a shelter.

Pit B (fig. 22)

Pit B measured 6 ft. by 2 ft. 6in. (1.83 × .76 m.) and lay on an east–west axis, north-east of Pit A. It was about 6 in. (.15 m.) deep and had a similar filling to Pit A. It was covered by the cobbles and contained only some animal remains. It is possible that it was a grave (see p. 41 above), but it contained no human bones.

Pits A and B and the three adjacent post-holes are of earlier date than the adjacent stockade and gully (see p. 82). The pits and post-holes were sealed beneath the cobbles, whereas the stockade and gully cut the cobbles. From samian fragments in the pits it is possible to attribute them to the late second century. The presence of second-century pottery so far south of the main house would suggest that further occupation may be found in the area, and this is further confirmed by the discovery of an enamelled brooch (SF 27, fig. 55), close to Pit A. Whether this occupation was contemporary with Building C is uncertain.

DISCUSSION

In Period 4 the villa grew in size with the addition of the outer wings. This development may have followed fairly swiftly after the construction of Building A. The industry or trades carried out in these buildings is uncertain, although the plan and character of the western wing denote its use as a barn and living quarters for staff. Apart from the corn-drying oven, and possibly Pit A further south, no other ancillary buildings were associated with this period and none were found in the courtyard. Apart from seven irregular post-holes mid-way between the wings, the courtyard seems to have been deliberately kept clear of work surfaces and structures; a sufficient depth of soil remained over the courtyard to have retained evidence of any features that might have existed. It is possible the area was being farmed in Roman times since early plough furrow marks were found in the area.[1] Further evidence that the courtyard was kept clear, apart from the two areas of lime slurry and the water-conduits, was the lack of rubbish pits;[2] the only pit found was the clay pit south-west of Building B (Plan, fig. 20. Section W–X, fig. 21).

The reason why the corridors of Buildings A and B should have been subdivided into small rooms is uncertain. They may indicate either a growth in the main family, or an increase in the staff; but for staff to be accommodated in the main house while there were out-buildings is unlikely. It will be obvious from later periods that the baths were a major feature of the house, and the rooms in the corridors may have been built to accommodate guests. Perhaps it is not mere coincidence that the rooms were possibly added at the same time as the cold plunge-bath (Room 13).

[1] Shown on plan, fig. 22.
[2] The absence of features in the courtyards compares with the courtyards at Latimer and High Wycombe. It has been postulated that the courtyards of these villas were laid out with gardens or orchards, so perhaps the courtyard at Gadebridge was similarly farmed.

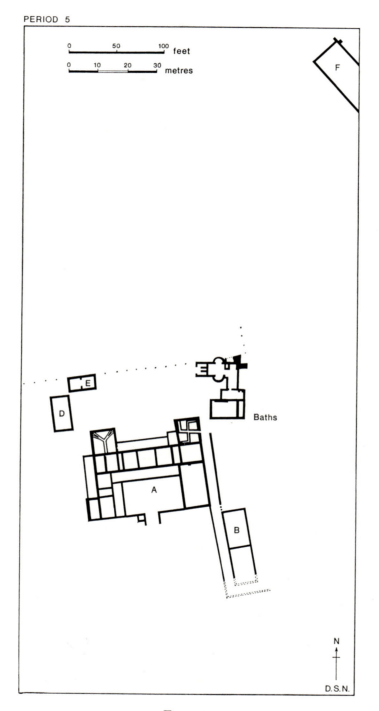

PERIOD 5

Baths

FIG. 27

PERIOD 5 (fig. 27; reconstruction drawing of Periods 5 and 6, fig. 30)

The villa was extensively modernized in the early fourth century by the enlargement and addition of rooms and by the construction of three new farm buildings. A gatehouse was built leading into the inner courtyard. The outer wings were probably destroyed and the courtyard transferred to the north side of the house. The baths were now connected to the villa.

All the walls of this period, dated to the early Constantinian era, were constructed in flint and bright yellow mortar and were about 2 ft. 6 in. (.76 m.) wide. Many alterations and additions were made to the villa; they included Room 34 on the west; a gatehouse leading into the inner courtyard; the two large rooms on the northern side (Rooms 18 and 27); and Buildings D, E and F. The baths also had extensive repairs, which included the enlargement of the plunge-bath (Room 13), alterations to the *praefurnium* (Room 10), *caldarium* (Room 9) and *tepidarium* (Room 2), and the construction of two flint features north-east of Room 1.

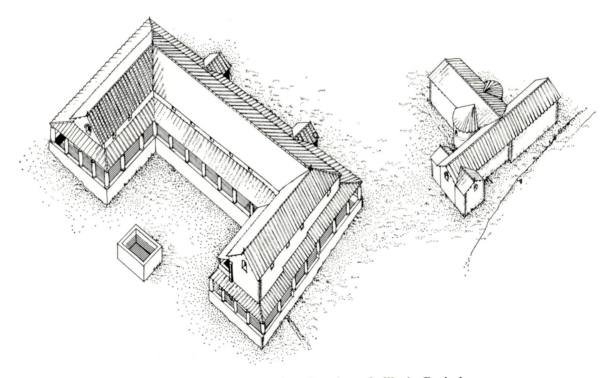

FIG. 28.   Reconstruction drawing of villa in Period 3

The architects also moved the axis of symmetry of Building A to the west (plan, fig. 5; reconstruction of alterations to front elevation of Building A, fig. 29). This was achieved by extending the villa (Room 34) over the western corridor and placing the gatehouse off-centre to the earlier courtyard. The measurement from the east side of the gate to the outer corridor wall of Building B was almost equal to the measurement from the west side of the gate to the west wall of Room 34.

Room 20 was enlarged by the destruction of the arcades. This enabled the room and those upstairs to be widened over the western corridor. The eastern corridor on the west wing was also demolished, for this explains why it was blocked from the main range of rooms. However, the corridor was never reduced to the same level as the courtyard surface. With the demolition of the corridor, the gatehouse would have had a symmetrical relationship to the courtyard.

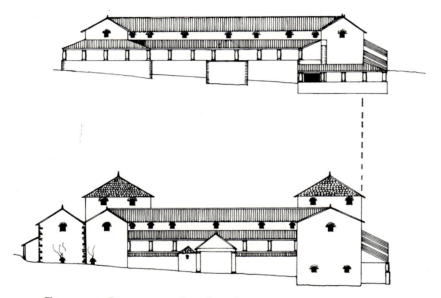

Fig. 29. Reconstruction drawings of front elevations of Building A in Periods 3 and 6

The plan of the villa was further altered by the extension of both the east and west wings, over the line of the original south corridors. The southern wall of the west wing was dissected to reveal the Period 5 masonry constructed over the narrower corridor wall (pl. XIIIa). A similar use of the corridor wall as a foundation was also made in the east wing; however, the south wall of Room 20 was not dissected as it survived to a height of 3 ft. (.91 m.). Building C was probably demolished in this period and the flints used in the rebuilding. Whether Building B was retained is uncertain. Certainly the northern corridor went out of use, and perhaps the western corridor also, but unlike the outer west wing no extensive robbing had taken place. The balance of evidence is on the side of the retention of Building B.

It appears from the construction of the gatehouse, that the outer courtyard wall was no longer regarded as the southern perimeter of the estate. The construction of Buildings D and E to the north-west of the villa, balancing the bath-house on the eastern side, formed, probably quite intentionally, a new northern courtyard. It would appear therefore that

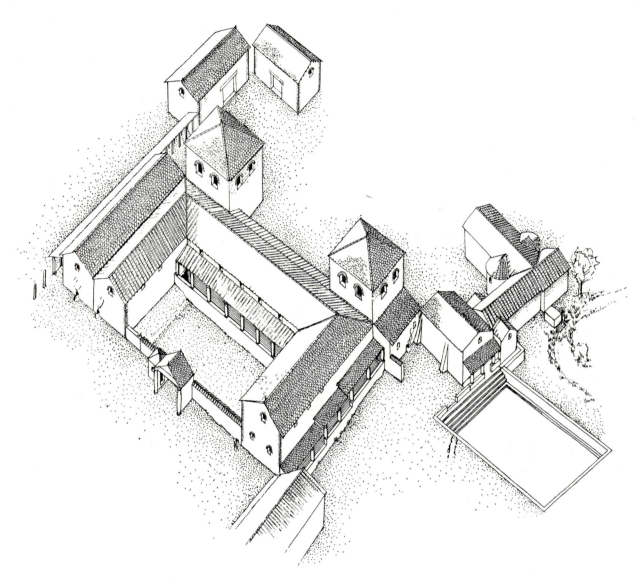

FIG. 30.   Reconstruction drawing of villa in Period 6

there was a tendency for farm buildings to be moved out of sight of the front of the villa, so as to allow the main building and the gatehouse the maximum effect.[1]

It is probable that the gatehouse was mainly for show; it had no function apart from leading into the courtyard, and giving access to an enlarged Room 20, for no evidence has been found for steps leading up to the higher level of the main east–west range and the west wing. However, it is possible access was by means of a staircase situated in Room 20.

[1] For further discussion on this subject see p. 96.

It has been stated above under Period 4 (p. 31) that the approach-road to the villa was never from the south, but more probably from the south-west, and that a track entered the original southern outer courtyard between Buildings A and C. Access to the villa in Period 5 still appears to have been from the south-west, but now by means of a cobbled path leading into the northern courtyard between Buildings A and D.

BUILDING A (fig. 5)

Room 18

Room 18 was an irregular-shaped room built on the north-east side of the villa, measuring 23 ft. by 20 ft. 6 in. (7.01 × 6.24 m.), reducing on the south side to 19 ft. 9 in. (6.02 m.). The walls varied in thickness from 2 ft. 6 in. (.76 m.) to 4 ft. (1.22 m.) — the widest wall found in any of the villa buildings. The south-east wall of the room was not constructed in yellow mortar as used in the other walls, but in a white mortar; it is probable therefore that the wall was associated with the conversion of the corridors into rooms in Period 4. The original outer corridor-wall ran beneath the floor, but the eastern wall of the porch had been destroyed by the western wall of the room. In Period 5 the room was paved with a red-brick tessellated pavement which was repaired in the south-west corner with irregular pieces of tile. The repairs were necessitated by the subsidence of the corridor make-up around the old corridor wall. In Period 6 the floor was cut by the construction of a swastika-shaped hypocaust. This will be described below, under Period 6 (p. 63).

Room 19

The hypocaust in this room probably belonged to Period 5 as the type of *pilae* and the bedding mortar were similar to the other Period 5 works. The stoke-hole was in the western wall, and was 3 ft. 9 in. (1.15 m.) wide; it appeared to be too wide for a normal stoke-hole entrance, so it is probable that the sides of the furnace were constructed in tiles which have since been robbed. A burnt tiled area outside the stoke-hole was probably the hearth floor. The *opus signinum* floor close to the stoke-hole was also burnt, so severely that its surface was destroyed and its flint make-up revealed. A denarius of Trajan was found close to the surviving tiles and may at one time have been sealed by them.

Room 20 (fig. 31)

In Period 5 Room 20 was totally rebuilt. Both the east and west walls of the room were extended towards the south, by 10 ft. (3.05 m.), over the line of the southern corridor, and the piers supporting the first-floor wall demolished. Consequently the western corridor alongside the upper storey must have been dismantled. The original south wall was demolished (pl. XIIIb) making the overall measurements 23 ft. 9 in. by 43 ft. (7.24 × 13.11 m.). Both the east and west walls were rebuilt, that on the eastern side to within 12 in. (.31 m.) of the north wall. The whole of this wall was not demolished, however, because a rebuilding line ran from this point down the wall, at an angle of about 25° to the ground. A similar rebuilding line was not observed on the western wall, since it was robbed.

ROOM 20   PERIOD 5.   Raised floor

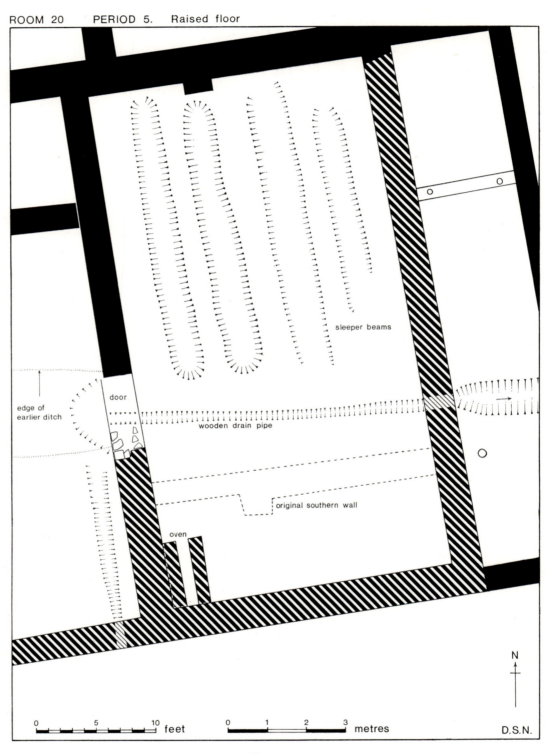

sleeper beams

edge of
earlier ditch

door

wooden drain pipe

original southern wall

oven

0   5   10 feet   0   1   2   3   metres

N

D.S.N.

FIG. 31

When the south wall of the room was demolished, the door was transferred to the west side (pl. XIVa). The frame was 5 ft. 3 in. (1.60 m.) wide and had a massive timber threshold laid on a bed of tiles and mortar. The step was built into the door-jamb for approximately 6 in. (.15 m.). The reason for such a solid step was to bridge the loose ditch-filling that ran underneath, and to cover a timber drain, laid as another attempt to cure the continual flooding of the room. The drain did not continue west beyond the door-step, and was designed to collect water from immediately west of the door. The timber pipe ran at an angle across the room and out on the eastern side, where it discharged into an open gully that ran towards the river. The pipe rested on the clay floor and no attempt was made to protect it. Whether the original conduit leading into the east side of the room was still functioning is not known; it had probably gone out of use.

The northern extent of the eaves-drip on the western side of the wing was filled with chalk, but its southern extent remained in use. A channel bridged with roofing tiles was made through the courtyard wall, 1 ft. 6 in. (.46 m.) from the west wall of the room. The channel was 12 in. (.31 m.) high and 6 in. (.15 m.) wide.

A raised timber floor was built in the northern area of the room, north of the door (pl. VIa). The floor was laid on four massive joists resting in shallow U-shaped trenches, 2 ft. 6 in. (.76 m.) wide and about 24 ft. (7.32 m.) long, which ran on a north–south axis parallel with the east and west walls (pl. VIa). The trenches probably represent the shape of the floor joists, split tree trunks. The provision of a raised floor, which would allow air to circulate beneath it, may indicate that this part of the room was a barn or granary, although it is possible it was installed merely to provide a dry floor.

The buttress against the north wall was cut back flush with it, and only the lower 12 in. (.31 m.) was left. Subsequently the scar on the wall was rendered with mortar and covered with white painted plaster, which also covered the original Period 3 imitation ashlar blocks. The painted plaster on the north wall did not cover the lower 1 ft. 2 in. (.35 m.), probably because, when applied, it had to respect the level of the raised floor. This explains why the buttress was not fully dismantled, as the lower 12 in. (.31 m.) remained beneath the floor boards. It would be reasonable to assume that when this floor was laid, the Period 3 bases no longer survived.

An oven 5 ft. 6 in. (1.68 m.) long by 3 ft. 6 in. (1.07 m.) wide was constructed in the south-west corner of the room (pl. XIIIb). It had a flue set between two parallel stands and was built of blocks of Totternhoe-stone. It was demolished in Period 6 and amongst the remains were a number of voussoirs possibly used to vault the roof. The uppermost course of flints in the adjacent west wall (pl. XIVb) appeared to arch over towards the oven (they were not disturbed by the plough), so it is possible they acted as a support for the voussoirs. If this were the case, the total height of the oven would have been about 4 ft. 6 in. (1.37 m.). As this southern area had no raised floor and was equipped with an oven it was presumably a kitchen.

Room 27 (pl. XVa, b)

Room 27 was built on the north-west side of the villa and was 23 ft. (7.01 m.) square with walls about 2 ft. (.61 m.) thick. The west side of the room was terraced into the slope of the

E

ground, so that the foundation on this side was 12 in (.31 m.) deep, whereas those on the eastern side were built directly on to the natural clay and marl subsoil. Compared to Room 18 the room was more regular in plan, and the walls more even in thickness. The walls were built on to a triple offset foundation with a total width of about 3 ft. (.91 m.). Even though there were these differences between the two rooms they are possibly contemporary, since the yellow mortar and the herringbone technique of laying the flints were the same. Their placing at either side of the villa, given the assumption that the architect intended the building to present a balanced view, would also suggest their being associated.

The room was heated by a channelled hypocaust in the plan of the letter Y, the arms of which divided in a fish-tail arrangement, terminating at niches in the walls, which originally contained flue-tiles. The floor of the hypocaust was 2 ft. 6 in. (.76 m.) below the surface of the floor, and was constructed in flint resting on a triple course of tile, set in pink tile-mortar. The walls of the channel were 8 in. (.20 m.) thick, and the flue about 12 in. (.31 m.) wide; little of the hypocaust survived as it had been robbed for tile. Cutting the north wall of Room 26 was the stoke-hole, which had been partly constructed in Barnack limestone, fragments of which were found in the rubble filling of the stoking-pit. The room was also built over the corridor, the north wall of which ran beneath the make-up for the floor; the porch was also built over by an extension of the east–west corridor wall. A door-step 2 ft. 6 in. (.76 m.) wide was found in the eastern wall of the room opening into the corridor; this was probably the only door into the room — it is unlikely to have been entered from Room 26, which contained the stoke-hole.

The floor of the room was surrounded with a quarter-round moulding and was paved with a large mosaic bordered with red-brick *tesserae*. The border *tesserae* were of two types — those closest to the wall were much larger than those around the mosaic: therefore it is possible the floor was originally paved throughout with plain red brick *tesserae*, and that the mosaic and small border *tesserae* were inserted later. Room 18 was also paved with brick *tesserae* in Period 5 and was paved with a mosaic in Period 6. The mosaics were probably contemporary with one another. As no major rebuilding was carried out in the room in Period 6, the mosaic will be described here.

It was of the early fourth century but had gone out of use after A.D. 353. It was approximately 16 ft. 6 in. (5.02 m.) square, but was extremely damaged by ploughing and by the robber trench cut into the hypocaust channels; sufficient remained, however, to attempt a reconstruction drawing (pl. XVI).

It was a large geometric pavement bordered by treble braided guilloche, and divided into nine 8-lozenge star patterns. Set between the patterns were four squares, one of which partially survived: this enclosed a guilloche mat. To the sides of the pavement were eight half-squares, also bordered by guilloche, four of which contained fragmentary designs — these included, describing the illustration clockwise from the top right-hand side: (a) a short length of guilloche; (b) an encircled guilloche knot set in a frame; (c) a short twist of guilloche, shorter than (a); and (d) traces of two leaves or petals set stalk to stalk. Between each square and half-square were small squares set lozengewise. These were bordered by guilloche and contained two triangles set apex to apex. Only three squares survived, sufficient however to tell that the three pairs of triangles were not identical in colouring. The eight lozenges within each star pattern were extremely well executed. Their colours, red, yellow, blue/grey and pink, were deliberately shaded to obtain a perspective effect, and only the colours in the opposing lozenges repeated. In the centre of the lozenges were small infilling motifs comprising circles and spirals, some with red petals set on either side.

Although square, the mosaic was not laid in the centre of the room, but to the south, so in order to secure a symmetrical relationship to the walls a make-up panel of guilloche was included against the northern edge of the mosaic. This guilloche differed in style from that on the mosaic as it was worked in pale yellow and red *tesserae*, and enclosed small circles worked in dark grey, red, and light grey consecutively.

A most unusual feature of the mosaic was that it was made almost entirely of terracotta *tesserae*. Only the single band of dark grey *tesserae* which formed the framework of the pattern was in natural stone. Whereas in other Hertfordshire mosaics the white *tesserae* are of lime-stone, especially in backgrounds, here all the background *tesserae* were either pale yellow or pale pink terracotta. The pink and pale grey *tesserae* were so even in their colouring as to suggest that clays were deliberately mixed and fired to make them. Broken tile was used to form the red and yellow *tesserae*. White limestone *tesserae* were used to patch the floor on its western side.

The all-over pattern of nine 8-lozenge stars of the mosaic is unparalleled in Britain, although the pavement from Great Staughton[1] has similarities. Here the overall scheme comprises twelve 8-lozenge star patterns (enclosing no filling motifs), the central four of which have been halved in order to surround an octagonal panel. Sufficient remained of the Gadebridge pavement to establish that no similar central panel existed. A close parallel to the perspective colouring of the lozenges within the star patterns on the Gadebridge pavement occurs on a side panel to the Orpheus mosaic from Barton Farm.[2] On this pave-ment the mosaicist also shaded the lozenges to obtain a perspective effect.

Even though there are similarities between the Gadebridge pavement and mosaics from Great Staughton and Barton Farm, there is insufficient evidence to attribute Gadebridge to either the Durobrivan or Corinian schools.[3]

Only the northern area of the pavement was sealed by rubble. The latter comprised flint, slate, tile, and yellow mortar, amongst which were fragments of carved Barnack limestone (SF 692 and 693, fig. 82), which may have formed a cornice decorating the interior of the room. Also cutting the floor were five post-holes, filled with flint packing, attributed to Period 7.

It is probable that the trenches for the offsets of the north and west walls were used as eaves drips, because the filling in them consisted of silty earth. Two coins were found in the yellow mortar rubble sealing the silt, one of which was dated to A.D. 350–5 and the other to A.D. 388–95.

The foundations of both Rooms 27 and 18 were very wide when compared to the other walls in the villa. For this reason it is possible that the rooms may have had another storey, or at least that the ceilings were higher than the smaller rooms in the villa, and consequently

---

[1] *J.R.S.*, XLIX (1959), 118, fig. 15.
[2] J. Buckman and C. H. Newmarch, *Remains of Roman Art in Corinium* (1850), p. 32, pl. VIII.

[3] For discussion on the mosaics of the Corinian school, see Dr D. J. Smith's article (ed. Rivet, pp. 71 ff.). The author is indebted to Dr Smith for discussing the date of the mosaic and stylistic affinities.

E1

the roofs were also higher. The effect created would have been that of twin towers on either side of the villa, probably bearing pyramidal roofs of Collyweston roofing slates.

Rooms 25 and 26 (fig. 16)

Room 25 was originally a passage linking the northern and southern corridors, and was paved with an *opus signinum* floor. However, in Period 5 its west wall was dismantled to 8 in. (.20 m.) below the level of the adjacent floors which, together with the dismantled wall, gradually became covered with soot from the hypocaust in Room 27.

It is unlikely that the east wall of the passage was also demolished, because Room 24 was not also covered with soot. Room 26 was reduced in size by the construction of a Period 5 north–south wall: the overall dimensions of the room were not greatly affected — the room was reduced to 18 ft. 6 in. by 17 ft. 9 in. (5.64 × 5.40 m.). The Period 5 north–south wall probably formed part of the hypocaust furnace; its northern extent was cut by the robbery of tile from the hypocaust, and the eastern face of the wall close to the stoke-hole had a rendering of pink tile-mortar, the same as that used to bond the tile and flint in the hypocaust channels. The wall cut the *opus signinum* floor. On the east side of the wall was another which ran parallel to it; this may have belonged to the original Period 3 villa, because it appeared to bond with the north wall of the room, was cut by the Period 5 stoke-hole, and appeared to have been covered by the *opus signinum* floor. Evidence of this floor was only found over the south-west corner of the wall. The wall was extremely irregular in plan, however, and was of totally different character from other Period 3 walls. Apart from slight evidence of Period 5 rebuilding in the southern section, the wall was breached in two places. The wider breach was 3 ft. 6 in. (1.07 m.) wide, the narrower 12 in. (.31 m.) wide, and the intermediate length of wall about 2 ft. (.61 m.): no wall foundations existed in the breaches. Surrounding the intermediate stump of wall was a layer of green sand which also covered the hearth. The purpose of the wall is uncertain. Because the wall was so different to known Period 3 walls, it should be classed as belonging to a doubtful period, although earlier than Period 5.

Cutting through the *opus signinum* floor on the eastern side of the stoke-hole were two concentric circles of stake-holes (pl. XVIII*a*); the total diameter of the circles was 6 to 7 ft. (1.83–2.13 m.). The stake-holes were from 2 to 6 in. (.05–.15 m.) wide and 6 to 7 in. (.15–.18 m.) deep. Within the circle was an area of burning, more scorched to the north, although occurring throughout.

The juxtaposition of the stake circle and the hypocaust furnace would suggest some association; it is probable that the stake circle was a receptacle for ash raked out of the furnace. A similar feature was found in the Period 2 *praefurnium* in Room 7 (fig. 10) and another was associated with the stoke-hole (Rooms 6 and 7) on the nearby villa at Boxmoor.[1] Whether hot ash was simply dumped into the receptacle to cool is uncertain, since if it was hot enough to scorch the floor, then it would have been hot enough to burn the stakes. The stakes therefore may have been laced with wattles and covered with daub, although no trace of daub was found. It may, alternatively, have been used for cooking or heating water.

[1] Situated in Room 6 (*Brit.*, 1 (1970), plan facing p. 162).

A number of pits and post-holes also cut the floors in Rooms 25 and 26. The numbering of pits follows in sequence. Pits A and B have already been discussed (p. 41).

Pit C

Pit C was almost rectangular in plan, measured 3 ft. 6 in. by 2 ft. 6 in. (1.07 × .76 m.) and was 1 ft. 2 in. (.36 m.) deep. It was filled with pure brown earth, which became more stony in its upper level.

Pit D

This pit was oval in plan and 2 ft. 3 in. (.69 m.) long, 4 in. (.10 m.) deep and filled with brown soil. It lay 2 ft. (.61 m.) north of the south wall.

Pit E

This was semi-circular in shape, measured 1 ft. 6 in. (.46 m.) in diameter and may originally have cut the south wall, although this is not certain because the wall at this point had been robbed. The pit was 8 in (.20 m.) deep and filled with brown soil.

Pit F

Pit F lay to the east of Pit E, was oval in plan and 2 ft. (.61 m.) long by 5 in. (.13 m.) deep. It was filled with black earth and contained a coin of A.D. 320–4. Its filling would suggest it to have been a Period 7 post-hole.

Pit G

This lay at the southern edge of the old passage, Room 25, and was roughly rectangular in plan. It was 3 ft. 6 in. (1.07 m.) long by 2 ft. 6 in. (.76 m.) wide, and partially cut the north edge of the wall. It was 1 ft. 6 in. (.46 m.) deep and was filled with a layer of gravel and a layer of black soil. The gravel may indicate it to have been a soakaway. A coin dated to A.D. 346–50 was found in the black filling. This pit also probably belongs to Period 7.

Pit H

This pit lay immediately to the north of Pit G, and was 1 ft. 3 in. (.38 m.) wide, 7 in. (.18 m.) deep, and filled with brown soil; it did not cut the wall.

Pit I

Pit I lay half way along the east wall of the passage. It was 1 ft. 9 in. (.53 m.) in diameter, 7 in. (.18 m.) deep, and filled with brown soil.

Pit J

This was 1 ft. 3 in. (.38 m.) in diameter and filled with black soil similar to the filling in the Period 7 post-holes; it should probably be regarded as such.

Pit K

This was also a Period 7 post-hole as it was filled with black earth and packing flints. It was 1 ft. 6 in. (.46 m.) in diameter and 6 in. (.15 m.) deep.

The reduced area of Room 26 west of the north–south Period 5 wall was surfaced throughout with *opus signinum* and skirted with a quarter-round moulding. Cutting the floor to the north of the room was a beam slot, 8 ft. (2.44 m.) long by 1 ft. 2 in. (.35 m.) wide, and 1 ft. 2 in. (.35 m.) deep. It cut the foundation trench for the north–south Period 5 wall, but did not continue up to the west wall; a paved gap of 6 in. (.15 m.) was left between the wall and the beam. A coin of Valens was found in the filling of the beam slot. Whether the floor was contemporary with the Period 4 floor in the western corridor, and the sleeper beam contemporary with the re-arrangement of the rooms in the corridor is uncertain. It is possible the beam supported a staircase rising into an upper storey over Room 27. The space north of the beam was too small for a room.

A layer of black earth, associated with hundreds of small flint chippings, all of which were burnt, was found throughout Rooms 25 and 26. It is possible that the chippings were fractured from the walls by the heat of a fire. If there was a fire, it was probably confined to these rooms since no flint chippings were found elsewhere.

Room 28 (fig. 5)

The Period 3 ovens went out of use. The room was cut by an east–west wall and the ovens sealed by a layer of chalk and a tessellated pavement. Beneath this pavement were two radiate coins, nos. 34 and 90, the latest of which was an irregular dated to *c.* A.D. 270. Most of the pavement survived, but the *tesserae* in the south-east side of the room were destroyed by ploughing.

Room 29 (fig. 5)

The room was extended from the new south wall of Room 28 over the southern corridor and measured 14 ft. by 29 ft. (4.25 × 8.84 m.). The southern corridor wall was used as the foundation for the extension (pl. XIIIa) and the original south wall of the wing was demolished. A layer of chalk capped with a tessellated pavement (in a manner similar to that of Room 28) was put down throughout the room over the trench of the Period 3 division wall.

A Period 7 post-hole cut the tessellated pavement on the north-west side of the room. No floor survived on the eastern or southern sides because it had been destroyed by ploughing and by a later Period 6 Y-shaped hypocaust. The room suffered from subsidence as the floors had sunk into the filling of the early ditch (Ditch 1).

Room 34 (fig. 5)

Room 34 was built on to the south-western side of the wing, over the western and southern corridors and over the masonry corridor-division of Period 4. The room measured 10 ft. by 18 ft. 6 in. (3.05 × 5.64 m.) and was constructed in flint and bright yellow mortar. Its walls varied in thickness from 3 ft. 6 in. (1.07 m.) to 2 ft. (.61 m.); this was because the west and south walls had been built over an existing foundation. The north wall had no earlier foundation and was only 2 ft. (.61 m.) wide. Apart from its earlier *opus signinum* pavement, no floor survived. The room was demolished in Period 6 prior to the construction of a massive hypocaust on the west side of the villa. The room was also cut by a post-hole 1 ft. 6 in. (.46 m.) wide, filled with black earth and flint packing. This is probably associated with Period 7.

THE GATEHOUSE (fig. 5, pl. VIIIa)

The gatehouse and courtyard wall were bonded to one another and both were built in flint and yellow mortar. They were also bonded to the south walls of the wings. The gate was 12 ft. (3.65 m.) wide and flanked on both sides by two walls which extended south 10 ft. (3.05 m.) beyond the outer face of the courtyard wall. On the western side was a small 'porter's lodge' (Room 36) which occupied the right-angle enclosed by the western flank, and which measured 5 ft. by 4 ft. (1.52 × 1.22 m.) internally. Only the flint make-up for its floor survived; on it were a bronze balance and a lead weight (SF 47, fig. 56). On the east side of the wall were the remains of a lime-slurry, possibly associated with the Period 5 rebuilding.

THE BATHS (fig. 8)

Plunge-bath, Room 13 (fig. 19)

The plunge-bath (Room 13) was abandoned for a period of time; its floor was covered with a layer of soot and cut by 7 stake-holes from 3 to 5 in. (.08 to .13 m.) wide. The probable reason for the abandonment is that Room 12 subsided and cracked. The south wall of Room 13 may also have subsided; it was reinforced by two buttresses. In the course of rebuilding the west wall was almost entirely rebuilt in flint and yellow mortar, set on a layer of crushed tile. Room 12 was abandoned and filled with rubble which was mixed with white mortar of Periods 3 or 4; the rubble contained no yellow mortar of Periods 5 or 6.

The east wall of the bath was extended 8 ft. (2.44 m.), increasing its width from 17 ft. 6 in. (5.33 m.) to 25 ft. 6 in. (7.77 m.). A timber (which had been charred prior to being laid and was presumably a seat) was set on a layer of crushed tile against the north side of the bath and rendered with plaster. It was not built up to the west wall, but stopped 3 ft. (.91 m.) short of it. Its eastern extent is not known because here the upper levels of the bath had been destroyed.

The area was then paved throughout with a new *opus signinum* pavement. A quarter-round moulding was laid around the walls and the timber. A lead drain was constructed through the east side of the south wall, and a corridor to Room 6 was built against the east side of the bath. The foundation of the outer corridor wall was slight, presumably because it was not load-bearing; it rested on large blocks of flint and Hertfordshire Puddingstone, set directly on loose make-up soil. The south wall was an extension from the plunge-bath, and had no butt joints. It was also constructed over the line of the earlier outlet for the bath.

E2

Stoke-hole, Room 10 (fig. 8)

Some minor improvements were made in the stoke-hole where the space between the northern flue and the wall was filled with flint and mortar, and the space between the southern flue and the wall blocked by a wall running north–south. The upper hypocaust floor was also relaid; numerous *pila* tiles were replaced, especially in the *tepidarium* (over the original *caldarium*, Room 1). The hypocaust in the southern area of the *tepidarium* (Room 2) was rebuilt when a flint and yellow mortar wall 2 ft. 6 in. (.76 m.) wide was built over the lower hypocaust floor against the existing walls. This enclosed four *pilae*, three of which survived. Why this hypocaust was reduced in size is not known.

Two large foundations of flint were also constructed to the north of the baths. These will be discussed in connexion with the water leat under Period 6 (p. 69).

BUILDING D (fig. 32, pl. XVII)

Building D lay north-west of Building A, ran on a north–south axis, measured 20 ft. (6.10 m.) by 41 ft. (12.50 m.), and was constructed in flint and bright yellow mortar. The slope of the hill was terraced to secure a level platform on which to erect the building (Section II–JJ–KK, fig. 33). The east wall was on the same alignment as the west wall of the massive Period 6 hypocaust built against the main house (Room 35); and the south wall was on the same alignment as the north wall of Room 27, attributed to Period 5. The asymmetrical character of the Period 6 hypocaust — there was more space on the west side of the hypocaust flue than on the east side — suggests that the west wall of the hypocaust may have been constructed to align with an existing foundation, the east wall of Building D. For this reason and the similarities of the mortar, the building is believed to belong to Period 5. The east wall was built over an earlier pit, Pit L.

The entrance into the building was in the centre of the east wall and was about 8 ft. (2.44 m.) wide. A bedding layer of mortar and recesses in the walls which originally held a timber door-step were found.

The outside ground surface was covered with small flint cobbles. East of the entrance were the remains of a wall running on a north-east/south-west axis, built in flint and Barnack limestone resting on natural marl. Whether it was part of an earlier building is uncertain; only a 4-ft. (1.22-m.) length of wall survived. It is possible the wall was built in front of the door merely as a screen, and that it was contemporary with the building.

The building was divided into two rooms by two sleeper beams set end to end. They were set at right-angles to the west wall. The western beam was 4 ft. 6 in. (1.37 m.) long by 9 in. (.23 m.) wide by 3 in. (.08 m.) deep, and started 1 ft. 3 in. (.38 m.) from the west wall of the building. However, the eastern slot was slightly narrower and separated from the western slot by a gap of 1 ft. 5 in. (.43 m.). It was 6 in. (.15 m.) wide, and was only a slight surface feature with virtually no depth. The space between its eastern limit and the entrance probably marked the position of a door opening into a kitchen. This kitchen area had an oven on its east side (pl. XVIII*b*), 2 ft. 6 in. (.76 m.) in diameter: its stoke-hole was lined with tiles and was about 4 ft. long by 12 in. (1.22 × .31 m.) deep. None of the superstructure survived, except for the tile bridging the neck of the flue.

Buildings D & E . Period 5

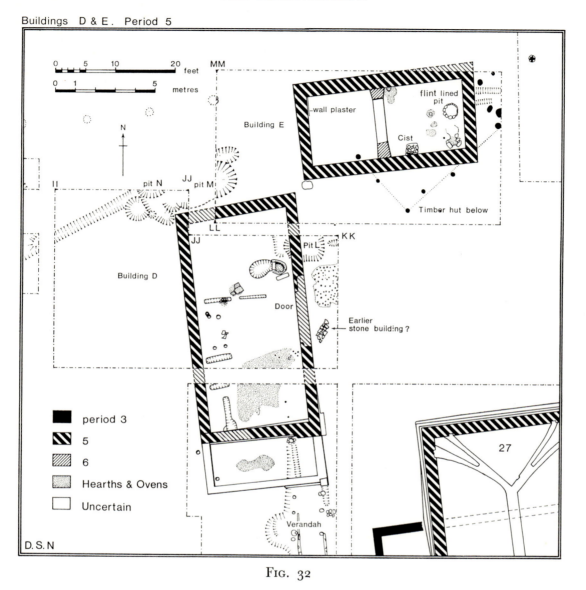

FIG. 32

A hearth was situated in the gap between the sleeper beams. It had consisted of four tiles, of which three survived; they were scorched and cracked by heat. Adjacent to it, over the line of the western beam, were the remains of another hearth. Their relationship is uncertain. Whatever the sequence, the sleeper beams must have been removed before the construction of the hearths because no charred wood was found beneath them.

South of the more westerly sleeper beam was another of similar size, at a distance of 9 ft. (2.75 m.). Between them were two pairs of post-holes, each about 9 in. (.23 m.) wide and filled with chalky earth. The north-western post had been replaced, as here there was a double post-hole. In the south-west corner of the room were two more sleeper beams, one running at right-angles to the west wall, parallel to the sleeper beams already described and about 3 ft. (.91 m.) long, and another at right-angles to the south wall, almost 6 ft. (1.83 m.) in length. Since the filling of the beam slots was the same as that of the post-holes, they were probably contemporary with one another. A burnt hearth area occurred in the south of the building in association with a number of stake-holes.

The northern room was probably a kitchen and servants' quarters but the character of the sleeper beams in the southern room suggests it had other uses, and that the sleeper beams supported a work-bench or raised platform. Apart from the more common domestic iron objects such as knives, fragments of two saws (SF 355 and 360, fig. 70) were found in the occupational rubbish. The building therefore may also have been used as a carpenter's shop. Certainly wood-working was being practised on the estate as a number of other saw blades were found.

In a later phase, the building was extended 12 ft. 6 in. (3.81 m.) over the line of the Period 6 verandah. Where the south-east corner of the extension ran over the verandah bank, the wall was strengthened by an off-set and a block of Barnack limestone. The original south wall was breached by a door. The only features found in the extension were a post-hole on the western side and a hearth.

Pit L (Section II–JJ–KK, fig. 33) beneath the east wall of Building D was apparently a cesspit: the clay filling (L 19) was deposited in thin sealing layers, and the bottom of the pit was stained green. Unfortunately only one sherd was found in the pit, a jar-rim in pale grey fabric with orange surfaces, a form similar to Pot no. 225 (fig. 103) which occurred in an early third-century context from the well. Prior to the construction of the east wall, the pit had been filled with a layer of brown earth, stones and tile (L 18) covered with a layer of rammed chalk (L 17).

BUILDING E (fig. 32, pl. XIX*a*)

Building E lay at right-angles to Building D; its south wall was almost on the same alignment as the north wall of Building D. The building was 29 ft. (8.84 m.) long by 16 ft. 6 in. (5.02 m.) wide, and terraced on its western side 12 in. (.31 m.) into the hill slope. The walls were approximately 2 ft. 6 in. (.76 m.) wide, and constructed in flint with odd blocks of Hertfordshire Puddingstone and chalk, bonded with bright yellow mortar. Many of the flints had white mortar on them which suggested that they had been stripped from other buildings, possibly the abandoned Outer West Wing, Building C. The house had been constructed over the site of an earlier hut.

TIMBER HUT

Its post-holes lay diagonally to Building E, on a north-east/south-west axis, but its overall dimensions were not established because only its east, west, and south sides were found. Its north side ran beneath the later building and all but one of the post-holes were destroyed by the terracing. The south side of the hut was 23 ft. (7.01 m.) long. The posts were 9 to 12 in. (.23–.31 m.) wide and 6 to 9 in. (.15–.23 m.) deep, and were filled with earthy clay. The only feature that may have been associated with the hut was a flint-lined pit, 2 ft. (.61 m.)

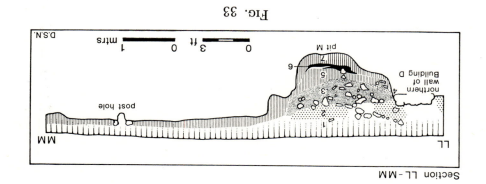

Section LL-MM

Fig. 33

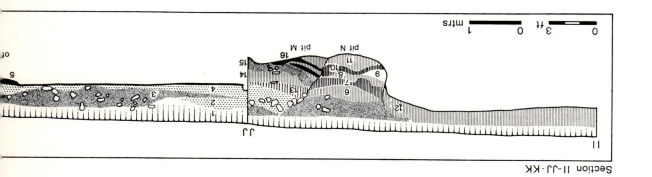

Section II-JJ-KK

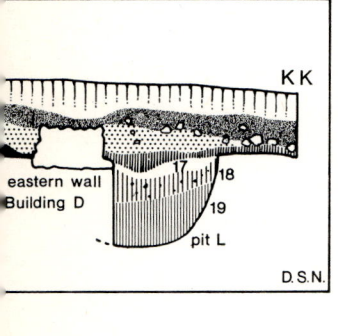

Layer No.	Description of layer	Pottery Nos. illustrated
1	Ploughsoil	—
2	Yellow mortar	—
3	Black earth with flint rubble	—
4	Yellow mortar	380–5
5	Black occupation material over floor	377–9
6	Hillwashed clay	—
7	Grey silt	—
8	Clay seal	—
9	Clay and chalk slip from side of pit	—
10	Black soil	—
11	Clay	—
12	Hillwashed clay	—
13	Grey silt with flint pebbles	—
14	Clay and chalk seal	—
15	Dark grey soil	—
16	Black earth with a layer of clay between	—
17	Rammed chalk capping to pit with grey silt above	—
18	Brown earth with stones and tile	—
19	Clay with fragments of tile	—

Layer No.	Description of layer
1	Ploughsoil
2	Yellow mortar with flint rubble
3	Black silty soil with flints
4	Thin mortar layer possibly associated with the construction of Building D
5	Light brown earthy clay mixed with small stones and charcoal
6	Charcoal
7	Chalk and clay

wide, beneath the eastern room of the later building. It was filled and covered with clay which seems to have been put over the pit prior to rebuilding.

The masonry building was originally a single room, later divided into two by a wall constructed of flint and chalk. The opening between the rooms was 7 ft. (2.13 m.) wide. The eastern room had three hearths, two ovens and a cist, whereas the floor of the western room was totally devoid of features. The clay and marl floors were never paved, although the walls in the western room were originally rendered in white-painted wall-plaster, some of which was found *in situ* on the west wall, the remainder having collapsed over the floor. No collapsed plaster was found over the east room so it was probably not similarly rendered. None of the plaster bore evidence of decoration.

The main oven in the eastern room (pl. XIX*b*), occupied the south-east corner and was constructed in tiles, slate, and blocks of Barnack limestone — materials which would suggest that other buildings were falling into disrepair and being robbed. West of the oven were the remains of a slate-lined cist (pl. XIX*c*), the south edge of which butted against the wall. A cooking pot (Pot no. 392, fig. 111) and the remains of another oven were found in the north-west corner of the eastern room. Pottery nos. 386–98 (fig. 111) were found in the filling of this building.

PIT COMPLEX NORTH OF BUILDING D (Section II–JJ–KK, fig. 33)

The pits north of Building D were probably cesspits; there were traces of cess in the lower silt, and the pits contained very little pottery. Pit M was the earlier, being cut by Pit N. The filling of M comprised alternate layers of clay and chalk; L 14 contained four coins, the latest of which was dated A.D. 341–6. As Pit N (see coin Appendix D, p. 119) cut the rubble collapse over M, it would seem that Pit N was associated with the late occupation in Building E (see below) and that the rubble through which it cut represented the debris from Building D.

DATING OF BUILDINGS D AND E (see coin appendices B and C, pp. 118–19)

A total of thirteen coins were found in the occupation spread in Building D; the majority were Constantinian, but the latest was dated A.D. 351–3. Ten coins were found in the destruction rubble, the latest of which was probably the core of a plated siliqua of Julian (*c.* A.D. 361–3). The rubble inside and outside the building was uniform, but beneath the rubble outside were five coins, the latest of which was dated to A.D. 364–78.

In Building E a total of twenty coins were found, the majority of which came from the second half of the fourth century. The latest coin found in the occupation debris, sealed beneath the collapsed wall plaster, was dated to A.D. 388–402. Another coin of the same date was found in the rubble. As the coins in Building E are later in date than those found in Building D, it is probable that D had fallen into decay whilst E was still occupied, and that the later groups of coins outside Building D were associated with the occupation of Building E. The latter building was certainly occupied until the end of the fourth century and occupation could well have extended into the fifth.

THE STOCKADE (figs. 8 and 32)

On the same alignment as the north wall of Building E was a row of post-holes (Group A) set at 10 to 11 ft. (3.05 to 3.35 m.) intervals; it extended east across the courtyard to the baths and west up the hill. The stockade is attributed to Period 5 because the Period 5 masonry feature which cut Room 7 (fig. 8) was also on the same alignment; an attempt appears to have been made to align all buildings on this side of the courtyard. The post-holes on the west side of Building E continued west for about 130 ft. (39 m.) but were cut midway by a chalk quarry (U) (fig. 46). The stockade and quarries are discussed in detail below (pp. 76–87).

BUILDING F (fig. 27)

Building F lay 300 ft. (91.50 m.) north of the villa, close to the west bank of the River Gade. It was discovered during the road construction in 1962, after the upper levels had already been bulldozed. Only its lowest footings survived. The building was 35 ft. (10.67 m.) wide by 70–90 ft. (21.34–27.45 m.) long, and lay on a north-west/south-east axis, with walls approximately 2 ft. 6 in. (.76 m.) wide, constructed in flint and bright yellow mortar. No finds were made. The size of the building suggests that it was either an aisled house or a barn. The north-west corner had been reinforced by two buttresses, each about 4 ft. (1.22 m.) square.

PERIOD 6 (fig. 34)

A large bathing pool was built on to the bath-house and a massive heated room built on to the west side of Building A.

Hitherto the economy of the villa appears to have been based on farming, but the scale of the massive bathing-pool constructed on the east side of the baths suggests the possibility that the bathing establishment now became the primary attraction of the settlement. This period has a *terminus post quem* of A.D. 319 (a date based on a coin sealed beneath a Period 6 mortar floor in the courtyard) and continued no later than A.D. 353. Further additions were also made to the villa (fig. 5): an enormous hypocaust, Room 35, was constructed on its west side, a Y-shaped hypocaust built into the south-west wing, an extension built against the eastern wall of Room 18, and Room 18 itself provided with a hypocaust in the plan of a swastika. Room 20 was divided into four rooms, and the plunge-bath (13) paved with yet another floor. All the walls of this period measured about 1 ft. 6 in. (.46 m.) wide and were constructed in flint and yellow mortar, this being more orange than Period 5 mortars. The main characteristic of the construction of this period was the widespread use of blocks of chalk in the buildings.

Room 18

This room was enlarged on its eastern side by the addition of a narrow room measuring about 9 ft. by 23 ft. (2.75 × 7.01 m.), the east wall of which extended over the eastern

PERIOD 6

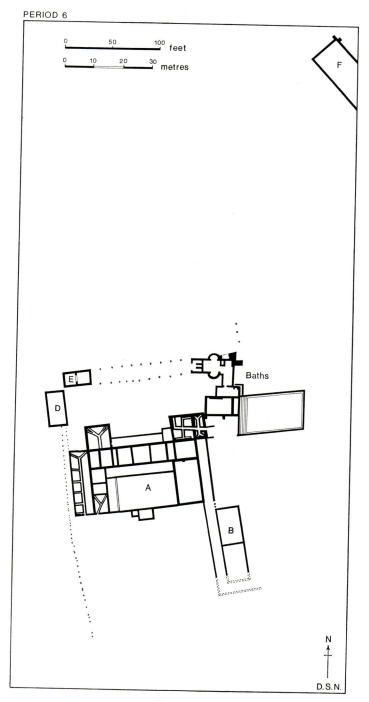

Fig. 34

ROOM 20   PERIOD 6.   phase A & B

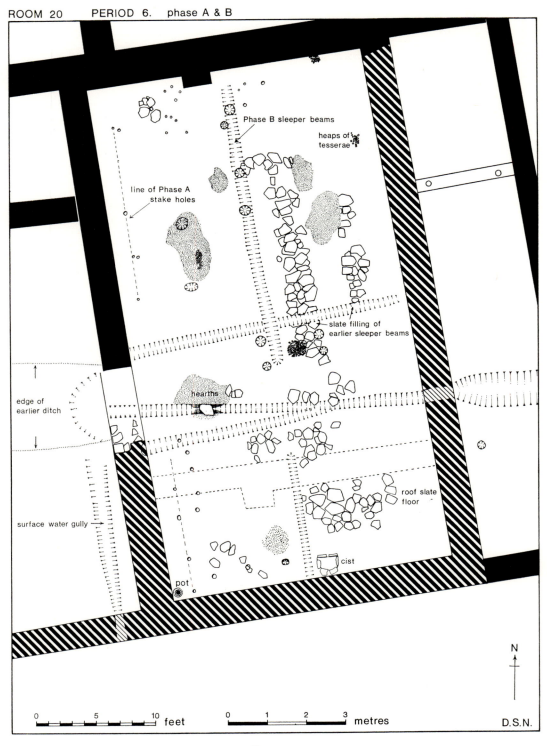

Phase B sleeper beams

heaps of
tesserae

line of Phase A
stake holes

slate filling of
earlier sleeper beams

edge of
earlier ditch

hearths

roof slate
floor

surface water gully

cist

pot

N

0   5   10 feet   0   1   2   3 metres   D.S.N.

Fig. 35

corridor. Both rooms were cut by a channelled hypocaust, that in the main room in the plan of a swastika, and that in the addition in the plan of a double Y (pls. XX*a, b*). Both were heated from a central flue running on an east–west axis, with a stoking-pit on its eastern side. The swastika-shaped hypocaust cut the existing brick tessellated pavement, and was constructed in flint (laid herringbone fashion) and blocks of chalk. At the end of the flues which were about 2 ft. 4 in. (.71 m.) deep were niches for box-tiles, none of which remained in position. The extension to the main room was probably a heated ante-chamber: the remains of a pink tile-mortar door-step were found in its south wall. No floor survived, as it had been destroyed by ploughing; but from a number of coloured *tesserae* found in the hypocaust channels it would appear the room was originally paved with a mosaic. When the hypocaust was abandoned it was used by foxes — a number of their bones were found.

Running at right angles to the east wall of the extension to Room 18 were two walls (pl. II*a*) both built over earlier footings. The northern was an extension to the north wall of the flue, and the southern an extension of the south wall of the room. The former projected 9 ft. (2.75 m.) and the latter 6 ft. (1.83 m.). Their position on either side of the stoke-hole would suggest that they acted as a screen to hide the grimy stoking area. The two walls were not parallel to one another; the northern wall aligned with an entrance pier in the bathing pool, and the southern aligned with its south wall.

Room 20

Phase A (fig. 35, pl. XXI*a*; Section L–M, fig. 6)

The oven and raised floor were demolished and a number of stakes erected along the line of the west wall; several of the stakes cut the remains of the oven. The stake-holes were irregularly spaced; their purpose was not determined. The exposed area of the wall behind the oven was covered with mortar and plain off-white painted plaster. Similar plaster covered all the walls of the room, and on the northern side where it survived to a greater height, it was decorated with a crudely executed pattern: a dado, 2 ft. 6 in. (.76 m.) high, flecked with purple, yellow and red (pl. XXI*b*) and above it the remains of a lattice pattern also in purple, resting on a horizontal band (fig. 89*a*) and flecked with the same colours as the dado. This design was painted over an earlier white wall scorched by fire. It is uncertain whether this plaster belonged to Period 5 or 6 because it also appeared to respect the level of the raised floor.

After the floor was removed, possibly as a result of fire, the joist trenches were filled with earth and Collyweston roofing slates and covered with a yellow mortar floor. However, since a layer of ash was found in the westernmost joist, associated with a row of iron nails, it is possible this joist was never removed; it may have been too heavily charred.

Phase B

A passage, 7 ft. (2.13 m.) wide, was built from the door towards the east wall, where a similar door may have existed. Although no structural evidence was found for this, a layer of silt had run in from the east over the line of the surviving wall: similar silting had also occurred over the western door (L 5, Section L–M, fig. 6) and was caused by water washing down from the courtyard.

On either side of the passage were two rooms. Those to the north measured 11 ft. 6 in. by 22 ft. (3.50 × 6.70 m.), and those to the south 11 ft. 6 in. by 13 ft. (3.50 × 3.96 m.). The positions of the doors between the passage and the rooms were not found, but the entrance linking the southern rooms was set in the north of the partition wall.

The sleeper beams dividing the northern rooms rested on the yellow mortar floor that covered earlier joist trenches and were visible only because another yellow mortar floor was laid against them. The walls were from 6–9 in. (.15–.23 m.) thick, and were probably constructed with wattles faced with mortar and strengthened by 9 in. (.23 m.) wide posts. The irregular spacing of the posts and their absence in the southern half of the room suggest that they were not load-bearing. Wattle impressions were found on the back of many fragments of wall-plaster, which presumably came from the wall. The plaster was decorated in a similar style to that on the north wall, but the design was double bands of lattice with circles in the vacant lozenges (fig. 90).

The sleeper beam dividing the two southern rooms differed from that in the northern section; it was narrower (6 in. (.15 m.) wide) and was sunken into the clay floor and packed with flints. It is assumed that they were both contemporary, since they were on the same alignment.

Midway along the passage were two pairs of post-holes, all with a filling of grey silt; the posts may have supported a staircase rising to an upper storey. The post-holes' width and filling resembled those of the post-holes associated with the northern partition; the latter extended south into the east–west passage and stopped between the sets of posts. The southern rooms were different to the northern mainly because they lacked mortar floors and were much cleaner. The western room had a pebbled clay floor, a hearth and a large cooking-pot (Pot no. 315, fig. 107) standing on the remains of the oven. The eastern room was paved with old roofing slates and a number of re-used tiles from herringbone floors, and had a small cist lined with flints and roofing slates in its western corner. The mortar floors in the northern rooms, however, had a number of hearths and the floors were covered by a thick black occupational deposit mixed with ash, iron slag, sherds, bones, and trinkets. Apart from living quarters the rooms also appear to have been used as a workshop, for a farrier's butteris (SF 345, fig. 69), a tool used for cleaning horses' hooves, was found in the occupational material. It is possible therefore that horses were brought into the passage to be shod and that the hearths and the iron slag were associated with a smithy. A hearth in the passage was superimposed on the timber drain, and as a result, the pipe was burnt (pl. XIVa). The drain certainly ceased to function when this occurred, if it had not already silted up.

In between the post-holes in the passage was a heap of red-brick *tesserae*, possibly used to patch floors. Three similar groups were also found in the northern rooms, one against the northern wall of the east room, one a little further south, and another roughly in the middle of the west room. The *tesserae* were probably being made from old roofing tiles.

Dating

The Period 6 floor was covered by a thick silty black occupation level (L 5, Section L–M, fig. 6), covered by yellow mortar silt (L 3) washed out from the rubble layer above (L 2).

A total of 37 coins was found in the room (see coin report (Appendix A, p. 118) for detailed list); two coins (one of Gallienus and another of Victorinus) were found sealed below the Period 6 mortar floors. Eighteen coins were found in the black occupational deposit covering the floor, and seventeen in the rubble filling. The earliest coin in the occupation (L 5) is dated A.D. 318–20 and the latest A.D. 348–50; the earliest found in the rubble (L 2) is dated A.D. 270–3 and the latest A.D. 353+.

The numismatic evidence above and below the floor would suggest that the Period 6 partitions could not have been laid earlier than A.D. 268, and are likely to have been laid in the Constantinian period; and that this occupation was terminated in the middle of the fourth century by the collapse or destruction of the room.

GATEHOUSE AND INNER COURTYARD (fig. 5, pl. VIII*a*)

The entrance through the gatehouse was blocked by two walls, one linking the southern piers, and another linking the northern. It is possible therefore that the gate was turned into a room. A mortar surface which covered a coin dated A.D. 319–20 was spread over the courtyard, and a sump dug opposite the gatehouse over the line of the earlier ditch. The purpose of the sump was probably another attempt to cure the flooding in Room 20. Presumably the timber drain in this room had already ceased to function. A total of sixteen coins were found over the courtyard, mostly sealed by the destruction rubble. The latest coin was dated A.D. 341–8.

Room 35 (fig. 5, pls. XXII*a, b*)

A massive hypocaust was built on to the western side of the villa over the line of the corridor and over Room 34 (Section U–V, fig. 37). The room was 17 ft. (5.18 m.) wide by 65 ft. (19.82 m.) long, and was heated by a channelled hypocaust, with two stoke-holes, one set at either end of the main flue. The northern stoke-hole was probably constructed later, after it was realized that one stoke-hole was insufficient to heat such an enormous room.

All the flues, which were about 18 in. (.46 m.) high, were constructed in flint and chalk blocks, capped with both bonding and roofing tiles; at one point a large block of Barnack limestone was used. The main north–south flue was not symmetrical with the walls of the room; there was more space on its western than its eastern side. The reason may have been a desire to align the west wall of the room with the east wall of Building D, or to make the frontage of the villa truly symmetrical. The old corridor wall was used as the foundation for the western side of the flue. Five subsidiary flues ran west from the central flue, terminating at comb-patterned box-tiles (SF 717 and 718, figs. 86–7) set into the walls (pl. XXIII*a*). Another flue ran from the southernmost east–west flue to the southern wall of the room. No flues existed on the east side, probably because it would have involved cutting vertical niches out of an existing wall. The northernmost point of the central flue terminated in a Y, the western arm of which linked with the northern stoke-hole.

Little of the southern stoke-hole survived because it had been robbed; but it was probably constructed in flint and tile. Its stoking pit measured about 5 ft. (1.52 m.) in diameter, and

F

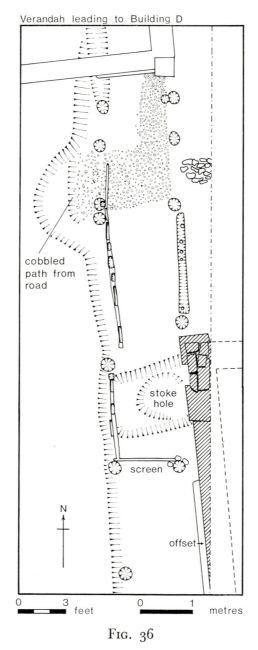

Fig. 36

was filled with black ash and pottery forms 168, 316, and 342. The flue of the northern stoke-hole (pl. XXIIIb), however, was in a superb state of preservation; it was constructed of three blocks of Northamptonshire limestone. These had been previously used elsewhere as they had been partly shaped, and had holes (not lewis holes) cut into them: whether they came from the villa is not known.

The room had no paved floor; the only level resembling one was a layer of chalk and a layer of yellow sand which had probably leached out of the rubble. This was not an eroded floor, since the mortar over the hypocaust channels had not also eroded.

The Verandah (fig. 36)

Parallel to the western side of Room 35 was a path and a row of post-holes which extended south of Building A, over the kitchen area in Building C (fig. 22), and north towards Building D. The post-holes, which were set at the foot of a bank and spaced at irregular intervals of between 6 and 10 ft. (1.83 and 3.05 m.), probably marked the positions of posts which supported a lean-to verandah. The verandah, however, must have been free-standing between Room 35 and Building D, because here there was a double row of posts. The single row of posts over Building C was probably a fence.

On the south and west sides of the northern stoke-hole was a screen made from a row of vertical planks each about 9 in. (.23 m.) wide and 2 in. (.05 m.) thick. They must have been nailed against horizontal bars fixed between the verandah posts. When this feature was constructed, it blocked access along the verandah to Building D. The screen stopped short of Building D at a point where there was a cobbled path (presumably leading from the track-way) running down the bank into the northern courtyard. The bank at this point had been worn, so that its angle was less steep than elsewhere. It would appear that when the screen was constructed between the verandah posts, it partially blocked access along the path. Whether this was intentional, and a gate constructed here, is uncertain.

Pottery forms similar to Pot nos. 284, 288, 299, 316 and 358 were found on the verandah floor.

Room 29: Y-shaped Hypocaust (fig. 5, pls. XXIIa, b)

The southern room of the west wing was reduced in size when it was divided by a chalk wall. The new room measured 14 ft. by 17 ft. (4.25 × 5.18 m.) and contained a channelled hypocaust in the plan of a letter Y, the arms of which terminated at flues set in the northern corners of the room. It was constructed in flint and blocks of chalk, and heated from the south side. The remains of a door-step or position for a wooden threshold survived in the north wall and measured 2 ft. 9 in. (.84 m.) wide.

The mouth of the flue was constructed in tiles and measured 1 ft. 6 in. (.46 m.) wide. The stoking pit was 4 ft. (1.22 m.) in diameter. The main flue of the hypocaust did not run at right-angles from the south wall, but was built diagonally from the south-west corner, probably to keep both stoke-holes as close together as possible for convenience of stoking. The single stoke-hole serving Rooms XIV and XV at Park Street[1] had a similar purpose. The floor had been destroyed by the plough, but the presence of coloured *tesserae* in the filling of the hypocaust channels suggests that the room had been paved with a polychrome mosaic.

[1] *Arch. J.*, CII (1945), 21.

Bathing Pool (fig. 8, pls. XXIV*a*, *b*; Sections C–D–E, and F–G, fig. 38)

The bathing pool was constructed in flint and chalk, which were faced with pink tile-mortar. It was built on to the eastern side of the baths. The west and possibly the east walls were built parallel with the baths, but the north and south walls were constructed parallel with the east–west axis of Building A. Consequently the pool had a parallelogram plan. The reason for this is uncertain, but it may have been an attempt to tidy the frontage of the baths, which hitherto had developed in rather an haphazard plan.

The pool was terraced into the river bank, so that its west side was about 6 ft. (1.83 m.) below the surface of the natural clay, which acted as a substantial support against which to erect the walls. The north side of the pool, however, was disturbed by the water leat, and it was necessary for the builders to build a bank of clay (L 12 in Section C–D–E, fig. 38) against the loose leat filling, prior to building the wall against it. It is possible, however, that the clay was deposited to act as a dam to prevent the area being flooded during building operations.

The pool measured 40 ft. (12.20 m.) wide by 68 ft. 6 in. (20.89 m.) long, and was constructed against the corridor wall alongside the plunge-bath. Two entrances led into the pool, one through this corridor wall, and the other further south between the corridor walls from Room 18. Five steps led into the pool, but the bottom step turned and ran around the interior walls, possibly for use as a seat. The steps were about 1 ft. 6 in. (.46 m.) wide and about 12 in. (.31 m.) high and were moulded on their edges.

Level with the floor in the north-west corner were six holes each about 5 in. (.13 m.) square in cross-section: three ran through the west step and three through the north step (pl. XXV*b*) and all were about 2 ft. (.61 m.) deep and filled with silty clay. Their purpose is problematical, but similar features exist on a number of *piscinae* on continental examples, i.e. that in the Portico of Pompeia at Vaison la Romaine in Gaul. On this example the features are believed to have been places of refuge for fish. Presumably the fish sheltered in the holes either when the pool was being used by bathers or possibly when the water level was lowered during times of cleaning. Since no pavement was found over the floor (it was natural clay), it is reasonable to assume that there had been a made surface, and that it had been robbed. The only material resembling a surface was a layer of pink tile-mortar close to the steps, but this was probably collapsed rendering.

Water entered the pool from an inlet which skirted the east wall of the *apodyterium* (Room 6, pl. XXV*a*). The inlet must have been constructed after the pool had been built, for its southern end ran over the north wall of the pool. The water probably flowed in continuously, for in the south wall was an overflow (pl. XXV*c*), capped with pink tile-mortar, 4 ft. 6 in. (1.37 m.) above the floor. This height was the same as staining on the plaster lining the sides of the steps. To empty the pool there must also have been an outlet level with the floor, and this may have existed somewhere in the south-east corner, because the level of the floor fell 6 in. (.15 m.) from the foot of the steps to the eastern edge of the excavation. Whether this fall in levels was maintained towards the eastern side is not known.

Running parallel to the north wall was a drain (L 12, filling of, Section C–D–E, fig. 38) which from its alignment appeared to be contemporary with the pool. This was not the case, however; so long as the drain was in use it must have been left uncovered, for it was never provided with capping tiles; but the clay bank (L 12) covered it. No pipe collars were

Layer No.	Description of layer
1	Modern turf level
2	Clay make-up for road works
3	Old ploughsoil
4	Brown soil with small quantities of Roman building rubble
5	Black silty soil with flint rubble
6	Shown on Section C-D-E only
7	Flint rubble mixed with brown earth and yellow mortar
8	Shown on Section C-D-E only
9	Black silty soil
10	Clay and brown earth
11	Flint rubble with yellow mortar
12	Shown on Section C-D-E only
13	Shown on Section C-D-E only
14	Yellow-orange mortar
15	Orange-brown rubble filling foundation trench
16	Chalk floor; ploughed over west wall of bathing pool
17	As no. 4

Layer No.	Description of layer	Pottery Nos. illustrated
1	Modern pavement surface	—
2	Make-up for pavement	—
3	Ploughsoil	—
4	Brown soil with small quantities of building rubble	—
5	Black silty soil with flint rubble	348-71
6	Flint rubble mixed with silty soil	—
7	Flint rubble with brown earth and yellow mortar	—
8	Gravel filling water leat	339-47
9	Black silty soil	—
10	Clay and brown earth	332-8
11	Flint rubble and yellow mortar	330-1
12	Clay revetment to north wall of bathing pool	328-9
13	River washed clay	324-7

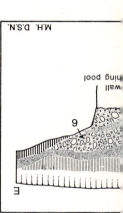

Layer No.	Description of layer	Pottery Nos. illustrated
1	Ploughsoil	—
2	Flint rubble mixed with black soil	—
3	Yellow mortar with flint rubble	—
4	Red brick tessellated pavement over Room 28 covering layers of rubble, chalk and clay	372-6
5	Charcoal filling of Oven C	—
6	Flint and chalk rubble with yellow mortar	—
7	Hillwashed clay	—
8	Grey silt filling of eaves drip running parallel with Period 3 outer corridor wall	—

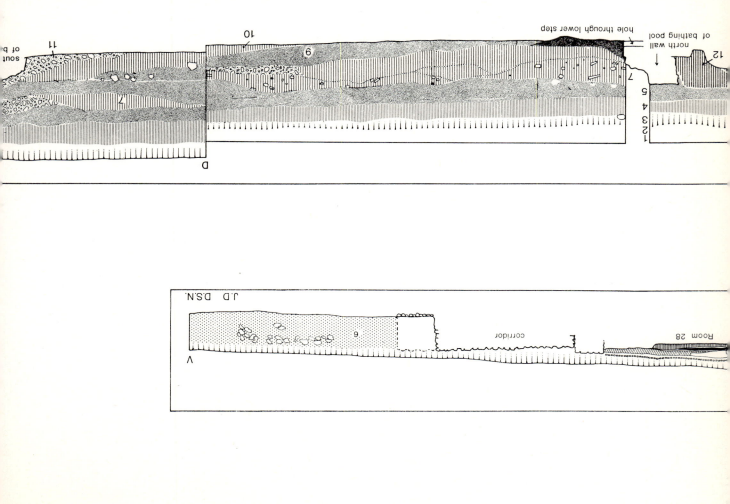

Fig. 38

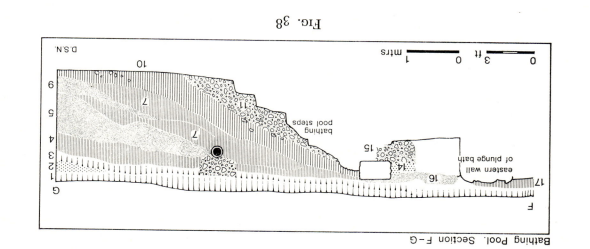

Fig. 38

Bathing Pool. Section F-G

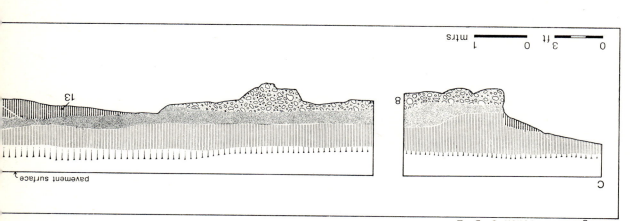

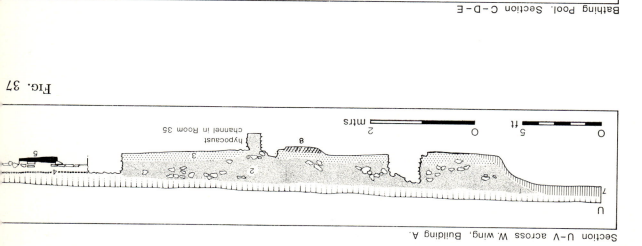

Bathing Pool. Section C-D-E

Fig. 37

Section U-V across W. wing, Building A.

found, and the sides of the drain were covered with scale deposited by running water; so it is unlikely to have been a timber conduit. The drain probably ran from the *apodyterium* (Room 6).

The Leat (fig. 39)

The water for the pool came from the River Gade via a leat, the bank of which is still a surface feature. It appears to have been of two periods: (a) a water course earlier than the bathing pool, probably serving the bath-house and dated to the late first century A.D.; (b) re-direction, contemporary with Period 5 or 6. The course of the early leat is uncertain but it appears to have run in a south-westerly direction from the river, probably on the line of the surface feature shown on fig. 2. The course of the later leat was probably the same, but it was made to turn east sooner — about 27 ft. (8.23 m.) north of the pool. Evidence for there being two periods was found just north of the pool where the leat was deeper than at a point further north (Section H–I, fig. 40) and was filled with white mortar rubble, presumed to have come from the conversions of the earlier bath building. However, the rubble filling of the leat further north contained only yellow mortar — the destruction rubble of either Period 5 or 6. Not all the functions of the early leat are apparent; it obviously served the bath-house, but it may also (a) have constituted a source of water additional to the well (that is for the villa); and (b) have served an earlier bathing pool. This would explain why the pool was built parallel to the earlier drain and the foundation beneath the corridor from Room 18. The overflow may have been the overflow for an earlier pool (unless it was just a drain from the plunge-baths); this would explain why it contained first- and second-century pottery, and why its floor was on a higher level than the leat further north. Also in the overflow was a coin of Antoninus Pius and the lagena (fig. 93, c) dated *c.* A.D. 60–80.

To the north of the pool were two large foundations of flint, groups of post-holes, and a rectangular building (Building 16). The northernmost foundation (fig. 8) cut the *tepidarium* (Room 7) and measured 7 ft. by 6 ft. 6 in. (2.13 × 1.98 m.). It was not rectangular; the northern side, instead of running at right-angles to the adjacent walls, ran on the same alignment as the fence between the baths and Building E. It was also parallel to the north wall of the pool.

The other foundation (pl. IV*c*) was built against the east wall of the baths, outside Room 1, and measured 8 ft. by 6 ft. (2.44 × 1.83 m.); it too was constructed parallel to the walls of the bathing pool. It was built adjacent to the leat, and was associated with a puddle of yellow mortar which rested directly on the bank. The surface of this mortar bore an impression of a lead pipe that ran into the leat (fig. 39). It is more probable that a costly lead pipe was used to draw fresh water than as a drain; thus the foundation on the eastern side of the baths may have supported a pumping device that drew water from the leat into a tank, which would have been supported either on the same foundation or, more probably, on the foundation cutting Room 7. The total absence of chalk in the construction of these foundations, combined with their deep footings, would suggest they were constructed during Period 5.

F1

THE BATHS. Detail to north of pool

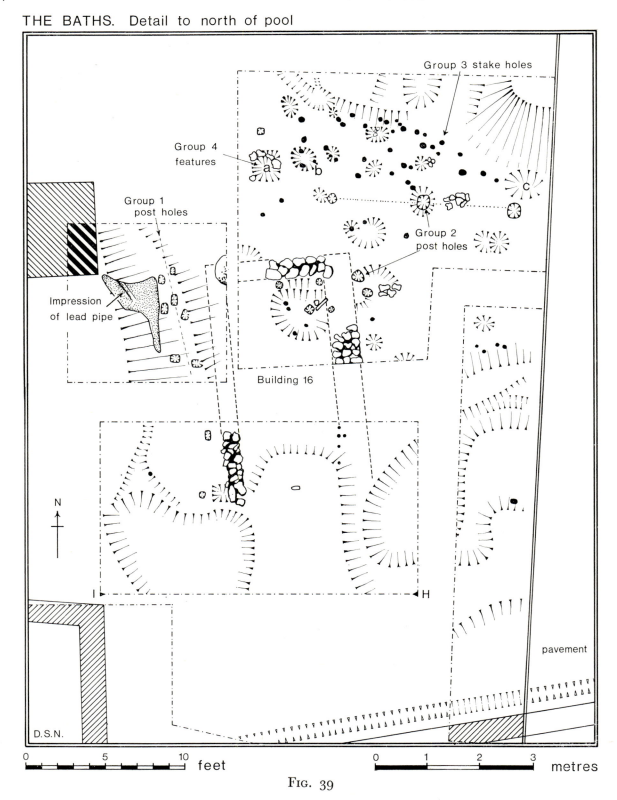

FIG. 39

Section E-F

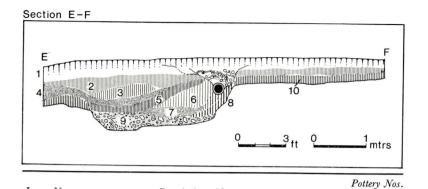

Layer No.	Description of layer	Pottery Nos. illustrated
1	Ploughsoil and road make-up	—
2	Brown soil with small quantities of building rubble	—
3	Flint rubble mixed with black earth	—
4	Black silty soil with flint rubble	158–61
5	Light brown-grey silt with small chippings of flint, tile and mortar. Probably overflow gully from bathing pool	
6	Brown earth	—
7	Loose dark grey rubbly soil	148–57
8	Black layer with charcoal	—
9	Gravel at bottom of water gully	144–7
10	Clay upcast from water gully	—

Section H-I

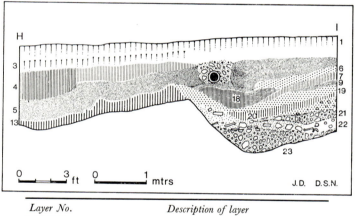

Layer No.	Description of layer
1	Modern turf level
2	Clay make-up for road works
3	Old ploughsoil
4	Brown soil with small quantities of Roman building rubble
5	Black silty soil with flint rubble
6	Yellow mortar
7	Brown soil with tile fragments and yellow mortar
8	Shown on section C–D–E. Fig. 38
9	Black silty soil
10	Shown on Section C–D–E. Fig. 38
11	Shown on Section C–D–E. Fig. 38
12	Shown on Section C–D–E. Fig. 38
13	River washed clay
14	Shown on Section C–D–E. Fig. 38
15	Shown on Section C–D–E. Fig. 38
16	Shown on Section C–D–E. Fig. 38
17	Shown on Section C–D–E. Fig. 38
18	Brown soil with 'pea-gravel'
19	White mortar
20	Grey clay
21	White mortar with flint rubble
22	Clay with rubble and mortar
23	Fine river washed gravel

FIG. 40

BUILDING 16 (fig. 39)

The building, or such as remained of it, was constructed in flint, Hertfordshire Pudding-stone and chalk, and was about 9 ft. (2.75 m.) wide by at least 15 ft. (4.57 m.) long; the southern extent was not traced owing to the poor state of preservation. All that remained of the walls were short lengths on its west, east, and north sides. The floor was an even layer of unmortared gravel about 6 in. (.15 m.) thick.

Beneath the floor was a hollow, 2 ft. (.61 m.) deep, lined with large flints, tiles, and roofing slates, all of which were water-worn. The side of the hollow was cut by a number of post-holes belonging to Group 2 (see below). The hollow appeared too deep and wide for a post-hole and the question arises whether it was created by a natural spring. A radiate coin was found beneath the floor.

The purpose of the building is uncertain; it is possible it supported gear designed to raise water into the pool (the levels indicate the necessity for raising the water). The floor of the pool was 12 in. (.31 m.) deeper than the bottom of the leat which had a depth of water of between 12 and 24 in. (.31 and .61 m.). As the water level in the pool was 4 ft. 6 in. (1.37 m.) above its floor, it would have been necessary to have raised the water at least 1 ft. 6 in. (.46 m.) just to the required level. To get the water into the inlet it would have been necessary to have raised the water over 5 ft. (1.52 m.).

At the bottom of the leat were four groups of post-holes which may have formed four separate alignments:

Group 1

This group occupied the eastern bank, close to the puddle of mortar. In all there were nine post-holes, each about 6 in. (.15 m.) square, arranged roughly in pairs. The main group was about 12 in. (.31 m.) deep, but the two post-holes further south were about 3 ft. (.91 m.) deep. They were filled and covered with gravel. The division of the posts into pairs would suggest that horizontal planks ran between them, of the kind used for revetting the sides of rivers or canals.

Group 2

This comprised six post-holes arranged into two rows of three posts, running east–west. They were similar in size and filling to those in Group 1 and lay south of the north wall of the rectangular building, underneath its floor — they are therefore earlier in date. Another row of three posts, indicated on the plan by a dotted line, may also belong to this group, although they were larger in size, about 9 in. (.23 m.) square, and about 2 ft. (.61 m.) deep. The eastern post-hole had the remains of an oak post left *in situ*, preserved by the waterlogged conditions. As these posts were set into the bottom of the leat it is possible they supported a bridge.

Group 3

Group 3 was a complex of stake-holes (shown in black dots) measuring 3–4 in. (.08–.10 m.) wide, and mainly confined to the north-east bank. Their greatest number ran on a north-west/south-east axis, and may be contemporary with similar stake-holes throughout the rest of the trench. The stakes must have been too slight to have supported a substantial structure; they were presumably leat revetting.

Group 4a, b, c

None of this group can be confidently called post-holes; they were shallow hollows about 2 ft. (.61 m.) square, cut into the clay, and were filled either with flints or with masses of corroded iron nails. The features were mainly confined to the north-eastern bank, but appeared to have no set interval or alignment. Another was found in the northern trench cutting the leat (fig. 8). As the hollows were too shallow to have been post-holes it is more probable they were piers supporting a bridge. Their construction was similar to the rectangular building (16).

Besides the large number of nails there were 173 bronze coins, mostly dated to the House of Constantine; none was later than A.D. 353. They were found mainly in the lowest river gravels (L 8, Section C–D–E, fig. 38), but some of contemporary date were also found in the black earth over it (L 5). Even though this layer (L 5) ran over the primary filling of the bathing pool, the coins in it were only found north of the pool, and therefore must have become dispersed by water action from the layer below. Also found in these two layers, but mainly in L 8 were fragments of 15 bronze bracelets, 11 bronze rings, fragments of 4 bronze penannular brooches, 2 toilet tweezers, a fragment of silvered bronze mirror, a bronze spoon, numerous fragments of worked bronze and a number of broken iron knives. It is unlikely that the group of coins represents a scattered hoard, because it is improbable that such a large group of trinkets would have been associated with them; possibly the finds were deliberately thrown into the water as a tribute to a water deity.

DISCUSSION

Such an enormous bathing pool would have been unnecessarily large for the ordinary requirements of the villa (which is by no means large) especially as the baths were already provided with a plunge-bath large enough to have been used for swimming. Apart from the large plunge-baths on the villas at Eccles, Kent[1] and High Wycombe, Bucks.,[2] which are both believed by their excavators to have been sufficiently large for bathing, the only other pools are those associated with religious spas, such as Bath, Somerset[3] and Well in Yorkshire,[4] and pools in public or military bath-houses, such as Wroxeter,[5] and Caerleon.[6] It will be apparent from the outlines of the dimensions of these baths (fig. 41) that the pool ranks in size with the largest public bathing pools; it would be reasonable, therefore, to assume that the pool was intended for public rather than private use.[7]

---

[1] *Arch. Cant.*, LXXVIII (1963), 125–41; LXXIX (1964), 121–35.
[2] *Records*, XVI (1953–60), 227.
[3] B. Cunliffe, *Roman Bath*, Society of Antiquaries Research Report no. XXIV, 1969.
[4] R. Gilyard-Beer, *The Romano-British Baths at Well*, Yorkshire Roman Antiquaries Committee Research Report no. 1, 1957.

[5] For plan see Current Archaeology no. 14, p. 84.
[6] *J.R.S.*, LVII (1967), 175.
[7] Room XXXII at Lydney (interpreted as an ante-room) may also have been a bathing pool, since it was entered down a flight of steps and had a bench around its sides. The room measured 50 ft. × 16 ft. internally.

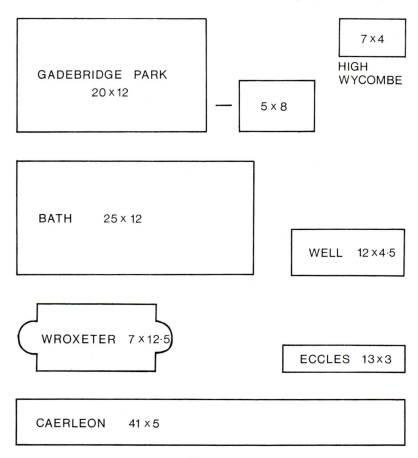

COMPARISON OF BATHING POOL SIZES (IN METRES)

GADEBRIDGE PARK
20 × 12

7 × 4
HIGH
WYCOMBE

5 × 8

BATH 25 × 12

WELL 12 × 4·5

WROXETER 7 × 12·5

ECCLES 13 × 3

CAERLEON 41 × 5

FIG. 41

It is uncertain whether the pool had religious associations; no temple was discovered, although the deposit of coins and the associated finds would suggest that offerings were being made to a water deity. The only cult object found was a bronze axe-head (SF 73, fig. 57) found in Building A. Although the pool was filled with water from a leat, there may also have been a sacred spring nearby; this would also help explain the votive deposit. Modern artesian wells have lowered the water table so that natural springs no longer survive in the area; but they once abounded in the vicinity, and many were used to feed the local watercress beds. The only active spring known to the author is just north of Water End (Grid Reference, TL 034107, Sheet 160).

From a notice of sale, dated Friday, 3 July 1840, of property in Piccotts End, it would appear that the springs were then regarded as having medicinal properties.

'Piccotts End, where as well as at Noke Mill, in the vicinity of the town, there are Saline and Chalybeate Springs, the water of which is said to be similar to that of Cheltenham.'

A writer in the Victoria County History,[1] states: 'Medicinal springs have been fitfully exploited at East Barnet, Hemel Hempstead and other places.' Where the V.C.H. writer got his information is not clear, because the reference 'A Topographical and Statistical Description of the County of Hertford' (1825) makes no mention of the springs at Hemel Hempstead.

If the qualities of the water were exploited in the eighteenth and nineteenth centuries, it is not impossible that the waters were considered curative in Roman times. The only conclusive evidence to suggest the site was a spa would have been the discovery of a temple and a larger group of votive finds, and they have not been found. Furthermore, analysis of water from the remaining spring by the Uxbridge and Rickmansworth Water Board[2] proved no excessive saline or chalybeate properties.

The number of toilet articles found in the villa complex is high: 5 bronze tweezers, 7 nail cleaners, 1 ear scoop, 16 cosmetic spatulae, 3 toilet razors, 2 fragments of silvered bronze mirrors, and 17 bronze and 24 bone pins, all of which are illustrated. Many more fragments of pins were found, but are too small to be drawn. These finds would appear to be more numerous than might be expected for a collection of toilet articles from a villa, but it is perhaps unwise to form comparisons between groups within this report, for it must be remembered that the site is one of the few that has been totally excavated. In the light of present evidence the pool can be assumed to have been for public use, but whether it had religious associations is far from clear.

It may be that the main house was also of a semi-public nature and was occupied by a landlord or bailiff responsible for administering the estate. His tenants may have been allowed to use the bathing facilities,[3] perhaps after paying their taxes — these may have been paid at the gatehouse for it would explain the balance (SF 47, fig. 56) found in the 'Porters Lodge'. The purpose of the heated room on the west side of the villa is also problematical: it appears to have been too large for the ordinary requirements of a family. Mr John Smith has suggested that the room may have been a meeting hall for villa workers,[4] although it is possible it was merely connected with farming, and served as a warming or drying shed. Alternatively, it could have been a barn because a villa of this size could be expected to have had one, and none, with the possible exception of Building F, has been found. However the storage of grain under heated conditions is unlikely, because there would have been a possibility of the grain germinating (this would depend of course, upon how far the grain had been artificially dried before storage). The fact that corn was grown on the estate is attested by the corn-drying oven to the west of Building C.

It is uncertain how the occupation of the villa ended. The bathing pool went out of use; its north and south walls were deliberately pushed inwards and covered with earth. The large deposits of coins mentioned above, dated no later than A.D. 353, were covered by the black deposit (L 5) which also covered some primary filling of the pool. This would suggest

[1] V.C.H. *Herts.*, IV (1914), 245.
[2] I am most grateful to the Rickmansworth and Uxbridge Valley Water Company for testing a sample of water from the spring in question, and for the following information — Chloride 14.0 ppm, Iron .01 ppm; both perfectly normal and similar to the water at Piccotts End.

[3] Mr Hartley also considered that the large and isolated bath-house at High Wycombe (*Records*, XVI (1953–60), 242) was so situated to allow tenants to use the bathing facilities.
[4] I am grateful to J. T. Smith, F.S.A., for this interpretation.

the bath had been abandoned soon after this period. The leat did not appear to have been deliberately filled; it probably silted up.

The whole bath complex must also have been abandoned, for covering the flue in the stoke-hole, Room 10, was a mortar floor, cut by stake- and post-holes attributed to Period 7 (fig. 43, pl. V*a*). A similar situation in this period was also found in the main villa where Rooms 20, 27 and the inner courtyard were either demolished or falling into decay. The latest coins in these rooms and the courtyard were similar in date to those north of the pool, and none was later than about A.D. 353. The contrast in dates between the latest coins found in Building A, Building D and the baths, and those found in Building E, is apparent (pp. 118–19): it would appear that Building E remained standing while the main villa was ruinous. Whether the villa was attacked by marauding Picts in about A.D. 367, as has been suggested happened at Park Street,[1] is doubtful. Certainly the picture of coin loss for the period immediately succeeding A.D. 353 in no way compares with that obtaining at Park Street where Fel Temp (fallen horseman) copies of the late 350s abound. It is highly probable that had destruction occurred as late as A.D. 367 there would have been a higher proportion of coins later than A.D. 353 sealed within or beneath the rubble.

Placing the villa into an historical context can only be reasoned guesswork but bearing in mind that the villa was probably ruinous soon after the 350s it is possible that it may have been owned by a supporter of the rebellion of Magnentius, and that the estate was confiscated during the political purges carried out after his defeat in A.D. 353. The villa site remained in use to the end of the fourth century and possibly into the early fifth century, but it never reached its previous affluence; Period 7 is characterized by wooden buildings and compounds designed for herding large numbers of sheep or cattle.

Whether this change in prosperity was political or caused by lack of trade, staff or demand, is not known, but the land use may not have altered considerably. Even though the main house was demolished a similar farming economy could still have been practised on the estate in Period 7.

PERIOD 7 (fig. 42)

All buildings except Building E were destroyed. Timber stockades were then built over the areas of the northern and southern courtyards.

Timber buildings were constructed over the northern courtyard, the baths, the west side of Building A, and over the site of Building C. All that remained of the original estate was Building E and possibly the Group A posts between Building E and the baths. The time gap between the destruction of the villa and the construction of the timber buildings is uncertain, but the coin evidence shows no sign of there having been a period of abandonment. If the villa was abandoned, it may only have been for a few years.

[1] *Arch. J.*, CII (1945), 30.

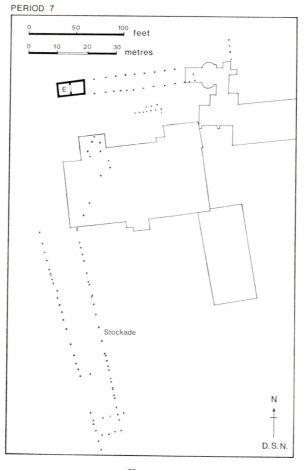

FIG. 42

THE NORTHERN COURTYARD AND BATHS (fig. 8, pl. XXVI)

Apart from Group A (which probably belong to Period 5) the post-holes in the northern courtyard cannot with certainty be attributed to any one period for there were several groups; however, they all cut the courtyard's gravel surface and were filled with black earth.

Group A

The post-holes of this group were set at intervals of 10 ft. 6 in. (3.20 m.); the alignment ran east–west between Building E and the baths and north from Room 8. They extended west of Building E for 210 ft. (64 m.) and turned neither north nor south, but the line was cut midway by a Roman chalk quarry (fig. 46). The post-holes did not cut the bath-house, and were therefore a stockade or fence that enclosed the northern courtyard. They varied between 2 and 3 ft. (.61 and .91 m.) wide, and contained posts measuring about 9 to 12 in. (.23 to .31 m.) thick.

The stockade on the eastern side of the Period 3 *tepidarium*, Room 8 (fig. 8), had similar spacing and packing to the Group A post-holes. Its purpose may have been to prevent cattle falling into the water leat, and to enclose an area of land north of the villa.

Traces of another two post-holes were found on the western side of the demolished *tepidarium*, Room 8, but they were very shallow features lacking packing materials, and their identification as post-holes is doubtful. The remains of the baths at this point may possibly have been converted into a dwelling; in the north-east corner of the building was a storage pit, Pit O. A post-hole also cut Room 7.

Pit O (fig. 10)

The pit measured 1 ft. 7 in. by 1 ft. 8 in. (.48 × .51 m.) by about 2 ft. (.61 m.) deep and had been cut through the clay build-up for the Period 3 floor. The top of the pit was lined with flints, chalk, and fragments of Barnack limestone. The pit was filled with brown earth containing hundreds of small snails' shells belonging to the species *Avianta arbustorum*. It is possible the snails were kept in the pit for food (see report on the mollusc shells, p. 262). The habitat of *Avianta arbustorum* is in damp lush vegetation in ditches or along streams. The proximity of the colony to the water gullies north and south, and to the water leat further east, would indicate that these conditions existed nearby and that the snails were easily gathered.

Group B (fig. 8)

This group of post-holes ran parallel with Group A, were spaced at intervals of 10 ft. 6 in. (3.20 m.), and were aligned with the south wall of Building E. They were also similar in type, filling and packing, but their depth was about 9–12 in. (.23–.31 m.) compared to

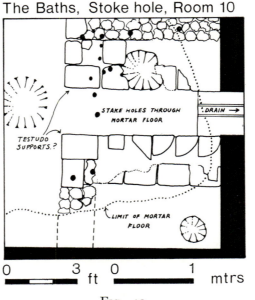

The Baths, Stoke hole, Room 10

FIG. 43

12–18 in. (.31–.46 m.) in the northern row. They did not appear to be contemporary with Group A, however, because (a) the posts were not set opposite one another, as might be expected had the structure been a verandah (although it could have been a lean-to structure); and (b) the post alignment continued east, over the western extent of the baths. Here, two posts were erected over the furnace and another was erected on a large block of Hertfordshire Puddingstone dumped over the south wall of the Phase 3 squaring of the former apse, Room 11. The posts were associated with a mortar floor laid over the hypocaust flues (fig. 43). This floor was cut by a number of stake-holes roughly aligned on a north–south axis. As no post-holes cut the *caldarium* (Room 9), the post-holes would appear to have been the end wall of a structure.

The structural state of the rest of the baths in this period is uncertain, apart from the filling-in of the bathing pool; but as there was no means of heating the hypocaust, the baths must have been abandoned. They were probably demolished, as is suggested by the block of Hertfordshire Puddingstone dumped over the wall. The erection of the posts of Group B should be attributed to Period 7 as they were later than the abandonment of the baths, and after *c.* A.D. 353.

Groups C and D (fig. 8)

These groups ran parallel to one another on an east–west alignment and were situated to the south of the courtyard. The post-holes measured about 1 ft. 6 in. (.46 m.) wide, and were spaced 5 to 6 ft. (1.52 to 1.83 m.) apart; each contained a post about 9 in. (.23 m.) thick, set 1 ft. 3 in. (.38 m.) deep and packed with blocks of chalk. The filling was black earth mixed with yellow sand: the latter was probably decayed mortar. Group C comprised three post-holes, and Group D eight, including one chalk post-base. Both groups ran parallel with a line of heavy cobbling, the surface of which was higher than the level of the courtyard and cambered as though it was a surface for a road or track. A single post-hole cut this cobbling, but was different from those of Groups C and D in that it was packed with flints and not chalk. Also associated with the post-holes was a spread of chalk blocks, but whether this was a collapsed wall that at one time ran between the posts or whether it was a spread of rubble put down for cobbling was not established.

The relationship of the separate groups to one another is uncertain, but as they had different types of post-packing it is unlikely they belonged to a single structure such as an aisled building, as their overall plan might suggest. It is more reasonable to assume, with the exception of the possible room in the *praefurnium*, that all groups were stockades or fences for the enclosure of herds of sheep or cattle. The date of these structures is not known. A coin of Constantine was found in one of the Group B post-holes.

The Drain (fig. 8)

A drain crossed the courtyard on a north–south axis, cutting both the cobbled courtyard surface and the water-conduit north of the post alignment of Group A. At its southern end its section was 9 in. (.23 m.) deep and 1 ft. 3 in. (.38 m.) wide, but it gradually became deeper and wider towards the north. Where it crossed the Group A post alignment it bulged from 1 ft. 6 in. (.46 m.) to 4 ft. (1.22 m.) wide, as though a chute entered from the east. The drain continued north from this point for a further 37 ft. (11.28 m.) and then turned east and ran towards the river.

As no trace of the drain was found leading from Building A, it is probable that it was dug to drain surface water from the courtyard, and possibly to act as a channel for dung. It was probably regularly cleaned, for it contained no finds whatsoever; it was filled with black silty soil. The drain apparently belonged to Period 7. Its right-angled axis to the villa must have been a coincidence; but why it should run so far north in a diversion to clear the baths, which in this period were abandoned, is puzzling; perhaps too much walling was still standing or it was an attempt to follow the contour, so as to effect better drainage from the uphill slope. The alignment of the post-holes on the villa is also a problem; how much of the main house and baths remained standing is not known, but sufficient must have survived to govern later building work.

Fence (fig. 8)

Cutting the southern edge of the water-conduit were twenty-five stake-holes, some of which divided into groups of three. They measured approximately 4–6 in. (.10–.15 m.) wide and about 9 in. (.23 m.) deep. The stakes could hardly have been large enough to support a heavy structure, but it is possible that they framed a wattle fence.

The Gully (fig. 8)

South of the Group B post-holes, and west of the drain, was a shallow U-shaped gully running on an east–west axis. It was not traced on the eastern side of the drain, nor in the trench further west; consequently its purpose is doubtful, but it was probably a surface-water gully flowing into the drain. Two coins, the latest of which was dated A.D. 330–48, were found in its filling.

Pit P (fig. 8)

Cutting the southern conduit was a circular pit 4 ft. (1.22 m.) in diameter, 12 in. (.31 m.) deep and filled with white mortar. It was probably a lime slurry.

Pit Q (fig. 8)

This pit was situated due north of Pit P and ran beneath the section of the trench. It was about 3 ft. (.91 m.) in diameter, 4 in. (.10 m.) deep, and filled with black earth. Its purpose was not established.

Pit R (fig. 8)

Pit R was south of the Group A post alignment and west of the drain. It was about 3 ft. (.91 m.) square, 9 in. (.23 m.) deep and filled with rammed chalk. To the north-east of it was an irregular cutting, lying east–west, filled with dark earth; how or if they were related was not established. Neither feature yielded any finds.

Pit S (fig. 8)

Further north was another pit, oval in plan, 5 ft. (1.52 m.) long, between 6 to 9 in. (.15 to .23 m.) deep, and filled with gravel and dark earth. The proximity of the pit to the water-conduit suggests that there may have been an outlet at this point.

Pit T (fig. 8)

Pit T lay north-west of the courtyard, was irregular in plan, being wider at the eastern side than the western, and was 9 ft. (2.74 m.) long. Its greatest width was 3 ft. 6 in. (1.07 m.). The gravel courtyard surface stopped a few feet north of the conduit and gave way to natural clay into which the pit had been dug. The sides of the pit were burnt and it may therefore have been an oven but, apart from some burnt clay, no solid building materials were found in its filling. At its widest point it was 1 ft. 6 in. (.46 m.) deep, and at its narrowest 12 in. (.31 m.). Six feet (1.83 m.) to the north was a small post-hole measuring 6 in. (.15 m.) wide, packed with fragments of a Jurassic limestone quern.

Bathing Pool

After the abandonment of the bathing pool, the steps were partially demolished and covered with a layer of rammed earth and rubble (L 11, Section F–G, fig. 38). Cutting this layer was a cluster of twenty-one stake-holes each about 3 in. (.08 m.) wide (fig. 44). These encircled two post-holes about 6 in. (.15 m.) wide, one of which cut the partially demolished corridor wall. Their purpose was not established; they may have been associated with two post-holes cutting the bathing pool steps further north (fig. 8) and formed another stockade.

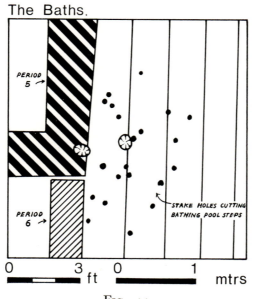

Fig. 44

Outer Western Wing (fig. 22, pl. XII*a*)

It is certain that Building C was demolished prior to the construction of the verandah alongside Room 35 since its post-hole alignment continued south, over the kitchen area in Building C. This fence was also removed in Period 7 to make way for a stockaded enclosure that ran almost on the same axis as Building C, but extended south from at least the south wall of Room 35 for 226 ft. (69 m.). The enclosure at its northern end measured 36 ft. (10.97 m.) wide, but tapered to 26 ft. (7.93 m.) wide at the south. The post-holes that formed the limit of the structure were spaced at intervals of approximately 10 ft. (3.05 m.) and were generally arranged in pairs, set 1–3 ft. (.31–.91 m.) apart. It is unlikely that the double posts indicate replacements, for the filling and packing were the same in both. They were normally about 1 ft. 6 in. (.46 m.) wide, and contained a post 9 in. (.23 m.) thick, packed with flints, chalk blocks and old roofing slates (the materials suggest the destruction of masonry buildings). The post-holes on the north-east side of the structure cut through the footings of the corridor wall of Building C, and two others cut through the walls in the western side of the building. The northern end of the stockade is in doubt, for a post-hole was found cutting the massive Period 6 hypocaust in Room 35 and others cutting floors in Rooms 28, 26 and through the mosaic in Room 27. The stockade probably turned and continued on a north-easterly line across the villa; it presumably extended to the stockades in the northern courtyard.

The structure was probably never roofed, since it lacked central ridge-supports and its small posts are unlikely to have supported a span of 36 ft. (10.97 m.). However, the southern-most area of the stockade may have been roofed; an area 16 ft. by 26 ft. (4.87 × 7.93 m.) was enclosed by post-holes. No occupational material was found in this area or elsewhere within the enclosure, but cobbling did occur at the southern end. If the enclosed area was a room, then it may have been intended as a shelter for stockmen or shepherds rather than as living-quarters. No evidence was found for a tiled or slate roof although it could have been of thatch.

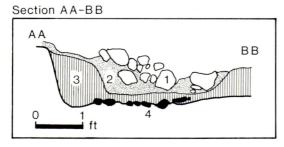

Section AA–BB

Layer No.	Description of layer
1	Possible remains of flint wall
2	Black silty soil
3	Brown-grey clay silt with pebbles
4	North wall of Building C

FIG. 45

The northern end of the stockade may also have included a shelter; the remains of a secondary flint wall were constructed over the line of the north wall of Building C (Section AA–BB, fig. 45). Unfortunately it is not known whether it had return walls enclosing a room.

Running along the western side of the stockade was a shallow U-shaped gully that was traced from the south-west corner of the courtyard wall, of Period 4, Phase D, southwards for a distance of about 200 ft. (61 m.), where it was cut by the modern Galley Hill road. The gully was not continuous, however, for after 80 ft. (24.40 m.) it stopped for a distance of 14 ft. (4.25 m.) before it continued southwards. As the break occurred close to the shelter at the south end of the stockade it probably indicated an entrance. Another entrance may have existed just south of the courtyard wall; this would explain both why the gully was filled with flints, and the absence at this point of post-holes on either side of the enclosure. The flint filling petered out towards the south and gave way to a filling of black earth containing no significant pottery or finds, apart from a bronze needle (SF 230, fig. 64). The purpose of the gully was probably to drain water from the uphill slope so as to prevent the inside of the stockade from becoming too muddy.

DISCUSSION

It has already been stated that the stockade enclosure was probably associated with stock-raising, but whether the economy of the estate was based on sheep or cattle is uncertain. From the evidence of the bone report it would appear that more cattle bones than sheep bones were found in the fourth-century deposits; this may indicate that cattle were the primary business of the estate in this period; on the other hand, grain would still have been grown, for it was necessary to provide for the needs of the household.

A stockade of this size would have enclosed a large number of cattle, but whether it was designed as a nightly or winter refuge, or as a corral for cattle due to be taken to the market, is not known. Certainly the area enclosed points to a number of head of cattle far greater than the needs of the estate and sufficient to supply the needs of a town abattoir. The presence of one bronze needle is insufficient evidence to suggest that the business of the estate in this period was weaving and therefore the enclosures intended for sheep.

How late the timber structures are is highly doubtful. If they were associated with the occupation of Building E, then a late fourth-century date is certain, and an early fifth-century date probable. To suggest an even later date, on the evidence of a possible Romano-Saxon sherd (Pot no. 367) from the upper filling of the bathing pool, cannot be reliable.

That occupation in the Chiltern villas possibly continued into the fifth century is suggested at Latimer,[1] where a cruck-type building was constructed. Some villas must have remained operational, albeit less efficiently, to have supplied the needs of Verulamium.

CHALK QUARRIES (overall plan, fig. 3)

To the west of the villa were a number of chalk quarries which were in use throughout the whole history of the villa.

Six chalk quarries extended from the western side of Building D, southwards to the corn-drying oven. The quarries varied in size from a collection of small pits forming a continuous series, and measuring about 24 ft. (7.31 m.) in diameter, to much larger workings measuring at least 70 ft. (21.35 m.) in diameter. The quarries were situated on the hillside,

---

[1] *Med. Arch.*, XII (1968), 1.

Chalk quarry pits west of Buildings D & E

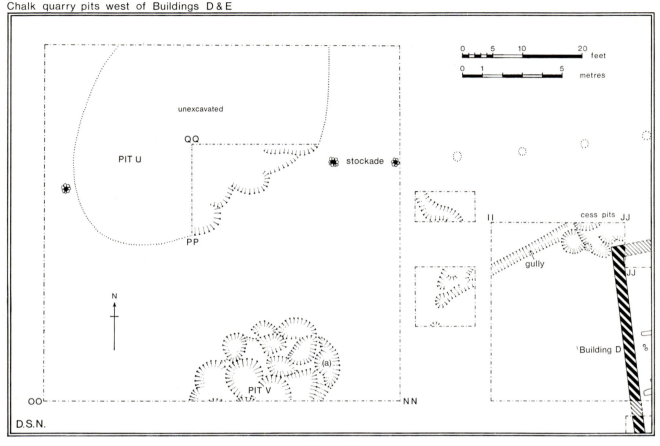

FIG. 46

and followed the 320 ft. (97.60 m.) contour. None was found below this level, nor above the 350 ft. (106.75 m.) contour. The quarries were probably cut into the hillside because the quarriers had to dig less deeply to obtain hard chalk, and because the side of the hill had less covering of clay than the top. The chalk was probably extracted for building and for making lime.

Pit U (fig. 46, Section PP–QQ, fig. 47)

This was oval in plan, about 34 ft. (10.36 m.) wide by at least 48 ft. (14.63 m.) long, and cut the alignment of the Period 5 stockade (Group A) which ran west from Building E. Almost the whole area of the quarry was exposed by a bulldozer but only a quadrant was excavated. Reaching a maximum depth below the natural chalk surface of 4 ft. 6 in. (1.37 m.), the quarry had an even floor which would suggest that it had reached its greatest depth, and that the chalk was being obtained from pits cut into its face. Its lower filling comprised a layer of waste chalk and clay (L 6), which in turn was covered by a layer of

Chalk Quarry, Pit U. Section PP–QQ

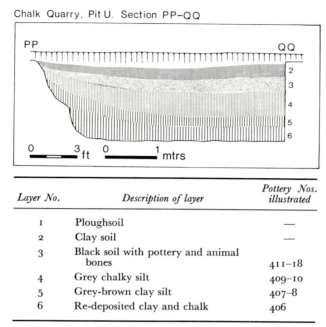

Layer No.	Description of layer	Pottery Nos. illustrated
1	Ploughsoil	—
2	Clay soil	—
3	Black soil with pottery and animal bones	411–18
4	Grey chalky silt	409–10
5	Grey-brown clay silt	407–8
6	Re-deposited clay and chalk	406

FIG. 47

Chalk Quarry, Pit V Section NN–OO

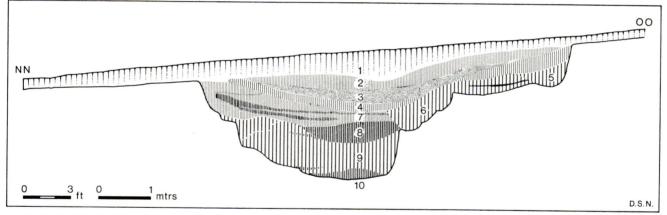

D.S.N.

Layer No.	Description of layer	Pottery Nos. illustrated
1	Ploughsoil	—
2	Hillwashed clay	—
3	Black soil	421
4	Brown clay	—
5	Yellow clay with mortar and tile	—
6	Chalky earth with traces of yellow mortar	419–20
7	Thin layers of chalk and clay	—
8	Brown earth and clay	—
9	Orange clay seal to pits not shown on section	—
10	Chalk silt	—

FIG. 48

light brown clay silt (L 5), a layer of grey chalky silt (L 4), a layer of black soil (L 3), and a layer of clayey soil (L 2).

In all, nineteen coins were found in the quarry together with a number of fine grit-stone pestles (SF 704, fig. 84) in association with mortaria and other pottery (Pottery nos. 406–18, fig. 112). Two coins of Allectus (A.D. 293–6) were found in L 5; 14 coins, the latest of which was dated A.D. 341–8, were found in L 3. It would appear therefore that the quarry was being worked by the first quarter of the fourth century, and filled by the middle of the century.

Pit V (fig. 46, Section NN–OO, fig. 48)

This pit was of different character to Pit U; a large pit, 24 ft. (7.32 m.) wide and 8 ft. (2.44 m.) deep, was formed by a multitude of smaller workings varying from 3 to 6 ft. (.91 to 1.83 m.) wide. After the extraction of chalk they were probably used as cess pits. They were later filled by layers of mixed chalk and clay. The exception was (a), which was filled with layers of fine brown soil, sealed by layers of chalk. Apart from a fragment of a column-drum (SF 688, fig. 82) and a bone pin (SF 313, fig. 67), the lower levels of the pit were barren of finds. A quantity of mid fourth-century pottery was found in a deposit of black earth (L 3) in the upper levels.

Pit W (fig. 3)

This quarry was found in a small trench (measuring 10 ft. by 5 ft. (3.05 × 1.52 m.)) put down to find the western extent of the ditch beneath Building A. The ditch was not found; the subsoil gave way to disturbed marl, apparently the filling in a quarry. It was excavated to a depth of 5–6 ft. (1.52–1.83 m.), but its bottom was not found, nor its overall dimensions established.

Pit X (fig. 49, Section RR–SS, fig. 50)

Two trenches running on an east–west axis were dug on the west side of Building C to determine the alignment and width of the incoming road to the villa. The width of the road was about 18 ft. (5.48 m.), but it was also discovered that the road had been constructed over the filling of a large chalk quarry, and consequently had subsided into it. Only the southern trench traversed the quarry, the limits of which are uncertain but it was estimated that its south side was about 14 ft. (4.25 m.) south of the trench. This distance was deduced by the angle of tip lines which fell from south to north, indicating that the side of the quarry was near.

No evidence was found for its northern limits, but as the quarry was turning on its north-eastern side it was estimated at being not less than 80 ft. (24.40 m.) long by 65 ft. (19.82 m.) wide. It was about 11 ft. (3.35 m.) deep. The sides of the quarry were not cut by smaller pits as in quarries U and V, but were almost sheer. The level of the quarry floor in the southern trench was 3 ft. (.91 m.) higher on the western side than the eastern, yet both floors were level. It is probable therefore that a working face existed between the two levels, and that the quarry was worked from east to west.

The road cobbles (L 8) were built directly over a clay bedding layer which contained three fragments of decorated samian in the style of Butrio and dated c. A.D. 120–45. The

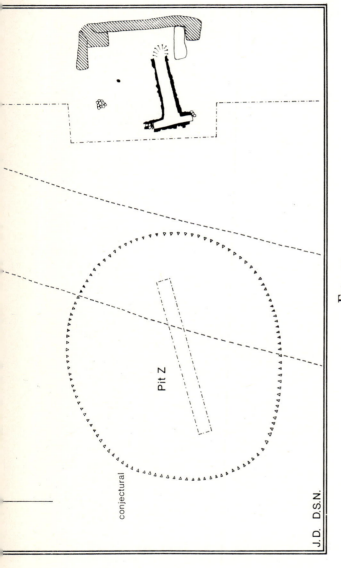

Pit Z

conjectural

J.D.   D.S.N.

Fig. 49

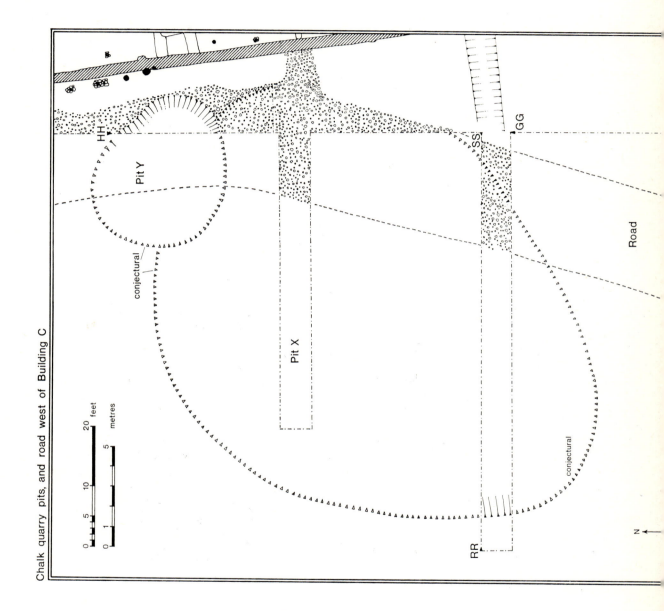

Chalk quarry pits, and road west of Building C

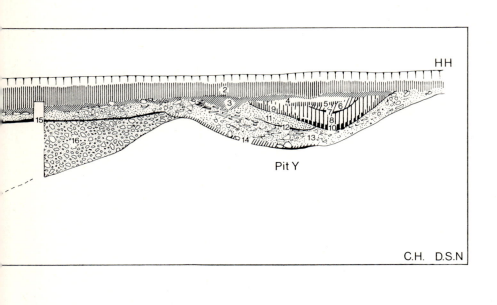

HH

Pit Y

C.H. D.S.N

Layer No.	Description of layer
1	Ploughsoil
2	Hillwashed clay soil
3	Dark brown chalky soil with building rubble
4	Marl
5	Dark grey soil
6	Grey silt
7	Black refuse layer
8	Dirty orange clay
9	Grey-brown soil with chalk, tile, and mortar building rubble
10	Black refuse layer
11	Yellow mortar
12	Black refuse layer
13	Building rubble with yellow mortar, tile and Collyweston roofing slates
14	Black silt
15	Cobbled road surface
16	Clay with cobbles, the latter similar to those used in the road (L 15)

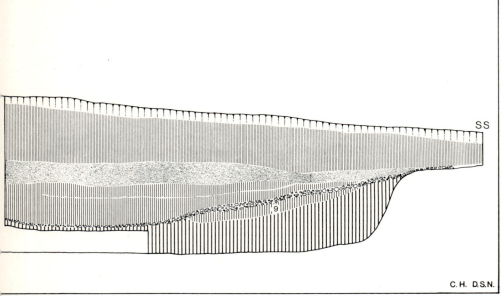

SS

C.H. D.S.N.

Layer No.	Description of layer
1	Ploughsoil
2	Hillwashed clay
3	Grey chalky earth
4	Black earth with flints
5	Clay filling of small secondary pits cut into disturbed clay and chalk
6	Yellow clay
7	Grey-brown chalky clay
8	Cobbled road surface.
9	Clay with charcoal flecking
10	Mixed clay and chalk

Chalk Quarry, Pits X & Y   Section GG – HH

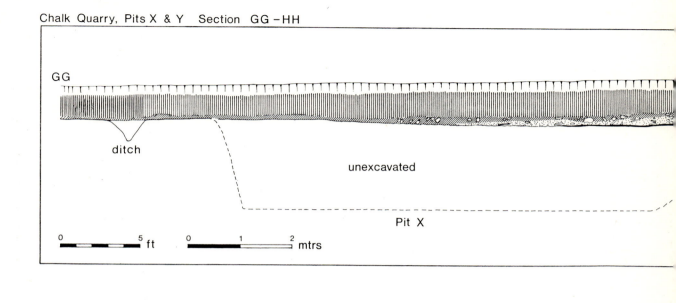

GG

ditch

unexcavated

Pit X

0   5 ft   0   1   2 mtrs

Chalk Quarry, Pit X,   Section RR – SS

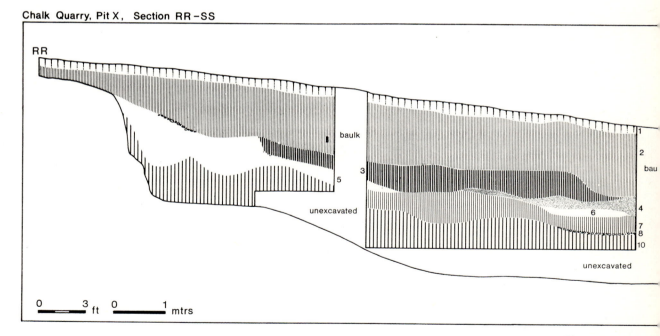

RR

baulk

5

3

unexcavated

1

2

bau

4

6

7
8

10

unexcavated

0   3 ft   0   1 mtrs

FIG. 50

bedding layer was directly over the chalk filling of the quarry (L 9). Covering the road were deposits of chalk and clay (L 7) which may have been thrown out of adjacent workings, for the road was cut by Pits Y and Z. Above layer 7 was a deposit of black earth (L 4) containing quantities of pottery (p. 252), and a coin of Carausius, A.D. 286–93.

Pit Y (fig. 49, Section GG–HH, fig. 50)

This pit cut the road cobbles, and the eastern edge of Pit X. It was approximately 24 ft. (7.32 m.) in diameter and about 4 ft. (1.22 m.) deep, and was filled with building rubble (L 11 and L 13) which was cut by a subsidiary pit filled with black earth (L 10) containing mid fourth-century pottery and a necklace (SF 75, fig. 58). The pit may have originally been a chalk quarry.

Pit Z (fig. 49)

A trench 26 ft. (7.93 m.) long by 2 ft. 6 in. (.76 m.) wide, was dug on the western side of the corn-drying oven in order to locate the road. This was not found for the subsoil gave way to disturbed marl, believed to have been the upper filling of another quarry; the trench was abandoned. Had this feature been a quarry, which is most probable, it must have cut the road; its diameter and depth were not established. The road originally ran through the area, for it was discovered in a small trench further south (the southernmost trench on fig. 3).

CONCLUSIONS

The quarries were dug for chalk possibly used in the construction of the villa, but the chalk used in the Period 6 hypocaust and bathing pool was hard, and must have been obtained from quarries deeper than any of those found on the site. It is possible therefore that the chalk was quarried either for burning into builders' lime, or for marl to spread over the fields. The former suggestion would imply that a kiln or furnace must have existed on the site; but none has been found, although the temporary furnace built into the water-cistern (fig. 5) south of Building A may have been used for this (p. 27).

From the size of the quarries known and conjectured it has been estimated that at least 62,000 cubic feet of chalk was quarried from them. Chalk weighs about 120 lb. per cubic foot, which would give a total weight of about 3,400 tons. With present-day methods, 100 lb. of chalk will make 56 lb. of quicklime;[1] but in Roman times the ratio might have been closer, since the lime is unlikely to have been as well refined as today. Taking a minimum estimate of 50 lb. of quicklime to 100 lb. of chalk, the total yield of lime from the quarries would have been about 1,700 tons.

This would seem a high figure for the needs of the estate throughout its history, so it may be possible that the manufacture of lime was one of the industries of the villa and that it may have been sold to adjoining villas, or to builders' merchants at Verulamium.

[1] Information from the Welwyn Hall Research Association.

G2

GENERAL DISCUSSION

By R. GOODBURN and DAVID S. NEAL

The form and exact site of the earliest dwelling-house at Gadebridge is unknown. This is possibly the result of the intensity of the building activities during the later Roman period, for the works associated with the later main house, Building A, would easily have obliterated traces of an earlier building. Perhaps Room 17 (figs. 5 and 8) was part of this early house, although the northern limit imposed by the Period 1 baths would have made it very small, at least in a north–south sense. Another possibility is that the earliest house lay north of the baths complex, for the later Building F (fig. 4, Period 5) shows that occupation probably extended over a vast area in this direction, at least in the early fourth century and perhaps in earlier centuries also. However trial-trenches north of the main villa complex produced no finds, and no pottery was noted in spoil from the recent road-building activities. All the first- and second-century finds made during road works were east of Buildings A and B.

The earliest house was associated with a bath-house (fig. 8) of the very simplest type, with a cold room, and hot and tepid rooms heated by a single furnace. There were apparently no plunge-baths, their absence qualifying Gadebridge Period 1 as one of the most elementary bath-houses known. This is not to say primitive, because the structure was well-built and apparently incorporated roller-stamped box-tiles (pp. 14–15). The use of these implies a fairly sophisticated establishment which organized the purchase of tiles from specialist craftsmen who were possibly producing them in the Verulamium area.[1] The earliest pottery from the site is dated to *c.* A.D. 75 and the earliest coins — although we are warned that reliance should not be placed on these as straightforward dating evidence (p. 101) — from *c.* A.D. 64. It seems that the box-tiles here are among the earliest of the type produced in Britain.

The dating evidence seems strong enough to place Gadebridge among the earliest of villas in Britain and, although perhaps not as grand as, for example, Eccles, certainly not a tardy or second-rate copy of the earliest examples. What the owner could afford to do, he did well.

Growth in the owners' wealth was quite slow, for during the seventy or eighty years following the erection of the bath-house, the only alterations made were to provide plunge-baths and basins (fig. 8) and to improve the stoking area. Presumably improvements would also have taken place in the main house. Some measure of the extent of the changes made during the first century of the existence of the villa is suggested by the number of different alignments of features (fig. 9) — the ditch under the later Rooms 25 and 26, Room 17 and the pair of parallel ditches (p. 7) to the south, the plough-marks between these (fig. 22), and the bath-house itself — if one can assume at least a slightly different date for each of these four alignments.

The form of the early house is not to be guessed. It would most certainly be wrong to suggest that the winged corridor house of Period 3 grew out of a simple rectangular block of

---

[1] Lowther, fig. 4.

FIG. 51. Comparative villa plans

a. Lockleys.   d. Park Street.   g. High Wycombe.
b. Boxmoor.   e. Ditchley.   h. Hambleden.
c. Gadebridge (Period 3).   f. Box.   i. Gorhambury.

rooms located in the same spot, which was first given wings and then surrounded by corridors. This possibility is dismissed by the evidence produced by the excavation. The excavations of the villas at Park Street near St Albans,[1] and Lockleys (fig. 51a) near Welwyn,[2] produced plans in which more complex houses derived from simple rectangular structures. The development sequence from rectangular building to winged corridor house (with two or four wings) and possibly to courtyard villa is so neat and logical that over the years it has been applied to many sites, sometimes with more imagination than insight. It is true that the sequence is genuine in some cases, for example at Chedworth, Gloucestershire,[3] and possibly North Leigh, Oxfordshire;[4] but the picture is complicated by economic and other factors. At Little Milton, Oxfordshire,[5] it seems that the building never grew beyond the simple rectangular stage (although in the absence of excavation this might be explained by a short life-span). On the other hand, the earliest houses at Boxmoor, Herts.[6] (fig. 51b) (late first or early second century), and Folkestone, Kent,[7] were perhaps of winged corridor type. In short, the initial form taken by a house depended upon the means and wishes of the inhabitants and not upon the development of new types of structure.

Thus it is no surprise that the Gadebridge Period 3 house appears as a unitary structure of winged corridor form (fig. 51c). The Period 1/2 house (or houses) eludes us. It may have been of timber or of stone. It may have been a simple rectangular structure or a winged corridor house. We may not jump to a conclusion.

The changes which took place in Period 3, dated to the late Antonine era, were so sweeping as to suggest a change in ownership, marked by an influx of capital and new ideas. The new house was not created by rebuildings or additions, but by building an entirely new structure.

We might consider here whether some other houses were not of winged corridor type from the first. In the earliest masonry phase at Park Street, St Albans[8] (fig. 51d), there was a single range of rooms on a north–south alignment, the most northerly of these being a cellar. On the western side, nine feet (2.75 m.) away from the building, was a short length of wall interpreted by the excavator as being a screen for a number of rubbish pits further west. It is conceivable, however, that the wall belonged to a corridor along the western side of the building.[9] Now, although the cellar was attributed to the earliest masonry phase, the section drawing[10] and plan show two walls separating the cellar from Room V and neither of these walls was bonded to the other. This evidence would suggest that the cellar was built later than the main block. The width of the cellar from the south side of the north wall to the line of division between the two walls separating the cellar from Room V corresponds to within about three inches to the measurement between the west wall of the house and the supposed screen. It seems quite likely that the cellar was dug into a corridor which ran along the north and west sides of the block. The construction of a cellar in an existing corridor is paralleled at Faversham, Kent.[11]

[1] *Arch. J.*, CII (1945), fig. 3, facing p. 23.
[2] *Antiq. J.*, XVIII (1938), pl. LXX.
[3] R. Goodburn, *The Roman villa of Chedworth* (The National Trust, 1972).
[4] Collingwood, p. 143.
[5] *J.R.S.*, XL (1950), pl. VI.2; ibid., XLIII (1953), 94.
[6] *Brit.*, I (1970), plan facing p. 162.
[7] Collingwood, p. 138, fig. 47b.
[8] *Arch. J.*, CII (1945), fig. 3 facing p. 23.
[9] J. Liversidge, *Britain in the Roman Empire* (1968), p. 240.
[10] *Arch. J.*, CII (1945), 41, fig. 5, section H–H.
[11] *Faversham*, p. 69 and fig. 21.

It is reported that the Ditchley, Oxon.[1] (fig. 51e) villa was of winged corridor type from the first. A corridor was added first to the north, and then around all sides of the house, but it is specifically stated[2] by the excavator that it was in part divided into rooms from the first, unlike Gadebridge.

Ditchley is similar to the house at Gadebridge in the high degree of symmetry of the house and the placing of the water supply. The well itself could not be placed between the wings at Gadebridge because it would have been cut into impermeable clay. Its siting further west meant that it was sunk into the chalk. The provision of a cistern gave the same architectural effect as the Ditchley well, and also provided a ground-level reservoir.

The plan of the house at Box, Wilts.[3] (fig. 51f), is similar to that of Gadebridge Period 3. There was an east–west range of eight rooms with deep wings running south. The building was surrounded by a corridor which may have been part of the original design of the house, since two passages in the main range and one in each of the wings were set directly opposite the corridors bordering the inner courtyard and connect with the outer corridor. There may also have been a corridor at the south end of the east wing.

Whether a building existed at Box prior to the winged corridor layout is problematical. The northern wall of the main range of rooms was very wide and apparently the dividing walls of the latter rested on massive buttress-like foundations abutting the north wall. Had the buttresses belonged to an earlier house the main body of rooms must have lain under the later northern corridor, and no walls that could have belonged to this were found. A possible reason for the buttresses may be found by consideration of the levels of the corridors and rooms in relation to the outside ground level. The north side of the house had been considerably made up and the builders may have deemed it prudent to construct buttresses and a massive northern wall to avoid subsidence. Accepting this, an original plan complete with corridors can be suggested.

The house at High Wycombe, Bucks.[4] (fig. 51g), was also of winged corridor type, but elaborated still further by having shallow wing rooms on both sides of the building which thus had an H-plan. The building was dated to the mid-second century and was of a single constructional phase apart from the addition of porches on the north side which matched existing porches on the south side. The house at Hambleden, Bucks.[5] (fig. 51h), had a similar plan although it differed in the layout of the rooms in the main range. The rooms at High Wycombe were not as usefully designed since it was probably necessary to use one room as a corridor to connect the others. Whether the Hambleden house began as a single range of rooms as is suggested in the report is far from certain. Whatever the sequence of ground-plans, it is reasonable to assume that a corridor bordered the eastern side in an early phase since the report describes[6] this corridor wall as having a secondary wall added outside the original. Clearly this is not merely a reinforcement or damp-proofing, as suggested in the report, but a new corridor wall superseding an earlier one. This earlier wall is probably identical with that which divides Room A from Room B. The wall would appear from the published photograph[7] to have existed before these rooms were constructed and to have

---

[1] *Oxon.*, I (1936), 30.
[2] Ibid., 35.
[3] *W.A.M.*, XXXIII (1903–4), plan facing p. 244.
[4] *Records*, XVI (1953–60), 229.

[5] *Arch.*, LXXI (1921), pl. XIII.
[6] Ibid., 145.
[7] Ibid., pl. XIV, fig. 2.

been used as the side wall of a tile-lined chute emerging from the south side of Rooms A and B.

The house at Gorhambury, Herts.[1] (fig. 51*i*), near Gadebridge, was also a winged corridor building in its initial phase. Until a final report on this site is published interpretation of the plan must be unreliable, but there are two major masonry periods. Period 1, dated to the early second century, appears to have comprised a range of rooms bordered on the east and west sides by corridors. The most southerly room was a cellar. The Period 2 villa, dated to *c.* A.D. 160–80, was constructed on the same alignment as the earlier house, but lay further to the west. It had a range of rooms also bordered on the east and west sides by corridors; the western corridor appears to have had a porch and a simple bath suite. The east wall of the main range of rooms was probably constructed over the outer wall of the corridor belonging to the Period 1 house. It is also probable that the west wall of the Period 1 range of rooms was used as a foundation for a corridor bordering the east side of the later building.[2] Further evidence, perhaps, that the Period 2 house was bordered on both sides by corridors is the passage (Room 4) running from east to west. The plan suggests (unless further excavation proves otherwise) that this house was from the first a building with corridors. It may be noted here, too, that the construction of the Period 2 house immediately adjacent to the earlier building is similar to the relationship of the masonry dwelling to the early timber house at Boxmoor.

Let us now return to the consideration of the developments at Gadebridge.

One of the most striking things about the Period 3 house plan (fig. 51*c*) is its symmetry, which has been compared above to that of Ditchley. The wings have virtually the same dimensions; the northern porches are of equal size and are disposed at equal distances from the corners of the house. The cistern on the south is placed exactly between the wings. Also, although it was not considered necessary to demolish the baths and build a completely new set (shown on fig. 12), the additions on the western side of the baths are symmetrical about an east–west axis, as well as respecting the existing alignment of the suite. As a rule it was the public buildings in towns[3] which displayed the greatest degree of symmetry, both individually and in their interrelationships. Symmetry was one of the badges of Romanization. It is thus perhaps worth emphasizing the symmetry of the Gadebridge Antonine house as a likely indicator of the Romanized attitude of mind of the man who lived in it.

In this house, Room 20 (fig. 5) can be classed as a cellar since it was terraced into the ground to a greatest depth of *c.* 7 ft. (2.13 m.). In general, cellars were only constructed in villas in south-east Britain: for instance Lullingstone[4] and Faversham[5] in Kent. Gorhambury[6] and Park Street[7] in Hertfordshire had cellars too, and Lockleys, Welwyn,[8] had a half-underground room which must have been very similar to that at Gadebridge. Cellars are a very common feature of continental villas and a large number can be seen, for example, in the plans contained in R. de Maeyer's *De Romeinsche Villa's in België* (Antwerp, 1937). In

[1] *T.S.A.H.A.A.S.*, 1961, 21–30. Since 1972 further excavations have continued on this building, and two phases of timber buildings of the first century discovered.
[2] This was confirmed during the 1972 excavations. Mid-first-century timber buildings have also been discovered.
[3] Verulamium forum and basilica, and temple and theatre, for example. *Antiq. J.*, XXXIX (1959), 2.
[4] *Lullingstone*, pp. 59–64.
[5] *Faversham*, p. 69 and fig. 21.
[6] *T.S.A.H.A.A.S.*, 1961, 22–5 and pls. 1–3.
[7] *Arch. J.*, CII (1945), pl. VII.
[8] *Antiq. J.*, XVIII (1938), pl. LXIX, section C–D.

British villas however, they seem to be confined to the first two centuries A.D. and mainly to the south-east (on civil sites). It seems fairly clear that cellars were a continental development which did not find much favour in Britain, perhaps because the technical difficulties and expense of construction were too great when measured against utility. The towns form a separate case. Verulamium[1] for example, has at least one third-century cellar, but here building land was at more of a premium than in the countryside and there was a strong incentive to use building land as fully as possible. We might conclude from this discussion that Gadebridge came under some continental influence in the Antonine period, even if not at first hand.

In spite of the neat plan, Gadebridge was not a rich house in the later second century. Most of the rooms had *opus signinum* floors and most had plain undecorated plaster on the walls. Nor are any of the rooms of really impressive size (for the largest, Room 20, it is suggested, was quite probably a stable). No room presents itself as obviously being the dining room, although Room 28 was probably the kitchen (fig. 16); perhaps it was Room 26, but no room has a particular claim by virtue of its size or shape.

At this time it is likely that the house faced south (fig. 12). A courtyard generally forms the focus of the dwelling ranged around it in Roman as in other buildings. The careful placing of the cistern, and also the fact that the entrance to the possible stable was on the south side, lend support to the contention. The hypothesis is strengthened by the building works of Period 4, dated between the late second and the early third centuries (fig. 18). The barn-like Buildings B (on the east) and C (on the west) were erected so as to create a large yard entered on the west side and eventually closed by a wall on the south side. The overall plan bears a resemblance to that of the Hambleden, Bucks., complex.[2]

All the indications are that the villa was growing steadily at this time. The number of rooms in the main house, Building A, was increased by dividing the western corridor into the tiny Rooms 30–3 (fig. 5) by means of rather flimsy partitions. It was at this stage that the first small swimming-bath was built (Room 13). Both of the new work-buildings were apparently designed also to accommodate staff. Building B (fig. 19) on the east, had a hearth and oven in the northern end of its barn area, and its north-eastern room also held a hearth and two ovens. It is suggested that these may have been kitchen areas in part at least, although it is possible that small-scale industrial work requiring heat sources was also carried out here.

The western Building C (fig. 22) started out as a simple rectangular barn, but before the end of its life (it lasted for rather less than one hundred years) it may have been converted piecemeal into an aisled building of sorts. In this respect it is reminiscent of the simple rectangular Building A on the south of the villa yard at Winterton, Lincs.[3] This was used to form the nave area of an aisled building, B.

At Gadebridge, Building C, like Building B, had a domestic area with cooking facilities at its northern end. Close by the east wall of the early building was discovered the skeleton of a newly-born infant; doubtless the building was the home of at least some of the estate workers and this was one of their progeny who died young. The large number of infants

---

[1] *Verulamium*, 1972, 103 ff.
[2] *Arch.*, LXXI (1921), pl. XIII.
[3] *Antiq. J.*, XLVI (1966), 72–7.

buried at the Hambleden, Bucks., villa led the excavators to surmise the deliberate extermina-
tion of unwanted female babies of the workers there.[1] The actual buildings at Gadebridge
cover an area comparable with that at Hambleden and we might suspect that this would
indicate a comparable number of estate workers. Hambleden, however, is still a unique
case and many sites have produced just one or a few infant burials; for example, Saunderton,
Bucks.; Wendens Ambo, Essex; Ely, Glamorgan; and Winterton, Lincs. Thus it seems that
Gadebridge is to be included among the 'normal' sites in this case, although quite what are
the implications for the organization of the labour force on these estates is not clear.

In the context of the villa work-force we might mention here the *graffiti* (see p. 254,
fig. 113). These seem mainly to be property marks on pottery vessels (a, c, e and l at least)
and may indicate a number of literate workers spanning the life of the site. The Greek
name Peirithous hints at the presence of immigrant specialists. The *graffiti* as a whole warn
us not to assume that all villa employees were necessarily illiterate merely because most of
the work on the estate could have been performed by uneducated manual labourers.

The prosperity of Gadebridge continued to grow after the beginning of the fourth century.
Period 5 is dated to the late third century, the building work being completed by *c*. A.D. 300.

The area of floor space was increased, partly by building over more of the original corridors
(fig. 5). New corridors were not built around the new rooms, presumably because this would
have made the new building plans more expensive and because the more essential lengths of
corridor still remained.

The cistern now no longer existed. It was apparently temporarily converted into a kiln
to make lime from the chalk produced from the quarry pits on the west for use in the new
works. In the completed version of Period 5 the cistern was replaced by a wall and gate.
Building A had been extended to the west by building over the south end of the earlier
corridor of the west wing and the east corridor of this wing had been removed, perhaps to
enlarge the courtyard which must have seemed very cramped once the fourth side had been
closed in. This moved the axis of symmetry of the house to the west and so the gate was
placed somewhat west of the site of the cistern to maintain the symmetry of Building A
(fig. 5; see also reconstructions of front elevations, fig. 29). The room-space was also extended
to include the corridors across the southern ends of the wings. The effect of all these alterations was to lengthen the façade and the distance between the two wings whilst preserving
the symmetry of the southern aspect of the house.

The most impressive additional room-space provided was the large square northern
Rooms 18 and 27 which formed heated wing rooms. These may have stood much higher
than the rest of the building, because their foundations were wider than usual, indicating
that a heavy load was being carried; also, Room 27 perhaps had a second storey attained by
means of stairs set at the north-west corner of Room 26: a ground-sill trench suitable for
this purpose can be seen in plan (fig. 5). Obviously these rooms would preserve the symmetrical aspect of the house and the reconstruction is similar to that in fig. 30 (although
note that this depicts the site in Period 6, not 5). The reconstruction demonstrates how towers
would have been visible on approaching the house from the south, enhancing what otherwise
would have been a rather blank façade.

---

[1] *Arch.*, LXXI (1921), 150; S. S. Frere, *Britannia* (1967), pp. 266–7.

The existence of towered villas in the Roman provinces is attested by depictions of them, for example on North African mosaics, mainly of the fourth century A.D. Mosaics from Tabarka[1] and El-Alia[2] in Tunisia depict country houses with towers at either end of a range of rooms. The fragmentary wall-painting from Trier[3] may prove the existence of such buildings in the north-western provinces, although the central feature may be a gateway rather than a range of rooms. The modern reconstruction of a fairly broad horizontal median strip of the plaster makes certainty impossible. Elsewhere in the northern provinces, it is suggested by E. B. Thomas's *Römische Villen in Pannonien* (Budapest, 1964) that a large proportion of villas had tower rooms, although there usually seems to be no especial thickening of the foundations; compare, for example, the plans on her pages 67, 120 and 275, with the drawings on pages 68, 121 and 276.

In Britain, it has been shown that one villa apparently had an upper storey. At Lockleys, not far from Gadebridge, Room 8[4] was thought to have carried a second storey over half of it, for there were 'two concrete floors which lay the one almost immediately on top of the other, as if the flat roof had fallen first and carried the ceiling of the lower room as it fell'.[5] However, the excavator did not consider the room to be a tower[6] as suggested for Gadebridge Rooms 18 and 27. The parallel is rather with Gadebridge Room 20, for the upper room was thought to have been built because the natural ground surface sloped down under Room 8 to five or six feet below the level of the other rooms 'and this fall was balanced by the addition of an upper room above it'.

The villa at Keynsham, Somerset,[7] may have had rooms of greater than single storey height. At the north and south corners of its courtyard were two groups of rooms, each ranged around a central hexagonal room. Since these groups were set on the outside of the courtyard, their external appearance could only have been admired from the courtyard by building them higher than other rooms. Fragments of tufa blocks were in fact found among the rubble in both areas (and Bath stone voussoirs in the northern suite) which suggests that the rooms had vaulted roofs. Could these groups of rooms have been of the same type as, although on a less grand scale than, the fountain hall of the Domus Aurea[8] of Nero in Rome? A structure similar to the Keynsham hexagons is the Holcombe, Devon bath-suite[9] and similar arguments there apply. The massive buttresses supporting the walls of the octagonal plunge-bath at Lufton near Yeovil, Somerset[10] are quite possibly indicators of walls of unusual height, for none of the other walls of the house came to need such support.

Absolute proof of the existence of towers at Gadebridge is not possible, but it is possible that rooms higher than those of normal single storey dimension were built for the reasons cited above.

To return to a consideration of Gadebridge in Period 5, there is difficulty in deciding where exactly were the approach and entrance to the house. Since a gate was built, we would

[1] P. Gauckler, *Inventaire des mosaïques de la Gaule et de l'Afrique*, 2 (1910), no. 940.

[2] Ibid., no. 93.

[3] E. M. Wightman, *Roman Trier and the Treveri* (1970), pl. 6*b*.

[4] *Antiq. J.*, XVIII (1938), pls. LXVIII, 2 and LXIX, section C–D.

[5] Ibid., 347. It does seem possible, though, that the putative fallen floor of the upper storey may have been a secondary floor inserted on top of debris lying on the original *opus signinum* floor.

[6] *Antiq.*, XIV (1940), 317–20.

[7] *Arch.*, LXXV (1924–5), 109–35.

[8] A. Boëthius, *The Golden House of Nero* (1960), p. 98, fig. 53.

[9] *Arch.*, XLV (1877), pl. XXXVIII.

[10] *P.S.A.N.H.S.*, XCVII (1952), 90, 97–103.

suppose that the old south-west road was still in use, but that it was re-routed as it neared the house so as to lead to the gate. If this were not so, there would have been little point in constructing a gate in the wall. The difficulty arises when we try to locate the point of entry into the house from the courtyard; the floor levels of most rooms were rather higher than that of the yard but there is no trace of any steps. One possibility is that Room 20 was converted from a stable into a large reception room in this period for it may now have been decorated with garish painted plaster which would have been out of place unless a change to domestic accommodation had been effected. On the other hand the raised wooden floor and furnace (fig. 31) suggest that it may have been a kitchen and store-room. A further problem is that we do not know whether or not there was a door in the east wall of Room 20. Such a door would have been necessary to give access to the baths *via* the corridor of the east wing. Whether or how Room 20 connected with the rest of the house, unless along this same corridor, or by means of a staircase in Room 20, is unknown. The first tessellated pavements were laid in Period 5 (p. 47) and were of plain red *tesserae*.

There would have been little point in improving the southern aspect of the house if this were only visible from a yard as in Period 4. Thus it was that the work-building C on the west and possibly also Building B on the east were demolished at this time. The removal of Building C alone (fig. 27, p. 43) would enable the house to be admired from the road from the south-west. The main yard seems now to have lain north of the house, for two new work-buildings D and E were erected; these, together with the Rooms 18 and 27 and baths, enclosed an area there. The new yard was entered at its south-western corner from the south-west road between Building D and Room 27. Along the northern side of the yard the series of post-holes indicate that an animal enclosure lay here. Hardly any rebuilding of the baths was found to be necessary in Period 5. The main task was the enlargement of the plunge-bath 13 which now formed the largest villa bath yet known in Britain.

Buildings D and E were much smaller than B and C, but we must remember that not only did Building B possibly still survive but also Building F, 300 ft. (91.50 m.) north of the excavated complex, was probably built at this time: it was noted as having been constructed with the same type of mortar as the known Period 5 buildings (fig. 27). Since Building F was a chance discovery, it is necessary to allow for the possibility of further structures north of the known group, at least in this period and later.

Building D (fig. 32) may have comprised both workshop and dwelling. It held three tiny hearths and an oven or furnace and possibly a bench along the west wall. Two saws as well as knives were found here.

Building E also had an oven, built of re-used materials, on the eastern side of its north–south division. A second oven, three hearths and a slate-lined cist were also found and are equivocal evidence of a dwelling, but the presence of wall-plaster on the western wall may indicate that it was, at least originally, a habitation.

It seems possible that in Period 6, which began *c*. A.D. 319 and ended *c*. 353, the southern frontage of the house declined in importance. The carefully balanced façade was spoiled partly by widening the western wing, partly by constructing two hypocaust stoke-holes at the end of that wing and also perhaps by blocking[1] the gate (fig. 34). Thus it seems that the

---

[1] But these could be sleeper walls.

transference of the yard to the northern side in Period 5 was followed by an increase in the importance of the northern aspect of the house itself in Period 6. This can be compared with the history of the Winterton, Lincs.,[1] villa and possibly that of Hambleden[2] in Buckinghamshire.

In the Antonine period at Winterton the corridor house faced east and was approached through a yard by a straight road running along the line of the east–west axis of the house. In the fourth century, however, the eastern entrance was disused and built over by an apsidal *triclinium*. Possibly this phase may be connected with a yard on the west; at least one building corresponding to those flanking the eastern yard lay on that side.

It is an oft-repeated statement that the Hambleden villa turned its face from the squalor of its yard on the east, which was full of corn-driers and of unpleasant aspect, but there is no proof of this change in the report. House 1 may always have faced east, for in so far as the structural sequence can be followed in the report there is no proof of a literal volte-face.

Period 6 at the Gadebridge house was a time of increase in the amount and comfort of accommodation provided, apparently at the expense of external appearances. The stoke-holes which spoiled the façade of the west wing increased the comfort within. Room 29 was now warmed, and Room 35 formed a vast new heated apartment. Such rooms are not uncommon elsewhere. A much smaller version of a similar type is Room 4 at Titsey, Surrey.[3] Room III at Rockbourne Park, Hants,[4] although it has a pillared hypocaust, is, like Gadebridge (fig. 5) and Titsey, located in a wing. The closest parallel to Room 35 at Gade-bridge is Room F at West Dean, Hants.[5] The area of the room (c. 1100 sq. ft.) is virtually the same as that at Gadebridge although it is broader and shorter. Again it is placed in one of the wings of the house, for an architect would be severely limited in his choice of location for a room of such a size. The differences between the two rooms are that at West Dean the hypocaust channels branch from both sides of the main flue, and there is only one stoke-hole there. The Gadebridge and West Dean houses were doubtless similar in plan as a whole.

Whether these very large heated rooms had any special purpose is unknown. They are all included within the main house and so probably did not have an industrial use. Perhaps they were reception rooms or were possibly divided into smaller areas above the floors.

It seems that the first geometric mosaics were laid in Period 6 (pl. XVI). These are dated to c. A.D. 319 and were thus among the first of the flood of British fourth-century mosaics. Fragments of carved limestone were found over the pavement in Room 27 and may have been contemporary with it. Decorated stone is, on the whole, rare at Gadebridge (see pp. 191–3). This does not mean that we can compare this villa with, for example, Gloucestershire villas and conclude a relative lack of luxury. Good stone is rare in the district and is reflected in the lack of worked stone even from Verulamium.[6]

The trend towards comfort and convenience is reflected elsewhere in the Period 6 house. The swastika-shaped hypocaust was inserted into Room 18 at this time. Also Room 20 had perhaps been found to be rather an extravagant use of space in Period 5, for it was now divided into four rooms by light partitions (fig. 35) and adapted for more utilitarian purposes.

[1] *Antiq. J.*, XLI (1966), 72–84, and I. M. Stead, forthcoming (H.M.S.O.).
[2] *Arch.*, LXXI (1921), 141–57.
[3] *Arch.*, LIX (1905), 214.
[4] A. T. Morley Hewitt, *Roman villa, West Park, Rockbourne* (1969), centre plan.
[5] *W.A.M.*, XXII (1885), plan facing p. 244.
[6] *Verulamium* 1936, pl. XCIIIB; *Verulamium* 1972.

H

A number of hearths were made and slag, together with other rubbish, and a farrier's butteris (SF 345, fig. 69) deposited on the floors. Room 20 was obviously used partly as a smithy. A number of heaps of *tesserae* were found and were perhaps being manufactured here. This activity was also carried on at the Rudston, Yorks., villa[1] and we can presume that the *tesserae* were for use on the spot.

Period 6 produces one of the most puzzling features of Gadebridge in the shape of the huge swimming pool (fig. 8) which is only exceeded in size by the Great Bath of *Aquae Sulis*. Its vastness leads us immediately to suspect public rather than private use although it is not proven that Gadebridge ever was a spa or religious centre. The finds do not include any series of votive objects left at a cult centre; there was no temple, and there was no large-scale accommodation for patrons (cf. Lydney, Glos.)[2] unless the large Room 35 has some relevance here. It is possible, however, that other buildings, perhaps to the north of the main complex, would shed some light on the problem. A factor which may at least partly explain the presence of such a large bath is the availability of water. The leat (p. 69), used from the earliest times, was large and doubtless could supply a large volume of water. At the risk of putting the cart before the horse, we may wonder whether the plenitude of water was a factor in the decision to construct a really impressive pool.

At this time more fencing was erected along the western side of the building complex, presumably to exclude stock from the area immediately around the house. This could imply that the herds had increased in size and were now being kept both north and west of the villa, and further that the farming aspect of the villa continued to flourish and was perhaps providing the necessary funds for additions and alterations to the house.

Period 6 seems to have ended suddenly in the mid-fourth century when all the buildings excepting E were razed. The coin series of the hoard (fig. 53) ends in *c.* A.D. 353 and we wonder if this termination at the end of the reign of Magnentius is of particular relevance. Ammianus Marcellinus says that after the death of Magnentius, Constantius' state secretary Paulus was 'sent to Britain to fetch some officers who had dared to conspire with Magnentius [and], since they could make no resistance he autocratically exceeded his instructions and, like a flood, suddenly overwhelmed the fortunes of many, making his way amid manifold slaughter and destruction, imprisoning freeborn men and even degrading some with handcuffs'.[3]

On the face of it we seem to have here a neat correlation between the archaeological record and an historical source; but why should Paulus the Chain have caused the villa to be razed? If it had belonged to a pro-Magnentian, it would surely have been confiscated, not destroyed. In any case, the signs are not those of a haphazard bloody destruction but of dismantling in a fairly regular fashion: no burning and no bodies. It may be that the villa had a special purpose and that the events of A.D. 353–4 were sufficient to upset a delicate balance; or perhaps the site was now included within an estate with its headquarters elsewhere and most of the Gadebridge buildings were no longer required. In this context we are reminded of the leaden sealing[4] from Boxmoor which may imply the location there of an imperial estate. Perhaps the demise of the Gadebridge buildings was connected with the

---

[1] *Y.A.J.*, XXXII (1934–6), 216–17; ibid., XXXIII (1936–8), 81–4.

[2] *Lydney*, pl. LI.

[3] *Ammianus Marcellinus*, XIV, 5, 6 (Loeb Translation by J. C. Rolfe, Vol. I, p. 33).

[4] *Brit.*, I (1970), 162 and pl. XIII B, C.

re-arrangement of imperial estate boundaries after confiscations of private lands — if this is the kind of activity which Ammianus can be taken to be implying.

After the great demolition, only Building E of the known stone buildings survived; the coin-finds indicate that it remained in use until *c.* A.D. 388–402. This does not, of course, preclude the existence of buildings elsewhere in the vicinity, although if the area were now part of a larger estate, E could have been spared as quarters for stockmen out from the main estate centre. There was still much activity in this place (fig. 42). Timber structures were erected over the northern courtyard, the baths, the western side of Building A and the site of Building C. The post-holes form the outline of a series of stockaded enclosures and not roofed buildings, except perhaps for an area of 16 by 26 ft. (4.87 × 7.93 m.) at the southern end of the largest enclosure (fig. 22). Here no occupational debris was found; the place may have been a small pen for special treatment of animals. The length of time during which the site remained in use is indeterminate. Such light occupation leaves few datable traces. Few of the post-holes of this latest phase seem to have been replaced more than once, which could give a terminal date in the late fourth or very early fifth century.

We can now consider some aspects of the economy of the Gadebridge villa. The report on the animal bones (pp. 256–61) seems to indicate a swing from mainly sheep-rearing in the first and second centuries to mainly cattle-raising in the fourth, with a decline in the number of pigs from the early to the late periods. But the maximum number of individual animals available for study is rather small as the foundation for sweeping conclusions, especially if the villa were producing large numbers for sale (presumably on the hoof or as carcases, no doubt in Verulamium). Only animals slaughtered and eaten or dying of disease can appear in the archaeological record of the site itself. If the herds were healthy or if disease-ridden carcases were buried well away from any habitation (which would be likely), the bone-finds must show an apparently small number of animals. Thus in postulating stock-rearing it is the study of the stockaded enclosures and other non-skeletal remains which is important and the bones paradoxically assume less importance. However, the bones should tell us something of the dietary habits of the people who lived on the spot, and here we might detect an increase in the number of cattle consumed and a decrease in the number of sheep and pigs from the earlier to the later period.

The evidence for the arable economy is as follows. The plough marks (fig. 22) of an early date tell us that crops were being grown from the earliest times. A later indicator of arable farming is the grain-drying oven (fig. 25). Or at least that is what the structure seems to be; no carbonized grain was found in it and perhaps it was used for some other purpose; pottery dates it to the later second century.

Slags and other waste show that metal-working was being practised, mainly in the earlier periods and in the vicinity of the main Building A, but also in the late period in the north courtyard, in Room 20 and near the water-leat. This evidence is not surprising in view of the number of finds of, for example, iron objects. Doubtless many tools had to be repaired and horses needed to be shod. Special pieces of equipment may have needed manufacture too, but there seems little evidence to suggest that metal goods were made for sale elsewhere.

Six quarry-pits were examined and coins of *c.* A.D. 300–50 were found among rubbish dumped in them. This would suggest dates late in the third or early in the fourth century (with the exception of Pit X which is dated to the second century) for their excavation.

It seems probable that at least some of the chalk was converted into lime in the old cistern for use in Period 5 construction work. There was perhaps a surplus to be disposed of elsewhere. It is also possible that some of the chalk was used in the marling of arable land.

The Gadebridge villa is situated about five miles from Verulamium, which is by a considerable margin the nearest urban settlement. This fact has already prompted the suggestion that the stock raised on the estate was sold in Verulamium. Presumably the latter was also the market for grain and any other saleable surpluses produced by the villa. The successive structural phases of the house show how it grew in prosperity. Money continued to be available to pay for the alteration and elaboration of existing buildings and the construction of new ones. The development began at an early date and throughout the villa's existence there was a notable tendency to build in a symmetrical fashion which was typically Roman. These observations lead us to wonder whether the villa was the country property of people having opportunities to observe and adopt Roman attitudes in Verulamium, perhaps a series of decurions. We would suspect, perhaps, that the buildings were designed to impress visitors as well as to please the eye of the owner. The swimming pool would certainly be included in the former category. If the owner of Gadebridge in the mid-fourth century were an important and well-known person, perhaps an administrative official in the city, the apparent sudden demise of the grand complex of buildings would perhaps be more comprehensible.

Considering the proximity of Verulamium to the Gade valley,[1] its known density of Romano-British settlement is quite low compared with the number of sites near other Chiltern rivers feeding the Thames. Gadebridge, five miles from Verulamium, is the only villa certainly known in the upper valley of the Gade, although a villa was discovered below the Gade–Bulbourne confluence on the east bank at Abbots Langley.[2] In the Bulbourne valley there is, of course, the Boxmoor villa,[3] with another building a few hundred yards to the north-west at Hemel Hempstead station.[4] Apart from these sites, only traces of Roman occupation are known, for example at Great Gaddesden[5] (TL 028113) and Little Gaddesden[6] (SP 995139; pottery), Box Lane, Hemel Hempstead[7] (TL 037057; burial), and Moor End roundabout[8] (TL 055064; pottery).

Doubtless there are also more sites to be found on higher ground away from the Gade and Bulbourne, especially nearer to Verulamium. A recent discovery is the building at Wood Lane End,[9] Hemel Hempstead (TL 083078) but its exact nature is undetermined. At Potters Crouch[10] (TL 116052) pottery has been found. Closer yet to Verulamium and in the Ver valley is the Gorhambury villa.[11]

It would be of remarkable interest if a number of sites in the area were examined in as great detail as Gadebridge. This and the Boxmoor house have already suggested a number of possibilities of interrelationships and of associations with Verulamium. Further work on rural Romano-British settlement around Verulamium will increase our knowledge not only of the histories of particular sites but also of how this part of the province developed and then declined as an economic entity.

---

[1] See fig. 1, p. 2 and *Arch. J.*, CXXIV (1967), fig. 1, facing p. 152.
[2] *V.C.H. Herts.*, IV (1914), p. 147.
[3] *Brit.*, I (1970), 156–62.
[4] *Arch.*, XXXIV (1852), 394–8; *Brit.*, I (1970), 156.
[5] R.C.H.M. *Herts.* (1910), p. 100.
[6] *Viatores*, pp. 155–6.
[7] *Arch.*, XXVII (1838), 434–5.
[8] *Brit.*, I (1970), 158.
[9] *J.R.S.*, LVII (1967), 188.
[10] *Viatores*, p. 138.
[11] *T.S.A.H.A.A.S.*, 1961, 21–30.

PART II

The Finds

INVENTORY OF FINDS

A large number of finds were made during the excavation and these have been fully illustrated. Many unidentifiable fragments, or duplicates such as bronze studs and tacks, have not been illustrated. The deposit of finds in the water leat north of the pool has been published as a separate group. Measurements are either in millimetres or centimetres, and have been taken from the furthest points of the object, unless stated otherwise. In some cases examples of the same type of object of different materials have been published together, so as to provide a complete list of objects of that type. Where possible, the place of discovery and layer number is followed by the relevant section, figure number and measurement. Layer is abbreviated to 'L'.

THE COINS

By P. E. Curnow, f.s.a.

THE excavations of 1963–8 produced a total of 309 Roman coins as site finds — a substantial number for a villa in the Home Counties even allowing for the size of the villa complex and the completeness of its excavation.

A further 173 coins are suggested as being the dispersed contents of a votive deposit found in one-time waterlogged levels north-west of the bathing pool, although the possibility of this group of coins being a dispersed hoard should not be ignored. This group of coins is discussed separately below (see p. 105). The fairly distinctive condition of these coins and their localized find-spot make it very improbable that any appreciable number of them figure in the site list.

The site list which contains nothing of intrinsic numismatic interest is, however, large enough to provide evidence which helps to illustrate the economic history of the villa, although in the present state of knowledge coin evidence must be used with caution. It will be seen from the list and accompanying histogram (List I and fig. 52) that while under one-third of the coins (96) belong to the period up to A.D. 300, over one-half are dated to the period A.D. 300–48 (165) and less than one-sixth to the second half of the fourth century (48).

The numismatic evidence cannot really be used alone to support the idea of first-century occupation of the site;[1] thus great weight should not be attached to the Flavian issues

---

[1] But see below Appendix E.

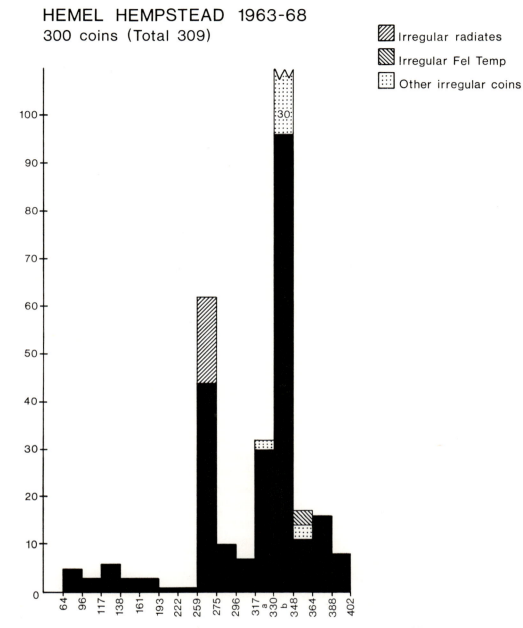

FIG. 52.   Coin histogram for Gadebridge Park villa

(nos. 1–5). These could easily remain in circulation for many years and it should be noted that three of the four coins of Domitian were badly worn as also were the two bronze pieces of Trajan.

Allowing for the relative scarcity of second-century coinage which is normal to this period as compared with the later third and fourth centuries, the second century seems to have been a high point of activity, for apart from those earlier issues probably still in circulation, the coinage of the Hadrian–Antonine period is represented by twelve pieces.

The issues of the first half of the third century are poorly represented, but, as on most sites, the radiate series of the second half is plentiful. The distribution is quite evenly spread from Gallienus to Allectus and the proportion of regular to irregular is high, 52:18. Even representation, implying a steady rate of coin loss, compared with that on sites where there is an emphasis on the coinage of the Tetrici and/or irregular issues, suggests activity throughout this period.

It is in the fourth century, however, that the rate of coin loss leaps. The heavy concentration of coinage of the House of Constantine I is not an uncommon feature but at Gadebridge it completely overshadows the radiate coinage in numbers.

The pre-A.D. 317 period produced seven folles evenly spread in date, and from A.D. 317 to 330 examples of most of the common issues totalled 32 coins, but between A.D. 330 and the commencement of the Fel Temp Reparatio coinage of A.D. 348, no less than 126 coins are listed, including 29 irregular copies. Although the western mints of Trier, Lyons and Arles produced the great bulk of the coinage with Rome, Siscia and Aquileia also represented, there are two pieces from the Eastern mints — a POP ROMANVS from Constantinople and a GLORIA EXERCITVS (1 std.) from Heraclea.

Most of the current issues were present and the spread over the whole period is again quite even; the numbers are as follows (excluding two uncertain Constantinian):

A.D. 330–5/7: 53
- GLORIA EXERCITVS (2 stds.) 11 + 8 irregular
- VRBS ROMA + CONSTANTINOPOLIS 20 + 14 ,,

A.D. 335/7–41: 42
- GLORIA EXERCITVS (1 std.) 22 + 5 ,,
- others................. 14 + 1 ,,

A.D. 341–8: 29
- VICTORIAE DD AVGG Q NN 26 + 2 ,,
- others................. 1

In the succeeding period the Fel Temp Reparatio coinage of A.D. 348–50 with two 'Hut' and four 'Phoenix' reverses contrasts with the 'Fallen Horsemen' reverses of A.D. 353–61. The regular issues, of the latter of which there were two, are not common as site finds, but irregular copies, often found in profusion, rather surprisingly yielded only three examples. The earlier Hut + Phoenix types, rarely abundant, suggest that the activity of the preceding period ran on into the early 350s, and may have included the reign of Magnentius, A.D. 351–3, which produced three regular and two irregular coins. The subsequent re-assertion of power by Constantius II after A.D. 353 may mark a distinctly unfavourable political and economic climate, and it is worth noting that the hoard or (?) votive deposit also ends with two Magnentian issues. Further, in the case of the deep room (Room 20, fig. 5) where the occupation soil yielded 18 coins and the overlying rubble 17, the distribution is shown in Appendix (A) (p. 118).

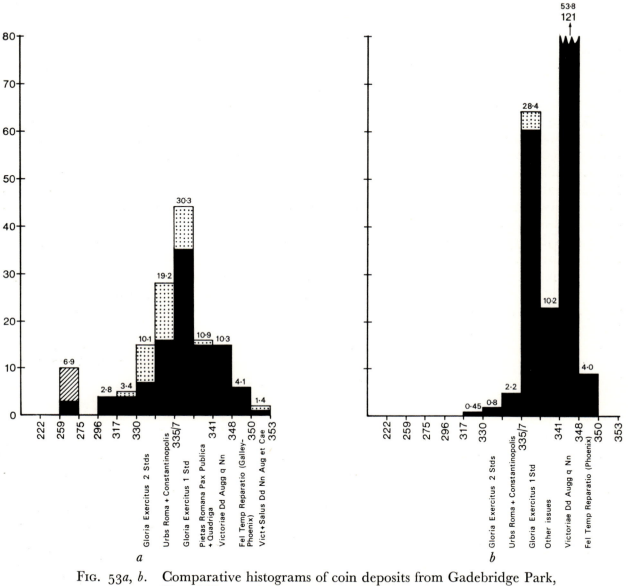

FIG. 53*a, b*.   Comparative histograms of coin deposits from Gadebridge Park,
Hemel Hempstead and Great Weldon Roman villas

While the numismatic evidence certainly supports the view that there was a considerable
reduction in the prosperity of the villa in the mid-fourth century, coins of the House of
Valentinian I (16) and the House of Theodosius (8) indicate continuity of occupation,
albeit on a reduced scale.

This becomes more apparent if the actual find-spots of the late fourth-century coins are isolated. In the small building (Building E, fig. 32) and a pit (Pit N) sealed by its destruction rubble, to the north-west of the villa proper, a total of 23 coins was recovered. The distribution was markedly different from that encountered on other parts of the site. Eight coins were of the House of Valentinian I, A.D. 364–78, and two were Theodosian, A.D. 388–402.[1] These account for one half of the total finds of the former and one quarter of the latter. In this building evidence for late fourth-century occupation must be seen as unequivocal. In contrast the small neighbouring building (Building D, fig. 32) produced much the same pattern of coinage as the deep room (Room 20) already mentioned; the series of thirteen coins from occupation soil ending with a single coin of Magnentius (A.D. 351–3).[2]

The provenance of the remainder of the later fourth-century coinage provides no single instance of a properly stratified coin from an occupation layer. Of five coins from the main villa site, one, of the House of Valentinian I, was found in a sleeper beam trench in Room 26; this trench had cut through an earlier floor. Another of Theodosian date was found in black soil within Building B. Other coins were found in contexts which the excavator concludes must imply that the villa had been at least partly demolished at this time. Apart from Building E itself, the greatest concentration of later coinage came from the north courtyard which produced five coins — four House of Valentinian I and one Theodosian. The former were amongst the rubble in the courtyard whilst the latter lay on silt in an eaves drip gully just to the north of Room 27.

The numismatic evidence for the last phases of the villa seems to point clearly to the existence of a severely reduced scale of occupation, with most or all of the residential villa in ruins and economic activity limited to one or more outbuildings and perhaps parts of the wings of the villa re-used.

There is no positive numismatic evidence for fifth-century occupation in any part of the site and the Theodosian Ae 4 issues are divided 7 : 1 in favour of the earlier Victoria Auggg type as against the longer-lived Salus Reipublicae coinage.

The fourth-century coin deposit

The archaeological context of this coin deposit has been discussed by the excavator (see p. 73) and mentioned above (p. 101). Its composition (List II) does provide internal numismatic evidence, however, and this is summarized in the accompanying histogram (fig. 53a), which attempts to show the chronological distribution, the main issues represented and the proportion of irregular coins present. This has resulted in a slight inconsistency in the form of the histogram due to the placing of contemporary issues alongside each other rather than superimposed on the vertical scale. In any event an exactly proportional histogram giving a uniform horizontal scale is of doubtful value in a case like this where a maximum of information for the purposes of comparison is required.

Several interesting points emerge when the Gadebridge deposit is compared with a hoard from Great Weldon (fig. 53b), Northants.,[3] which covers an almost identical range of

---

[1] See Appendix C.
[2] See Appendix B.
[3] The report on the excavation of this villa 1953–6 by Dr D. J. Smith is in preparation and I would like to thank

the excavator for allowing me to use the information which the writer of the note had prepared for the Weldon coin report in advance of publication.

coins. The latter, recovered during excavations on a substantial villa in 1955, had been in part scattered, but the 225 identifiable coins (out of a total of 230) can safely be regarded as the bulk of the hoard. The villa at Great Weldon included a winged residential block of some pretension, but not on the spacious scale of Gadebridge, an attached bath-suite, ancillary barns, etc., and an enclosed courtyard. The economic backgrounds of the two sites are thus similar and both sites show a noticeable decrease in coin loss subsequent to the dates of the two deposits. The terminal dates of the two groups are very close; at Gadebridge the series ends with the two coins of Magnentius, a regular SALVS DD NN AVG ET CAES of A.D. 351–3 and an irregular VICTORIAE DD NN AVG ET CAE also of A.D. 351–3 which must be regarded as a contemporary copy. A terminal date of c. A.D. 353 would seem to be likely in view of the lack of 'Fel Temp' — 'Fallen Horsemen' types. At Weldon no fewer than nine 'Fel Temp' — Phoenix types of A.D. 348–50, with nothing later, suggest a date soon after Magnentius' seizure of power in A.D. 350.

The points which emerge when the two groups are contrasted can be summarized as follows: at Gadebridge there is a more even spread with the peak of numbers (41.2%) represented by the GLORIA EXERCITVS (1 std.) and commemorative issues of A.D. 335/7–341; this compares with the overwhelming preponderance (53.8%) of the two victories type of A.D. 341–8 at Weldon. This type, one of the commonest of the Constantinian issues, is nevertheless rarely dominant in site finds, but it could easily predominate in a hoard formed at a time when it would form the most plentiful and freshest up-to-date currency, i.e. c. A.D. 350.

The presence of radiate coinage is not particularly surprising in the Gadebridge deposit, but seven out of the ten pieces are irregular and hardly desirable coins in a selective hoard, as witness the complete lack not only of radiates but also the finer but hardly current folles of the period up to A.D. 330 in the Weldon hoard. In the latter, the single pre-A.D. 330 piece is a IOVI CONSERVATORI of A.D. 324 which is a small module piece, comparable in size to the issues of A.D. 330–5/7.

Almost as striking as the difference in the distribution pattern of the issues between the two groups is the difference in the proportions of irregular coins present. At Gadebridge 27% of the total is made up of irregular copies — mainly of the earlier issues — whereas at Weldon only four copies were identified (this could be a slight under-estimate, but the numbers involved would be relatively insignificant), representing only 1.7%.

At Gadebridge a number of the irregular Constantinian issues were AE 4 or minim size, and amongst the 28 faulty or wholly unidentifiable coins not shown on the histogram, six were AE 4 or minim size, two were cut pieces and six were fragmented. Even amongst the identifiable coins a number were broken. Unfortunately, due to the nature of the water-logging which reduced many of them to the consistency of mud, it was difficult to establish how many had been broken before being deposited.

The Weldon coins on the other hand were generally of a like module and were in fair condition. It may be argued that the Weldon hoard is not typical — nevertheless I think it possible to draw valid conclusions from the distinguishing characteristics of the two collections. The Weldon hoard was a collection of the best AE coinage available at the time of its deposition, and is unlikely to have been a savings hoard of slow accumulation. On the contrary the Gadebridge deposit surely contains a large number of coins which a saver would least like to retain — many obsolete, many small and irregular pieces and containing a few examples of notably greater module than the rest. The early Constantinian folles (nos. 11–14) and the Magnentian AE 1 (no. 144) are an ill assorted group at best and do not accord well with the remainder.

On numismatic grounds alone the nature of the Gadebridge deposit makes its identification as a 'normal' (i.e. consisting of current coin — intended for future use) hoard at least questionable failing any other alternative. The anomalous archaeological circumstances of its finding do, however, suggest an alternative. The levels containing coins covered the area of a leat or water-course which joined the river to the baths. This seems to have been destroyed or to have gone out of use at the same time as the large bathing pool in the 350s. Of several layers of fill which contained the coins one extended from the leat area to the bathing pool. Thus, it would appear that if the coin deposit had been a hoard it would have had to have been dispersed and found its way into not less than two superimposed layers of waterworn and waterlogged gravel and debris within a period which is archaeologically indistinguishable from that of its presumed initial deposition.

The period of accumulation of this deposit, if such it was, must have been short — perhaps the decade c. A.D. 340–50 — perhaps even shorter.

Perhaps even more significant is the association with the coins of a considerable number of small bronze objects; rings, fragments of bracelets, penannular brooches and toilet implements, together with small pieces of bronze wire (figs. 65–6), as well as a number of unidentifiable iron fragments.[1] Although there is a good deal of variety in the make-up of Roman votive offerings a number do show a general similarity in the juxtaposition of coins and small metal objects. These offerings, rather like bent pins in wishing wells, were often inferior objects, miniatures, or were sometimes purposely broken, and it is perhaps worth noting that in this instance a number of the bronze objects seemed to have been broken in antiquity.

In this case the evidence of both content and context suggest the strong possibility that this deposit originally formed a collection of votive offerings connected in some way with the supply of water, or perhaps its qualities. As regards context, fountains, cisterns and nymphaea all play a conspicuous part in Roman life and minor deities were not uncommon in Roman Britain.

In 1911, Ward[2] commented, 'It would be strange if here and there some wealthy proprietor did not grace the spring or stream which supplied him with water, and honour the divinities who dwelt in or by it, with a shrine'. At Gadebridge no evidence for a nymphaeum such as existed at Chedworth was found but the lack of evidence on the ground for small local or household water cults is not really surprising, for total excavation not only of the complete building complex but also of natural features would be required before evidence could be recovered. Gadebridge must be one of the few sites where this has been largely accomplished due to the close physical and archaeological relationship of the water supply with the bath-suite. On the other sites local sources of water supply could easily be too remote, inaccessible

[1] At Brigstock, Northamptonshire a circular shrine yielded a large collection of coins together with numerous small bronze and iron objects of miscellaneous character apart from the more particular bronze cult objects. E. Greenfield, 'The Romano-British Shrines at Brigstock, Northants.', Antiq. J., XLIII (1963), 228 ff.

[2] T. Ward, Romano-British Buildings and Earthworks (1911), p. 249.

or unidentifiable. That local water cults existed in quantity in England as well as Gaul is not in doubt[1] but few have left traces in the form of identifiable structures. Conversely the rather grand establishments known from Gaul[2] often lack the adequate publication of associated small cult objects of votive deposits as well as detailed coin lists and small finds reports.

[1] J. P. Alcock, 'Celtic Water Cults in Roman Britain', *Arch. J.*, CXXII (1965), 1–12.

[2] A. Grenier, 'Les Monument des Eaux' in *Manuel d'Archéologie*, Pt. VI (1960).

Coin List I: SITE FINDS

No.	Obverse Type	Date A.D.	Denomination	Reference (see page 122)
1	Vespasian	69–79	As	763
2–5	Domitian	81–96	Sest [2], Dup [2]	350, + 2 Sest + 1 Dup illeg.
6–8	Trajan	98–117	Den, Dup [2]	91 (Den) + 2 Dup illeg.
9–14	Hadrian	117–38	Sest [3], Dup [2], As	594b, 562b, cf. 914 (Exercitus type as pps. 458–62), 617, 699 + 1 Dup illeg.
15–17	Antoninus Pius	138–61	Dup, Asses [2]	660a, 934, ?934
18–20	M. Aurelius	161–80	Sest [2], Dup	861/898, 909, 1232
21–2	Illegible first and second century	—		Sest, + cut and hammered fragment of Sest
23	Julia Domna (Septimius Severus)	196–211	Den	572 (Den)
24	Severus Alexander	222–35	Den	178 (Den)
25–33	Gallienus (sole reign)	259–68	Ant	$179(8k)\frac{}{X}$, $193(8A[2]8k)\frac{s}{}$, $\frac{}{\perp}[2]$, $214(8k)\frac{}{XI}$, $227\frac{ᴣ}{}$, $230(8k)\frac{}{B}$, $287(8k)\frac{ε}{}$, $320/30(8k)$,
34–8	Claudius II	268–70	Ant	15(4k), 48/9, 56, 104 + 1
39–42	Posthumous Claudius II	270	Ant	261[2], 266[2]
43	Irregular Claudius II	270 +	—	cf. 261
44	Quintillus	270	Ant	$33\frac{}{Γ}$
45–6	Postumus	259–68	Ant	64, 85

No.	Obverse Type	Date A.D.	Denomination	Reference
47–52	Victorinus	268–70	Ant	45, 67/112 (5F), 71(5C), 112–14, 114 $\frac{*|}{*}$, 118 (5C) $\frac{V|}{}$*
53–64	Tetricus I	270–3	Ant	56/7, 87(2C), 87/90, 100(A)[2], 125(C), 127, 136(2C)[3], 148(2C), + 1
65–8	Irregular Tetricus I	270 +	—	cf. 86, cf. 100[2] + 1 Pax type
69–71	Tetricus II	270–3	Ant	255, 272, + 1 Pietas type
72	Irregular Tetricus II	270 +	—	Pax type
73–8	Carausius	286–93	Ant	101 $\overline{ML}$, 149 $\frac{B|E}{MLXXI}$, 300(1A) $\frac{S|C}{}$, cf. 498 $\frac{S|C}{}$, (but PROVIDE), cf. 915–17 (overstrike) + 1
79–82	Allectus	293–6	Ant	22(F) $\frac{S|A}{ML}$, 33(2C, 2F) $\frac{S|P}{ML}$ [2], 94 (2C) $\frac{S|P}{C}$
83–4	Illegible Radiate	third century	Ant	O and R illegible
85–96	Irregular Radiates	c. 270 +		Uncertain [5], AE4 [3] (2 Pax type), minims [4] (2 Pax types, 1 Pietas, 1 Spes)

No.	Reverse Type	Date A.D.	Mint	Obverse Type	Reference
97	GENIO POPVLI ROMANI	c. 303–5	London	CS. I	37a
98	MARTI PATRI PROPVG	307–10	London	C. I	108
99–101	SOLI INVICTO COMITI	312–13	London Trier	C. I C. I [2]	284 875, 865–76

No.	Reverse Type	Date A.D.	Mint	Obverse Type	Reference
102–3	GENIO POP ROM	316	Trier	L. I [2]	121, 123 (but obv. B 5)
104–8	VICTORIAE LAETAE PRINC PERP	318–20	London Trier Arles	C. I C. I [3] C. I	168 208A, 209, 221 191
109–10	Irregular Vict Laetae Princ P	318 +	—	cf. C. I [2]	cf. 229 + 1
111–12	VIRTVS EXERCIT	320–1	Trier Arles	C. I L. II	266 206
113–21	BEATA TRANQVILLITAS	321–4	London Trier Lyons —	C. II, Cr. C.I [2], C.II, Cr. C.I [2] C. II	211, 236 303, 308, 382, 389 155 (but vs?M AVG), 198 —
122–4	SARMATIA DEVICTA	323–4	London Trier	C. I [2] C. I	290 [2] 429
125–7	VOT X CAESARVM NOSTRORVM	321–4	Trier Arles Siscia	C. II Cr. C. II	441 225 182
128	VOT XX D N CONSTANTINI MAX AVG	322–3	Arles	C. I	252
129	Uncertain Votis type — Wreath	c. 320	—	C. I or II	—
130–4	PROVIDENTIAE AVGG/CAESS	324–30 327–30	Trier Ticinum	C. I [2], C. II, Cs. II Cs. II	L.R.B.C. I, 28s, 34p, 38p, 39s, 486s
135	Wreath — CRISPVS CAESAR	324–30	Trier	Cr. ? Irregular	cf. 17p but wreath instead of star

No.	Reverse Type	Date A.D.	Mint	Obverse Type	Reference
136–46	GLORIA EXERCITVS (2 standards)	330–5	Trier	C. I [2], C. II [2], Cn. + 1	60, 67s, 73p, 84p, cf. 48, cf. 49
			Lyons	C. II [2], Cs. II	187p, 213p, cf. 209
			Arles	C. I	373p
			Aquileia	C. II	663s
147–54	Irregular Gloria Exercitus (2 standards)	330 +	—	Types of C. II [4], + 4	[8]
155–62	Wolf and Twins	330–5	Trier	U.R.	58s, 65s, 70p, 70s
		330–7	Lyons		195p, cf. 184
		330–7	Siscia		750A
		330–7	—		—
163–6	Irregular Wolf and Twins	330 +	—	cf. U.R.	AE 4[3] + 1 minim
167–78	Victory on Prow	330–5	Trier	C'opolis	59p, 59/71, 66p [2], 71p [2], 71s, cf. 52 [2]
		330–5	Lyons		185p, 206s, + 1
179–88	Irregular Victory on Prow	330 +	—	cf. C'opolis	AE 3 [6] (inc. 2 hybrids with Obv. of Cs. II and Cn.)
					AE 4 [3] + 1 minim
189–210	GLORIA EXERCITVS (1 standard)	335–7	Trier	C. II [5], Cn.	88p, 88s, 88/93 [2], 93, 95p
			Arles	C. II	411
			Rome	Delmatius	570s
		337–41	Trier	Cs. II [4], Cs. II or Cn.	125p, 126p, 130s, 132/3s
			Lyons	Cs. II [3]	242p, 248p, 252s
			Arles	Cs. II	428
			Heraclea	Cs. II	949
			Arles or Trier	H. of Const. I	134 or 434–7
		335–41	Trier	H. of Const. I	—[2]
			Arles	H. of Const. I	—

No.	Reverse Type	Date A.D.	Mint	Obverse Type	Reference
211–15	Irregular Gloria Exercitus (1 standard)	335 +	—	—	AE 3 type of Cn., AE 4, + 3 minims
216–22	PAX PVBLICA	337–41	Trier	H.	cf. 112, ?119p, 128p, 128s
				H.	— [3]
223	Irregular Pax Publica	337 +	—	cf. H.	A 4
224–9	PIETAS ROMANA	337–41	Trier	Th.	113p, 120p, cf. 120 [2] + 1
				Th.	—
230	VIRTVS AVGVSTI	337–41	Rome	C. II	602p
231	Star in Wreath	341–8	Constantinople	POP ROMANVS	1067
232–57	VICTORIAE DD AVGG Q NN	341–8	Trier	Cs. II [2], Cn. [15], Cs. II or Cn. [2]	139p, 140s, 140ap, 140a, 148p, 148, 148/50, 149, 150p, 150s, 150, 151, 152/5, 155s, 158s, 158–64, 159, 164p, 164s
			Lyons	Cs. II [3]	26op [2], 266p
			Arles	Cs. II, Cs. II or Cn.	455, 455–7
			Rome	Cn.	cf. 642
			—	Cn.	— (but mm. ⋙ ∕∕∕∕∕)
258–9	Irregular Victoriae Dd Augg Q Nn	341 +	—	types of Cn.	— [2] (but cf. 138, + 158/274)
260–1	House of Constantine I	—	—	—	— [2] (1? Vict dd)
262–3	FEL TEMP REPARATIO (hut)	348–50	Trier / Rome	Cn. / Cn.	L.R.B.C. II, 29p / II, 604T
264–7	FEL TEMP REPARATIO (phoenix)	348–50	Trier	Cn. [3], Cs. II	33p [2], 33s, 34s
268	GLORIA ROMANORVM	350–1	Lyons	Mg.	214p

I

No.	Reverse Type	Date A.D.	Mint	Obverse Type	Reference
269–70	VICTORIAE DD NN AVG ET CAE	351–3	Lyons	Mg. Mg.	221p —
271–2	Irregular Victoriae Dd Nn Aug et Cae	351 +	—	Type of Mg. or Dec., Mg.	AE3, AE4 (as *L.R.B.C.* 8)
273–4	FEL TEMP REPARATIO (fallen horseman)	353–61	Trier —	Cs. II Cs. II	76 —
275–7	Irregular Fel Temp Reparatio (fallen horseman)	353 +	—	—	AE 3, minims [2]
278	Irregular Vot X Mult XX	361 +	—	cf. Julian	Core of plated siliqua
279–85	GLORIA ROMANORVM	367–75 364–7 367–78 367–75 364–75	Lyons Arles Arles Aquileia —	V. I, Gr. [2] V. I Vn. Vn. V. I	338, 343/7, 351 $\left(\text{but } \dfrac{\text{O}|\text{F II} \quad |\text{R}}{\text{LVGS}}\right)$ 484 526 1018
286–92	SECVRITAS REIPVBLICAE	364–78 367–75 367–78	Lyons Arles —	Vn. [3] V. I, Vn. Vn., H. of V. I	328, 340, + I (cf. 280) 477–527p, 523 — [2]
293–4	GLORIA NOVI SAECVLI	367–75	Arles	Gr. [2]	511T, 529
295–8	VICTORIA AVGGG	388 +	Trier Arles —	T. I, Ar. Ar. Ar.	169, 167/70 566/9
299–302	House of Theodosius I	388 +	—	Ar. [2] + 2	?Victoria Auggg [2], ? Salus Reipublicae, + I Æ 4
303–5	Illegible fourth century	—	—	—	AE 4 [3]
306–9	Illegible	—	—	—	AE 3, AE 4 [3]

MODERN COINS

1–2.	Charles I Maltravers ¼d.	1635–49	Brooke, p. 212 + pl. xlix, 16
3.	Illegible token ½d.	1651	—
4.	Napoleon III (2 centimes)	1855	—

Coin List II: THE FOURTH-CENTURY COIN DEPOSIT (1968)

No.	Obverse Type	Date A.D.	Reference
1	Claudius II	268–70	cf. 60–3
2–3	Tetricus I	270–3	100 + 1
4–10	Irregular Radiates	c. 270+	[7] (cf. Tet. I Laetitia, Tet. II Salus, Pax, + 1 Spes, 1 Pax, 1? Fortuna type + 1 uncertain)

No.	Reverse Type	Date A.D.	Mint	Obverse Type	Reference
11	GENIO POP ROM	316–17	Trier	C. I	—
12–14	SOLI INVICTO COMITI	313–17	London	C. I [2]	cf. 10, 91 (but IMP in obv. legend)
	SOLI INVICTO COMITI	—	—	—	—
15	VICTORIAE LAETAE PRINC PERP	319–20	London	C. I	157
16	Irregular VICTORIAE LAETAE PRINC PERP	c. 319	—	as C. I	cf. Trier 224 $\frac{X}{STR}$
17	CAESARVM NOSTRORVM	321	Arles	C. II	232
18–19	BEATA TRANQVILLITAS	322–3	Trier	C. II	384
		321–4	—	C. I	—
20–26	GLORIA EXERCITVS (2 standards)	330–5	Trier	C. I, C. II, C. II or Cs. II	53s, 68p, 68/9s
			Lyons	C. II	198p
			Arles	C. I	352p
			—	C. II + 1	— [2]

No.	Reverse Type	Date A.D.	Mint	Obverse Type	Reference
27–34	Irregular GLORIA EXERCITVS (2 standards)	330 +	—		AE 3 [4], AE 3–4 [2], AE 4 [2]
35–9	Wolf and Twins	330–5 / 330–5 / 330–7	Trier / Lyons / —	U.R. / U.R. / U.R.	58p, 58s / 195s / —[2]
40–3	Irregular Wolf and Twins	330 +	—	U.R. Type	AE 3, AE 3–4 [2], minim
44–54	Victory on Prow	330–5 / 330–5 / 330–7	Trier / Lyons / —	C'opolis / C'opolis / C'opolis	71p + 1 / 191p [2], 201p / —[6]
55–60	Irregular Victory on Prow	330 +	—	C'opolis Type	AE 3 [2], AE 3/4 [2], AE 4 [2]
61–2	Irregular Victory on Prow or Wolf and Twins	330 +	—	U.R. or C'opolis	AE 4 [2]
63–8	GLORIA EXERCITVS (1 standard)	335–7	Trier / Lyons / —	C. II / C. II [2] / C. II [2], Delmatius	93p / 229p, c.f. 226 / —[3]
69–84	GLORIA EXERCITVS (1 standard)	337–41	Trier / Aquileia / —	C. II [2], Cs. II [5], Cn. [2], Cs. II or Cn. [3] / Cn. / Cs. II, Cn., Cs. II or Cn.	107s, 125p, 126p, 126s [2], 126/7, cf. 126, 130p, 130/1, 132s, 132–3, ?134 / 694s / —[3] (one Trier or Arles)
85–97	GLORIA EXERCITVS (1 standard)	335–41	—	—	—[13] (inc. 9 broken or fragment)
98–106	Irregular GLORIA EXERCITVS (1 standard)	335 +	—	—	—[9] (inc. type of Cs. II [2], and Cn. [1])
107–10	PAX PVBLICA	337–41	Trier / —	H. / H.	128p / —[3]

No.	Reverse Type	Date A.D.	Mint	Obverse Type	Reference
111	Irregular PAX PVBLICA	337 +		cf. H.	—
112–19	PIETAS ROMANA	337–41	Trier	Th.	129p, 113p [3], 113s, cf. 113
			—	Th.	—[2]
120–2	Quadriga	337–41	Trier	Div. C. I	114p
			—	Div. C. I	—[2] (1? Lyons, cf. 245)
123–37	VICTORIAE DD AVGG Q NN	341–8	Trier	Cs. II, Cn. [6], Cs. II or Cn.	138, 141, 148, 149s, 149, 148/50, 145–50 + 1
			Arles	Cs. II, Cn., Cs. II or Cn.	444, 454p, 461/2p
			Thessalonica	Cs. II	859 E
			—	Cs. II, Cs. II or Cn. [2]	⟫⟫ [2], + 1
138–42	FEL TEMP REPARATIO (Phoenix)	348–50	Trier	Cn. [4], Cs. II or Cn.	33p [2], cf. 32–5, 36s, 39p
143	FEL TEMP REPARATIO (Galley)	348–50	Trier	Cn.	43p
144	SALVS DD NN AVG ET CAES	351–3	Trier	Mg.	62
145	Irregular Vict Dd Nn Aug et Cae	351 +		Type of Mg.	AE 2–3 size (cf. 5 mint of Amiens)
146–51	H. of Constantine	330 +		—	Uncertain type [6]
152–8	Illegible fourth century	—		—	? H. of Const. [4] uncertain [3]
159–65	Irregular fourth century	—		—	cf. H. of Const. AE 4 [2], minims [4]
166–73	Illegible	—		—	Fragments [6], cut pieces [2]

APPENDIX A
STRATIFIED COINS FROM BUILDING A, ROOM 20
(figs. 5, 6)

Occupation level (layer 5)	Date A.D.	Coin No.	Destruction level (layers 2 and 3)	Date A.D.	Coin No.
VICTORIAE LAETAE PRINC PERP	318–20	108	Tetricus I	270–3	64
BEATA TRANQVILLITAS	321–4	117	Irregular Radiate	c. 270	85
BEATA TRANQVILLITAS	321–4	120	BEATA TRANQVILLITAS	321–4	115
VOT X CAESARVM NOSTRORVM	321–4	127	GLORIA EXERCITVS (2 standards)	330–5	143
CRISPVS CAESAR	324–30	135	GLORIA EXERCITVS (2 standards)	330–5	146
GLORIA EXERCITVS (2 standards)	330–5	137	Irregular Gloria Exercitus (2 standards)	330 +	147
GLORIA EXERCITVS (2 standards)	330–5	145			
Irregular Gloria Exercitus (2 standards)	330 +	148	Irregular Gloria Exercitus (2 standards)	330 +	149
Wolf and Twins	330–5	155	Wolf and Twins	330–5	158
Victory on Prow	330–5	167	Wolf and Twins	330–7	159
Victory on Prow	330–5	173	Wolf and Twins	330–7	161
Irregular Victory on Prow	330 +	179	Victory on Prow	330–5	171
Irregular Victory on Prow	330 +	182	Victory on Prow	330–5	172
Irregular Victory on Prow	330 +	183	Victory on Prow	330–5	174
GLORIA EXERCITVS (1 standard)	337–41	205	Irregular Victory on Prow	330 +	180
PAX PVBLICA	337–41	218	GLORIA EXERCITVS (1 standard)	335–7	189
VICTORIAE DD AVGG Q NN	341–8	246	Irregular Pax Publica	337 +	223
FEL TEMP REPARATIO (Hut)	348–50	263	Fel Temp (f.h.) minim	353 +	278

APPENDIX B
STRATIFIED COINS FROM BUILDING D
(Section II–JJ–KK, fig. 33)

Occupation level (layer 5)	Date A.D.	Coin No.	Destruction level (layers 3 and 4)	Date A.D.	Coin No.
Claudius II (posth.)	270	40	Gallienus (sole reign)	259–68	31
VIRTVS EXERCIT	320–1	112	Irregular Tetricus I	270 +	65
GLORIA EXERCITVS (2 standards)	330–5	136	PROVIDENTIA AVGG	324–30	132
Irregular Gloria Exercitus (2 standards)	330 +	147	Victory on Prow	330–5	168
			GLORIA EXERCITVS (1 standard)	337–41	198
Irregular Wolf and Twins	330 +	163	VICTORIAE DD AVGG Q NN	341–8	239
GLORIA EXERCITVS (1 standard)	335–7	190	VICTORIAE DD AVGG Q NN	341–8	243
GLORIA EXERCITVS (1 standard)	335–41	208	VICTORIAE DD AVGG Q NN	341–8	253
PAX PVBLICA	337–41	216	FEL TEMP REPARATIO (f.h. 3)	353–61	274
PAX PVBLICA	337–41	219	? Irregular VOT X MVLT XX	361–3	278
VIRTVS AVGVSTI	337–41	230			
VICTORIAE DD AVGG Q NN	341–8	234			
VICTORIAE DD AVGG Q NN	341–8	242			
VICTORIAE DD NN AVG ET CAE	351–3	269			

APPENDIX C

STRATIFIED COINS FROM BUILDING E

(fig. 32)

Occupation level	Date A.D.	Coin No.	Destruction level	Date A.D.	Coin No.
GENIO POPVLI ROMANI	303–5	97	Irregular Radiate	c. 270	86
SARMATIA DEVICTA	323–4	122	GLORIA EXERCITVS (1 standard)	335–41	208
Uncertain Votis type	c. 320	129	GLORIA EXERCITVS (1 standard)	337–41	203
Victory on Prow	330–5	171	FEL TEMP REPARATIO (f.h. 3)	353–4	273
PIETAS ROMANA	337–41	229	Irregular Fel Temp		
VICTORIAE DD AVGG Q NN	341–8	238	Reparatio minim	353 +	276
GLORIA ROMANORVM	367–75	281	Irregular Victoriae Dd		
SECVRITAS REIPVBLICAE	367–75	286	Nn Aug et Cae	351 +	272
SECVRITAS REIPVBLICAE	367–75	289	GLORIA ROMANORVM	367–75	279
SECVRITAS REIPVBLICAE	367–78	291	GLORIA ROMANORVM	367–78	283
VICTORIA AVGGG	388–402	299	VICTORIA AVGGG	388–402	300

APPENDIX D

PIT N SEALED BY DESTRUCTION MATERIAL

OF BUILDING E

	Date A.D.	Coin No.
Irregular Victory on Prow	c. 330	?
Upper pit fill: GLORIA ROMANORVM	367–75	280
Upper pit fill: SECVRITAS REIPVBLICAE	367–78	292

APPENDIX E

Coins found at Gadebridge Park, c. 1851

Included in John Evans's report on one of the Boxmoor villas (*Arch.*, xxxiv (1852), 397) is a list of coins found 'at various times' in a field a little to the north-west of the town of Hemel Hempstead. That these coins came from the vicinity of the Gadebridge villa, there can be no doubt in view of the location marked on the O.S. 6-in. map, but there is no evidence to connect them in any way with the villa itself. The possibility of a precursor to the excavated villa must nevertheless be borne in mind. The coins themselves, however, suggest that they formed all or part of a hoard of *denarii* deposited after A.D. 73.[1] At this period one would expect to find a large proportion of republican pieces; early imperial *denarii* with their high silver value, on the other hand, rarely survived in circulation after the Neronian revaluation of the *denarius*. The plentiful silver of Vespasian is only represented here by pieces from the early part of the reign and the date of the last piece is A.D. 73. Although there are only nineteen coins in all, four are of Vespasian and it may be regarded as more than coincidental that they were minted between A.D. 69 and 73. A date soon after A.D. 73 is therefore suggested for the deposition.

In order to gather all the material relating to Gadebridge together, Evans's list is reproduced here with the addition of dates and references. For the pre-Augustan coinage references are to *R.R.C.*; for the imperial issues references are to *R.I.C.*, i and ii.

One further coin from the area has been brought to my notice by the excavator. It came from the garden of 125 Marlin's Turn (a road about ¼ mile to the west of the site) during 1971 and was identified at the British Museum as a republican *denarius* of the moneyers Piso and Caeopio (*R.R.C.*, no. 603)[2] and dated *c.* 96–91 B.C. In view of the lack of a precise location for the first-century hoard just described, it is possible that this is a stray coin from that hoard, if not it may be adduced as further evidence for early activity in the area.

Moneyer

M. Baebius Tampilus   *c.* 155–120 B.C.
    Obv. TAMPIL. Head of Rome to the left; in front x.
    Rev. M. BAEBI. Q. F. ROMA. Apollo in a quadriga.   *R.R.C.*, p. 59, no. 489

Mn. Fonteius C. f.   *c.* 84 B.C.
    Obv. M. FONTEI. C. F. A laureate head: below, a thunderbolt and A.P.
    Rev. Cupid riding on a goat; above the caps of Dioscuri, beneath, the thyrsus; the whole within a garland.   *R.R.C.*, p. 114, no. 724a

---

[1] Another local hoard of *denarii* containing numerous republican pieces but terminating as late as Hadrian came from Beech Bottom dyke, St Albans (*Verulamium 1936*, pp. 17–18).

[2] Published in full in *Herts. Arch. Review*, Autumn 1971, p. 71.

P. (Sulpicius) Galba Sulpicia   *c.* 65 B.C.

    Obv. A veiled female head; behind, s.c.

    Rev. P. GALB. AED. CVR. The secespita, simpulum, and axe.   *R.R.C.*, p. 138, no. 838

Faustus (Cornelius Sulla)   63–62 B.C.

    Obv. s.c. Head of Hercules.

    Rev. A globe between four garlands, the acrostolium, and an ear
          of corn.   *R.R.C.*, p. 146, no. 883

C. Hosidius C. f. Geta   *c.* 60 B.C.

    Obv. (GETA) III. VIC. Bust of Diana.

    Rev. C. HOSIDI C. F. A boar pierced with a spear and assailed by
          a dog.   *R.R.C.*, p. 149, no. 904

Q. Cassius   *c.* 57 B.C.

    Obv. Q. CASSIVS VEST. Head of Vesta.

    Rev. The temple of Vesta between an urn and a tablet inscribed
          A.C.   *R.R.C.*, p. 152, no. 917

Mn. Acilius   55 B.C.

    Obv. SALVTIS. Laureate female head.

    Rev. MN. ACILIVS III. (VIR) VALETV. A female standing; in her
          right hand a serpent, her left resting on a column.   *R.R.C.*, p. 154, no. 922

Paullus (Aemilius) Lepidus   55 B.C.

    Obv. PAULLVS LEPIDVS. CONCORDIA. A veiled head, with diadem.

    Rev. . . . PAULLVS. Three captives standing opposite a figure
          erecting a trophy.   *R.R.C.*, p. 154, no. 926

Lucius Scribonius Libo Scribonia   55 B.C.

    Obv. BON. EVENT. LIBO. A female head.

    Rev. PVTEAL SCRIBON. The Puteal with a lyre suspended on each
          side.   *R.R.C.*, p. 155, no. 928

Q. Caepio Brutus L. Sestius   43–42 B.C.

    Obv. (L. SESTI PRO Q.) Laureate heads.

    Rev. Q. CAEPIO BRVTVS PRO COS. A tripod between an axe and
          simpulum.   *R.R.C.*, p. 202, no. 1290

P. Petronius Turpilianus   Augustus 18 B.C.

    Obv. TVRPILIANVS III. VIR FERON. Head of Feronia.

    Rev. CAESAR AVGVSTVS SIGN. RECE. A Parthian presenting a
          standard.   *R.I.C.*, I, no. 99

IMPERIAL COINS

M. Antonius (32–31 B.C.) Legionary denarius of Mark Antony

Obv. ANT. AVG. III. VIR R.P.C. A galley.

Rev. LEG. VII. The eagle between two standards. *R.R.C.*, p. 196, no. 1224

Augustus

c. 14 B.C.   Obv. Head of Augustus.

Rev. CAESAR AVGVSTVS. Two branches of laurel. *R.I.C.*, I, 268

14–12 B.C.   Obv. AVGVSTVS DIVI F. Head of Augustus.

Rev. IMP. X. A bull butting. *R.I.C.*, I, 327

2 B.C.–A.D. 14 Obv. CAESAR AVGVSTVS DIVI F. PATER PATRIAE.

Rev. C. L. CAESARES AVGVSTI F. COS. DESIG. PRINC. JVVENT. Caius and Lucius standing, with spears and shields; the lituus and capeduncula. *R.I.C.*, I, 350

Vespasian (A.D. 69–79)

A.D. 70–2   Obv. IMP. CAES. VESP. AVG. P. M. Laureated head of Vespasian.

Rev. TRI. POT. A seated and veiled figure; in her right hand a simpulum. *R.I.C.*, II, 36

A.D. 69–71   Obv. IMP. CAESAR VESPASIANVS AVG. Head.

Rev. COS. ITER. TR. POT. A seated figure; in her right hand a branch, in her left a caduceus. *R.I.C.*, II, 10

A.D. 69–71   Obv. IMP. CAESAR. VESPASIANVS AVG. Head.

Rev. COS. ITER. FORT. RED. Fortune standing, in her right hand the prow of a ship, in her left a cornucopiae. cf. *R.I.C.*, II, 4 (but holding prow as 276)

A.D. 73   Obv. IMP. CAES. VESP. AVG. CENS. Head.

Rev. PONTIF. MAXIM. A seated figure; in his right hand a branch, in his left a hasta. *R.I.C.*, II, 65

REFERENCES

Unless otherwise indicated references to coins are as follows:

to A.D. 324 *R.I.C.*, I–VII.   from A.D. 324 *L.R.B.C.*, I, II.

Abbreviations for fourth-century Emperors are as follows:

C. I	= Constantine I	Vn.	= Valens
C. II	= Constantine II	G.	= Gratian
Cr.	= Crispus	V. II	= Valentinian II
Cs. II	= Constantius II	T. I	= Theodosius I
Cn.	= Constans	Ar.	= Arcadius
Mg.	= Magnentius, Dec. — Decentius	Hon.	= Honorius
V.	= Valentinian I		

OBJECTS OF BRONZE

1. THE BROOCHES

By S. A. BUTCHER, F.S.A.

(figs. 54–5)

1. 'One-piece' brooch from early level east of Building A. Black occupation over L 10, Section S–T (fig. 6). 4.1 cm.

2. Fragment of 'one-piece' brooch from south of Building C (Phase B). 2.3 cm.

3. Spring from 'one-piece' brooch. Found beneath cobbled surface of courtyard. Between L 8 and L 13, Section N–O (fig. 6). 2.8 cm.

4. 'One-piece' brooch from south of Building A. 3.6 cm.

   1–4. Examples of 'one-piece' brooch. It is most commonly found in deposits dating from the first half of the first century A.D., as at Hod Hill and Camulodunum, but can also occur later in that century: e.g. *Wroxeter*, III, pl. xv, 1 and *Newstead*, pl. LXXXV.

5. 'Colchester' brooch. From verandah floor west of Building A. L 3, Section U–V (fig. 37). 5 cm.

6. 'Colchester' brooch from filling of ditch beneath Building A. L 12, Section N–O (fig. 6). 3.5 cm.

7. 'Colchester' brooch from lower filling of early water leat north of bathing pool. L 23, Section H–I (fig. 40). 5.2 cm.

8. Bow fragment of 'Colchester' brooch. From filling of water leat. Could be part of the votive deposit, but may be survival from filling of original leat. L 8, Section C–D–E (fig. 38). 4.4 cm.

   5–8. Examples of the 'Colchester' brooch. This occurs in levels of *c.* A.D. 10–65 at Camulodunum (*Camulodunum*, p. 309).

9. Fragment of brooch spring. From filling of chalk quarry Pit X, L 4, Section RR–SS (fig. 50). 3.9 cm.

10. Iron brooch. It has a broad flat bow and a narrow tube at the head in which the pin was hinged. The foot is obscured by corrosion but was probably plain. There are parallels from Camerton, one of which was in a deposit dated A.D. 60–90. Found in cobbles covering inner courtyard, Building A. L 8, Section N–O (fig. 6). 6.7 cm.

11. From early levels beneath floors in Room 25. 2.5 cm.

12. Plain bow brooch with spring of six turns held by the chord passing through a lug on the head. The only decoration is an off-centre groove down the bow, with slight notching either side. The catch-plate was pierced and there is a groove down the back of the bow. The type is generally of the second half of the first century A.D. (cf. *Camulodunum*, pp. 310–11). Filling of eaves drip alongside western corridor of Building A, L 8, Section U–V (fig. 37). 4.1 cm.

13. A 'dolphin' brooch with pierced lug at the head to hold the chord of the spring, now missing. There are two unusual hooks near the ends of the side wings. The bow is decorated with a series of grooves and is flat at the back. The type occurs at Hod Hill and Camulodunum and therefore must begin by the middle of the first century, but it probably continued until the early second century (cf. *Wroxeter*, III, p. 23). Unstratified. Found during road works in 1962. 4.2 cm.

14. Bow brooch decorated by two grooves down the centre, flanked by four raised pellets on either side. The spring has six turns and its chord passes through a lug projecting from the head. The wings are semi-cylindrical and have solid ends into which a bar holding the spring is inserted.

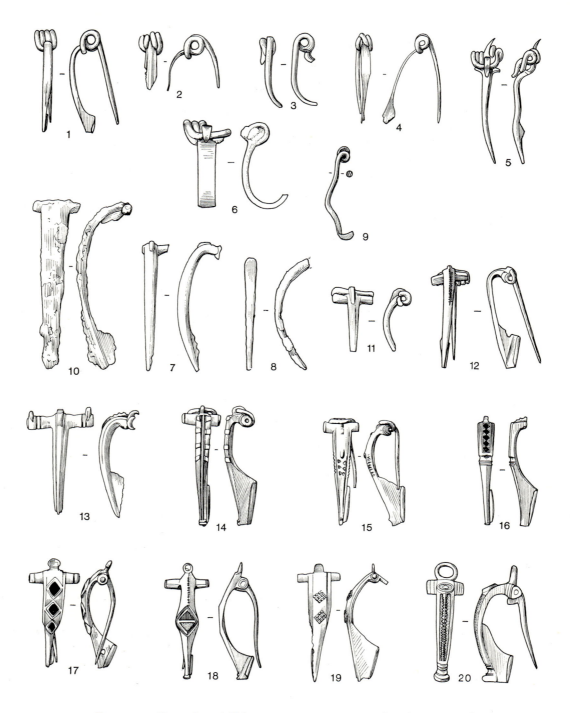

Fig. 54.   Brooches (all bronze, except no. 10, iron).   Scale $\frac{2}{3}$

The back is flat and the catch-plate springs from one side of the bow. A brooch from Rotherley (*Rotherley*, pl. xcvii, 1) has similar decoration but the pin is hinged. Another comes from Wroxeter (*Wroxeter*, ii, fig. 4, 2) but in this the grooves do not extend to the foot of the bow. See 15 and 16 below. Sealed beneath destruction rubble south of Building A.   4.8 cm.

15. Similar in construction to nos. 14 and 16, but of poorer workmanship. It is decorated by a group of triangular pits in the centre of the bow (which appear never to have held enamel) and has a slightly toothed edge to the same zone. Very similar brooches have been found at Rushall Down (*Devizes*, pl. lxvi, 4), Caerleon (*Caerleon Amphitheatre*, fig. 13, 8) and Woodeaton (*Oxon.*, xiv (1949), fig. 2, 5) and there is one in Bath Museum. In early turf layer covering outer courtyard, east of Building C.   4.3 cm.

16. Narrow bow with panel of five lozenges of dark blue enamel in field of (?) white enamel. The top of the brooch is missing but there is part of a stepped crest which probably held the chord of a spring. The back of the bow is flat and the catch-plate springs from one side. From bottom of gully crossing Room 7.   4.4 cm.
The three brooches (14, 15, 16) are of similar construction and in the absence of dated parallels it is suggested that on typological grounds they probably belong to the first half of the second century A.D. In spite of their general similarity visual inspection shows that the finish of each is very different and suggests that they come from different workshops.

17. Tapering bow brooch with unperforated tab at head and panel of three lozenges with traces of green enamel. The pin is hinged on a bar which is completely enclosed in a tube forming the cross piece at the head. The back of the bow is concave behind the decorated panel and the catch-plate springs from one side and is pierced. This appears to be a south-western type: several from Charterhouse in Bristol Museum are very similar and one has the hole in the catch-plate, as does one from Ashwick in Taunton Museum and another from Caerleon (*Caerleon Amphitheatre*, fig. 13, 10). There is also a close parallel from Nornour (*Nornour*, fig. 11, 7A). None of these is dated but the type probably belongs to the second century. From black silt covering natural hollow beneath Building C, L 8, Section S–R (fig. 6).   4.3 cm.

18. The bow is decorated with a double triangle in the centre, the pin is hinged in a tube at the head, and there is a small head tab roughly pierced. The back of the bow is flat and the catch-plate springs from one side. There are remains of turquoise coloured enamel in the upper triangle and red in the lower. There are ten very similar brooches from Nornour (*Nornour*, fig. 13) and direct comparison of the Gadebridge specimen with these suggests very strongly that it came from the same source. Other parallels are given by Mr Hull on page 35 of the Nornour report: they are all south-western. None are dated but, as with 17, the type is likely to belong to the second century A.D. From clay L 12 over chalk floor of early occupation east of Building A. Section S–T (fig. 6).   4.6 cm.

19. Tapering bow decorated with two cross-hatched raised lozenges. The pin is hinged in a tube and there is an unperforated tab at the head. The upper part of the bow is slightly concave at the back and the catch-plate springs from one side. The brooch appears to have been tinned. There are close parallels at Nornour (*Nornour*, fig. 11, 6) and in the collection from Charterhouse at Bristol Museum. It closely resembles no. 17 in details of workmanship and like that, should belong to the second century. From chalk filling of southern ditch (Ditch 2), L 1, Section EE–FF (fig. 7).   4.7 cm.

20. A 'head-stud' brooch (Collingwood type Q). The head loop and stud are cast in one piece with the rest and the pin is hinged in a tube. The back of the bow is flat and the catch-plate central. The stud has a disc of enamel within an outer rim of bronze, and there is a central spot of bronze.

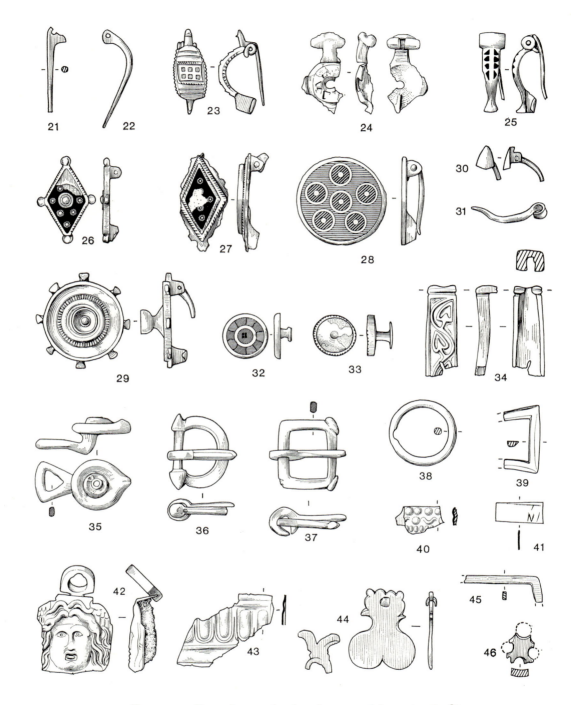

FIG. 55. Brooches and other bronze objects (scale $\frac{2}{3}$)

There is also enamel (possibly white although it now appears green) in two strips down the bow, divided by a toothed rib of bronze.

This type derives from more elaborate examples such as that found at Richborough (*Richborough*, IV, pl. XXVIII, 34) which itself had an analogy in a pit dated *c*. A.D. 75–90; but the simpler versions were evidently produced at about the same time since another brooch from Richborough (*Richborough*, IV, pl. XXVIII, 36), which has the head loop and stud cast in one with the rest, was found in a pit of *c*. A.D. 80–90.

The type as a whole has a very wide distribution; if it is eventually possible to ascribe it to more than one centre of production the decoration on the foot of the Gadebridge example may be significant: it is less common than a panel of enamel divided into triangular and lozenge-shaped fields, but is also seen on some trumpet brooches (e.g. Gloucester Museum A111 and A1112, Taunton Museum 51 A38, and Norwich Museum, Hockwold 15). There is a very similar head-stud brooch with this decoration, which also came from Hertfordshire (Braughing), now in the museum at Haslemere. Found in black occupation and cobbled layer east of Building A. Over L 10, Section S–T (fig. 6). 4.7 cm.

21. Brooch pin from black silt over cobbled spread, west of Building B. 3.4 cm.

22. Brooch pin from floor make-up in northern corridor, Building A. 3.9 cm.

23. Belongs to a class of brooch mid-way between bow and plate which is more common on the continent. The broad plate is curved almost to a semi-circle and has narrow projections at either end which bear the catch-plate and the spring. The spring has two turns and is pinned through a lug projecting at the back. The principal decoration is a rectangular panel containing six small squares, three of which are inlaid with turquoise enamel and three with translucent material now greenish in colour. It is clearly related to continental brooches with rather more elaborate decoration (Exner, fig. 10.1, p. 88; *Mandeure*, no. 129; *Besançon*, no. 272–4), but there is a very similar brooch from Charterhouse in Bristol Museum and it is likely that both are British products. Another, generally similar, was associated with pottery of *c*. A.D. 110–40 at Caerleon (*Caerleon Amphitheatre*, fig. 14, 19). From black occupation and cobbled layer east of Building A, in association with SF 20. Over L 10, Section S–T (fig. 6). 3.4 cm.

24. An unusual brooch, only part of which survives. The thin disc is formed in one piece with a more substantial short 'bow' of D section joined to a semi-circular head plate, behind which is the tube in which the pin is hinged. The decoration — a ring of alternating triangles, probably once enamelled — suggests a date within the second century. From the northern courtyard. 3.2 cm.

25. 'Knee' brooch (Collingwood type T). The spring has four turns and is attached by means of a bar passing through it and inserted in the ends of the semi-cylindrical head. The back of the bow is flat and the catch-plate central. The shape is quite typical of knee brooches commonly found in late second–early third-century contexts (especially on the continent) but the decoration, two rows of triangles inlaid with blue enamel, is unusual and probably marks it as a British product. At Traprain (*P.S.A.S.*, L (1915–16), figs. 22.4, 23.3) rather similar brooches were found which have been ascribed to the early second century (*P.S.A.S.*, LXXXIX (1955–6), 160) and Wroxeter (*Wroxeter*, III, 23) has two in deposits of that date. From black silt over cobbled spread west of Building B. 3.2 cm.

26. Lozenge-shaped plate brooch with rounded lugs at each corner. The back is flat except for the catch-plate and two lugs between which the pin was hinged. There is a moulded central knob of bronze but otherwise the entire plate is filled with enamel: a field of dark blue bearing rings of red in which there was another colour, now missing but probably white. There is a very close parallel from Charterhouse in Bristol Museum (F.1963) and many similar brooches have been

found on the continent, e.g. Exner, fig. 12. Nornour also shows a wide range of plate brooches with similar patterns, though none are identical. See 27 below. Over cobbled area north-east of Room 27.   3.4 cm.

27.   Plate brooch bearing raised central lozenge surrounded by mouldings. The edge probably had a series of circular flat lugs but most are now broken off. At the back there is a sharply moulded circular depression with central pit (cf. a similar depression, just visible below the enamel on the face of no. 26). The pin is hinged between two lugs. The central lozenge is filled with enamel of the same colours and pattern as no. 26 and no doubt the brooch comes from the same workshop, which in view of the large group of essentially similar brooches from Nornour may well have been in south-west Britain. There is no dating evidence in Britain but brooches of the same type have been dated to the late second century in Pannonia (Sellye, pl. xx, 17) and Czechoslovakia (Thomas, fig. 8.2). Found close to the northern side of Pit A, southern courtyard. 3.9 cm.

28.   Flat enamelled disc brooch. The pin is on a spring of two turns between two lugs. The face is decorated in a simple pattern of red circles on a background now green but possibly originally white. Each circle is outlined by a broad rim of reserved metal, and contains a central bronze dot. It is a common type: similar (though not identical) brooches have been found at Zugmantel (*S.J.*, v, fig. 22, 18), Woodeaton (*Oxon.*, xiv (1949), pl. ii, B 9), and Hockwold (three, in Norwich Museum). Found in Roman turf level south of the water cistern, Building A.   3.5 cm.

29.   Disc brooch of the type often called 'buckler'. The centre rises to a cupped stud and there are eight lugs round the edge. The pin is hinged between two lugs. The type occurs widely, e.g. Neuss (Exner, fig. 17, 11), Newstead (*Newstead*, pl. lxxvii, 15, p. 331), *Besançon*, no. 293, and Wroxeter (*Wroxeter*, iii, pl. xvi, 12). The Wroxeter example was in a deposit dated before A.D. 120, whereas Exner (p. 67) refers to it being common in graves of the second half of the second century in Belgium. Found in the filling of early water leat, south of bathing pool. L 7, Section E–F (fig. 40).   3.6 cm.

30.   Fragment of a plate brooch. It may be related to the 'fusiform' brooches from Nornour described by Mr Hull (*Nornour*, fig. 23, p. 56) though it lacks the enamelled stud which they bear at each end. Over cobbling in northern courtyard.   9 mm.

31.   Pin from penannular brooch. Such brooches occur from the first century onwards and are not closely datable. Found in filling of well in association with coin of Julia Domna, A.D. 196–211, and a coin dated A.D. 388+, L 2, Section X–Y (fig. 17).   3 cm.

2.   MISCELLANEOUS OBJECTS OF BRONZE
By David S. Neal and S. A. Butcher
(figs. 55–66)

32.   Enamelled bronze stud with central circular field of red enamel with traces of black mosaic. Surrounding this is a bronze band, and a circular band of enamel dividing into alternating areas of red and blue. From upper filling of clay pit, south west of Building B. L 2, Section W–X (fig. 21).   1.8 cm.

33.   Bronze stud, originally decorated with enamel. The outer edge of the object is decorated with notches. Destruction rubble south-west of Building A.   1.7 cm.

Similar studs are found on many sites; they were presumably used as buttons. Compare Sellye, pl. VI, 10, and *Newstead*, pl. LXXXIX; *Nornour*, fig. 8, no. 25, has a very similar disc to no. 32, but it is not clear that it ever had a shank.

34. Bronze plate with leaf-scroll design reserved against an enamelled field. The form of the plate is paralleled at Richborough, Wroxeter, and Jewry Wall, Leicester, where plates with enamelled decoration on one side have similar flanged sides and one end turned over, presumably to fit on to some core of wood or leather (*Wroxeter*, III, pl. XVI; *Jewry Wall*, fig. 84, 12; *Richborough*, IV, pl. XL, 152 (dated to before *c.* A.D. 85)).
The leaf scroll appears on several enamelled vessels thought to have been made in Britain (e.g. the Braughing bowl now in the British Museum) but the workmanship of the Gadebridge plate is much coarser than these. Black occupation over northern courtyard. 3.6 cm.

35. Fastener, with circular top plate, which was possibly enamelled in centre; triangular foot. Belongs to J. P. Wild's Class III (*Brit.*, I (1970), 137 ff.). Moulds for making similar objects were found at Traprain Law (*P.S.A.S.*, LXXXIX (1955–6), no. 233). Similar examples also occur at Hockwold, Norfolk, Sawbench temple site, now in Norwich Castle Museum, Ilkley, in an Antonine context (*P. Leeds Phil. & Lit. Soc.*, XII, part II, fig. 13.2), and at Wroxeter (*Wroxeter*, II, fig. 5, 16). Found in eastern corridor of Building B. 3.8 cm.

36. Semi-circular buckle with conical knobs on either end of the hinge bar. There is a close parallel to this at Zugmantel, and it seems to be a type associated with the army (*S.J.*, XV (1956) fig. 3.2). Destruction rubble south of Room 20. 3.1 cm.

37. Rectangular buckle with oval shaped knobs on the corners opposite the hinge bar. Post destruction turf layer over Building C. Early fourth century. 2.8 cm.

38. Circular buckle worn on inner side by pin. In Period 6 mortar floor of Room 20. 2.7 cm.

39. Fragment of post-medieval buckle with traces of silvering, L 4, Section F–G (fig. 38). 2.7 cm.

40. Fragments of bronze with lead backing, decorated in repoussé. The design comprises a row of circles, a row of alternating circles and wave patterns, and a row of smaller ovals, one beneath the other. Filling of Room 20, L 3, Section L–M (fig. 6). 1.9 cm.

41. Trapezoid sheet with traces of *graffito*. $\overset{\text{I}}{\text{NII}}$. Filling of Room 20, L 3, Section L–M (fig. 6). 1.9 cm.

42. Escutcheon from bucket or bowl, decorated in repoussé with head of Medusa. Described in detail by Professor J. M. C. Toynbee, F.S.A. (p. 151). From west side of Building A.

43. Irregular piece of bronze, decorated in repoussé with ovolo pattern. Chalk quarry, Pit U, L 3, Section PP–QQ (fig. 47). 4.6 cm.

44. Bi-circular furniture fitting surmounted by rectangle, decorated on edges with mouldings. Circular hole in rectangle with remains of bronze rivet. Another fragment of decorated bronze sheet was found associated with above, and may form part of decoration for same object. Tracery design with incised circles. From Ditch I beneath Building A. 3.1 cm.

45. L-shaped strip of bronze, possibly fragment from buckle. Floor of Room 20, L 5, Section L–M (fig. 6).

46. Fragment of cast bronze, perforated by four holes. Possibly from colander. Rubble over Pit N, L 3, Section II–JJ–KK (fig. 33). 1.3 cm.

47. Bronze steelyard with lead weight. The steelyard is octagonal in section and broken at one end. The arm is graduated on one side by Roman numerals marked I, II, III, IIII, V, and spaced 2, 2.2, 2.4 and 2.7 cm. apart respectively. The reverse side of the balance arm is divided by equally spaced digits set 9 mm. apart, and divided in turn by a dot. The arm of the balance

terminates with a ring, through which is passed a hook that originally supported a scale-pan. The lead balance shows little sign of wear and is cylindrical in section with a conical base and apex. Set into the latter is an iron ring. The weight was suspended from the balance by a bronze hook, permanently attached to the lead weight, but with a loop at its top so that it could slide along the steelyard arm. Zugmantel has a similar graduated arm (*S.J.*, III (1912), Taf. XIV). The object was found in the rubble filling of the porter's lodge (Room 36) associated with the gatehouse and is no later than *c.* A.D. 350. The situation of the find would possibly suggest that the balance was used to weigh taxes brought to the estate. The height of the lead balance including bronze hook is 7 cm., weight 114 gms.

48. Lead steelyard weight, cylindrical in section, with conical apex, terminating with the remains of an iron hook. The latter passes through the weight and emerges through the base. Found in northern trench across chalk quarry, Pit X. Level corresponding to L 4, Section RR–SS (fig. 50). Width of weight 4.7 cm. Weight 300 gms.

49. Large bronze hook, probably from steelyard. The upper end of the hook is looped and wound round the stem. The point of the hook folds back on itself. See *Richborough*, III, pl. XIV, 44. From rubble filling of Room 20.   8 cm.

50. Circular bronze disc, ornamented with depressed boss, and three concentric incised lines. The underside of the object has a band of solder where it was originally affixed to another bronze plate. Disc brooch? From subsoil over western wing of Building A. Probably fourth century. 3.8 cm.

51. (a)   Iron knife with bronze binding for leather sheath. The binding was secured to the leather sheath by two rivets, one of which survives. From filling of Pit E in north-west corner of kitchen area, Building C (fig. 23).   8.4 cm.
      (b)   Another fragment of bronze was found in Pit Y west of Building C, and may be the scabbard tip for the above knife. It has a V-shaped section with a flange on either side, and the remains of three rivet holes. Another similar shaped piece would have been riveted to it as shown on illustration. L 10, Section GG–HH (fig. 50).   6.4 cm.

52. Remains of circular bronze disc, ornamented with depressed boss, pierced by a rivet hole. The outer edge of the disc is flanged. Probably either a wood or leather fitting. Also found in Pit Y as 51b. Original diameter 5.5 cm.

53. Silver mounting with beaded decoration. Lower filling of Pit Y. L 14, Section GG–HH (fig. 50). 4.4 cm.

54. Length of bronze wire with loop at one end. Possibly used to suspend weight from steelyard. Early levels, east of Building A.   4.2 cm.

55. Bronze strip with curved and flanged section. Object originally straight. Possibly furniture fitting. Rubble over western corridor, Building C.   13.4 cm.

56. Bronze ferrule of 'poppy head' shape, with remains of iron tang. Possibly a furniture fitting. From filling of bathing pool, L 7, Section F–G (fig. 38).   1.8 cm.

57–61.   Selection of bronze studs.

62. Conical headed rivet. Filling of water conduit south of Building A.   9 mm.

63. Bronze nail with slightly flared head, and incised grooves. Filling of Pit A south of corn-drying oven.   1.7 cm.

64–8.   Selection of dome headed rivets. Maximum size 4 cm., minimum size 1.4 cm.

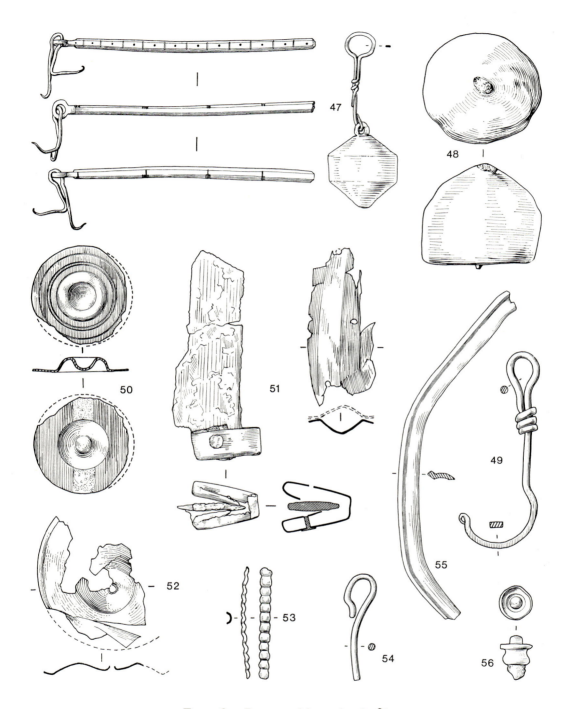

FIG. 56. Bronze objects (scale $\frac{2}{3}$)

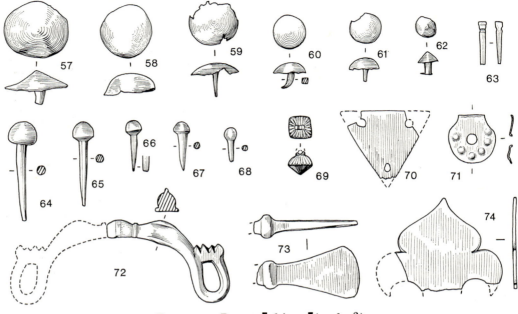

FIG. 57. Bronze objects (scale $\frac{2}{3}$)

69. Bronze ear ring or pendant, set with a cut green glass stone. The setting is decorated with a petal pattern radiating from the remains of a loop. Rubble over northern courtyard. 9 mm.

70. Triangular bronze sheet pierced in each corner by a hole. Two of the holes show signs of wear. Similar bone objects found at Richborough (*Richborough*, IV, 151, pl. LVI, 267) are recorded as being for the manufacture of braids. Rubble filling of water leat south of bathing pool. L 4, Section E–F (fig. 40). 3.5 cm.

71. Circular bronze disc, decorated with six small bosses, and pierced in centre by a hole. One side of the object flares out and is cut straight. Lid from seal box? Rubble over Room 35. 1.9 cm.

72. One half of bronze drop handle probably for use on a small wooden casket. Originally decorated in the form of two opposed dolphins. The tail of the dolphin forms the loop of the handle and is decorated with V-shaped cuts to imitate the flipper. The crest and side fins of the dolphin are formed by pinching out the body and the nose of the dolphin by a radial collar. There is a group from Trier which all show dolphins, some more recognizable than others, and it seems likely that handles of this type were made there (cf. H. Menzel, *Die romischen Bronzen aus Deutschland II, Trier*, nos. 302–17). One very similar to the Gadebridge example was found at Zugmantel (*S.J.*, III (1912), Taf. XIII, 1) and one found at Wilderspool shows the dolphins clearly but is in a different style (F. H. Thompson, *Roman Cheshire* (1965), fig. 20, 19). Rubble over eastern corridor, Building A.

73. A miniature votive bronze ?axe head; the object is too large for a toilet spatula. Shaft broken. Compare Brigstock (*Antiq. J.*, XLIII (1963), 43, fig. 5, 6); Woodeaton (*Oxon.*, XIV (1949), fig. 8) (not same shaped blade); *B.M. Guide*, fig. 37.4; *London*, fig. 36, 2. Robber trench of south wall of Room 26. 4.1 cm.

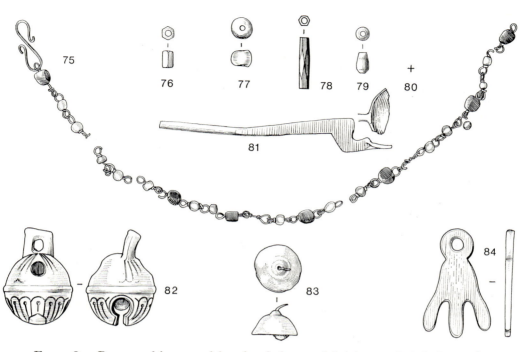

FIG. 58. Bronze objects and beads of glass and jet (nos. 76–80). Scale $\frac{2}{3}$

74. Trefoil shaped fitting made from sheet bronze. Sealed beneath tessellated pavement covering ovens in Room 28. Height 3.7 cm.

75. Bronze chain necklace with glass beads. A reconstruction drawing has been attempted on the basis of the distribution of the beads. A total length of 27 cm. of chain and 22 beads was found. At one end is an S-shaped clasp, but unfortunately no corresponding clasp was found on the other end, so the full length of the object is uncertain. It would appear however, that the matching of many of the beads into pairs would suggest that the necklace is virtually complete, except for a few smaller beads, and the corresponding clasp. Given below is a list of pairs of beads given in colours, working downwards from either end of the necklace:

Blue	Blue	Yellow	Yellow
Yellow	Yellow	Blue	Blue
White	White	Green	Green
—	Blue	Green	White
Dark green	Dark green	Blue	Blue
Pink	Pink	—	Yellow

The oval yellow, white, pink and dark green beads are of uniform size whereas the blue beads are larger. Found in secondary pit cutting Pit Y, west of Building C, L 10, Section GG–HH (fig. 50).

76. Green glass bead with hexagonal section. 6 mm.

77. Oval-shaped green glass bead. 6 mm.

78. Hexagonal jet bead, decorated with lozenge-shaped facets. 2 cm.

79. Pear-shaped green glass bead. 8 mm.

80. Green glass melon bead. Object unillustrated, missing.

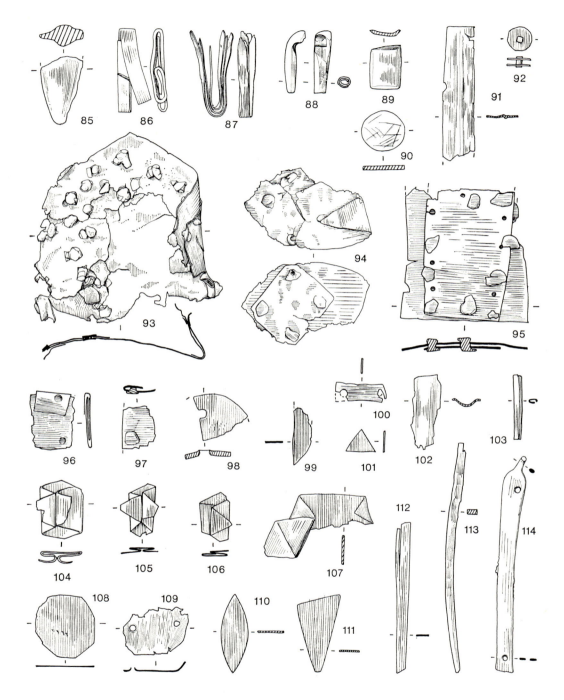

FIG. 59.   Bronze objects (scale $\tfrac{2}{3}$)

81. Handle and part of bowl of bronze spoon. Found in northernmost trench cutting water leat. In river gravel, possibly votive offering.   9.8 cm.

82. Spherical bronze horse bell of medieval date, with central rib, decorated above and below with arcaded pattern of incised lines containing line and dot motifs. The lower part of the bell is decorated with a shield, but the design is worn, and no arms can be seen. On either side of the shield and in the upper zone are three circular holes, the two in the lower half being linked by a narrow slit. The bell contains an iron striking ball. Surmounting the bell is a square handle with a circular hole. Apart from being worn, the bell is in a fine state of preservation and can still provide a tuneful noise. A very similar bell was found at Northolt (*Med. Arch.*, v (1961), fig. 76, 27). Unstratified.   3.8 cm.

83. Small bronze horse bell of medieval or post-medieval date, with remains of bronze hook attached to iron striker. From topsoil.   Diameter 1.9 cm.

84. Bronze trefoil-shaped pendant. Probably post-medieval horse brass. From topsoil. 4.3 cm.

85. Fragment of cast bronze tapering to point. Possibly foot of bronze vessel. Make-up for south corridor, Building A, L 9, Section N–O (fig. 6).   2.7 cm.

Miscellaneous fragments of worked sheet bronze

86. Single folded strip of bronze, cut at angle at one end. Occupation of eastern corridor. Building B. 3.3 cm.

87. Three identical-sized strips of sheet bronze placed one above the other, with bevelled ends and folded in the centre. Early stratum south of water cistern.   3.5 cm.

88. Wound sheet of bronze, pinched at one end and folded over. Building C.   2.5 cm.

89. Rectangular sheet of bronze bevelled on all sides. West of Building A.   1.8 cm.

90. Circular bronze disc with scratch markings on both sides. Use uncertain, possibly a weight. Chalk quarry, Pit U, L 3, Section PP–QQ (fig. 47).   1.7 cm.

91. Rectangular sheet of bronze decorated with a moulding. From Pit B south of corn-drying oven. 5.4 cm.

92. Circular bronze rivet, probably for leather. Edge of rivet shows signs of being cut by metal snippers. Unstratified.   1 cm.

93. Irregular sheet of bronze with three other bronze sheets riveted to it. The object is pierced by numerous rivets; the latter are formed from wound pieces of bronze inserted through the sheets and hammered flat. Probably patching for large bronze bowl or cauldron. From chalk quarry, Pit X, L 4, Section RR–SS (fig. 50).   7.5 cm.

94. Irregular sheet of bronze with square sheet of bronze riveted to it. Secured by four bronze rivets. South of gatehouse.   5.2 cm.

95. Sheet of bronze with rectangular sheet of bronze riveted to it. The latter appears to have been re-used as it is perforated with holes which do not penetrate the other sheet. Upper rubble in Room 20.   5.3 cm.

96. Strip of bronze, folded four times with two rivet holes. East of Building A.   2.4 cm.

97. Folded fragment of bronze secured with a rivet. Northern courtyard.   1.7 cm.

98. Fragment of cast bronze with square hole, probably pierced by nail. Occupation in verandah south of Building D.   2.3 cm.

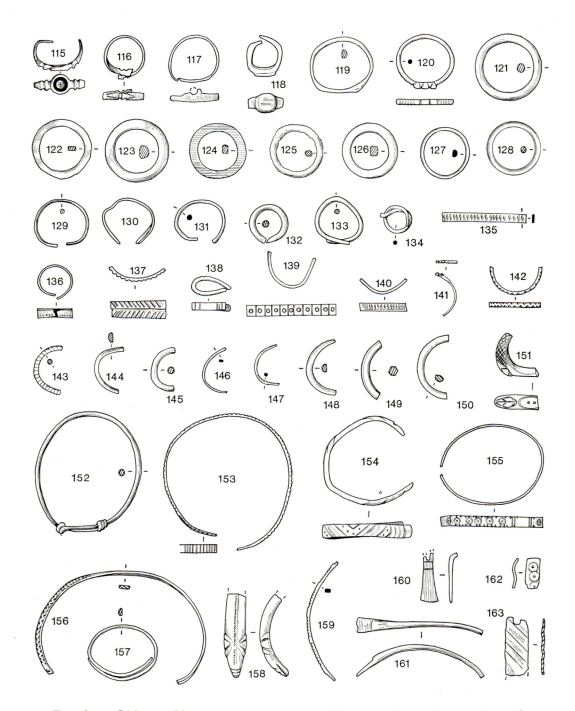

FIG. 60.   Objects of bronze, except nos. 120 (silver) and 151 (stone). Scale $\frac{2}{3}$.

99. Semi-circular fragment of sheet bronze with remains of guide line scored on it. Occupation in Room 20. L 5, Section L–M (fig. 6). 2.3 cm.

100. Trapezoidal fragment of sheet bronze with rivet holes at either end. Occupation in Room 20, as above. 2 cm.

101. Triangular piece of sheet bronze cut on all sides. On tessellated pavement over Room 28. Possibly inlay for box or furniture. 1.2 cm.

102. Fragment of bronze with semi-circular section, flanged on edges. Filling of Ditch 1 beneath Building A. 3 cm.

103. Bronze ferrule, possibly for leather thong. Rubble east of Building A, L 3, Section S–T (fig. 6). 2.6 cm.

104–6. Lozenge-shaped pieces of bronze sheeting, with the ends folded towards the centre and back again. Purpose uncertain, but probably improvised split pins or rivets for leather work; similar items occur on many sites, but are rarely published; see *Brough*, fig. 38, 26. 104 and 106 from verandah, west of Building A, 105 from chalk quarry, Pit U. Maximum size 2.3 cm.

107. Folded rectangular sheet of bronze. Verandah west of Building A. 4.4 cm.

108. Octagonal bronze disc, purpose uncertain. Verandah west of Building A. 2.5 cm.

109. Irregular shaped piece of sheet bronze with rivet holes on either side. Rubble east of Room 27. 2.5 cm.

110. Leaf-shaped snippet of bronze, possibly inlay ornamentation for box or furniture. Unstratified. 3.2 cm.

111. Trapezoidal piece of bronze. From beneath tessellated pavement, L 4, Room 28, Section U–V (fig. 37). 3.2 cm.

112. Strip of bronze with score line along one side, and partially cut by shears. Offcut from bronze working. Occupation in Building E. 6 cm.

113. Strip of bronze with hammer marks. Robber trench in western wing of Building A. 9.2 cm.

114. Length of bronze with rivet holes at either end, one of which tapers into narrow 'hook'. Purpose of object not known. Rubble in western corridor, Building B. 8.6 cm.

Finger rings of bronze: except 120 (silver) and 151 (stone)

For additional bronze rings see SF nos. 249–59 from water leat (fig. 65).

115. Ring of second-century type. Bezel decorated with dark blue enamel. Similar to ring at Nornour (*Nornour*, fig. 8, 13). South of water cistern, Building A. 2 cm.

116. Expanding ring, the terminals of which are decorated with V-shaped incisions. Unstratified. 1.6 cm.

117. Ring with setting for stone. Rubble filling of Building D, L 3, Section II–JJ–KK (fig. 33). 2 cm.

118. Child's ring with circular bezel. Northern courtyard. 1.4 cm.

119. Ring from Building D, L 5, Section II–JJ–KK (fig. 33). 2.5 cm.

120. Silver ring with flat bezel divided into three by V-shaped incisions and beading. Rubble in Room 20, L 3, Section L–M (fig. 6). 2.3 cm.

121–8. Selection of plain rings with various shaped sections.

129–33. Selection of expanding rings.

134.   Ring made from coil of bronze wire. Inner courtyard surface.   1.3 cm.

135.   Fragment of unfolded expanding ring decorated with S-shaped incisions. Silvered bronze. Verandah south of Building D.   3.3 cm.

136.   Expanding child's ring ornamented with horizontal line and chip decoration. Occupation, Room, 20. L 5, Section L–M (fig. 6).

137.   Fragment of ring decorated with oblique lines above and below central horizontal groove. Rubble filling of Room 35, L 2, Section U–V (fig. 37).   2.2 cm.

138.   Crushed ring ornamented with vertical incisions. East of Building D.   1.5 cm.

139.   Unfolded ring decorated with alternating lines and circles. Rubble over inner courtyard. 1.9 cm.   Mid fourth-century stratum.

140.   Fragment of ring with S-patterned incisions. Chalk quarry, Pit U, L 3, Section PP–QQ (fig. 47). 1.8 cm. Fragments of rings with similar decoration were found throughout the site.

141.   Very delicate penannular ring decorated on terminal with snake or lizard head. Filling of well, L 3, Section X–Y (fig. 17).   1.7 cm.

142.   Finger ring ornamented with zig-zag patterns. Occupation in Room 35. Below L 3, Section U–V (fig. 37).   2 cm.

143.   Ring made from two strands of twisted wire. Building B.   2 cm.

144–50.   Fragments of bronze rings.

151.   Fragment of stone ring originally decorated on either side of the bezel with serpents' heads. The narrowest part of the ring is decorated by a criss-cross design representing the skin of a snake. The bezel is outlined by an incision and at one time was probably mounted by a separate stone or jewel. Through the bezel are two rivet holes.

The following is the result of a qualitative spectrographic analysis kindly provided by Dr A. E. Werner, F.S.A. and Miss M. Bimson, F.S.A., of the British Museum Research Laboratory. Dr D. B. Harden, F.S.A., also advised on the ring.

It has a pale green colour and is made of a very finely textured material, which has a hardness of about 4 on the Mohs scale. Qualitative spectrographic analysis of a small sample showed that the main constituents were aluminium and phosphorus, and X-ray diffraction analysis showed the presence of the mineral variscite, i.e. hydrated aluminium phosphate, $Al\,PO_4\,2H_2O$. This is rather a rare mineral which is commonly pale green in colour but may be pale blue or white; this is the first time it has been identified here in an archaeological artifact. The European source of this mineral is confined to Saxony, Austria, and Bohemia and therefore it appears likely that this ring came from Central Europe. From occupation in Room 20, L 5, Section L–M (fig. 6).   2.5 cm.

Bronze bracelets

152.   Expanding bracelet made from single strand of wire. Upper filling of bathing pool, L 4, Section F–G (fig. 38).   4.2 cm.

153.   Bracelet decorated with vertical grooves. Fourth-century destruction rubble in Room 35, L 2, Section U–V (fig. 37).   5.1 cm.

154. Bracelet with alternating oblique fluting, groove-and-dot ornamentation. Sealed beneath tessellated pavement over northern corridor. Early fourth century. 3.5 cm.

155. Bracelet ornamented with rows of circles divided by pairs of vertical grooves. V-shaped chip carving on outer edges. Rubble filling of Room 20, L 3, Section L–M (fig. 6). 4.1 cm.

156. Bracelet decorated with zig-zag pattern. Terminal perforated with hole. Amongst rubble over Building E. Probably late fourth century. 6.8 cm.

157. Unornamented child's bracelet. From occupation in Room 26. 4.8 cm.

158. Terminal of heavy bronze bracelet decorated with head of serpent. Mouth formed by incision in side of terminal. Upper filling of chalk quarry, Pit U, L 3, Section PP–QQ (fig. 47). 3.3 cm.

159. Bracelet with crenellated pattern on outer edge. Rubble filling of hypocaust channel, Room 27. 4.7 cm.

160. Fan-shaped terminal of bracelet with catch hole, and incised line decoration. Rubble west of Room 20, L 3, Section L–M (fig. 6). 1.9 cm.

161. Fragment of bracelet with fan-shaped terminal. From occupation in Building E. Fourth century. 5.1 cm.

162. Fragment of bracelet ornamented with circles. Rubble east of Building D, L 4, Section II–JJ–KK (fig. 33). 1.2 cm.

163. Fragment of bracelet with oblique fluting. Unstratified. 2.4 cm.

164. Bracelet of two strands of twisted wire, beaten so that section is almost square. Chalk quarry, Pit U, L 3, Section PP–QQ (fig. 47). 4 cm.

165. Bracelet of two strands of twisted wire. Unstratified. 3.7 cm.

166. Bracelet of two strands of twisted wire. Unstratified. 4.3 cm.

167. Bracelet of two strands of twisted wire. Chalk quarry, Pit U, L 3, Section PP–QQ (fig. 47). 4.4 cm.

168. Bracelet of two strands of twisted wire. Chalk quarry, Pit V, L 2, Section NN–OO (fig. 48). 8.4 cm.

169. Fragment of bracelet of two strands of twisted wire with remains of hook. From filling of bathing pool, L 11, Section F–G (fig. 38). 2.8 cm.

170. Bracelet of two strands of twisted wire. Rubble over Building D, L 3, Section II–JJ–KK (fig. 33). 2.6 cm.

171. Terminal hook of bracelet decorated with incised lines. Chalk quarry, Pit U, L 3, Section PP–QQ (fig. 47). 2.4 cm.

172. Bent bracelet, the terminal of which is decorated with six incised lines. Hypocaust channel, Room 27. 9.9 cm.

173. Fragment of bracelet from filling of bathing pool, L 10, Section F–G (fig. 38). 3.9 cm.

Shale bracelets (fig. 61)

174. Bracelet, from robber trench, west wall of Room 20, Section L–M (fig. 6). Original diameter 7 cm.

175. Bracelet, from filling of bathing pool, L 5, Section F–G (fig. 38). Original diameter 6.1 cm.

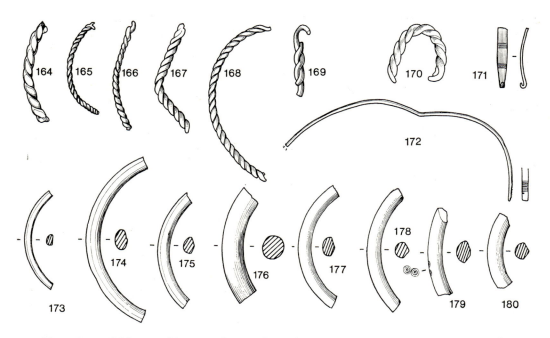

FIG. 61.   Objects of bronze (nos. 164–73) and shale (nos. 174–80). Scale $\frac{2}{3}$

176.   Bracelet with thick circular section. From filling of bathing pool, L 5, Section F–G (fig. 38). Original diameter 7.5 cm.

177.   Bracelet from filling of Room 35, L 3, Section U–V (fig. 37). Original diameter 6 cm.

178.   Bracelet from chalk quarry. Pit U, L 3, Section PP–QQ (fig. 47). Original diameter 6.5 cm.

179.   Bracelet with circle design on outer side. From sooty filling in gutted wall between Rooms 25 and 26. Original diameter 8 cm.

180.   Bracelet from soot beneath tessellated pavement (L 4) over Room 28, Section U–V (fig. 37). Original diameter 5.4 cm.

Toilet articles (figs. 62–3)

181.   Tweezers with incised line decoration, from Ditch I beneath Building A, L 12, Section N–O (fig. 6).   4.4 cm.

182.   Tweezers with incised line decoration. From east of Building A, L 12, Section S–T (fig. 6). 4.7 cm.

183.   Tweezers, badly corroded. From upper filling of corn-drying oven. Section CC–DD (fig. 26). 5.4 cm.

184.   Toilet set comprising ear scoop, nail-cleaner and tweezers. The nail-cleaner is decorated with two incised oblique crosses divided by a horizontal groove. The head is also decorated with horizontal grooves. Finds made within close proximity of one another, though not definitely a set. From filling of Ditch I below Building A. Nail cleaner 5.2 cm.

185.   Nail-cleaner decorated with incised lines. From rubble in inner courtyard, Building A.   3.5 cm.

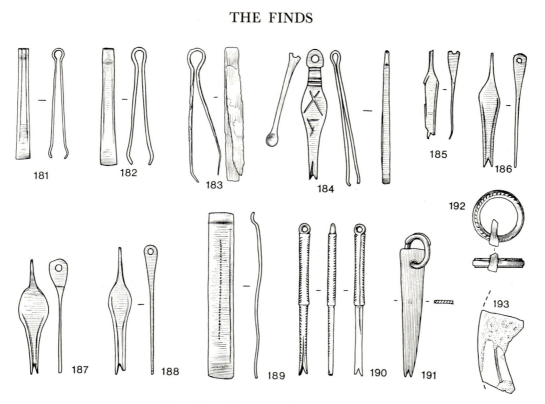

FIG. 62. Bronze objects (scale ⅔)

186. Nail-cleaner decorated with incised lines. East of Building A, L 10, Section S–T (fig. 6). 4.6 cm.

187. Nail-cleaner with incised lines. From east of Building A. As above. 4.6 cm.

188. Nail-cleaner with incised lines. South of Building A, in early levels. 5 cm.

189. Fragment of tweezers with incised line and dot decoration. Unusually large by comparison with other tweezers from excavation. Adjacent to porter's lodge in gatehouse. Fourth century. 6.6 cm.

190. Cylindrical nail-cleaner divided into two zones, the lower one of which is narrower. Oblique chip decoration on bevelled corners, excepting one side of the lower zone. Vertical groove on one side only and surmounted by ring. One of similar shape comes from the late fourth-century deposit in the theatre at Verulamium (*Arch.*, LXXX (1934), fig. 12, 17). Occupation level in Building E. Late fourth century. 6 cm.

191. Nail-cleaner made from piece of sheet bronze. With ring. Rubble filling of Room 20, L 3, Section L–M (fig. 6). 5.1 cm.

192. Silvered bronze ring with hexagonal section, decorated on one side with oblique incisions. Fragment of a bronze loop passes around it. Probably ring from a toilet set. From above gatehouse floor.

193. Fragment of circular mirror of speculum metal, decorated with two concentric lines. Filling of oven cut into south side of Ditch I beneath western wing of Building A. 3.5 cm.

194. Flat H bladed spatula from eaves drip alongside western corridor of Building A. See *London*, pl. XXXVII. L 8, Section U–V (fig. 36). 16.5 cm.

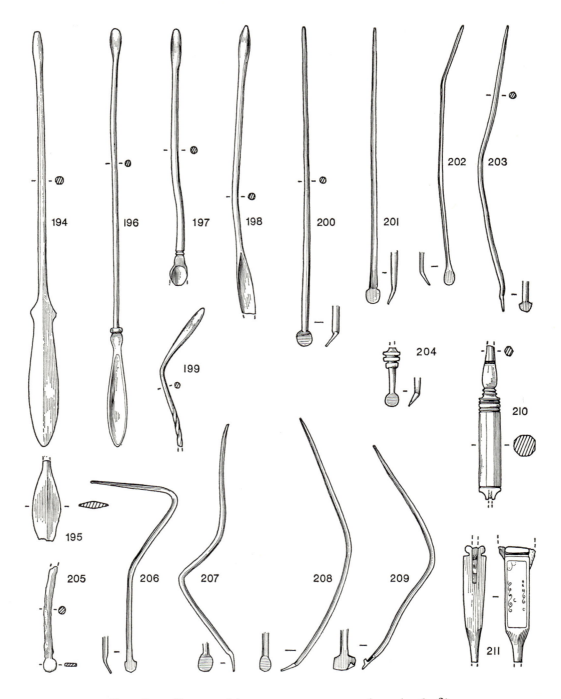

FIG. 63.   Bronze objects, except no. 205, iron (scale $\frac{2}{3}$)

195.   Fragment of flat-bladed spatula. Filling of well, L 8, Section X–Y (fig. 17).   3.2 cm.

196.   Spoon-shaped spatula with probe. Collar moulding above spoon. Filling of well, L 8, Section X–Y (fig. 17).   16.7 cm.

197.   Spoon-shaped spatula with probe. Broken. Decorated above spoon with two horizontal incised lines. South of Building A.   10.2 cm.

198.   Spoon-shaped spatula with probe. From filling of Ditch II beneath Building C, L 2, Section EE–FF (fig. 7).   11.5 cm.

199.   Fragment of spatula with probe. Twisted shaft. From rubble over western corridor of Building B. 5.6 cm.

200.   Unguent spoon. Unstratified. From 1962 road works.   12.8 cm.

201.   Unguent spoon from filling of Ditch I beneath Building A.   11 cm.

202.   Unguent spoon from destruction rubble east of Building A.   10.4 cm.

203.   Unguent spoon. Found on disturbed floor of bathing pool.   11.4 cm.

204.   Fragment of unguent spoon decorated with three collars, each of which is narrower towards the spoon. From filling of Ditch I beneath western wing of Building A.   2.3 cm.

205.   Fragment of iron unguent spoon. From filling of chalk quarry, Pit X, L 4, Section RR–SS (fig. 50).   4.2 cm.

206.   Unguent spoon from east side of Building A. In black occupation over L 10, Section S–T (fig. 6).   7.8 cm.

207.   Unguent spoon. Unstratified, from west side of Building A.   9.9 cm.

208.   Unguent spoon from cobbled surface of northern courtyard.   10.1 cm.

209.   Stylus or unguent spoon from east side of Building A, L 10, Section S–T (fig. 6).   9 cm.

210.   Bronze toilet razor with octagonal shaft or handle, with slot at lower end, in which is the remains of an iron blade. The upper end of the handle is circular and decorated with four horizontal grooves. It is surmounted by a bulbous stem which tapers from a circular to hexagonal section, and which is decorated with two horizontal grooves. From filling of well, L 8, Section X–Y (fig. 17).   6.2 cm.

211.   Bronze toilet razor, the handle of which is decorated on both sides with panels of silver, inscribed with a scroll pattern. Handle tapers at foot towards broken shaft. The iron blade of the razor is mounted in a deep slot that runs through the upper part of the handle. The latter is ornamented with a deep groove and roll moulding on either side of the blade. There is a very close parallel from Zugmantel: it has a panel of silver, engraved, and inset in the same position; and there is a similar slot for the blade, flanked, as in this example, by a roll moulding (cf. *S.J.*, III (1912), Taf. XIII, 17 and p. 50). From rubble in Room 20, L 3, Section L–M (fig. 6).   4.6 cm.

Bronze pins: except 214 (silver) (fig. 64)

212.   Conical-headed pin from destruction rubble L 3, east of Building A, Section S–T (fig. 6). 5.5 cm.

213.   Plain-headed pin inscribed with four horizontal lines. Filling of bathing pool, L 5, Section C–D–E (fig. 38).   8.2 cm.

214.   Spherical-headed silver pin from second-century levels in inner courtyard.   5.3 cm.

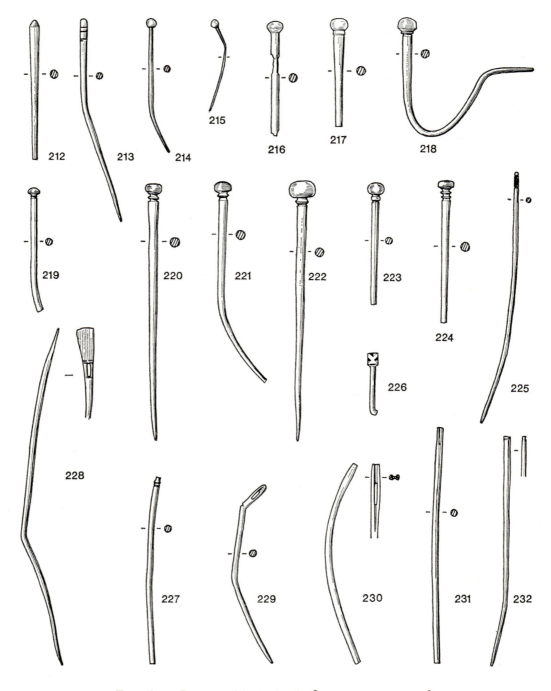

FIG. 64.   Bronze objects (scale ⅔, except no. 229, ⅓)

215. Spherical-headed pin from south of corn-drying oven.   3.6 cm.

216. Fragment of round-headed pin from soot filling of southern stoke-hole to Room 35.   5.5 cm.

217. Spherical-headed pin with single cordon below head. Chalk quarry, Pit V, L 3, Section NN–OO (fig. 48).   4.3 cm.

218. Spherical-headed pin with cordon and groove decoration. From Ditch I beneath Building A, L 12, Section N–O (fig. 6). Distorted; original length 10.5 cm.

219. Spherical-headed pin with cordon and groove decoration. From chalk quarry, Pit V, L 7, Section NN–OO (fig. 48).   5 cm.

220. Spherical-headed pin with double groove and single cordon. From rubble filling of bathing pool, L 11, Section F–G (fig. 38).   10.3 cm.

221. Spherical-headed pin with groove and cordon decoration. Found on courtyard surface, Building A, L 8, Section N–O (fig. 6).   8.2 cm.

222. Spherical-headed pin with groove and cordon decoration. In clay and chalk make-up for Room 22.   10.5 cm.

223. Spherical-headed pin with groove and cordon decoration. Unstratified.   8.8 cm.

224. Flattened spherical-headed pin with three grooves and two cordons. On cobbled courtyard floor, Building A, L 8, Section N–O (fig. 6).   5.7 cm.

225. Slender pin decorated with incised lattice pattern. Amongst rubble east of Building D, L 3, Section II–JJ–KK (fig. 33).   10.1 cm.

226. Square-headed pin decorated with V-shaped cuts. From Pit N, north-west of Building D, L 10, Section II–JJ–KK (fig. 33).   4.5 cm.

227. Pin with cordon and groove decoration, head missing. Unstratified.   7.5 cm.

Bronze needles: except 229 (iron) (fig. 64)

228. Spatulate-headed needle with incised line decoration above and below eye. On surface of northern courtyard.   13.5 cm.

229. Iron needle. Unstratified, possibly post-medieval.   14.3 cm.

230. Needle with vertical groove on either side of eye. From filling of gully west of Period 7 stockade (fig. 22).   8 cm.

231. Needle with vertical groove, head missing. From filling of water leat north of bathing pool. Could be associated with votive deposit. L 5, Section C–D–E (fig. 38).   9.4 cm.

232. Needle or pin with incised horizontal line decoration on remains of head. From clay spread over chalk floor associated with Period 1. L 12, Section S–T (fig. 6).   9.2 cm.

Votive deposit (all bronze unless stated otherwise) (figs. 65–6)

The finds in the following inventory were made in the water leat north of the bathing pool and were associated with 173 bronze coins (see Coin List II, p. 115) and numerous fragments of iron (listed after this section on the bronze, p. 149). The number of coins, and the type of objects found in the leat would suggest they were thrown into it as a tribute to a water deity. The bronze spoon SF 81 and the bronze needle SF 231, illustrated above, could also be

L

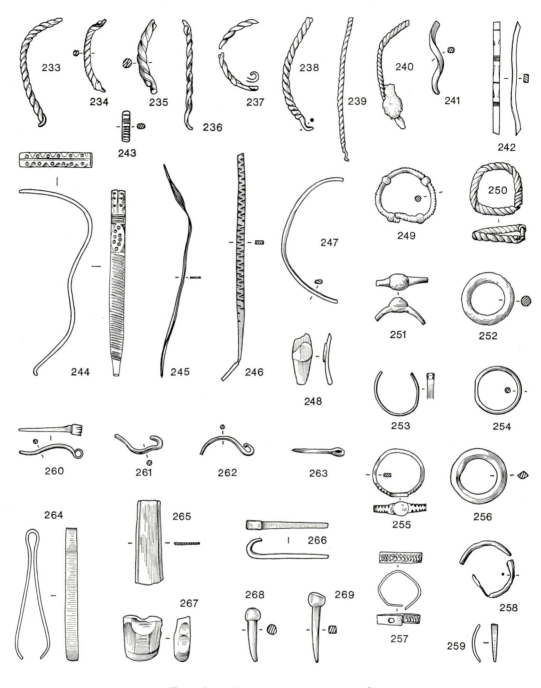

FIG. 65.   Bronze objects (scale $\frac{2}{3}$)

part of this deposit. The relevant section for all the finds is Section C-D-E (fig. 38). The layer number will follow the description of the object.

233–41.   Bracelets of two strands of twisted wire. All from L 8, except 235, L 5.

242.   Fragment of bracelet decorated with incised lines and V-shaped notches on edges. L 8. 4.5 cm.

243.   Minute fragment of bracelet decorated with incised lines. L 8.   1.2 cm.

244.   Distorted bracelet tapering towards hooked terminal. Decoration on outer side divided into three unequal zones. The longest is nearest the terminal and is decorated with oblique incised lines, followed by a short zone with an elliptical panel containing eight small circles. This in turn is followed by four incised lines and a wave pattern on both sides of the bracelet, divided by a groove and decorated with small circles. L 5.   7.5 cm.

245.   Undecorated fragment of bracelet L 8.   8.5 cm.

246.   Length of bracelet, tapering towards terminal, and decorated with zig-zag design created by alternating V-shaped cuts on either side of the bracelet. L 8.   9 cm.

247.   Undecorated fragment of bracelet. L 8.   5 cm.

248.   Terminal of bracelet decorated with circular disc. L 15.   2 cm.

249.   Ring with beading on outer edge and decorated with four spherical collars. L 8.   3.5 cm.

250.   Ring made from two strands of twisted wire with hook at one end. Possibly bent bracelet. L 10. 2.1 cm.

251.   Finger ring with oval shaped bezel. L 8.   2.1 cm.

252.   Plain finger ring. L 5.   2.1 cm.

253.   Expanding finger ring decorated on terminal with two incised lines and four wedge-shaped cuts, two on either edge of the ring. L 5.   2.1 cm.

254.   Plain finger ring with flattened bezel. L 8.   1.9 cm.

255.   Finger ring with plain circular bezel, decorated on either side with V-shaped notches. L 8. 2.1 cm.

256.   Undecorated ring with lozenge-shaped section. L 8.   2.2 cm.

257.   Expanding finger ring decorated with running S-pattern, with hole through one terminal. Traces of criss-cross markings on same. L 8.   1.7 cm.

258.   Fragments of broken ring. L 8. Original diameter 2.2 cm.

259.   Broken terminal of finger ring. L 8.   1.5 cm.

260.   Curved pin from penannular brooch or buckle. Hinge decorated with radial moulding. L 8. 2.5 cm.

261.   Bent pin from penannular brooch or buckle. L 8.   1.9 cm.

262.   Half fragment of penannular brooch with spiralled terminal. L 8.   2.2 cm.

263.   Buckle pin. L 8.   2.1 cm.

264.   Toilet tweezers. L 8.   5.3 cm.

265.   Fragment of toilet tweezers decorated with incised lines running parallel with the edges. L 8. 3.4 cm.

266.   Pin from penannular brooch or buckle. L 5.   3.2 cm.

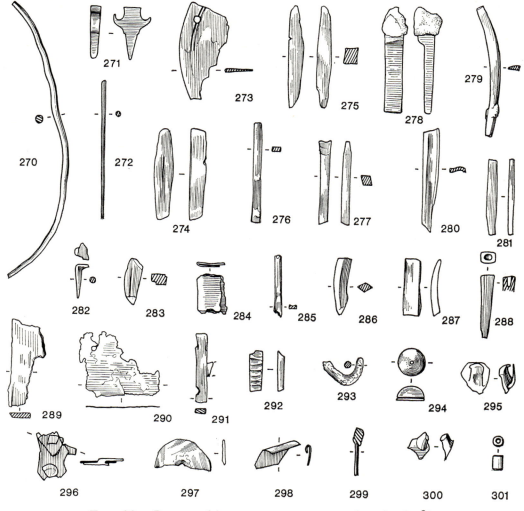

FIG. 66.   Bronze objects, except no. 301, glass (scale $\frac{2}{3}$)

267.   Fragment of ornamented cast bronze. Possibly from bronze vessel. L 5.   1.8 cm.

268.   Spherical-headed nail. L 8.   2.1 cm.

269.   Spherical-headed nail with flattened top.   2.7 cm.

270.   Strip of wire, possibly from bangle. L 8.   11 cm.

271.   Broken-off tongue of buckle. The tri-lobed type seems to have military associations throughout the Roman period; e.g. *Hod Hill*, fig. 4, A81, of the first century A.D. and Mrs Hawkes' buckles, type IIA, of late fourth-century date (*Med. Arch.*, v (1961), 25–6, etc.), but the present example is perhaps nearer in style to the plainer Hod Hill tongue. L 8.   2.1 cm.

272.   Shaft of pin or needle. L 8.   5.5 cm.

273.   Fragment of mirror of speculum metal, ornamented with small hole and concentric lines. L 8.   3.9 cm.

274-5. Two small ingots of cast bronze. L 8. 274, 3.6 cm. and 275, 4.1 cm.

276. Strip of worked bronze. L 8. 4 cm.

277. Bronze strip with flattened end. L 5. 3.3 cm.

278. Bronze strip with square section, reducing to rectangular section. The square end is encrusted with iron. L 8. 4.2 cm.

279. Curved piece of bronze. L 8. 5.2 cm.

280. Piece of bronze with S-shaped section. L 8. 4.1 cm.

281. Strip of bronze. L 5. 3 cm.

282. Rivet. L 8. 1.4 cm.

283. Fragment of cast bronze. L 8. 1.8 cm.

284. Folded bronze sheet. L 8. 1.6 cm.

285. Strip of bronze. L 5. 2.4 cm.

286. Curved fragment of bronze with lozenge-shaped section. L 8. 2.2 cm.

287. Fragment of bracelet? L 8. 2.3 cm.

288. Tapering rod with hollow section at one end. L 8. 2.5 cm.

289. Fragment of cast bronze. L 8. 3.5 cm.

290. Sheet of bronze with circular rivet hole. L 8. 3.8 cm.

291. Buckle fragment? L 8. 2.7 cm.

292. Strip of beaten bronze. L 8. 1.6 cm.

293. Fragment of bronze. L 8. 1.5 cm.

294. Dome-shaped object decorated with incised line and pierced with hole. L 8. 1.1 cm.

295. Rivet. L 5. 1.3 cm.

296. Riveted sheet of bronze. L 8. 2 cm.

297. Circular disc fragment with central hole. L 5. 2.2 cm.

298. Lozenge-shaped piece of inlay, folded on one side. L 5. 2 cm.

299. Bronze wire, wound at one end. Goad? L 8. 1.9 cm.

300. Rivet. L 5. 1.3 cm.

301. Cylindrical green glass bead. L 5. 6 cm.

Iron objects associated with this group

Fig. 71

387. Tumbler-lock slide-key.

390. L-shaped tumbler-lock lift-key.

394. Latch-lifter.

Fig. 72

423. Knife.

435. Knife.

438.   Knife.
446.   Knife.
447.   Knife.

Fig. 73
458.   Fragment of blade.
476.   Wedge.
477.   Bladed tool.
482.   Fragmentary blade.

Fig. 74
491.   Nail.
512.   T-staple.

Fig. 75
537.   Head of split spiked-loop.
539.   Head of split spiked-loop.
540.   Head of split spiked-loop.
541.   Fragment, probably the end of one arm of a split spiked-loop.
542.   Rod.
567.   Shoe cleat.

Fig. 76
575.   Fragment of horseshoe.
602.   Binding.

Fig. 77
632.   Fragment of strip.
641.   Fragment of rod.

Fig. 78
647.   Shaped strip.
648.   Fragment of bar.
654.   Joiner's dog.
662.   Fragment.

BRONZE MASK OF MEDUSA

By J. M. C. Toynbee, f.s.a.

The bronze mask of Medusa (pl. XXVII*b* and fig. 55, 42), topped by a stout bronze ring, was found unstratified. The whole object, including the ring, is 5.5 cm. high and would appear to be one of a pair of handle-escutcheons soldered on to a vessel of some kind, most probably a small pail or bucket, with a swing-handle, the ends of which would have been inserted into the two rings. Behind, the mask has been filled with lead, no doubt to strengthen it, and directly below the ring is a piece of metal bent back as though to fold it over the vessel's rim. Between the ring and the top of the head are the remains of a narrow horizontal band. There is no sign that the escutcheon once extended below the Medusa's chin. It now has a fine dark green patina.

As to the mask's identity there can be no uncertainty, since the headwings and the snakes entwined in the sinuous locks of hair are clearly visible. The face is very full and puffy, the eyes are large and staring, beneath markedly arched eyebrows, the nose is broad (but may have looked less so before it was somewhat flattened), the small mouth is closed and the lips are thick and protruding, the lower lip being considerably shorter than the upper one. The Roman craftsman would appear to have deliberately given his Medusa a somewhat unprepossessing aspect, perhaps to enhance the efficacy of its apotropaic function, and in this respect the Gadebridge Medusa differs from most Hellenistic and Roman Medusas who are, if sometimes fierce and glaring, by no means unhandsome.[1]

Of the pails or buckets with handle-escutcheons, carrying figured or other motifs, that have come to light in late La Tène and Romano-British contexts the ultimate models were Italian *situlae* with classical ornamentation — vessels from Etruria dating from the fourth century b.c.,[2] and similar, but later, pieces from Pompeii.[3] All these have double swing-handles. But another Italian *situla* from Italy, excavated at Boscoreale near Pompeii, has a single swing-handle and below the two rings, into which the ends of the handle are inserted, are two escutcheons, each displaying a female head with a scalloped 'bib' below it and the profile head of an animal, possibly a dog, on either side of it.[4] Bucket-escutcheons of British provenance dating from pre-Roman conquest Belgic times are classical only in the sense that they are representational and three-dimensional. Such are the two stylized heads of helmeted warriors that conceal the slots into which are fitted the ends of the single swing-handle of the famous bronze-mounted wooden bucket from Aylesford in Kent;[5] and the more naturalistic, but still formalized, heads of bulls and cows, each topped by a handle-ring and found without its bucket, from Felmersham in Bedfordshire.[6] Both sets of objects were obviously the work of Celtic craftsmen, whether working in Britain itself or in some nearby land.

[1] e.g. The Medusas carved on roundels in the Severan Forum at Lepcis Magna in Tripolitania (*J.R.S.*, xlv (1955), pls. 34, fig. 1; 36, fig. 1).
[2] *British Museum Guide to the Early Iron Age* (1925), pp. 27–8, fig. 24.
[3] V. Spinazzola, *Le arti decorative in Pompeii*, pp. 273–4.
[4] H. Willers, *Die römischen Bronzeeimer von Hemmoor* (1901), p. 130, fig. 56.

[5] J. W. Brailsford, *Later Prehistoric Antiquities of the British Isles* (1953), p. 70, pl. 21, no. 1.
[6] S. Piggott and G. E. Daniel, *A Picture Book of Ancient British Art* (1951), pl. 57; ed. W. F. Grimes, *Aspects of Archaeology in Britain and Beyond* (1951), pl. 7, figs. 3a, 3b; 4a, 4b.

On the other hand, a ring-topped bucket-escutcheon of precisely the same type as the escutcheons on the Boscoreale *situla*, found at Hod Hill in Dorset, may have come from a vessel imported into Britain from Italy not long after the Roman conquest.[1] Other examples of an identical or closely related type, some still adorning their single-swing-handled buckets, others isolated from them, have been discovered on a number of sites in northern Europe near, or far beyond, the imperial frontiers — in Norway,[2] in Denmark (Möen),[3] in Bohemia,[4] in Germany (Hagenow, Mecklenburg; Nettlingen, Marienburg);[5] and in Hungary.[6] A further such piece is in the Louvre.[7] Yet another single-swing-handled bucket, dating from the early first century A.D., with escutcheons very similar in general type to those just cited, came to light at Voerde-Mehrum (Dinslaken) and is now in the Bonn Museum.[8] There the escutcheons show each a female head, with waved hair parted in the centre, resting on a vine-leaf that spreads below it and to either side of it. The engraved plait-pattern that encircles the rim is continued on a horizontal, projecting band that separates (as in the case of the Gadebridge escutcheon) the crown of the head from the ring. This could well be an Italian import.

The motifs on other pail- or bucket-escutcheons of the Roman period in Britain are far more unlike the motif on the Gadebridge example than is that on the Hod Hill piece. On the miniature enamelled-bronze pail of globular shape from Barrow IV in the Bartlow Hills in Essex the escutcheons for the single-swing-handle, square in section, each take the form of a stylized leaf, topped by a ring, and there is no figured ornament.[9] The bronze-mounted wooden bucket from Mount Sorrel in Leicestershire has embossed shield-shaped escutcheons, from the surface of each of which projects boldly forward a ring-topped ox-head. These ox-heads are still in the late La Tène tradition, although the bucket was found in association with late third-century A.D. material.[10] A similar survival of the late La Tène style into the Roman period can be seen on an isolated bronze handle-attachment from Richborough. It is surmounted by a now broken ring and shows a head with human features and a bull's knobbed horns: there is a hook behind for folding over the vessel's rim.[11]

Closer to the Gadebridge piece than any Roman-age bucket-escutcheons of British provenance that are known to me are examples with classical figure motifs (other than those of the Boscoreale and closely related early types) from northern and western provincial, and from 'free-German' sites. From Roman Gaul come two ring-topped escutcheons, one carrying a beardless male head with closed eyes and a broad nose,[12] the other, what appears to be a tragic mask.[13] Nearer still to our Medusa are the escutcheons on two vessels in the

---

[1] *Hod Hill*, p. 15, no. 13, fig. 14.

[2] Willers, op. cit., p. 124, fig. 51.

[3] Ibid., p. 125, fig. 53.

[4] Ibid., p. 125, fig. 52.

[5] Ibid., p. 126, fig. 54 (Hagenow); p. 132, fig. 57 (Nettlingen); here a stylized leaf-pattern, below and at the sides, takes the place of the 'bib' and animal heads).

[6] A. Radnóti, *Die römischen Bronzegefässe von Pannonien* (1938), pls. 9, no. 47; 31, fig. 2 (fig. 5 on this plate closely resembles the Nettlingen escutcheons: see note 12 and cf. Willers, op. cit., pl. 4, fig. 5).

[7] A. de Ridder, *Les bronzes antiques du Louvre*, II (1915), no. 2898, pl. 102.

[8] *Auswahlkatalog des Rheinischen Landesmuseums Bonn* (1963), pp. 90–1, no. 47, pls. 56–7.

[9] *V.C.H. Essex*, III (1963), frontispiece. For a continental example of bucket-attachments with non-figured escutcheons, see M. H. P. den Boesterd, *Description of the Collections in the Rijksmuseum G. M. Kam*, V: *the Bronze Vessels* (1956), no. 149, pl. 15, where the decoration below the ring takes the form of an open-work *pelta*.

[10] Ed. Grimes, op. cit., p. 197, pls. 8, fig. B; 9, figs. i, 2.

[11] *Richborough*, III, p. 79, no. 17, pl. 10.

[12] P. Lebel, *Catalogue des collections archéologiques de Montbéliard*, III: *les bronzes figurés* (1962), pl. 39, no. 48.

[13] P. Lebel, *Catalogue des collections archéologiques de Besançon*, V: *les bronzes figurés* (1960), pl. 70, no. 7.

Rijksmuseum G.M. Kam at Nijmegen. One of these is a small pail, dated to the second or third century A.D. with a single-swing-handle and two shield-shaped escutcheons each topped by a ring and carrying what would seem to be the head of a Maenad.[1] The second vessel is a fluted bowl, assigned to the third or fourth century A.D., with a small single-swing-handle on either side and a large double-swing-handle above. The two escutcheons for the latter have each two holes for inserting the handle-ends and below them a Medusa-head with wings in the hair, snake-like locks framing the face, and a tapering leaf-like feature beneath the chin.[2] Identical escutcheons occur on a pail from Altenwalde in Germany.[3] Two more pails from Germany show respectively on their escutcheons a head crowned by a Phrygian cap (Stolzenau)[4] and a male bust coming down to a point in front (Westersode).[5] There would seem, then, to have been quite a wide variety of figure-motifs of classical content current under the middle and later Empire on the handle-escutcheons of buckets and pails from northern frontier lands, and the new Medusa motif from Britain takes its place readily enough among them.

If handle attachments of the Boscoreale and other early types are likely to have come for the most part from Italian workshops to the north, many, if not the majority, of the later pieces could well have been the products of provincial factories. One such provincial-Roman factory is believed to have been located at Gressenich, near Aachen, and to have been in production from about the middle of the second century onwards.[6] The Gadebridge escutcheon is of a definitely provincial style; and, in view of the apparent rarity of decorated buckets and pails of Romano-British provenance, the odds are in favour of its having been manufactured, not in Britain, but at a continental north-western bronze-working centre. Further than that we cannot at present go. Nor can anything more precise be said about its date than that it could have been produced sometime during the second or third century A.D. or even (but less probably) in the early years of the fourth century.

OBJECTS OF BONE
(figs. 67–8)

Bone pins (the shafts of the pins are circular except where illllustrated)

302. Conical-headed pin from rubble over western corridor of Building B.   5.8 cm.

303. Flat-topped pin with thick shank. Found in destruction rubble over western wing of Building A. L 2, Section U–V (fig. 37).   6.5 cm.

304. Flat-topped pin from above tessellated pavement (L 4) in Room 28, Section U–V (fig. 37). 9 cm.

305. Oval-headed pin. East of Building A, L 10, Section S–T (fig. 6).   7.6 cm.

306. Conical-headed pin with horizontal groove. In rubble filling of bathing-pool, L 11, Section F–G (fig. 38).   5.5 cm.

---

[1] Boesterd, op. cit., no. 152, pl. 6.
[2] Ibid., no. 196, pls. 8, 15.
[3] Willers, op. cit., p. 28, fig. 18.

[4] Ibid., p. 34, fig. 20; pl. 1, fig. 5.
[5] Ibid., pl. 1, fig. 1.
[6] *B.M. Guide*, p. 94; *J.R.S.*, XXVI (1936), p. 210.

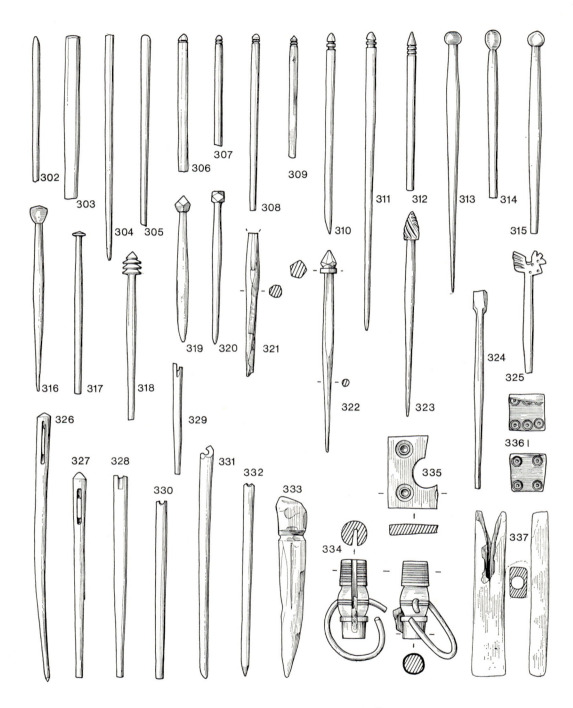

Fig. 67. Bone objects (scale ⅔)

307. Conical-headed pin with two horizontal grooves on neck. From burnt layer south of water cistern, Building A.   4.5 cm.

308. Conical-headed pin similar to above. From leat south of bathing pool, L 9, Section E–F (fig. 40). 7 mm.

309. Conical-headed pin with polygonal section and two grooves below head. From destruction rubble over baths.   4.9 cm.

310. Conical-headed pin with two wide grooves on neck. East of Building A, L 12, Section S–T (fig. 6).   8 cm.

311. Conical-headed pin with two grooves on neck. From west side of Building C.   11.9 cm.

312. Tall conical-headed pin, decorated with three grooves. From black occupation over cobbles east of Building A. Over L 10, Section S–T (fig. 6).   6.3 cm.

313. Spherical-headed pin from charcoal spread in chalk quarry, Pit V, L 7, Section NN–OO (fig. 48).   10.4 cm.

314. Oval-headed pin. From filling of north–south beam slot in Room 20, Building A.   6.7 cm.

315. Spherical-headed pin from above floor of eastern corridor, Building A.   8 cm.

316. Oval-headed pin with conical top, from northern corridor floor make-up, Building A.   7.4 cm.

317. Disc-headed pin from filling of bathing pool, L 5, Section F–G (fig. 38).   6.5 cm.

318. 'Pagoda'-headed pin, decorated with three discs surmounted by conical top. Location as above. 6.7 cm.

319. Pin with eight facets on head. From destruction rubble in baths.   10.5 cm.

320. Pin with thirteen facets decorating head. From filling of bathing pool, L 5, Section F–G (fig. 38). 6.1 cm.

321. Pin with missing head, shank crudely whittled. From filling of bathing pool as above.   10.7 cm.

322. Conical-headed pin, faceted, shank poorly whittled. From filling of bathing pool, L 3, Section F–G (fig. 38).   8.1 cm.

323. Conical-headed pin decorated with spiralled grooves. From occupation in Room 20, Building A, L 5, Section L–M (fig. 6).   8.2 cm.

324. Spatulate-headed pin from chalk quarry, Pit V, L 9, Section NN–OO (fig. 48).   8 cm.

325. Pin with head carved in the form of a cock, and decorated with tail feathers, and small drilled holes, one of which represents an eye. The holes do not penetrate to the other side. From western corridor of Building A. Below L 3, Section U–V (fig. 37).   4.8 cm.

Bone needles (the shafts of the needles are circular except where illustrated)

326. Conical-headed needle from filling of well. L 11, Section X–Y (fig. 17).   10.7 cm.

327. Conical-headed needle from filling of well. L 12, Section X–Y (fig. 17).   8.2 cm.

328. Needle with broken head and eye. From filling of robber trench, east wall of Room 28, Building A.   8.1 cm.

329. Needle with broken head and eye. In Ditch I below inner courtyard, Building A.   4.4 cm.

330. Needle with broken head and eye. From black occupation on eastern corridor floor of Building B.   7.1 cm.

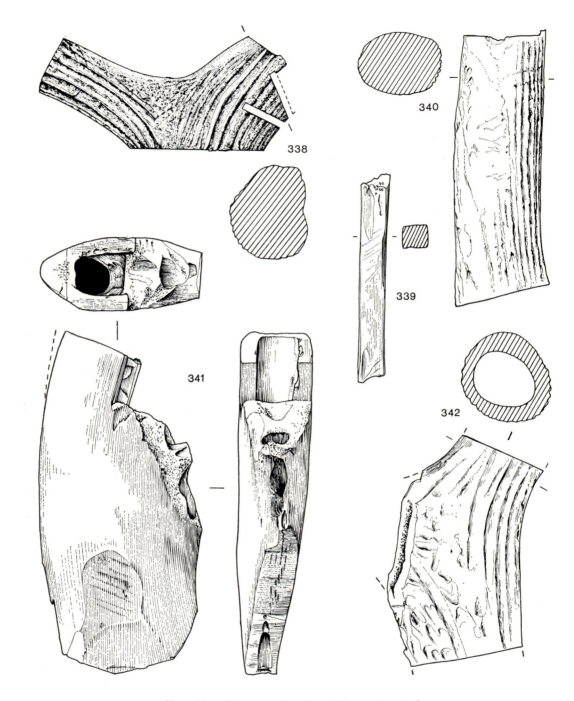

FIG. 68.　Bone and antler objects (scale $\frac{2}{3}$)

331.   Needle with broken eye. From chalk floor belonging to Period 1 occupation, L 13, Section S–T (fig. 6).   9.2 cm.

332.   Needle with broken eye. From black silt pre-dating Building B.   7.7 cm.

Miscellaneous objects of bone or antler (many fragments of sawn antler were found, but not all have been illustrated)

333.   Awl with horizontal groove below head. Whittle marks on shank. From upper filling of Pit N, north-west of Building D, L 3, Section II–JJ–KK (fig. 33).   7.2 cm.

334.   Cylindrical bone handle from toilet razor with deep vertical groove for seating iron knife blade, part of which still remains. The lower end of the object, beneath the collar, is strengthened by an iron ferrule. A penannular bronze ring passes through a hole in the bulbous centre zone, which is decorated with three horizontal grooves. The upper zone is decorated with nine horizontal grooves. From destruction rubble east of Building A.   3.1 cm.

335.   Fragment of game counter or decorative plaque originally marked with four circles, two of which survive. On cobbles of inner courtyard, Building A.   2.9 cm.

336.   Cubic dice marked on all sides with circles indicating numbers 1 to 6. Destruction rubble south of Building A.   1.5 cm.

337.   Bone handle, probably from knife. From rubble in bathing pool, L 11, Section F–G (fig. 38).   6.5 cm.

338.   Piece of antler, sawn on all three ends, with two deep saw cuts on right side. Filling of chalk quarry, Pit V, L 7, Section NN–OO (fig. 48).   10 cm.

339.   Long rectangular piece of worked bone with square section. Purpose unknown; from black occupation in Room 20, L 5, Section L–M (fig. 6).   8.2 cm.

340.   Length of antler, sawn at both ends. Upper filling of water leat, L 5, Section C–D–E (fig. 38).   10.9 cm.

341.   Mandible of an ox, the ramus of which has been partially curved with an axe — the alveolar region has also been cut and partially bored. The purpose of the object is uncertain, but it appears to have been a handle. The hole had no evidence of wear, nor that an iron object was slotted into it. It is possible it was a crude holder for a tallow candle. Filling of well, L 5, Section X–Y (fig. 17).   13.8 cm.

342.   Piece of sawn antler; possibly bored. From lowest gravel in water leat, L 8, Section C–D–E (fig. 38).   9.5 cm.

OBJECTS OF IRON

By W. H. MANNING, F.S.A.

(figs. 69–79)

In reports on the excavations of Romano-British sites it is customary to publish only a selection of the ironwork found, often only a very small selection, and to suppress the remainder. Much of the material found is fragmentary or repetitive, and on very large sites the fragments, scraps, nails and the like often cannot be dealt with without severely over-burdening the report. On sites where the finds are few they can all be published and often,

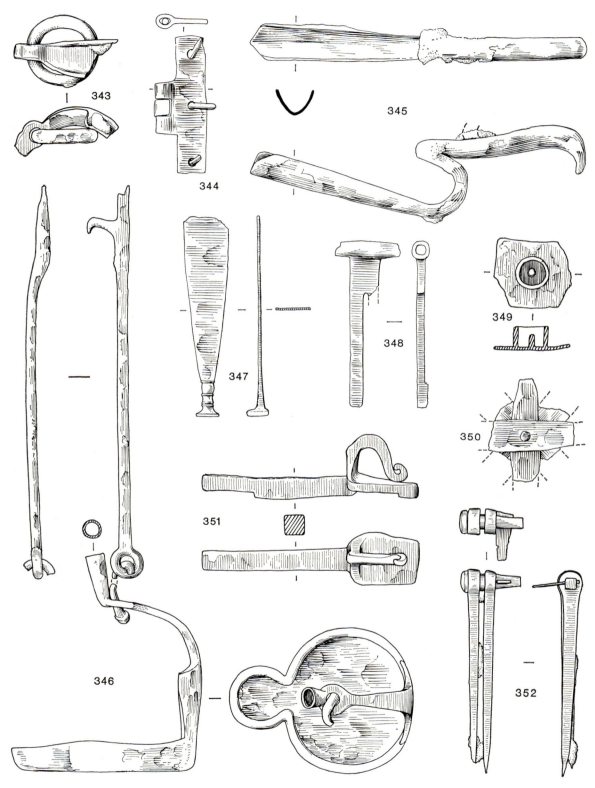

FIG. 69. Iron objects (scale ⅓)

though not invariably, are. Such sites as Gadebridge Park fall between the two extremes; a considerable, but not impossible, amount of ironwork was discovered and we have felt that it presented a worthwhile opportunity to illustrate it virtually in total. Only in this way can one obtain an idea of the full range of material from such a site.

REFERENCES. In order to reduce the length of references given in the text the following system has been used:

1. When the reference is to a work cited only once or twice the reference is given more or less in full. If the journal title is abbreviated the full title can be found in the list of references and abbreviations (p. xii).

2. When the reference is to material from a site which is quoted repeatedly, the site will be given in a shortened form; the full reference will be found under the name of the site in the list of references and abbreviations.

3. When a piece of iron is quoted for comparative purposes but is unpublished, the museum housing it is given in brackets.

343. Fragment consisting of part of a curving plate with raised edges narrowing into a neck at one end where it is pierced to receive a ring. It *may* be part of a handle from a vessel, in which case the plate must have been nailed or riveted in place through the part which is now lost. A pair of ring handles from a vessel with the ring separated from the nailed plate by a long, but straight, neck come from the Blackburn Mill hoard (*Blackburn Mill*, 42, fig. 11, B 15, B 16). Found west of Building A, L 7, Section U–V (fig. 37). 8.2 cm.

344. Half of a strap-hinge. The plate, which is exceptionally wide, is pierced by three nail holes, still retaining their nails. Strap hinges are not uncommon, but the normal form has narrow tapering arms, e.g. from the Lockleys Villa, Herts. (*Antiq. J.*, XVIII (1938), 355, fig. 3, 6), Richborough, Kent (*Richborough*, IV, 153, pl. LIX, 318), etc. From rubble in western corridor, Building B. 11 cm.

345. Farrier's butteris with a V-sectioned blade. These tools usually have a 'guard' in the form of a short, backward curving bar on the top of the handle, and the remains of such a guard can probably be seen on our example. The butt end of the handle *may* be intended to represent an eagle's head, a device quite common on these tools, but seen most clearly when they are made of bronze (e.g. on an example from Oundle, *Antiq. J.*, XLVIII (1968), 303). The blade usually has a V-section, although a few are known where the cross-section takes the form of a flattened U. They were used to pare horses' hooves in preparing the hoof before shoeing. Comparable examples come from Silchester, possibly with the handle in the form of an eagle's head (*Arch.*, LVII (1901), 248, fig. 6): Colliton Park House, Dorchester, Dorset (Dorchester Museum); Sandy, Beds. (*Sandy*, 53, fig. 2, 5) with a tang rather than a handle. All of these have V-sectioned blades, but examples with U-sections come from the Eckford hoard (*Eckford*, fig. 6, E 17), and Caerwent, Mon. (Newport Museum). Examples with bronze handles are known from Oundle (*Antiq. J.*, XLVIII (1968), 303), and various sites on the continent including Pompeii (*Arch.*, LVII (1901), 248). Occupation material in Room 20, Building A, L 5, Section L–M (fig. 6). 26.5 cm.

346. Open hanging-lamp with its hanger. The end of the lamp stem takes the form of a candlestick and a short swivel, now broken, links the lamp to the hanger. Lamps of this type are not uncommon. Despite frequent assertions to the contrary they are not lamp-holders but lamps in

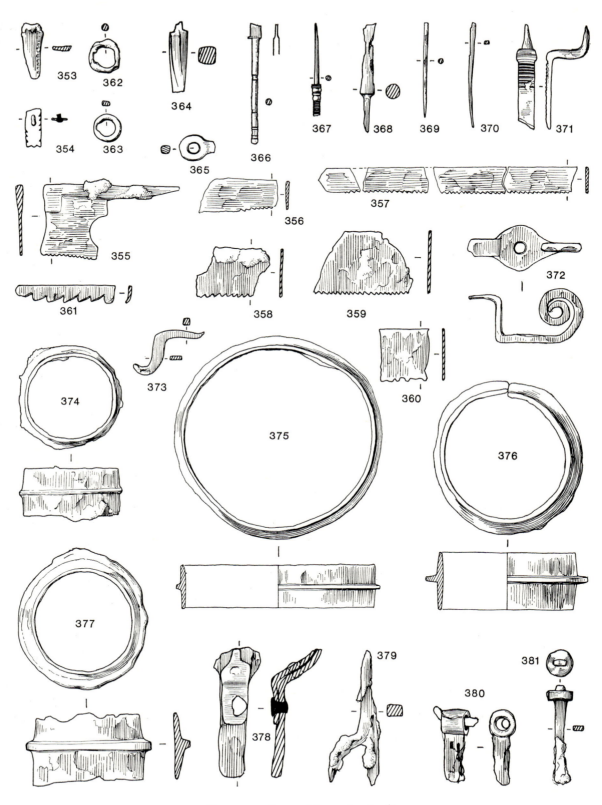

FIG. 70.   Iron objects (scale $\frac{1}{3}$)

themselves, comparable with the Scottish crusie. In a number of cases the short swivel which connects the lamp and hanger is developed into a distinct rod, while in others it is reduced to the minimal form seen here. Examples of the first type include lamps from Newstead (*Newstead*, p. 307, pl. LXXXIX, 6 and 7); the Bartlow Hills (*Arch.*, XXV (1834), 8, pl. II, fig. 10); Caistor-by-Norwich (Norwich Museum), etc.; while the second form is represented at Guilden Morden, Cambs. (Liversidge, *Britain in the Roman Empire*, fig. 70a, and *P.C.A.S.*, XXXVI (1936), 110 f., fig. 1, pl. II); Girton, Cambs. (E. J. Hollingworth and M. M. O'Reilly, *Anglo-Saxon Cemetery at Girton College, Cambridge*, p. 33, pl. XI); Baldock (*Arch. J.*, LXXXVIII (1931), 247 ff., pl. I, B). Other examples with fragmentary hangers or with the hanger lost come from the Blackburn Mill hoard (*Blackburn Mill*, p. 45, fig. 12, B 26); Bayford, Kent (*Arch. Cant.*, XVI (1886), 1–7); and Nettleham, Lincs. (Lincoln Museum). Of these, those from the Bartlow Hills, Guilden Morden, Girton, Baldock, and Bayford, come from graves and are clearly examples of the ancient practice of interring lamps with the dead. Another example of the uniting of a candle-stick with a lamp occurs on a standing lamp from Silchester (*Arch.*, LIV (1894), 153, fig. 20). Filling of well, L 13, Section X–Y (fig. 17). Hanger 31.5 cm. Lamp 17.3 cm.

347. Smoothing chisel with a moulded handle and wide, almost spatulate, blade, the edge of which is damaged. Such chisels are not struck but used with hand or shoulder pressure. The handle is commonly made in one piece with the blade, but the presence of mouldings on the handle is unusual. The blade width of smoothing chisels can vary considerably; our example is fairly broad and may be compared with examples from Caistor-by-Norwich (Castle Museum, Norwich), London (Guildhall Museum) and, in some numbers, Silchester (Reading Museum). Filling of secondary pit cut into Pit Y, L 10, Section GG–HH (fig. 50). 16 cm.

348. Fragment consisting of a cylindrical head with a double-armed stem. It may be the bolt of a barb-spring padlock which had lost its springs. Some of these padlocks have such a double stem, including examples from Rushall Down, Wilts. (*Devizes*, p. 237, pl. LXXIX, 9); Woodcuts (*Woodcuts*, p. 74, pl. XXIV, 10); and Maiden Castle (*Maiden Castle*, p. 284, fig. 95, 1–3). The form of the head would be uncommon in such a padlock but not impractical. From silt pre-dating Building B. Layer equivalent to L 8, Section P–Q, (fig. 6). 13.2 cm.

349. Fragment of a flat plate with a circular collar welded to it round a central spike. It is most probably the pivot for the key and circular ward from a lever lock, although whether from a lock or a padlock cannot be decided from such a small fragment. Lever locks are not common and when they are complete the details of the pivot and wards are hidden by the casing. Complete lever padlocks may be quoted from Caerleon and Lullingstone (*Bulletin of the Board of Celtic Studies*, XXII, pt IV (1968), 410); Fishbourne (*Fishbourne* II, pp. 140–3); Llantwit Major (*Arch. Camb.*, CII (1953), 153, pl. XIV, 2, 14); and in a more damaged state from Silchester (Reading Museum). Of these only the Lullingstone lock has been dissected sufficiently for the presence of a ward and pivot to be established beyond doubt. Continental examples of such locks may be quoted from Saalburg (Jacobi, *Das Römerkastell Saalburg*, p. 477, fig. 76, 13) and Stockstadt (*O.R.L.*, no. 33, Taf. X, 22). From destruction rubble over S wall of the west wing of Building A. Maximum width 6.1 m.

350. Fragment from a window grille in the form of a Maltese cross formed of four strips held by a central rivet. Grilles of this form have been discussed in detail by K. S. Painter and the writer (*B.M.Q.*, XXXI (1967), 122 ff.). Complete examples are known from Hinton St Mary (op. cit. 122 ff., fig. 1, and pl. XXXVIa), Wall, Staffs. (information from the excavator, Mr E. Greenfield), and Duston, Northants. (*Antiquity*, XXXIII (1959), 13, fig. 3). Fragments are common and a full list is given in the paper cited above, together with a list of similar grilles known on the Continent. Post destruction level over Building C. 8.3 cm.

M

351. Spatulate-headed linch-pin with a rebate at the lower end of the stem, and with the loop rising from the junction of the stem and head to curve back across the head. It is an unusual example of the commonest of all types of Romano-British linch pins; normally the loop rises from the top of the head; here its position is reversed. Many examples of the basic type could be quoted, including those from Newstead (*Newstead*, p. 293, pl. LXX, 1); Verulamium (Verulamium Museum); Caistor-by-Norwich (Norwich Museum); Silchester (Reading Museum), etc. It is equally common in Germany. From occupation level in Room 20, L 5, Section L–M (fig. 6). 17.3 cm.

352. Pair of dividers, with the arms held by a pivot with a wedge through its end. Similar examples are known from Caerwent (Newport Museum), and Silchester (Reading Museum). Other dividers are known where the arms are held by a double-headed pivot. From filling of chalk quarry, Pit U, L 4, Section PP–QQ (fig. 47). 16.3 cm.

353. Tip of a hand-saw blade(?). The teeth, if such they are, are too worn for comment. From clay floor of east corridor alongside Room 20, Building A. 4.4 cm.

354. Fragment of double-edged saw-blade with a rivet; it could be from either a hand- or bow-saw. The teeth are raked back towards the rivet; whether they were originally set cannot be told from this fragment. Double-edged saws are not common but a good example of the type is seen in the small hand-saw from Newstead (*Newstead*, p. 291, pl. LXVIII, 6). From destruction material over Building D, L 3, Section II–JJ–KK (fig. 33). 3.1 cm.

355. Small saw blade with a tang which continues along the back of the blade and turns down for a short way at the front to give rigidity to the blade. The teeth slope neither backwards nor forwards and are not set. The back of the blade below the tang has a large semi-circular notch in it. There are *c.* eight teeth/inch (3/cm.). It is a most unusual piece which was presumably made for a specialized function. The strengthening of the blade in this way is not normal Roman practise although it is reminiscent of the manner of straightening Roman scythe blades. From occupation level in Building D, L 5, Section II–JJ–KK (fig. 33). 10.8 cm.

356–60. These are all comparable fragments of saw blades, probably, though not certainly, from bow-saws. The pronounced slope of the teeth is a normal feature of Roman saws, particularly on hand-saws. A modern saw tends to cut on the forward thrust when the weight of the body is behind it rather than on the return, but when a saw blade is made of relatively thin, soft iron, as the Roman saw usually was, there is a strong possibility that it may buckle if it binds in the cut while being thrust forward. To avoid this the teeth were raked backwards to produce the maximum effect as it was drawn backwards towards the worker; the resistance of the blade in the cut served to keep the blade under tension. With a bow-saw the blade is automatically kept under tension and this effect is lessened, though not obviated. One cannot say that these fragments come from bow- or hand-saws with any certainty. Bow-saws using long blades with straight, parallel edges were very widely used in the ancient world, but hand-saws also tended to have straight blades with parallel edges (e.g. the tip of a saw from the site of the Bank of England, London, now in the Guildhall Museum (Acc. no. 13658), and the Iron Age saw blade with two rivets for the handle from Battlesbury Camp, Wilts. (*Devizes*, p. 92, pl. XXIV, C, 7)). Of all our fragments no. 357 would seem the most likely to be from a bow-saw; its relative thinness in comparison to its length would make it exceptionally liable to buckle if used without continuous tension.

356. Fragment of saw blade. There are *c.* seven teeth/inch (3/cm.) which are raked backwards but not set. From filling of well, L 12, Section X–Y (fig. 17). 6.5 cm.

357. Length of saw blade, almost certainly from a bow-saw. The teeth are raked backwards but not set. There are seven teeth/inch (3/cm.). From filling of well, L 12, Section X–Y (fig. 17). 20.6 cm. It is possible that this fragment is part of 356 above.

358. Fragment of saw blade with raked teeth. There are six teeth/inch (2.5/cm.). On natural clay to west of Building A, L 7, Section U–V (fig. 37). 5.8 cm.

359. Fragment of saw blade with raked teeth. There are seven teeth/inch (3/cm.). Filling of chalk quarry, Pit U, L 3, Section PP–QQ (fig. 47). 7.8 cm.

360. Fragment of saw blade too badly damaged for the details of the teeth to be clear. Occupation in Building D, L 5, Section II–JJ–KK (fig. 33). Length 3.60 cm.

361. Fragment of a ratchet(?). The blade is too narrow in comparison with the size of the teeth for it to be identified as a saw with any degree of probability. The use of this object is not immediately obvious. From filling of Pit V, L 3, Section NN–OO (fig. 48). 8 cm.

362. Small ring with a slight recess on the inner edge of one side; the edge facing this recess is almost straight. It is most probably a buckle which has lost the tongue. Buckles are not uncommon finds on Roman sites though few are published; however, two from Newstead are figured (*P.S.A.S.*, XLVII (1912–13), 391, fig. 6). I know of none of this exact form; normally they are rectangular (e.g. those from Caerwent in Newport Museum and from Silchester in Reading Museum), or semicircular with the tongue pivoting on a straight arm set across the ends of the arc (e.g. those from Newstead cited above and others from Hod Hill in the British Museum). On natural clay surface to east of chalk quarry, Pit V. 2.5 cm.

363. Small ring with a slight recess on the inner edge of one side; cf. no. 362 above. In occupation material in southern extension to Building D. Equates with L 5. Section II–JJ–KK (fig. 33). 2.2 cm.

364. Fragment of rod, possibly a punch. Filling of bathing pool, L 5, Section F–G (fig. 38). 5.5 cm.

365. Ring with a broken extension on one side; function uncertain. Filling of chalk quarry, Pit U, L 3, Section PP–QQ (fig. 47). 2.9 cm.

366. Stylus. The eraser has a small spur on one side at the junction with the stem; the stem itself is straight with four grooves around it; the point is missing. Iron styli, though common enough, are usually undecorated, although corrosion may have exaggerated the rarity of ornament. The small spur on the eraser can be matched on other styli (e.g. *Newstead*, p. 307, pl. LXXX, nos. 4, 7, 9). When they are decorated it normally takes the form of mouldings as here (e.g. *Richborough*, IV, p. 153, pl. LIX, 312, 316; *Maiden Castle*, p. 286, fig. 96, 1 and 2). Unstratified. 9.5 cm.

367. Point and part of the stem of a stylus. The stem is elaborately moulded. Ploughsoil over northern apse in western wing of baths. 7.3 cm.

368. Fragment of rod which narrows sharply at one end into a tang or stem, possibly a punch. See no. 364, above. Unstratified, found when road was constructed in 1962. 8.6 cm.

369. Tip of a needle or pin. In filling of Period 1 gully beneath Rooms 25 and 26, Building A. 7.5 cm.

370. Tip of a needle or pin. From black cobbled layer over L 10, Section S–T (fig. 6). 8.3 cm.

371. Cranked tang and fragment of the blade of a farrier's rasp (used for filing horses' hooves) or a carpenter's float (a form of coarse file). Similar tools are known from the Silchester 1890 hoard (*Arch.*, LIV (1894), 152) with a cranked tang; from Caistor-by-Norwich (Norwich Castle Museum) with a straight tang continuing the line of the blade; and from Hod Hill (*Hod Hill,*

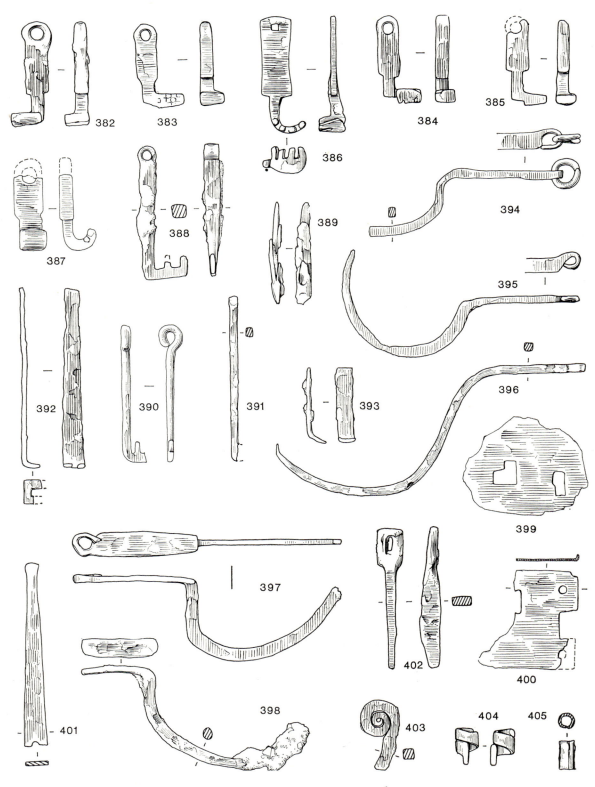

FIG. 71.   Iron objects (scale $\frac{1}{3}$)

p. 14, fig. 13, G 35, with a straight tang; and G 36, with a cranked tang). Unstratified. From L 3, Section F–G (fig. 38).   8.3 cm.

372. Fragment consisting of a diamond-shaped plate pierced by a nail hole with a spiral rising from it at one end, and an outward turning neck at the other, now probably broken short. Function uncertain. Unstratified. Found during road construction in 1962.   9 cm.

373. Tanged U-shaped hook. Such hooks are frequently found but rarely published; examples may be quoted from Verulamium (Verulamium Museum), Dorchester-on-Thames (Ashmolean Museum), Silchester (Reading Museum), Caistor-by-Norwich (Norwich Castle Museum), etc. A well-made example with a knob at the tip of the hook was in the Brampton hoard (*Brampton*, 30, no. 40). Uppermost level over Pit Y, L 3, Section GG–HH (fig. 50).   6.2 cm.

374–7.   These are all junction collars from wooden water-pipes. Such collars are characterized by the central ridge which may have served to ensure that roughly equal parts entered each length of pipe, although the act of driving the wooden pipes on to it probably tended to exaggerate the ridge. Examples are quite common on Roman sites, with both the pipes and their collars coming from London (*London*, p. 39, pl. XIII) and collars from Verulamium (*Antiq. J.*, XL (1960), 19–21), Caerwent (Newport Museum), Silchester (*Arch.*, LV (1897), 423), Wroxeter (Site Museum), etc.

374. Water-pipe junction collar. It has an unusually small diameter. From conduit linking the well with the water cistern (fig. 22).   8.1 cm.

375. Water-pipe junction collar. It has an exceptionally large diameter. From conduit running from the east into Room 20, L 10, Section S–T (fig. 6).   16.5 cm.

376. Water-pipe junction collar. From conduit cutting west corridor of Building B. Set into L 7, Section S–R (fig. 6).   11.9 cm.

377. Water-pipe collar junction. From conduit just south of Room 20. Collar from same conduit as no. 376 above.   10.3 cm.

378. Fragment consisting of two iron strips riveted together over a bronze sheet. From mortar floor, in east corridor alongside Room 20.   10.7 cm.

379. Fragment, probably from the top of a hanging lamp hook. See fig. no. 346 above. From northern courtyard.   10.7 cm.

380. Top of the arm and part of the rivet from a pair of dividers. See no. 352 above. Floor level associated with Period 3 occupation in Room 20.   6 cm.

381. Stem of a bolt from a barb-spring padlock. The springs were riveted to the top of the stem and when in position the cylindrical head blocked the loop at the end of the hasp, with the remainder of the stem serving to prevent whatever ran through the hasp from being removed. This type of lock is best seen in examples from the Great Chesterford hoard (*Gt. Chesterford*, 9, pl. 2,22). Basically similar bolts, though with more than one set of springs, come from Maiden Castle (*Maiden Castle*, p. 284, fig. 95, 2 and 3), and Rushall Down (*Devizes*, p. 237, pl. LXXIX, 9). The type continued into the middle ages. Destruction level south of Building A.   7.10 cm.

382. Tumbler-lock slide-key. The bit may originally have been a plain rectangle without teeth, but more probably this appearance is the result of corrosion. It may be compared with a similar key from Woodcuts (*Woodcuts*, p. 73, pl. XXIV, 2). Keys of this type are common both in bronze and iron. The arrangement and number of the teeth varies but the general principle remains constant. In destruction rubble a few feet south of the gatehouse.   8.3 cm.

383. Tumbler-lock slide-key. The remains of the teeth can be clearly seen. Comparable keys come from many sites; cf. *Verulamium 1936*, p. 219, pl. LXV B, 22, 23 and 27, *London*, pl. XXX B, 1–5, *Camulodunum*, p. 343, pl. CV, 18, etc. On rubbled surface of northern courtyard.   6.7 cm.

384. Tumbler-lock slide-key comparable with no. 383 above. On natural clay surface of inner courtyard. Building A.   7 cm.

385. Tumbler-lock slide-key comparable with no. 382 above. Black soil and destruction material over northern courtyard.   6.7 cm.

386. Tumbler-lock slide-key. The four teeth are set on a U-shaped bit. This form of key is a variant on the previous type but is less common, although a comparable example may be quoted from Verulamium (*Verulamium 1936*, p. 220, pl. LXV B, 26); while others with L-shaped bits come from London (*London*, p. 73, pl. XXX, 6, 7, 8) and Hod Hill (*Hod Hill*, p. 18, pl. XII, K 10), and with an S-shaped bit from Silchester (Reading Museum). From filling of well. L 12, Section X–Y (fig. 17).   9.2 cm.

387. Tumbler-lock slide-key with teeth on a U-shaped bit comparable with no. 386 above. From filling of water leat to north of bathing pool. L 8, Section C–D–E (fig. 38). Surviving fragment. 6 cm.

388. L-shaped tumbler-lock lift-key with two teeth. These are probably the commonest of all Roman keys. The number of teeth varies between two and four, but two is the commonest number. Examples come from many sites; cf. *Newstead*, p. 307, pl. LXXVIII, 2, *Blackburn Mill*, p. 42, fig. 11, B 9, *Verulamium 1936*, p. 220, pl. LXV B, 31, *London*, p. 73, pl. XXX, 3, 4, 5, etc. From L 12, Ditch I beneath Building A, Section N–O (fig. 6).   10.6 cm.

389. Fragment of spring from barrel padlock. From destruction level south of Building A.   8.1 cm.

390. L-shaped tumbler-lock lift-key with a broken bit. See no. 388 above. From filling of water leat to north of pool. L 8, Section C–D–E (fig. 38).   11 cm.

391. Fragment of rod, possibly the stem of an L-shaped tumbler-lock lift-key comparable with no. 388 above. In Ditch I beneath Building A, L 12, Section N–O (fig. 6).   13.2 cm.

392. Stem and fragment of the bit of a barb-spring padlock key. The bit would originally have been square, and the stem probably ended with a rolled loop. It may be compared with examples from Rotherley (*Rotherley*, p. 137, pl. CV, 13), Great Chesterford (*Gt. Chesterford*, p. 7, pl. 2, 25), and unpublished examples from Silchester (Reading Museum), Caistor-by-Norwich (Norwich Castle Museum), etc. Occupation in Room 35, L 3, Section U–V (fig. 37).   14.5 cm.

393. Fragment of strip, bent at one end, possibly part of a barb-spring padlock key similar to no. 392 above. Occupation material over floor of Building D, L 5, Section II–JJ–KK (fig. 33).   6 cm.

394. Incomplete latch-lifter with a ring through the loop at the end of the handle. This is the simplest form of key and is found in the Iron Age, e.g. at Glastonbury (*Glastonbury*, II, 375, pl. LXII, 156) and throughout the Roman period, e.g. at Woodcuts (*Woodcuts*, p. 76, pl. XXV, 5), Rotherley (*Rotherley*, p. 136, pl. CV, 5), Verulamium (*Verulamium 1936*, p. 219, pl. LXV B, 21), etc. In gravel at bottom of water leat. L 8, Section C–D–E (fig. 38).   17.5 cm.

395. Latch-lifter: like no. 394 it probably originally had a ring through the handle. Rubble filling of Room 20, L 3, Section L–M (fig. 6).   19 cm.

396. Latch-lifter. See no. 394 above. Clay pit to south-west of Building B, L 2, Section W–X (fig. 21). 25.5 cm.

397. Latch-lifter. See no. 394 above. Ploughsoil.   21.5 cm.

398. Latch-lifter. See no. 394 above. Ploughsoil over northern courtyard.   18.8 cm.

399. Fragment of a lock plate for a tumbler-lock opened by a slide-key which passed through the L-shaped hole. The second hole was presumably for a hasp, suggesting that the plate comes from a box rather than a door. In this event the tumblers will have been held down by a spring.

Such plates or escutcheons can be of bronze, e.g. that from London (*London*, p. 73, fig. 17, 1), or, less commonly surviving, of iron, e.g. that from Newstead (*Newstead*, p. 307, pl. LXXVIII, 12). Destruction level over Building C. 9.9 cm.

400. Fragment of a lock-plate originally, probably similar to the preceding. Two nail holes survive. Destruction level over Building B. 7.8 cm.

For additional keys omitted from the above section on keys and locks see SF 569 (fig. 75) and SF 672 (fig. 78).

401. Fragment of a tapering strip with the remains of a nail hole at one end. Rubble in Room 20, L 3, Section L–M (fig. 6). 14.5 cm.

402. Object with rectangular head with 'eye'. Of uncertain use. From southern branch of water conduit gully south of Building A. 11.1 cm.

403. Spiral, possibly from a pin or skewer of the type where the head divides into a pair of spirals, such as that from Richborough (*Richborough*, IV, 130, pl. XXXVII, 129). One may note, however, that the fragment 372 also has a spiral at one end, as no doubt had many other pieces of iron-work. Rubble east of Building D, L 3, Section II–JJ–KK (fig. 33). 5.6 cm.

404. Ox-goad with a spiral socket. For comparable examples see *Lydney*, p. 92, fig. 23, 189, *Woodyates*, p. 137, pl. CLXXXIII, 17, *Rotherley*, p. 137, pl. CV, 12, etc. Chalk quarry, Pit V, over L 5, Section NN–OO (fig. 48). 2.9 cm.

405. Ferrule binding. Cobbled surface to east of Building D. 2.3 cm.

406. Knife. The edge and the back are straight and parallel with the rod-like handle continuing the line of the back. The tang ends with a spiral. Similar knives exist unpublished in the collections from Margidunum (University of Nottingham Museum), Silchester (Reading Museum), Caerwent (Newport Museum), and Caistor-by-Norwich (Norwich Museum). Upper filling of chalk quarry, Pit V, L 3, Section NN–OO (fig. 48). 11.1 cm.

407. Knife. The tang continues the line of the back; the edge is straight but the back curves down to meet it at the tip. This is the commonest form of all Romano-British knives, and many examples could be quoted including those from Woodcuts (*Woodcuts*, pl. XXIII, 9), Bokerly Dyke (*Bokerly Dyke*, pp. 107–8, pl. CLXXVI, 12), and in some numbers from Silchester (Reading Museum), Caerwent (Newport Museum) and Caistor-by-Norwich (Norwich Museum). West of Building A. L 7, Section U–V (fig. 37). 14.4 cm.

408. Knife. The edge and part of the back are straight and parallel, with the back curving down to form the tip. There is a slight groove just below the back. It may be compared with examples from Newstead (*Newstead*, p. 282, pl. LX, 14), the Lockleys Villa (*Antiq. J.*, XVIII (1938), 355, fig. 3.1) and an unpublished example from Caistor-by-Norwich (Norwich Castle Museum). Filling of chalk quarry, Pit U, L 3, Section PP–QQ (fig. 47). 14.6 cm.

409. Knife of the same type as no. 407 above. Found during trial trenching in Easter 1963. Equates with L 4, Section H–I (fig. 40). 16.3 cm.

410. Knife. The curve of the back begins almost at the junction with the tang. Compare, for example, *Hod Hill*, p. 14, pl. VIII, G 60, and *Woodcuts*, p. 71, pl. XXIII, 2. Chalk floor associated with Room 35. 12.5 cm.

411. Knife. The blade is probably much shortened by repeated whetting; originally the back and edge were more or less parallel. Fourth-century destruction level to south of Building A. 12.3 cm.

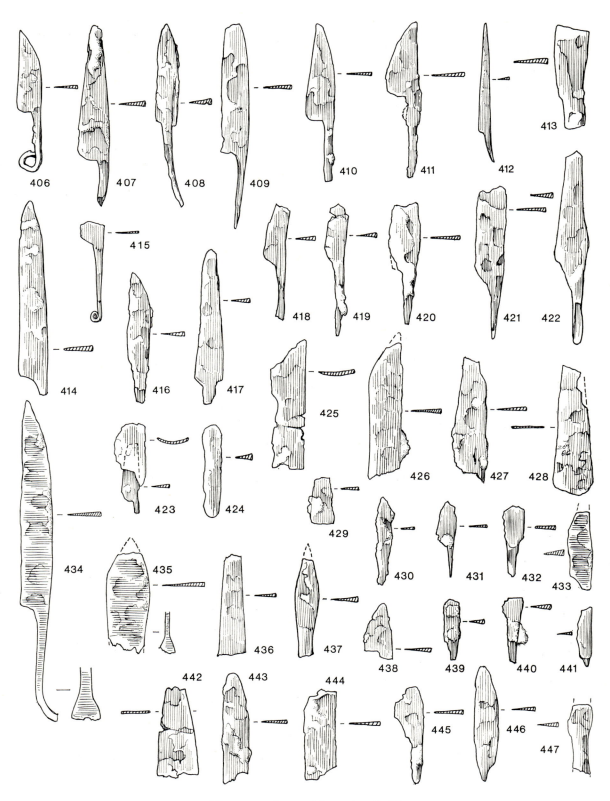

FIG. 72.   Iron objects (scale ⅓)

412. Knife or blade from a pair of shears. The back is straight while the edge runs to meet it in a sharp point. The tang continues the line of the back. A pair of shears with similarly shaped blades is in the Caerwent Collection in Newport Museum. Unstratified. From ploughsoil. 11 cm.

413. Fragment of a knife. Destruction level over Building E. 8.3 cm.

414. Knife. The edge and the back are almost parallel. It is basically similar to no. 407 above. Upper filling of chalk quarry, Pit U, L 3, Section PP–QQ (fig. 47). 15.5 cm.

415. Fragment of the blade and tang of a knife. The tang ends with a spiral. Filling of bathing pool. L 7, Section F–G (fig. 38). 8 cm.

416. Knife. The edge and part of the back are parallel except where the back curved down to form the tip. East of Building A. In black earth and cobbles above L 10. Section S–T (fig. 6). 10.4 cm.

417. Knife. The form of the blade has probably been deformed by whetting. Destruction level over north-east corner of Building C. 12.3 cm.

418. Fragment of tanged knife. East of Building A, L 12, Section S–T (fig. 6). 9.3 cm.

419. Fragment of tanged knife. Inner courtyard surface, Building A. 10.5 cm.

420. Fragment of tanged knife. Rubble filling of Room 35, L, 2, Section U–V (fig. 37). 9.6 cm.

421. Fragment of tanged knife. Destruction level of baths. 12.1 cm.

422. Fragment of tanged knife. Unstratified. 15.5 cm.

423. Fragments of two tanged knife blades fused together. Filling of water leat, L 8, Section C–D–E (fig. 38). 7.3 cm.

424. Fragment of knife blade. Upper filling of Pit L beneath Building D, L 17, Section II–JJ–KK (fig. 33). 7.5 cm.

425. Fragment of knife blade. Destruction rubble east of Building A. 10.4 cm.

426. Fragment of knife blade. Pit N, Section II–JJ–KK (fig. 33). 11.2 cm.

427. Fragment of knife blade. From ploughsoil. 10.1 cm.

428. Fragment of knife blade. Chalk quarry, Pit U, L 3, Section PP–QQ (fig. 47). 10.6 cm.

429. Fragment of knife blade. Destruction level over west wing of Building A. 3.7 cm.

430. Fragment of knife blade. Destruction rubble east of Building A. 7 cm.

431. Fragment of knife blade. Destruction rubble south of Building D. 6 cm.

432. Fragment of knife. Destruction rubble over inner courtyard. 5.7 cm.

433. Fragment of knife. Filling of well, L 13, Section X–Y (fig. 17). 6.3 cm.

434. Blade from a pair of shears. The end of the arm is bent and broken at the point where it widens into the spring. Here there are the remains of a hole. It may be compared with shears from Camulodunum (*Camulodunum*, p. 343, pl. cv, 7) and Blackburn Mill (*Blackburn Mill*, p. 45, fig. 12, B 29). Filling of well, L 13, Section X–Y (fig. 17). 25.7 cm.

435. Fragment of a wide bladed knife. A complete example of such a knife comes from Richborough (*Richborough*, IV, 154, pl. LX, 330) with a similar stop-ridge between the tang and blade, and another example is in the Caistor-by-Norwich Collection (Norwich Castle Museum). Gravel filling of leat, L 8, Section C–D–E (fig. 38). 8 cm.

436. Fragment of a knife. Probably modern; from ploughsoil. 8 cm.

437. Fragment of a knife. Destruction rubble Room 20, L 3, Section L–M (fig. 6). 7.9 cm.

438. Fragment of a knife. Gravel filling of leat, L 8, Section C–D–E (fig. 38). 4.5 cm.

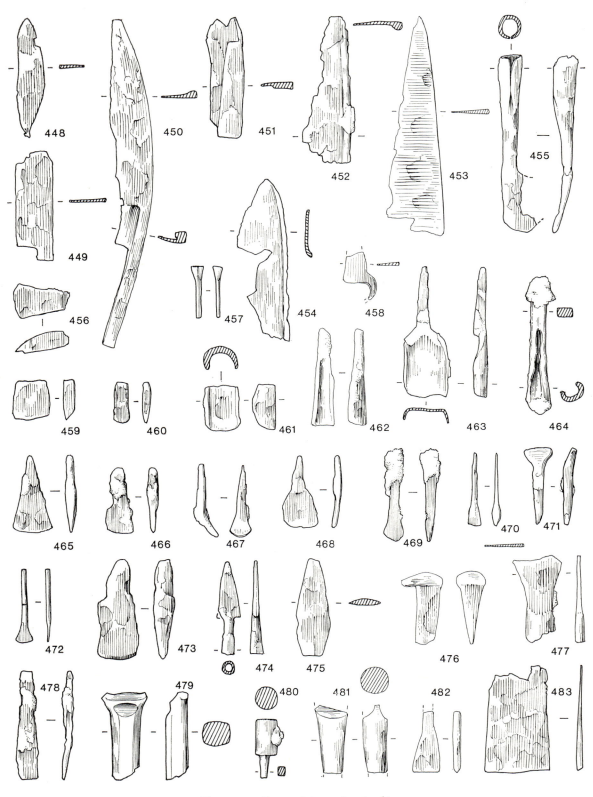

FIG. 73.   Iron objects (scale $\frac{1}{3}$)

439. Fragment of a knife, Filling of Room 35, L 2, Section U–V (fig. 37). 4.8 cm.

440. Fragment of a knife. Destruction rubble over western wing of Building A. 5.2 cm.

441. Fragment of a knife. Ploughsoil over Room 18. 4.2 cm.

442. Fragment of a knife. Occupation in Room 20, L 5, Section L–M (fig. 6). 7.2 cm.

443. Fragment of a knife. Filling of Pit M to north-west of Building D, L 14, Section II–JJ–KK (fig. 33). 8.8 cm.

444. Fragment of a knife. In chalk spread (upcast from well) to south of Building A. 7.2 cm.

445. Fragment of a knife. Destruction level south of inner courtyard. 7.7 cm.

446. Fragment of a knife. Filling of water leat, L 8, Section C–D–E (fig. 38). 9 cm.

447. Fragment of a knife. Filling of water leat, L 8, Section C–D–E (fig. 38). 5.5 cm.

448. Fragment of a knife. Destruction rubble south of Building A. 9.5 cm.

449. Fragment of a knife. Destruction rubble in Room 20, L 3, Section L–M (fig. 6). 8.7 cm.

450. Heavy knife or cleaver with an arched back and tang. There is a ridge on one side of the back of the blade. The edge of the blade was originally straight. Cleavers with a curved back and straight edge are known from Hod Hill (*Hod Hill*, p. 15, pl. VIII, G 91), and Kingsholm (*Kingsholm*, pl. XIII, 2), but they lack the strengthening ridge on the blade. Possibly modern. Unstratified. Said to have been found during road works in 1962. 30.4 cm.

451. Fragment of a sickle blade. Filling of bathing pool, L 7, Section F–G (fig. 38). 9.6 cm.

452. Fragment of a knife or a scythe blade. From Ditch I, beneath Building A, L 12, Section N–O (fig. 6). 11.7 cm.

453. Triangular blade from a knife or pair of shears. Possibly modern; from ploughsoil. 17.7 cm.

454. Fragment of knife blade. Beneath tessellated floor (L 4) in Room 28. Section U–V (fig. 37). 13 cm.

455. Socket and part of the blade of a small reaping or pruning hook. Small tools of this general type, though normally with the cutting edge beginning close to the tang, are quite common on Romano-British sites, including Rotherley (*Rotherley*, p. 138, pl. CVI, 2), the Walbrook in London (British Museum), and in some numbers from Caerwent (Newport Museum). Examples with very angular blades come from Hod Hill (*Hod Hill*, p. 15, pl. VIII, G 90) and Newstead (National Museum, Edinburgh). Possibly modern. Unstratified. 14.2 cm.

456. Fragment of unknown function. Destruction rubble east of Building A. 4.5 cm.

457. Stem with a circular cross section ending in a triangular plate, possibly the eraser of a stylus. Destruction rubble over west wing of Building A. 4.1 cm.

458. Fragment of unknown function. Gravel in water leat, L 8, Section C–D–E (fig. 38). 3.8 cm.

459. Fragment of a chisel blade (?). In eaves drip alongside Period 3 western corridor, Building A, L 8, Section U–V (fig. 37). 3.2 cm.

460. Fragment of a chisel blade (?). Period 1 water leat to south of bathing pool. 3.3 cm.

461. Fragment of a socket. Silt in Ditch I beneath Building A, L 12, Section N–O (fig. 6). 3.7 cm.

462. Fragment of a socket. Ditch I beneath Building A, L 12, Section N–O (fig. 6). 7.9 cm.

463. Tanged gouge-like blade. The blade is similar to that on a very large auger from the Brampton hoard (*Brampton*, p. 16, no. 12), but if the short stem is a tang it is difficult to see it as part of

an auger. On the other hand it may originally have been a stem which has been broken and corroded into its present form. In chalk upcast from well to south of Building A.   10.5 cm.

464.   Fragment of a socketed tool. Chalk quarry, Pit U, L 3, Section PP–QQ (fig. 47).   11 cm.

465.   Triangular blade tapering into a short tang. The tang is probably broken. It may have been intended for mounting in a block with the blade pointing upwards as are some mosaicists' tools used for cutting tesserae from prepared sticks. Destruction rubble in Building D, L 4, Section II–JJ–KK (fig. 33).   6.2 cm.

466.   Fragment of blade.   Destruction material to south of Building A.   5.3 cm.

467.   Fragment of blade (?). Occupation in Building E.   6 cm.

468.   Triangular blade tapering into a short tang. Compare no. 465 above and no. 471 below. Cobbled surface of northern courtyard.   5.9 cm.

469.   Fragment of a small chisel blade, probably from a firmer or paring chisel. Chalk quarry, Pit U, L 3, Section PP–QQ (fig. 47).   7.4 cm.

470.   Fragment of an awl (?). Ploughsoil.   5.9 cm.

471.   Triangular blade tapering into a short tang. Compare nos. 465 and 468 above. This example was almost certainly intended to be mounted in a block. Such tools can be used in a variety of trades including mosaic and metal working. Chalk quarry, Pit U, L 3, Section PP–QQ (fig. 47).   6 cm.

472.   Eraser and stem of a stylus. Compare with no. 457 above. Occupation level in Room 20, L 5, Section L–M (fig. 6).   5.8 cm.

473.   Fragment of bladed tool. Ploughsoil.   8 cm.

474.   Socketed arrowhead. This form of arrowhead with a triangular blade and well formed socket, is not common on Roman sites, though a few are known including some from Hod Hill (*Hod Hill*, p. 6, pl. VI, B 106). Filling of chalk quarry Pit Y, L 14, Section GG–HH (fig. 50).   8.4 cm.

475.   Fragment of a spear blade. It may be compared with those from Hod Hill (*Hod Hill*, pl. V, B 9–17), etc. Ploughsoil.   7.7 cm.

476.   Wedge or smith's set. Such tools are used for cutting metal or splitting wood or even stone. It may be compared with similar tools from Maiden Castle (*Maiden Castle*, p. 284, fig. 94, 7), and with unpublished examples from Silchester (Reading Museum) and the Chedworth Villa (Site Museum), etc. Gravel filling of water leat, L 8, Section C–D–E (fig. 38).   5.7 cm.

477.   Fragment of bladed tool. Gravel filling of water leat, L 8, Section C–D–E (fig. 38).   7 cm.

478.   Fragment of blade. Chalk quarry, Pit U, L 3, Section PP–QQ (fig. 47).   8.5 cm.

479.   Fragment of bar which widens at one end. Both the widening and the notch just before it are probably the result of cutting it with a chisel. Destruction rubble, Room 20, L 3, Section L–M (fig. 6).   7 cm.

480.   Short cylinder with a small, and probably broken, rod projecting at one end. It may be a small anvil intended for fine metalwork and used mounted in a wooden block. A similar object, but with a rectangular head, comes from Woodcuts (*Woodcuts*, pl. XXVIII, 12). From Roman turf level in outer courtyard.   4.7 cm.

481.   Fragment of tapering rod which has been notched at one end when it was cut. Inner courtyard surface.   5.1 cm.

482.   Fragmentary blade comparable with nos. 465, 468, and 471 above. Gravel at bottom of leat. L 8, Section C–D–E (fig. 38).   4.8 cm.

483. Fragment of strip. Destruction rubble south of Room 20. 8.4 cm.

484–504. Nails. The common forms of Romano-British nails have been classified by H. Cleere on two occasions when publishing the ironwork from the Brading (I.o.W.) Villa (*Brading Villa*) and the great hoard, mainly of nails, from Inchtuthil (*Inchtuthil*). Both classifications, however, include classes composed of rare types, one indeed so rare that it appears to be unique to Inchtuthil (Type F) and even there is represented by only 28 specimens out of a total of over 900,000 nails. For most purposes a more general classification is probably desirable. The vast majority of Romano-British nails are of one of two main types:

I: with a square-sectioned, tapering stem, the larger specimens having a round conical or pyramidal head, often flattened by hammering, the smaller examples having an almost flat head.

II: with a square-sectioned tapering stem and a triangular head no thicker than the stem. The top of the head is often rounded by hammering.

Nails of both types cover a wide and almost continuous range of lengths between one and fourteen inches (2.5 and 30 cm.). In classifying the nails from Inchtuthil, Cleere was able to take into consideration such factors as the thickness of the head, the section of the shank 0.5 inches below the head, and the weight in grammes. Unfortunately the majority of nails are not in the pristine condition of the best of the Inchtuthil nails and such detailed measurements are not meaningful with corroded specimens. Upon the whole a simple measurement of the length of the nail is sufficient, for this was clearly the controlling factor in the choice of the nail in Roman times as it is today, and the other factors reflect this main measurement. Cleere used his criteria to divide the nails into groups of varying lengths but until more work has been done on other large groups it is probably safer to avoid defining groups in this way and merely use the class (i.e. I or II) followed by the length of the nail. Our Class II nails were absent from Inchtuthil but a consideration of material from other sites indicates that they show as great a variation in length as do Class I nails, and are only slightly less common.

484. Tack with a domed head and short stem. Probably for upholstery. It can be compared with examples from the Baydon Villa, Berks. (*Devizes*, p. 194, pl. LXII, 6), and Woodcuts (*Woodcuts*, p. 93, pl. XXX, 1). Destruction rubble in Building D, L 4, Section II–JJ–KK (fig. 33). Originally 2.4 cm. long.

485. Small nail of Type I with an almost flat head. It may be compared with Cleere's Brading Type IIId (*Brading*, p. 58, fig. 3e) and Inchtuthil Group E (*Inchtuthil*, p. 957, fig. 1, second from right). Filling of Ditch I. 2.2 cm.

486. Nail with a very small flat head and round sectioned stem. Such nails are rare from Roman Britain; normally the stem is square sectioned. Filling of bathing pool, L 7, Section C–D–E (fig. 38). 4.2 cm.

487. L-headed nail with a square sectioned stem. A relatively rare form of nail; compare, for example, *Brading*, p. 57, fig. 2d and *Rotherley*, pp. 126–7, pl. CI, 13. Destruction rubble over western wing of Building A. 4.3 cm.

488. L-headed nail comparable with the preceding. Destruction rubble to south of Room 20. 5.8 cm.

489. Type I nail with an almost flat head. It is comparable with Cleere's Brading Type IIIc/d (*Brading*, fig. 3, c and d) and Inchtuthil Types D/E (*Inchtuthil*, p. 957, fig. 1, fourth from left and second from right). Destruction rubble in Room 20, L 3, Section L–M (fig. 6). 7 cm.

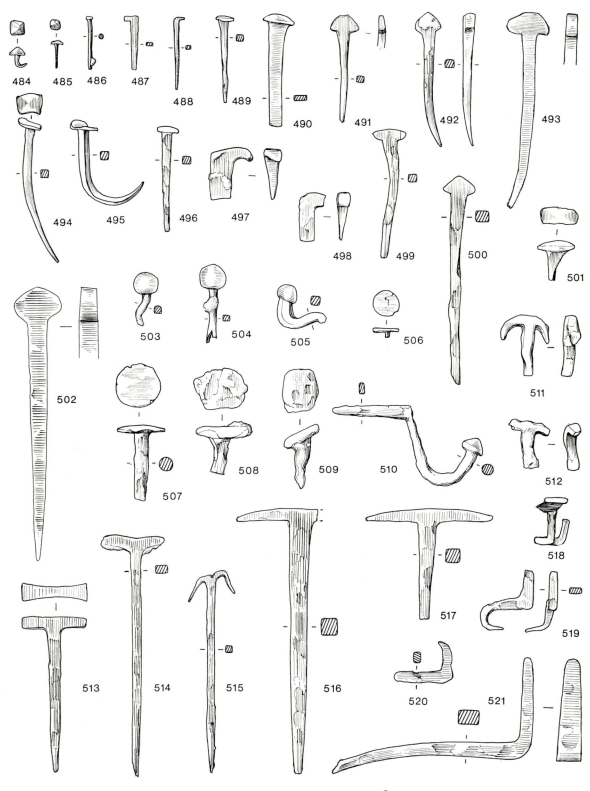

FIG. 74.   Iron objects (scale ⅓)

490. Nail with a domed head and wide, thin stem. Probably a variant on the common square-sectioned forms. Destruction rubble in Room 20, L 3, Section L–M (fig. 6). 9 cm.

491. Nail of Type II with a flat triangular head, slightly flattened by hammering. This is Cleere's Brading Type II (*Brading*, p. 57, fig. 2 *a, b, c*). Compare also *Woodcuts*, p. 93, pl. xxx, 4, 22 and *Bokerly Dyke*, p. 126, pl. CLXXXI, 1 and 2. The advantage of this form of head is that it can be driven right into the wood to make it almost invisible. Filling of water leat, L 5, Section C–D–E (fig. 38). 8.6 cm.

492. Type II nail, comparable with no. 491 above. Destruction rubble south of Building A. 10.9 cm.

493. Type II nail, comparable with no. 491 above. Ploughsoil. 15.7 cm.

494. Type I nail. On cobbled floor, to east, and associated with, Building C. 11.9 cm.

495. Type I nail. Destruction rubble in Room 20, L 3, Section L–M (fig. 6). Originally 10.3 cm.

496. Type I nail. Destruction rubble in Room 20, L 3, Section L–M (fig. 6). 8.4 cm.

497. Head of a large L-shaped nail, cf. no. 487 above. East of Building A. L 10, Section S–T (fig. 6). 4 cm.

498. Head of a large L-shaped nail, cf. no. 487 above. On clay floor of Period 3 corridor, east of Room 20. 4 cm.

499. Nail of Type II; the head is flattened by hammering. Occupation level in Room 20, L 5, Section L–M (fig. 6). 10.2 cm.

500. Type II nail. Filling of bathing pool, L 7, Section F–G (fig. 38). 16.6 cm.

501. Nail head, probably of Type I, though it may be from a small T-staple of the type of no. 512 below. Filling of gully skirting Room 8. 3.2 cm.

502. Large nail of Type II. Rubble filling Period 1 bath building. 22 cm.

503. Globular-headed tack, probably an unusual variant of no. 484 above. For a similar tack, see *Woodcuts*, pl. xxx, 7. Clay floor of Period 3 corridor, east of Room 20. 4.4 cm.

504. Globular-headed tack. Destruction level in Room 35, L 3, Section U–V (fig. 37). 7.4 cm.

505. Tip of hook (?). The relative proportions of the terminal knob and stem suggest that it is not a distorted tack. For a complete hook with a terminal knob see no. 510 below. Cobbled surface to east of Building A. Layer over L 10, Section S–T (fig. 6). 4.7 cm.

506. Nail or tack head. The size of the head when compared with the stem suggests that it is from a tack of the type found at Rotherley (*Rotherley*, p. 126, pl. CI, 16), Woodcuts (*Woodcuts*, p. 94, pl. xxx, 11), Newstead (*Newstead*, p. 289, pl. LXVII, 19), etc. From beneath feature 16 to north of bathing pool (fig. 39). Width 2.1 cm.

507. Head of Type I nail. Filling of well, L 11, Section X–Y (fig. 17). 6.1 cm.

508. Head of Type I nail. Cobbled surface associated with Period 7 stockade over eastern corridor of Building C. 4 cm.

509. Head of Type I nail. Filling of Period 1 water leat to north of bathing pool, L 20, Section H–I (fig. 40). 5.2 cm.

510. U-shaped wall-hook with terminal knob. Simple spiked wall-hooks are quite common and examples come from Verulamium (Verulamium Museum), Dorchester, Oxon. (Ashmolean Museum), Silchester (Reading Museum) and Caerwent (Newport Museum). An example with a similar terminal knob comes from the Brampton hoard (*Brampton*, p. 30, no. 40). Destruction rubble south of Building A. 12.5 cm.

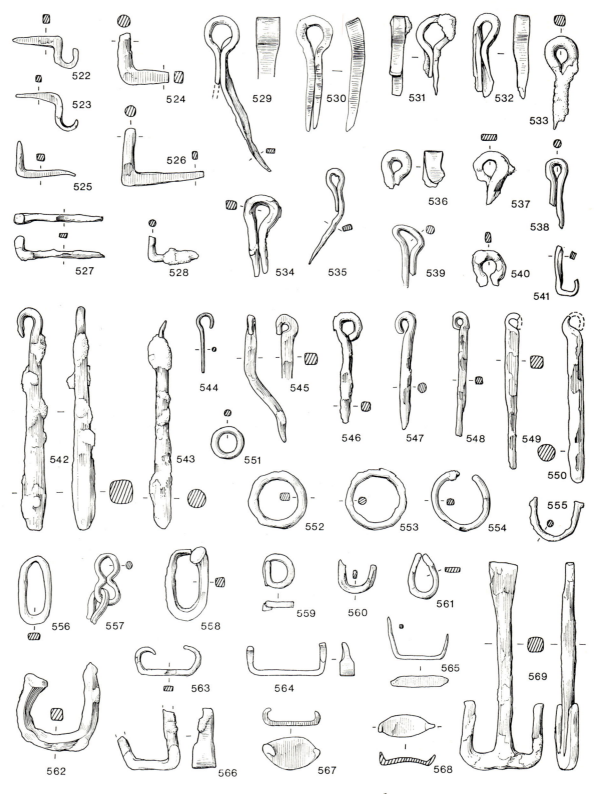

FIG. 75. Iron objects (scale ⅓)

511–17.   T-staples. These have a cross-bar set at the head of a tapering or chisel-edged stem. The exact form of the head varies as does the length of the stem. Many were used to hold tiles and box-flue tiles in place, while others, such as no. 511, appear to have been driven though pieces of wood with the arms of the head curved over. They are common finds, and the following examples with small heads may be quoted: *Brading*, p. 58, fig. 3*f*; *Rotherley*, p. 133, pl. CIV, 11; *Newstead*, p. 289, pl. LXVII, 4, etc.; for examples with larger heads see *Brading*, p. 58, fig. 3*g*; *Woodcuts*, p. 93, pl. XXX, 2; *Newstead*, p. 289, pl. LXVII, 1, etc.

511.   Head and part of the stem of a T-staple. The arms are curved and probably held a semi-circular bar. In filling of hypocaust channel, Room 35. Section U–V (fig. 37).   5.1 cm.

512.   Head and part of the stem of a T-staple. Filling of water leat. L 8, Section C–D–E (fig. 38).   4.4 cm.

513.   T-staple with well-formed arms. Occupation level in Room 20, L 5, Section L–M (fig. 6).   12.4 cm.

514.   T-staple. Destruction rubble south of Room 13.   19 cm.

515.   T-staple. Upper filling of bathing pool, L 4, Section F–G (fig. 38).   16 cm.

516.   T-staple lacking one arm. Rubble filling, Period 1 bath-house.   21.1 cm.

517.   Head and part of the stem of a T-staple. Rubble filling, Period 1 bath-house.   8.8 cm.

518.   Type I nail which has been driven through a wooden plank and then hammered flat. Filling of water gully west of Room 20.   3.8 cm.

519.   Distorted U-shaped wall hook of the general type of no. 510 above. Destruction rubble in Building D, L 4, Section II–JJ–KK (fig. 33).   5.9 cm.

520.   Small L-shaped wall-hook. Destruction rubble in Building D, L 4, Section II–JJ–KK (fig. 33).   5 cm.

521.   L-shaped wall-hook with the longer arm broken. It can be compared with examples from the Brampton hoard (*Brampton*, p. 31, no. 41), Newstead (National Museum, Edinburgh), etc. Ploughsoil.   18.2 cm.

522.   U-shaped wall-hook. Compare no. 510 (fig. 74). Destruction rubble over Building A.   5.5 cm.

523.   U-shaped wall hook. Destruction rubble south of Building A.   5.5 cm.

524.   L-shaped hinge staple with the longer arm broken. Such staples are characterized by the short arm having a round cross-section. They carried a U-shaped hinge attached to the door itself. Examples are common: see, for instance, *Woodcuts*, p. 87, pl. XXVIII, 20; *Carlingwark Loch*, p. 37, fig. 9, C 52, etc. Upper filling of chalk quarry, Pit U, L 3, Section PP–QQ (fig. 47).   5.3 cm.

525.   L-shaped hinge staple. Destruction rubble over Room 8.   4.8 cm.

526.   L-shaped hinge staple. On natural clay to west of Building A.   6.5 cm.

527.   L-shaped hinge staple. Destruction rubble south of Building A.   7 cm.

528.   L-shaped hinge staple. Rubble over cobbled surface to south of Building D.   4 cm.

529–41.   Split spiked-loops. In use they were driven into wood with the head remaining above the surface. If the ends of the arms projected on the other side of the wood they were usually hammered flat. They are very common; for published examples see *Blackburn Mill*, p. 45, fig. 12, B 24; *Carlingwark Loch*, p. 38, fig. 10, C 61; *Newstead*, p. 289, pl. LXVII, 11; *Woodcuts*, p. 85, pl. XXVIII, 1, etc.

529.   Split spiked loop. Filling of well, L 12, Section X–Y (fig. 17).   13 cm.

N

530.	Split spiked-loop. Chalk quarry, Pit D, L 9, Section RR–SS (fig. 50). 9.3 cm.

531.	Head of split spiked-loop. Chalk quarry, Pit U, L 3, Section PP–QQ (fig. 47). 6.4 cm.

532.	Head of split spiked-loop. Destruction rubble in Building D, L 3, Section II–JJ–KK (fig. 33). 6.7 cm.

533.	Head of split spiked-loop. Destruction rubble of Building C. 7.5 cm.

534.	Split spiked-loop. Level predating Building B, L 8, Section S–R (fig. 6). 6.5 cm.

535.	Split spiked-loop. Occupation material in Building E. 8 cm.

536.	Head of split spiked-loop. Occupation material in Building E. 3.2 cm.

537.	Head of split spiked-loop. Gravel filling of water leat, L 8, Section C–D–E (fig. 38). 4.2 cm.

538.	Head of split spiked-loop. Chalk quarry, Pit U, L 3, Section PP–QQ (fig. 47). 5.6 cm.

539.	Head of split spiked-loop. Gravel filling of water leat, L 8, Section C–D–E (fig. 38). 5 cm.

540.	Head of split spiked-loop. Clay bank of water leat, L 12, Section C–D–E (fig. 38). 3 cm.

541.	Fragment, probably the end of one arm of a split spiked-loop. Gravel filling of water leat. L 8, Section C–D–E (fig. 38). 4 cm.

542.	Rod ending in a small hook. Filling of water leat, L 5, Section C–D–E (fig. 38). 17.9 cm.

543.	Rod tapering at one end where it may originally have ended in a hook. Chalk quarry, Pit U, L 3, Section PP–QQ (fig. 47). 16.8 cm.

544.	Small hook. Possibly modern. Ploughsoil. 4.8 cm.

545.	Square sectioned rod tapering at its ends, one of which is turned over to form an eye. Probably intended as a ring-headed pin of the type of no. 546 following, or less probably the damaged handle of a latch-lifter of the type seen in nos. 394, 395, etc. (fig. 71). Clay build-up for floors in Room 23. 10.6 cm.

546.	Ring-headed pin. The function of these pins is uncertain but they may have been driven into wood and originally have held rings. It may be compared with examples from Woodcuts (*Woodcuts*, p. 90, pl. XXIX, 15) and another from the same site (pl. XXVII, 3) which although very small still retains a ring through the loop, and a similar example from Silchester (Reading Museum). Destruction rubble over west wing of Building A. 8.8 cm.

547.	Ring-headed pin. Chalk quarry, Pit X, Layer equates with L 10, Section RR–SS (fig. 50). 9.4 cm.

548.	Ring-headed pin. Below cobbled surface, south of Room 20. 10 cm.

549.	Ring-headed pin, or possibly the handle of a latch-lifter of the type seen in nos. 394 and 395 above, or the stem of a tumbler-lock lift-key of the type seen in no. 388 above. Upper filling of bathing pool, L 4, Section F–G (fig. 36). 12.6 cm.

550.	Fragment probably from the handle of a latch-lifter or tumbler-lock lift-key. Found during cable-laying over eastern side of bathing pool. 13.8 cm.

551.	Small ring. Clay floor of Period 3, Room 20. 2.7 cm.

552.	Ring with signs of wear on one side. Such rings could have many functions including the side rings of bridle bits. Filling of bathing pool, L 5, Section C–D–E (fig. 38). 4.6 cm.

553.	Rings with signs of wear on one side. Filling of well, L 13, Section X–Y (fig. 17). 4.9 cm.

554.	Broken ring. Cobbled surface, east of Building C. 5 cm.

555.	Fragment, probably from a broken ring. Destruction rubble south of Building A. 4.1 cm.

556. Oval link, probably from a chain. For the type, see for example *Camulodunum*, p. 383, pl. CV, 33, *Woodcuts*, p. 97, pl. XXXI, 1, etc. Possibly modern. From ploughsoil. 5.4 cm.

557. Figure-of-eight link from a chain with a fragment of another. For such chains see *Camulodunum*, p. 343, pl. CV, 14 and *Brampton*, p. 20, no. 18. Ditch I, beneath Building A. 5.7 cm.

558. Type I nail bent into a ferrule binding (?). For similar simple bindings see *Woodcuts*, p. 90, pl. XXIX, 20, and *Rotherley*, pl. CV.9. Period 3. Inner courtyard surface. 6 cm.

559. Simple ferrule binding (?). Occupation deposit in Room 35. Section U–V (fig. 37). 2.7 cm.

560. Fragment of ring or binding. Destruction rubble south of Building A. 3 cm.

561. Bent rod, possibly a simple binding. Occupation level in Kitchen Area, Building C. 3.7 cm.

562. Type I nail, now bent. Ploughsoil. 6.5 cm. wide.

563. Joiner's dog used for linking two pieces of wood; compare *Woodyates*, p. 139, pl. CLXXXIV, 7; *Bokerly Dyke*, pl. CLXXVI, 9, etc. Ditch I, beneath inner courtyard. 5.3 cm.

564. Joiner's dog comparable with the preceding. Ploughsoil. 6.3 cm.

565. Joiner's dog; compare *Rotherley*, p. 136, pl. CV.6 and *Woodcuts*, p. 86, pl. XXVIII, 14. Destruction rubble over bath-house. 5 cm.

566. Joiner's dog. Chalk quarry, Pit U, L 3, Section PP–QQ (fig. 47). 5 cm.

567. Shoe cleat. For similar examples see *Rotherley*, p. 190, fig. A; *Bokerly Dyke*, p. 128, pl. CLXXIV, 30; *Maiden Castle*, p. 284, fig. 94, 3, etc. Gravel filling of water leat, L 8, Section C–D–E (fig. 38). 4.7 cm.

568. Shoe cleat. Filling of bathing pool, L 10, Section F–G (fig. 38). 4.5 cm.

569. T-shaped lift key. Originally the shank probably ended with a loop. Compare *Brampton*, p. 34, no. 47; *London*, p. 73, pl. XXXA, 1; *Newstead*, p. 307, pl. LXXVIII, 4, etc. Fourth-century destruction rubble to south of Building A. 16.6 cm.

570. Hipposandal heel. Unfortunately one cannot tell the type of hipposandal from the heel alone. Such heels are common finds and there are many examples in the Silchester Collection in Reading Museum, for example, but they are rarely published. It can, however, be compared with an example in the Blackburn Mill hoard (*Blackburn Mill*, p. 45, fig. 12, B 20). Chalk quarry, Pit U, L 3, Section PP–QQ (fig. 47). 9.5 cm.

571. Hipposandal heel. Occupation material in Building D, L 5, Section II–JJ–KK (fig. 33). 8.8 cm.

572. Fragment of the wing and sole of an hipposandal. Filling of well, L 5, Section X–Y (fig. 17). 7 cm.

573. Fragment of binding. This piece and many of those listed below, could have so many functions that speculation is pointless and the quotation of parallels meaningless. From Period 1 occupation beneath Room 26. 6.8 cm.

574. Fragment of horseshoe with two nail holes. Very few Romano-British horseshoes are known from stratified contexts; two came from Camulodunum (*Camulodunum*, p. 342, fig. 64.3), both apparently dating from shortly before the Roman conquest, and a large and late group from Maiden Castle (*Maiden Castle*, p. 291, pl. XXXB). Both wavy and smooth outlined shoes occur in Roman Britain. This example may be a modern intrusion. Rubble to south of Room 20. 6.8 cm.

575. Fragment of horseshoe. Water leat, L 5, Section C–D–E (fig. 38). 5 cm.

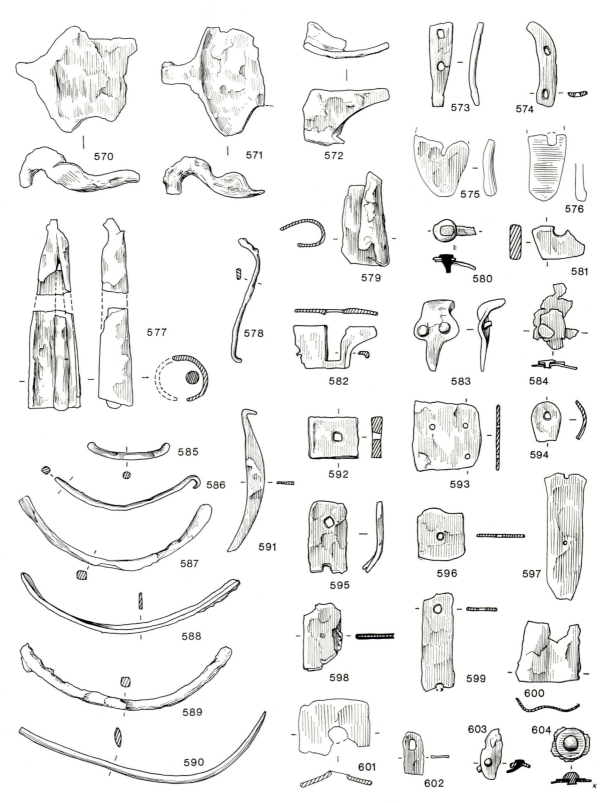

FIG. 76. Iron objects (scale ⅓)

576. Fragment of horseshoe. Filling in Ditch 2, to south of Building B.   5.3 cm.

577. Damaged ferrule which was held in place by a nail or spike jammed into the socket. Such ferrules are quite common; compare, for example, *Rotherley*, p. 138, pl. CVI, 10; *Woodcuts*, p. 90, pl. XXIX, 19; *Newstead*, p. 280, pl. LVIII, 6, etc. Occupational material in Room 25.   15.2 cm.

578. Fragment of strip. Occupation in Building D, L 5, Section II–JJ–KK (fig. 33).   10 cm.

579. Fragment of strip, possibly part of a ferrule or binding. Occupation in Kitchen Area, Building C.   7.5 cm.

580. Two fragments of strip held together by a nail; possibly part of a binding. Clay make-up for floor, Room 21.   3.5 cm.

581. Fragment. Occupation level in Building E.   4.3 cm.

582. Fragment with a rectangular slot cut into one edge. Destruction rubble in western corridor of Building B.   6.5 cm.

583. Fragment with a short tang and two rivets through it. Probably part of the handle of a composite tool such as a scraper, curry-comb or something similar. Turf level in outer courtyard associated with Building C.   5.7 cm.

584. Two fragments of plate riveted together. Ancient turf level over Building C. Associated with Period 5.   5.2 cm.

585. Small curving bar. Rubble over Building D, L 3, Section II–JJ–KK (fig. 33).   6.5 cm.

586. Curving bar with a hook at one end, possibly part of a small bucket handle; compare *Newstead*, p. 310, pl. LXIX, 4; *Brampton*, p. 27, no. 34, etc. Rubble over east wall of Building D, L 3, Section II–JJ–KK (fig. 33).   11.6 cm.

587. Curving bar, possibly part of a bucket handle. Destruction rubble over Room 26.   15.3 cm.

588. Fragment of curving strip, possibly part of a bucket binding; compare *Newstead*, p. 310, pl. LXIX, 4; *Woodcuts*, p. 85, pl. XXVIII, 4, 5, 6, and 673 below. Occupation level in Building D, L 5, Section II–JJ–KK (fig. 33).   17.4 cm.

589. Fragment of curving bar, possibly part of a bucket handle or latch-lifter. Secondary pit cut into Pit Y, L 10, Section GG–HH (fig. 50).   16.8 cm.

590. Curving strip. Destruction level south of Building A.   19.5 cm.

591. Semicircular fragment with a short tang at one end. Function uncertain. Chalk quarry, Pit U, L 3, Section PP–QQ (fig. 47).   11.5 cm.

592. End of a nailed strip or binding with one nail hole. Destruction level south of Building A.   4 cm.

593. Small plate with three nail holes. From clay spread covering Period 1 structure (Room 17) to east of Building A, L 12, Section S–T (fig. 6).   5.5 cm.

594. End of nailed strip or binding. Possibly modern, from ploughsoil.   3.2 cm.

595. Fragment of nailed strip or binding. Occupation in Room 20, L 5, Section L–M (fig. 6).   5.7 cm.

596. Fragment of nailed strip or binding. Occupation in Room 20, L 5, Section L–M (fig. 6).   4.2 cm.

597. Fragment of nailed strip of binding. From filling of well, L 11, Section X–Y (fig. 17).   10.1 cm.

598. Fragment of folded sheet binding. Late occupation over northern courtyard.   5.4 cm.

599. Fragment of nailed strip or binding. Associated with, and to south of, Building E.   7.8 cm.

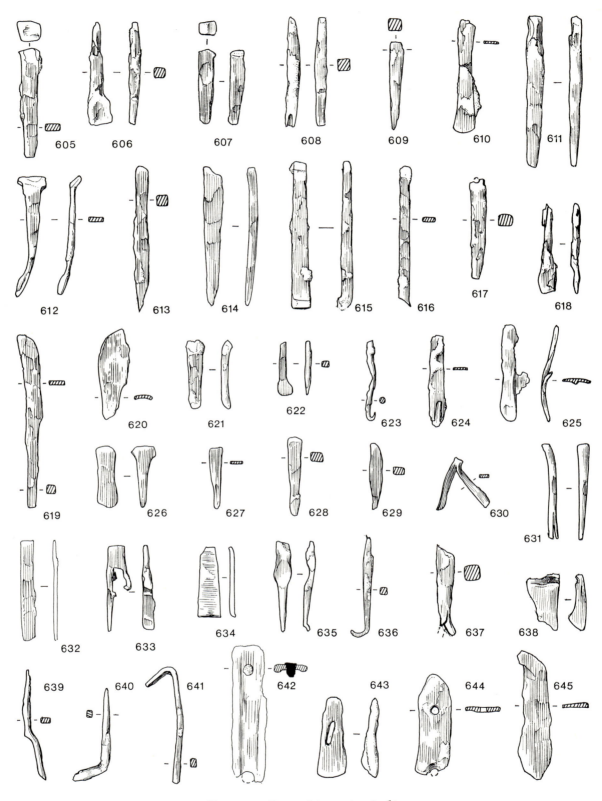

FIG. 77.　Iron objects (scale ⅓)

600. Fragment of strip. Filling of Period 1 water leat, L 23, Section H–I (fig. 40). 5.2 cm.

601. Fragment of nailed strip or binding, or a washer. Ditch 2, southern outer courtyard. 5.6 cm.

602. End of nailed strip or binding. Filling of water leat, L 8, Section C–D–E (fig. 38). 3.4 cm.

603. Fragment of strip with a nail through it. Period 1 occupation south of water cistern. 4 cm.

604. Fragment of strip with a washer held to it by a rivet. Destruction level over water cistern, pre-gatehouse. 3.2 cm.

605. Fragment of bar, possibly a damaged metal worker's chisel or punch. The head appears to be battered by hammering. It may be compared with a well-made punch or drift from Newstead (*Newstead*, p. 285, pl. LXIII, 7), and with examples from the Blackburn Mill hoard (*Blackburn Mill*, p. 48, fig. 13, B 47) and Rotherley (*Rotherley*, p. 137, pl. CV, 16). Ploughsoil. 8.7 cm.

606. Fragment consisting of a tang which widens asymmetrically into a flat blade, now broken; possibly from a knife. In northern corridor, Building B, L 6, Section P–Q (fig. 6). 8.2 cm.

607. Small metal-worker's punch or chisel, the point being broken. Compare with 605 above. Cobbled floor to east of Building D. Over L 17, Section II–JJ–KK (fig. 33). 5.9 cm.

608. Fragment of bar with a small gouge at one end. Filling of well, L 12, Section X–Y (fig. 17). 8.7 cm.

609. Small metal-worker's punch. Compare with no. 605 above. In northern corridor, Building B, L 6, Section P–Q (fig. 6). 7 cm.

610. Thin blade possibly from a paring chisel. Chalk quarry, Pit U, L 3, Section PP–QQ (fig. 47). 9 cm.

611. Fragment of bar. Rubble filling Period 5 drain, east of Room 20, L 3, Section S–T (fig. 6). 12 cm.

612. Tang and part of the flange of a tool. Destruction level to west of Building A. 9.6 cm.

613. Fragment of bar. Occupational material over northern courtyard. 11.6 cm.

614. Fragment of bar. Destruction rubble over bath-house. 11 cm.

615. Fragment of bar. Destruction rubble south of Building A. 11.6 cm.

616. Fragment of bar. Cobbled surface to south of Building D. 11.1 cm.

617. Fragment of bar with rivet hole at wider end. Chalk quarry, Pit U, L 3, Section PP–QQ (fig. 47). 8 cm.

618. Fragment of blade and tang, possibly from a knife. Period 5 mortar floor in corridor east of Room 20. 7.1 cm.

619. Tanged blade, possibly the remains of a much whetted knife. Chalk quarry, Pit V, L 8, Section NN–OO (fig. 48). 13.9 cm.

620. Fragment of blade. Rubble over northern courtyard. 7.3 cm.

621. Fragment of bar. Ploughsoil. 5.4 cm.

622. Fragment of small tanged blade. Occupation in Room 20, L 5, Section L–M (fig. 6). 4.3 cm.

623. Small hook (?). It is possible that the upturn of the hook is unintentional. Occupation in Building D. 6.3 cm.

624. Fragment of strip. East of Building A, L 12, Section N–O (fig. 6). 7.3 cm.

625. Fragment of strip. Destruction rubble south of Building A. 7.7 cm.

626. Wedge-like fragment. In gully between Rooms 13 and 17. 4.9 cm.

627. Fragment of strip. Pit M, to west of Building E, L 6, Section LL–MM (fig. 33).   5 cm.

628. Metal-worker's punch (?) (cf. 605 above). Chalk and clay make-up for floor in Room 21. Equates with L 10, Section N–O (fig. 6).   6.3 cm.

629. Fragment. Occupation in Room 20, L 5, Section L–M (fig. 6).   5.3 cm.

630. Fragment. Filling of bathing pool, L 5, Section F–G (fig. 38).   4.8 cm.

631. Small tapering rod dividing into arms at its narrower end. It could be a small claw for removing nails, but it seems almost excessively slight for such a function, although a claw no longer than this is in the Silchester Collection in Reading Museum. Filling of bathing pool, L 10, Section F–G (fig. 38).   7.7 cm.

632. Fragment of strip. Gravel filling in water leat, L 8, Section C–D–E (fig. 38).   7.9 cm.

633. Fragment with a rectangular hole through the centre. Ploughsoil.   6.7 cm.

634. Fragment of strip. Northern corridor, Building B, L 6, Section P–Q (fig. 6).   5.5 cm.

635. Tanged fragment. Ditch I, beneath Building A.   7 cm.

636. Small hook. Black silt in verandah west of Room 35. Section U–V (fig. 37).   7.11 cm.

637. Fragment of bar which appears originally to have divided at its end. East of Building A. Over L 10, Section S–T (fig. 6).   7.3 cm.

638. Fragment. Destruction rubble to east of Building A.   4.5 cm.

639. Fragment of rod. Chalk quarry, Pit U, Section PP–QQ (fig. 47).   9 cm.

640. L-shaped rod, possibly an L-shaped wall-hook (cf. nos. 520 and 521). Occupation in Room 20, L 5, Section L–M (fig. 6).   7.8 cm.

641. Fragment of rod. Filling of water leat, L 5, Section C–D–E (fig. 38).   9.3 cm.

642. Fragment of strip with its edges thickened and a rivet through one end; there appears to be the remains of a second rivet hole at the other end. Destruction rubble south of Building A.   11 cm.

643. Fragment with a rectangular hole through it. Clay spread over Period 1 occupation east of Building A, L 12, Section S–T (fig. 6).   6.4 cm.

644. Fragment of strip with two nail holes through it. Occupation in Room 20, L 5, Section L–M (fig. 6).   8 cm.

645. Fragment of strip. Rubble in Room 20, L 3, Section L–M (fig. 6).   10.3 cm.

646. Fragment of shaped strip. Gravel surface to south of west wing of Building A.   4.6 cm.

647. Fragment of shaped strip. Gravel filling of water leat, L 8, Section C–D–E (fig. 38).   8.2 cm.

648. Fragment of bar. Gravel filling of water leat, L 8, Section C–D–E (fig. 38).   5 cm.

649. Fragment of a joiner's dog. Chalk quarry, Pit U, L 3, Section PP–QQ (fig. 47).   4.2 cm.

650. Fragment. Pre-destruction silt layer to south of Room 20.   4.2 cm.

651. Ferrule binding. Rubble over Building B.   2.8 cm.

652. Fragment of bar, bent at one end. Rubble filling, Room 20, L 3, Section L–M (fig. 6).   8.7 cm.

653. Joiner's dog (cf. no. 563 above). Rubble filling, Room 35, L 2, Section U–V (fig. 37).   7.9 cm.

654. Joiner's dog. Filling of water leat, L 5, Section C–D–E (fig. 38).   7 cm.

655. Tang with a widened and pierced head. Basically this is the same as a ring-headed pin, and may be compared with a more regularly made example with a round head from Woodcuts (*Woodcuts*, p. 90, pl. xxix, 16). Destruction rubble to south of Room 20.   5 cm.

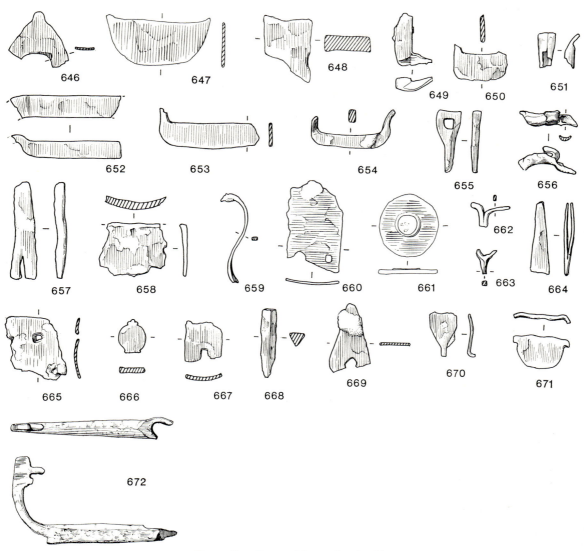

FIG. 78.   Iron objects (scale ⅓)

656.   Fragment. Chalk quarry, Pit U, L 3, Section PP–QQ (fig. 47).   4.6 cm.

657.   Fragment of rod divided at one end. The crudity of the work suggests that it is not a claw. Black deposit over ovens in north corridor. Building B, L 6, Section P–Q (fig. 6).   7.8 cm.

658.   Fragment of plate. Destruction rubble in inner courtyard, Building A.   5.3 cm.

659.   Curving fragment of rod. Filling of bathing pool, L 10, Section F–G (fig. 38).   7.2 cm.

660.   Fragment of strip. Silt over cobbled surface to south of Building D.   7.4 cm.

661.   Circular washer. Such washers could have many uses; for example, a holdfast from the Brampton hoard has a crescentic head at one end, and a similar washer at the other (*Brampton*, p. 34, no. 50). From conduit gully running from the well to the water cistern.   Diameter 5 cm.

Fig. 79.   Bucket (SF 673). Scale $\frac{1}{3}$

662. Fragment. Filling of water leat, L 5, Section C–D–E (fig. 38).   3.2 cm.

663. Tanged fragment which divides into semicircular arms. Destruction material south of Building A.   2. cm.

664. Simple tweezers. Better-made examples of tweezers are known from London (*London*, p. 77, pl. XXXIII, 6) with broad edges, and from Silchester (Reading Museum) with pointed arms. Destruction rubble to north of gatehouse.   6 cm.

665. Fragment of plate with single nail hole. Destruction rubble to north of gatehouse.   6.5 cm.

666. Small ornamental terminal consisting of a disc with a small trilobe device at its edge, probably from a strap binding. Door hinges not infrequently have ornamental terminals, although I know of none of this precise type. East of Building A, L 12, Section S–T (fig. 6).   2.7 cm.

667. Fragment of strip with nail hole. Occupation material in Building D, L 5, Section II–JJ–KK (fig. 33).   3.3 cm.

668. Fragment of triangular-sectioned rod. Destruction rubble to north of gatehouse.   5.6 cm.

669. Fragment of plate with a nail hole through it. Destruction material over Room 8 in bath-house.   5.7 cm.

670. Fragment. Rubble over Pit M to north of Building D, L 3, Section LL–MM (fig. 33).   3.7 cm.

671. Semicircular plate with short arms. Cobbled layer to west of Building A.   4.5 cm.

672. Tumbler-lock lift-key (cf. nos. 388 and 390). Filling of well. L 12. Section X–Y (fig. 17).   14.1 cm.

673. The iron fittings of a wooden bucket (fig. 79), consisting of the handle, still retaining a simple ring, the two handle straps and two hoops. Complete buckets come from Newstead (*Newstead*, p. 310, pl. LXIX, 4) and Silchester (Reading Museum), but the best parallel for our example is from a well at Woodcuts (*Woodcuts*, p. 85, pl. XXVIII, 3, 4, 5, 6). The usual form of bucket handle is a simple semicircular rod with hook ends; the loop in the centre of ours, which is also seen in the handle from Woodcuts, would prevent the rope or chain from sliding if the bucket was lowered into a well but has no very obvious advantage if it was not to be so used, which suggests that our example is a well bucket. The hoops are similar to those found on the other buckets cited above. The top hoop, which fitted outside the handle strap, was nailed in place through the strap, while the ends of the handle strap are folded out over the lower hoop. Turning the ends of the plates out appears to be an unusual feature; in the Newstead bucket the ends are turned under the bucket to give it support, and the handle straps found in the Brampton hoard (*Brampton*, p. 25, nos. 28 and 30) probably did the same. The nail is of our Type I. Filling of well, L 13, Section X–Y (fig. 17). Diameter of top hoop 37.5 cm.

For additional items of iron see brooch SF 10, unguent spoon SF 205, and needle SF 229.

OBJECTS OF LEAD
(fig. 80)

Numerous fragments of lead were found on the excavation and comprised mainly small sheets, snippets and fused droplets. Only the lead objects with form are illustrated.

674.   Triangular sheet, smooth on one side and rough on the other, with cut markings across angle. Appears to have been molten lead poured into matrix. Possibly lining to a bath. Rubble filling of Room 20, L 3, Section L–M (fig. 6).   11.4 cm.

675.   Irregular sheet with tongue of lead on one side. The tongue has not been applied, but is moulded from the sheet. Purpose unknown. Rubble filling of Room 20, L 3, Section L–M (fig. 6). 5.2 cm.

676.   Off-cut from lead sheet. Filling of bathing pool, L 4, Section F–G (fig. 38).   4.4 cm.

677.   Strip of lead with bulbous end, and semicircular section. Probably puddle of molten lead. Topsoil over Baths.   5.2 cm.

678.   Irregular wedge-shaped piece of lead, the wider end of which has been cut at an angle. Narrow end bent outwards. Rectangular section. Probably off-cut. Room 35.   5.3 cm.

679.   Thin triangular sheet with score line along one edge. Filling of bathing pool, L 7, Section F–G (fig. 38).

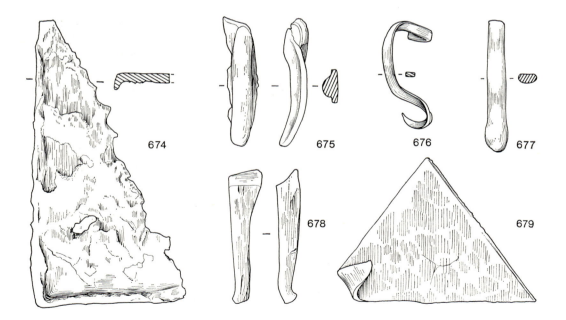

FIG. 80.   Lead objects (scale $\frac{2}{3}$)

OBJECTS OF STONE

PREHISTORIC FLINT ARTIFACTS
(fig. 81)

The seven flint artifacts[1] are all waste products, and do not include any implements. They comprise four blades, 680, 681, 682, and 683, two flakes 684 and 685, and a single platform blade core 686. It is not possible to attribute a date to the blades and flakes. A Roman date cannot be ruled out, since with the exception of 684 their condition is fresh and unpatinated.

The platform blade core 686 has flakes removed all around its perimeter and retains cortex on the platform. Worn. (?)Mesolithic.

680. Hillwash clay to west of Building D.   4 cm.
681. Water leat north of bathing pool, L 5, Section C–D–E (fig. 38).   4.9 cm.
682. Water leat north of bathing pool, L 5, Section C–D–E (fig. 38).   3.8 cm.
683. Western bank of water leat.   4 cm.
684. Early levels east of Building A, Beneath L 10, Section S–T (fig. 6).   3.3 cm.
685. Early levels east of Building A, Beneath L 10, Section S–T (fig. 6).   3.8 cm.
686. Ploughsoil. 5 cm. wide.

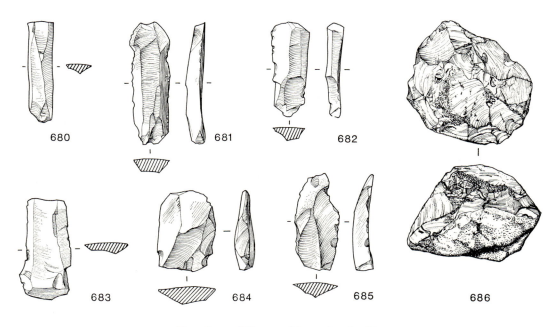

FIG. 81.   Flint artifacts (scale $\frac{2}{3}$)

[1] The writer is grateful to Dr G. J. Wainwright, F.S.A., for commenting on these items.

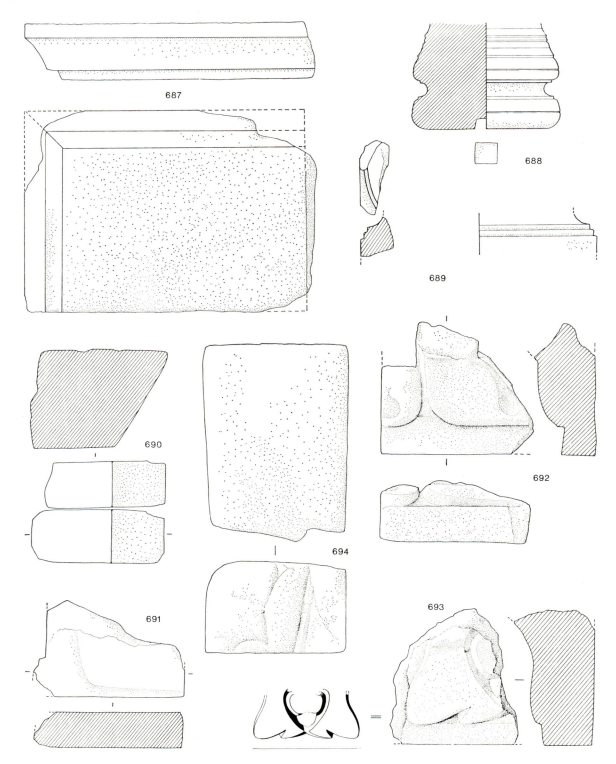

FIG. 82.   Architectural fragments (scales: $\frac{1}{8}$, except nos. 692 and 693, $\frac{1}{4}$)

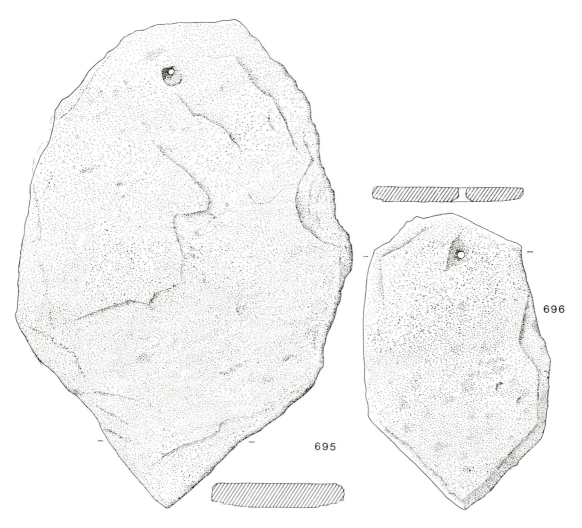

FIG. 83.   Roofing slates (scale ¼)

ARCHITECTURAL FRAGMENTS
(figs. 82–3)

687. Slab of Northamptonshire limestone moulded on two sides; the other sides are squared. The top is worked, the bottom unfinished. Possibly a cornice moulding, particularly the corner of a building. Rubble filling of bathing pool.   62 cm. × 43 cm.

688. Column drum worked in Northamptonshire limestone. Lathe-turned. Found in chalk quarry, Pit V. Fragments from two other drums of similar size were found on the site, one similarly moulded fragment from a robber trench cutting Room 7, and another undecorated fragment in the filling of the well. They were probably dwarf columns that supported a verandah roof. Width at base 31.6 cm.

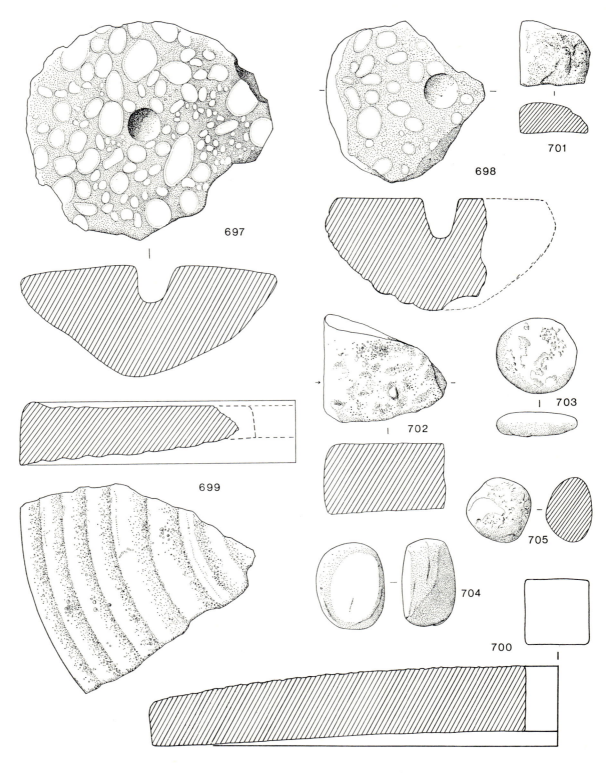

FIG. 84.   Stone objects (scale ¼)

689. Fragment of column base worked in Northamptonshire limestone. The base is square; the diameter of the lowest moulding is approximately 48 cm. Allowing another moulding before the shaft, the probable width of the drum would have been approximately 36 cm. The height of the column would have been approximately 3 metres, and therefore too tall for a dwarf column. The problem arises as to where this column type would have been situated. It could have been used to flank entrances through the verandah wall and therefore provide a clue to the height of the verandah. Found in the well, L 4, Section X–Y, fig. 17.

690. Two quoin stones worked in Northamptonshire limestone. Probably from a window opening, they were both found in the rubble filling the south side of the plunge-bath (Room 13). Maximum width of the largest stone 28 cm.

691. Moulded slab worked in Northamptonshire limestone. The upper side has evidence of having been painted in a wash of pink plaster, and also has the mortar impression of an angled quoin stone — an angle similar to 690. From Room 13. Maximum width 32 cm.

Decorated stone

692–3. Two decorated fragments of Northamptonshire limestone, possibly from a cornice.[1] A reconstruction of no. 693 has been attempted but it should be emphasized that since both fragments are small and eroded the reconstruction should *not* be regarded as certain. Maximum width: 692, 16 cm.; 693, 14.5 cm. Rubble in Room 27.

694. Block of Northamptonshire limestone with uncertain decoration at one end. The block appears to have been re-used; one side of the stone has been rounded off. From southern stoke-hole in Room 35.
Although evidence for decorated building at Gadebridge is slight, sufficient fragments have been found to presume that at least one building was of some pretensions. Unfortunately, which building is not known. It may be that the building has yet to be discovered since limestone blocks and fragments have been found re-used in Room 35, Building D and Building E.

695. Collyweston roofing slate. Used to fill Period 5 joist trenches in Room 20. 52.4 cm.

696. Collyweston roofing slate. Floor of bathing pool. 31.5 cm.

MISCELLANEOUS OBJECTS OF STONE
(figs. 84–5)

697. Base stone of quern of Hertfordshire Puddingstone. *In situ* south of Room 17, L 13, Section S–T (fig. 6). Diameter 26 cm.

698. Base stone of quern of Hertfordshire Puddingstone. Gravel at bottom of early water leat, L 23, Section H–I (fig. 40). Original diameter 24.5 cm.
Another fragment of quern (unillustrated) of Niedermendig basalt, similar in form to 700, was also found in this level. Diameter uncertain. Quern cut down, possibly for use as building stone. Part of a circular central hole remains.

[1] I am grateful to the late Professor D. E. Strong, F.S.A., for discussing these items with me, and to Dr F. W. Anderson for kindly identifying many of the materials.

o

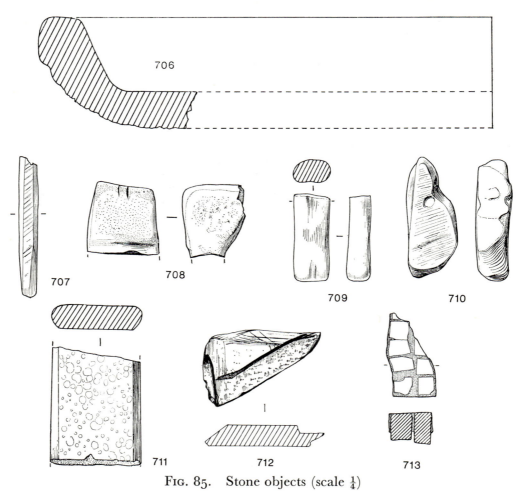

FIG. 85.   Stone objects (scale ¼)

699.   Upper quern of millstone grit, possibly from the Pennines. From east side of Building A. Original diameter 58.4 cm.

700.   Upper stone from quern of coarse gritty carboniferous sandstone. The central hole is square. Fragment. Filling of well, L 13, Section X–Y (fig. 17). Original diameter 86 cm.

701.   Fragment of quern of millstone grit used as a rubbing stone. Perhaps originally from a quern. Chalk quarry, Pit U, L 3, Section PP–QQ (fig. 47).   7.5 cm.

702.   Fragment of millstone grit used as a rubbing stone. The flat surfaces and side show wear. Probably once from a quern. Filling of Pit A to south of Building C.   13 cm.

703.   Flint pebble worn on both flat surfaces. Probably a rubbing stone. Fourth-century levels to south of Building A.   8.5 cm.

704.   Fine grit rubbing stone, considerably worn on all surfaces. Burnt. Chalk quarry, Pit U, L 3, Section PP–QQ (fig. 47).   9. 2 cm.
       A number of rubbing stones was found in this level, in association with mortaria in red fabric. Presumably they were used as pestles: some of the stones were burnt and therefore could also have been used as pot boilers.

705. River pebble with crazed burnt surface. Probably a pot boiler. Chalk quarry, Pit U, L 3, Section PP–QQ (fig. 47).   7 cm.

706. Rim fragment from basin of Purbeck marble, probably similar to that from Fishbourne (*Fishbourne*, II, fig. 21). The inside surface and outer rim are smooth. The underside surface is roughly tooled and therefore probably intended to be set into mortar. From filling of pipe gully east of Room 20. The fragment was used to support the corridor wall from collapsing into the drain beneath. Original diameter   72 cm.

707. Slate pocket hone from topsoil. Post-medieval.   11.2 cm.

708. Fragment of hone of fine grit. Extremely worn at narrow end, with two cut marks at butt. In clay over chalk floor of early occupation, L 12, Section S–T (fig. 6).   5.7 cm.

709. Rectangular hone of fine grit. Surviving end is slightly bulbous and has knife marking. Ditch I beneath inner courtyard.   7 cm.

710. Fragment of iron-stone, possibly used as hone. From rubble south-west of Building A.   9.6 cm.

711. Small slab of Purbeck marble, smooth on one side and partly worked on the other. The sides are semicircular. The purposes of the object is uncertain, for it is too thick and lacks the usual bevelled edges of a palette. It is possible that it is a fragment of a stone wall veneer. Filling of well, L 5, Section X–Y (fig. 17).   9 cm.

712. Fragment of palette in green slate. Scratch marks on one bevelled surface suggest it has been used as a hone. Unstratified.   5 cm.

713. Group of white limestone *tesserae* set in red tile-mortar. The length of the *tesserae* in relation to their width is unusual. Normally *tesserae* are roughly square. Upper filling of water leat. 6.8 cm.

For additional items of stone see jet bead SF 78 (fig. 58), Variscite ring SF 151 (fig. 60), and shale bracelets SF 174–80 (fig. 61).

OBJECTS OF TERRACOTTA
(figs. 86–8)

Flue-tiles

Many fragments of flue-tiles were found on the excavation and their decoration mainly comprised the W-chevron roller stamp pattern or simple combing. In all, three types of box-tiles were discovered.

714–15.   *Type A.* Rectangular tiles measuring approximately 41.5 cm. tall, 16.5 cm. wide and 11.5 cm. deep, decorated with either the W-chevron roller stamp design (pl. IV*b*) or simple wavy combing made from a comb with seven teeth. They had been made from a sheet of clay wrapped around a sanded mould, and have finger impressions on their corners. Rectangular holes, measuring 9.5 cm. by 5.5 cm. have been cut into their sides. Found as a drain (pl. IV*a*) beneath the Period 3 lower hypocaust floor of Rooms 1 and 9. Scorch marks, indicating that they were once used for their proper function, suggest that they may originally have been used in the Period 1 bath-house.

716.   *Type B.* Shorter rectangular tile measuring 38 cm. tall, 16.5 cm. wide and 11.5 cm. deep and decorated with a roller stamp pattern of radiating lozenges. Both sides of the tile are pierced with a pair of circular holes measuring 5–6 cm. in diameter.

FIG. 86.   Flue-tiles (scale ¼)

One complete example was found as the outlet pipe (pl. IV*c*) to the above drain (cf. 714–15). Only one other fragment of box-tile with this decoration was found: built into the corn-drying oven.

717. *Type C.* This tile is shorter than Types A and B. It measures 36.3 cm. tall, 18.5 cm. wide, 12.5 cm. deep and is decorated with an X combing, the comb used being eight-toothed. Both sides of the tile are pierced by a rectangular hole measuring 5 cm. by 7 cm. This is an early fourth-century type and was found *in situ* in Room 35.

718. This tile is somewhat larger than 717, but is probably Type C. It measures 38 cm. tall, 20 cm. wide and 15 cm. deep. It is decorated on both surfaces by three X comb patterns (made from an eight-toothed comb), with a comb line running through them. The sides are also decorated. One side only is pierced by a rectangular hole, measuring 5 × 4 cm. Found *in situ* in Room 35.

Miscellaneous objects of terracotta

719. Fragment of statuette[1] originally of the Venus or so-called pseudo-Venus type — the type that has the most numerous examples in the records of clay statuettes found in Britain. This particular example has only the lower part of the legs broken off below the knees and at the ankles. When complete, it was of a nude female personage holding a lock of her hair near her right ear, and supporting a sleeveless *tunica* or undergarment which hangs down to the ground by her left leg. Usually the definition of the details of the garment is rather sketchy, but the present example shows the lower parts of the creases in front in low relief, and down the front of the outer edge are incisions which may represent embroidery or stitching.

The fabric is not the pure white pipeclay of the Allier district, but is a whitish-buff fairly fine paste having a smooth whiter surface, which has the usual 'soapy' feel. It therefore came from some other district in Central Gaul which need not have been far from that important centre of production.

Viewed statistically, of the 153 recorded examples, 50% have been found in the south-eastern area of Britain, of which 67% come from Kent and London. This is undoubtedly due to the close proximity of these areas to Gaul, the immediate homeland of the cult these clay statuettes represented, and also the source of manufacture. It is also indicated that these statuettes were more popular in the civilian zone, for in the highland zone of Wales they are virtually absent and they are rare in the military zone of the Pennines.

Unfortunately the associated coinage with the present example does not provide a close date but it is fairly certain to have been Hadrianic–Antonine.

The piece of lead wedged between the two halves of the statuette is most interesting, for, as it is firmly in place and does not appear to have flowed in after the statuette was discarded and thrown away, it may well be that it is a repair prior to firing in the kiln, or perhaps a reinforcement. I know no other example of the use of lead in this manner, although perishable supports were sometimes used and were destroyed in the firing, leaving only the holes where they were placed. The closest parallels are Godmanchester, Hunts. (*Archaeological Newsletter*, 7 (1961), 11–12, fig. on p. 11) and London, Copthall Court (*London*, Inv. no. A249). Rubble filling of Room 20, L 3, Section L–M (fig. 6).   4 cm.

720. Fragment of tile used as a hone. Filling of bathing pool, L 7, Section F–G (fig. 38).   5.1 cm.

[1] I am grateful to Mr F. Jenkins, F.S.A., for the note on this object.

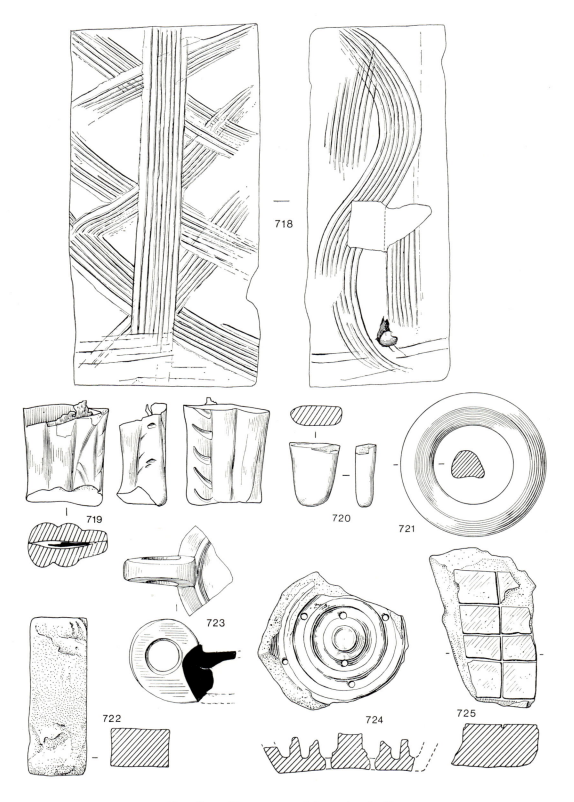

FIG. 87.   Terracotta objects (scale ¼)

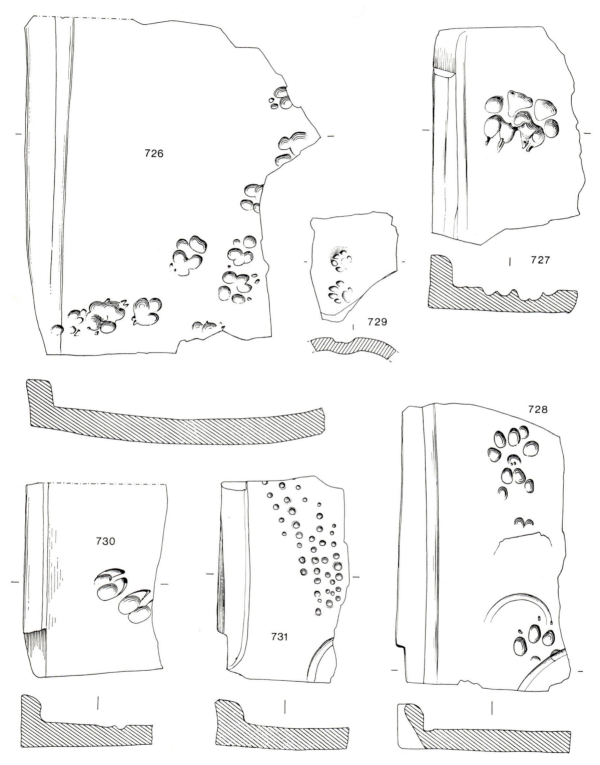

FIG. 88.   Tiles with impressions (scale ¼)

721.   Terracotta ring of uncertain use. Possibly kiln or oven furniture. Found in association with the two ovens in the northern corridor of Building B, L 6, Section P–Q (fig. 6).   5.8 cm.

722.   Herringbone floor-tile, one of many found patching the floor in Room 20.   12.6 cm.

723.   Handle from oil lamp. Pale orange-buff fabric with metallic grey slip. Ditch I beneath inner courtyard. Original diameter of bowl, 6 cm.

724.   Cheese or honey press in hard, coarse, dark grey fabric with reddish-brown surfaces. Burnt. Diameter at carination of base 10.5 cm. From east side of Building A. Black level over L 10, Section S–T (fig. 6).

725.   Fragment of tile, 3.5 cm. thick with (pre-firing) score lines across surface. Possibly the tile had been scored to make *tesserae* or was a gaming 'board'. Destruction material over baths.   11 cm.

726.   *Tegula* with imprints of paws of a dog crossing in two directions. Destruction material of Building A.   31 cm. wide.

727.   *Tegula* with dog paw imprints. Destruction level of Building A.   23 cm.

728.   *Tegula* with dog paw imprints. Destruction material over Building A.   30 cm.

729.   *Imbrex* with imprints of paws of a cat. Upper filling of bathing pool.   11 cm.

730.   *Tegula* with hoof imprints of a pig or goat. Built into corn-drying oven.   15 cm. wide.

731.   *Tegula* with hob-nail impressions from a boot or sandal. From oven beneath tessellated floor in Room 28.   22 cm.

WALL-PAINTING

By JOAN LIVERSIDGE, F.S.A.

Evidence for wall-painting was recovered from several areas.

A. (fig. 89a, pl. XXIb).   The lower part of an interior wall, dating to the fourth century, was found *in situ* in Room 20, the basement room. This was stippled in purple, red and yellow on a white ground. About 90 cm. above the ground level the lower edge of a trellis design survives, consisting of narrow diagonal purple lines.

B. (fig. 90).   On the Period 6 partition wall in Room 20, dated to c. A.D. 320–50, was another type of trellis design. This time yellow roundels were painted in the diamonds formed by the intersections of the double lattice. Other wall-painting includes fragments with foliate designs found in the swimming pool.

C. (fig. 89b, pl. XXVIIa).   Pieces recovered from the well (reconstructed by Dr N. Davey), and presumably from the late Antonine villa, have a far more elaborate design of shaded yellow and white bosses, each set in a framework of fine red lines connected by short diagonals. Each of the resulting squares forms part of a coffered design divided up by strands of guilloche outlined in red. Where the guilloche plait crosses at the corner, of each coffer, an awkward detail to depict, the crossing is covered by a four-petalled flower. Marks made by the artist's compass in laying out the guilloche are still visible.

The stippled plaster from Room 20 (fig. 89a) represents a type of decoration frequently found in Romano-British houses from the first century onwards. It was probably an attempt to imitate marble wall-veneers and was effective and economical for use near ground level,

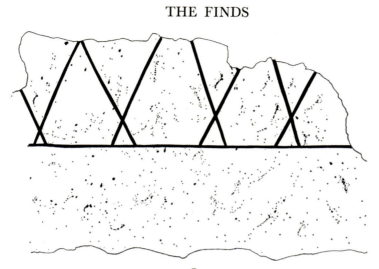

a

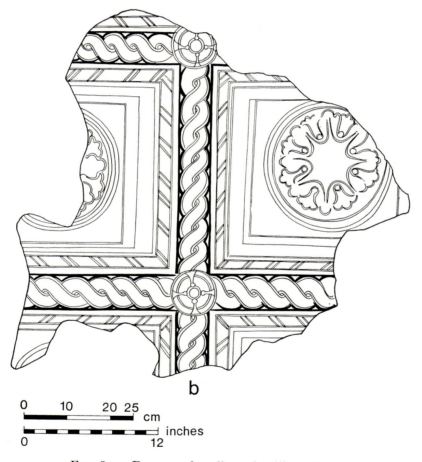

b

FIG. 89.   Decorated wall- and ceiling-plaster

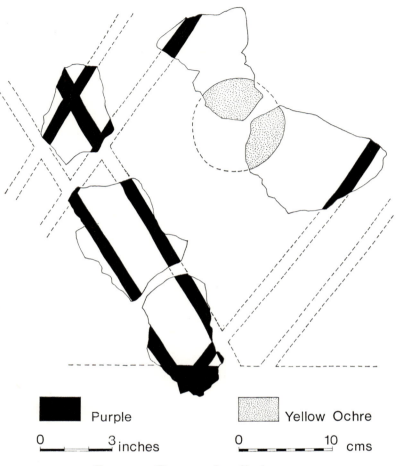

Purple   Yellow Ochre

0 _____ 3 inches   0 _____ 10 cms

FIG. 90.   Decorated wall-plaster

as it could easily be touched up when necessary. Parallels to the trellis design from higher up the wall include Flavian painting found *in situ* in the Farningham (Kent) villa. This consisted of stippling on a pale cerise ground for about 30 cm. above ground level. Above came a dark blue trellis outlining red diamonds on which were painted blue flowers.[1] Dado designs found at Martigny and Augst (Switzerland) are also decorated with a series of diagonals, and the Augst example has flowers where the diagonals cross and in the intervening space.[2]

Elaborate wall-painting of second-century date is known from several British sites, including Leicester and the city of Verulamium, not far from Gadebridge. Fig. 89*b* with its coffered effect seems more likely to come from a ceiling rather than from a wall, the shaded bosses recalling stucco ceilings surviving in Rome. Ceiling plaster with a design of octagons containing rectangles with birds and animal masks was found at Verulamium,[3] and may

[1] A. L. F. Rivet (ed.), *The Roman Villa in Britain* (1969), p. 134, pl. 4.9.

[2] W. Drack, *Die römische Wandmalerei der Schweiz* (1950), p. 44, fig. 94, pl. xxx. In some cases these designs with diagonals may have depicted the lower portions of a garden fence.

[3] *Antiq. J.*, xxxix (1959), 17, pl. 1).

have existed at the Winterton villa (Lincs.). The provincial cities of Carnuntum and Aquincum along the Danube have produced material also split up into rectangles and octagons. The guilloche frame, however, is most unusual and more suggestive of a floor than a ceiling. The only likely parallel known to me is some fragments of a heavy looking guilloche design found with the fourth-century Christian paintings from the Lullingstone (Kent) villa. These have not yet been fitted into the scheme of decoration, but they seem more suitable for a ceiling than a wall. Scraps of painted guilloche known from other sites may merely continue a floor mosaic in paint on the lowest part of the walls, or may be an attempt to depict wall mosaics.[1] A design such as fig. 89b would surely appear rather odd and heavy on a wall.

THE GLASS
By DOROTHY CHARLESWORTH, F.S.A.

Window glass (fig. 91)

The greater part of the glass found on this site is window glass and several of the pieces are of considerable interest as they indicate shape and methods of fixing as well as differences in appearances which must be linked with different methods of production. In no case was it possible to restore a full pane.[2]

Among the pieces of first- and second-century glass, distinguished by its green-blue colour, its thickness of *c.* 3–5 mm. and its one smooth and one rough surface, believed to be the result of pouring the molten glass into a flat mould,[3] the most interesting are the edge fragments. Some show traces of the mortar which held them in place. Sometimes this is on the rough surface (examples from the filling of the bathing pool, and in the well) sometimes on the smooth (an example was found in the packing material of a post-hole associated with Building C, and another from the filling of the bathing pool) but more often the edge is clean and it must be presumed that it was held in a wooden frame, or with an iron grille similar to that found at Duston.[4]

The corners of the panes are generally a rounded-off right angle, sometimes with tooling marks where the metal has been drawn out to the corner of the mould. Examples of this were found in Pit A, and in the occupation material in Room 26 (Fig. 91a). Four corners which had been cut to an acute angle, possibly for a diamond-shaped pane were also found. Two, one from the northern courtyard to the west of the baths, and another from the water leat to the north of the bathing pool (fig. 91b) had been cut to an acute angle and showed traces of mortar. Two others, one (fig. 91c) from L 5 in the well (Section X–Y, fig. 17) and another (fig. 91d) from the filling of the corn-drying oven, were also cut to a point but had no fixing material adhering to them.

The later window glass is generally thinner, colourless metal and smooth on both faces. It is thought to be blown glass, a cylinder which was cut and allowed to unfold in the

[1] Rivet, op. cit., p. 134, pl. 4.3b.
[2] *A.A.*[4], XXXVII (1959), 166: pane estimated .6 × .6 m.
[3] *Glastechnische Berichte*, VIII, 8 f.; *J. of Glass Studies*, VIII (1966), 41 f.
[4] *Antiq.*, XXXIII (1959), 10 f.

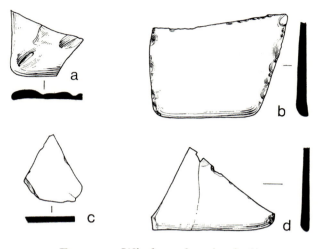

FIG. 91.   Window glass (scale ½)

annealing oven. There is less of this third–fourth-century window glass at the site than of the first–second-century type. The edge fragments that were found are all smoothly rounded and more than less straight. There are no corner pieces and no edge with any mortar for fixing. It may be assumed that wood or metal frames were used.

Bottle glass (fig. 92)

About 50 vessels are represented by fragments of blue-green and green bottle glass, typical first–second-century metal. In general the pieces are small and featureless so that it is not known for what sort of utilitarian vessel they come, bottle, flask, jar or bowl. Only the few that can be identified are mentioned individually.

Three fragments are from the bases of square bottles, each with a moulded marking of concentric circles, and two are from the shoulders of square bottles. Another bottle fragment (a) from L 13 in the well (Section X–Y, fig. 17) is rim, neck and the top of the handle only, so its shape cannot be determined. There is also a handle fragment (b) from a cobbled surface to the south of Room 20. The square body is the most common shape, but cylindrical bottles run a close second and hexagonal and octagonal (in section) bodies are also used. All are blown glass, normally formed in a mould, made *c.* A.D. 70–130 but lasting in use until late in the second century.[1]

There is one rim of a small jar in green glass, probably an ointment jar, (c) found in rubble to the north of Building A, and one neck from a small perfume flask (d) found to the west of Building E. The small flat strap handle (e) from L 5 Section C–D–E (fig. 38), also in poor quality greenish glass, probably comes from a small jar. Its date is not certain. It could be of the third or fourth century.

[1] *J. of Glass Studies*, VIII (1966), 26 f., and *Studies in Glass History and Design* (ed. R. J. Charleston, W. Evans, A. E. Werner), pp. 6 f.

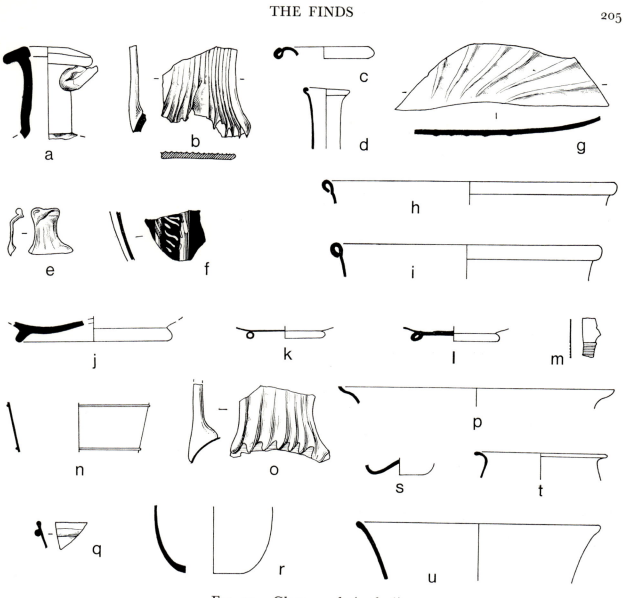

FIG. 92.   Glass vessels (scale ½)

Millefiori (fig. 92)

Only two fragments of this very distinctive metal, both from the same pillar moulded bowl were found, one from the west side of Building C and another (f) from beneath the west corridor of Building B. The matrix is emerald green and has rods of opaque white in it giving a marbled effect. The bowl is not likely to have been made after the middle of the first century A.D. At Camulodunum many fragments of these vessels were found in Claudian to Neronian contexts.[1] They also occur on early military sites, e.g. in an Agricolan context

[1] *Camulodunum*, pp. 292 f.; *Colchester*, p. 79.

at Newstead[1] and Trajanic at Nether Denton. On villa sites millefiori of any sort is rare. A small piece was found atWitcombe villa (Glos.)[2] and another at Chiddingfold.

Coloured glass: first–second century (fig. 92)

There is not very much deliberately coloured glass on the site and the only two colours are green and amber. The intentional green can be distinguished from the natural green of the bottle glass. It is generally more of an olive colour. The fragments of this olive green glass on this site are all from flagons of a type made in the Seine/Rhine area *c.* A.D. 70–150 (Isings form 52). Two were found in the destruction rubble south of Building A, another from the early levels to the west of Building B, and another in rubble west of Building C. The amber fragments may be from a similar flagon or from a globular jar (Isings form 67c) made at the same time. The pieces of a ribbed body from the filling of the bathing pool (g) could be from either a flagon or jar. The hollow tubular rimmed bowl, a very common vessel in the later first to third century is represented by two rim fragments in green glass (h) from the inner courtyard, and (i) from Building C. They are possibly from the same vessel.

Colourless glass: first–third century (fig. 92)

Most of the fragments are unidentifiable pieces from the sides of convex vessels. In quality the colourless glass varies from the thin metal with pinhead bubbles, for example, the fragment of an indented beaker (Isings form 32 or 35), to the thick, perfectly clear metal of the base ring from the rubble in Building D (j), which may have been moulded and has certainly been polished. Another base ring in equally good glass, but much thinner, a coil ring on a free blown vessel (k) from the filling of the bathing pool, L 6, Section C–D–E (fig. 38), and a second coil ring (l) from the water conduit gully north of Building C, have been distorted in a fire on the site. There are two decorated fragments each from a straight sided beaker, one with a group of five cut lines (m) from the occupation in Room 20, the other, with two thin trails running around the side, from Building E (n).

The handle of the third-century cylindrical bottle (o), reeded like those of the first–second-century bottles but unlike them in metal, is quite distinctive. The vessel may be either plain or decorated. From Room 26.

Fourth-century glass (fig. 92)

This is generally thin greenish metal, although one bowl rim fragment (p) from Room 20 is colourless with striations, bubbles and other defects in the glass. One small fragment (q) found in the filling of the water leat, from a flagon or jug with a trail below the rim, is probably of the first half of the middle of the fourth century, but other pieces are of middle to late fourth-century date. One base in greenish glass from Room 29 (r) is from a type of beaker often decorated with blobs of coloured glass. Another base (s), unfortunately unstratified and much greener in colour, is from a taller conical beaker (Isings form 106b). The two rounded rim fragments (t and u) from L 3, Section GG–HH, fig. 50, and L 8, Section C–D–E (fig. 38)

---

[1] *Newstead*, p. 272.   [2] *T.B.G.A.S.*, LXXIII (1954), 59.

respectively, are probably from beakers of the last quarter of the fourth century when the rounded rim tends to replace the cut rim, exemplified here by the bowl fragment (p).

For additional items of glass see pendant SF 69 (fig. 57), necklace and beads SF 75–7 and 79–80 (fig. 58), and bead SF 301 (fig. 66).

Distribution of glass

The location of both second- and fourth-century window glass was plotted on an overall plan of the site, and it was found that in some instances second- and fourth-century glass fragments were found in the same deposit. This was particularly the case in Room 20, where second-century glass predominated. It is possible that the glass had been re-used in later windows, since this room was rebuilt in the Constantinian period. Second-century glass also predominated in the filling of the bathing pool, but since the coin and pottery evidence proves conclusively a mid fourth-century backfilling, the most logical explanation is that the windows in the second-century bath buildings, up until their destruction, retained their original glazing. A large quantity of second-century window glass was also found in the gully to the south of the Period 3 caldarium (Room 9), suggesting that a window existed somewhere here. Another large quantity of second-century glass was found associated with building rubble thrown down the well.

Fourth-century glass was relatively less common, but an even scatter occurred over most of the area of Building A. The largest quantity was found in Building D; here there were two groups: one mid-way along the western wall, and another scattered about the south wall. It could be assumed that windows existed at these points. Building E also produced a quantity of fourth-century glass mainly confined to the eastern side of the building. A small quantity of second-century glass was also found outside the building. [D.S.N.]

THE SAMIAN

By G. Dannell

(fig. 93)

1. Form 30. Probably by cinnamvs (cf. *C.G.P.*, pl. 159.23). The lion is O.1421. Antonine. C.G. From L 6, Section P–Q (fig. 6). Another fragment was found over the western corridor of Building B. Equates with L 5, Section S–R (fig. 6).

2. Form 37. bvtrio style (cf. *C.G.P.*, p. 55, fig. 13, ovolo 2, and large rosette 10). The face masks are O.1330 and the smaller one to the right, both shown in the same figure. The candelabrum can be seen in *C.G.P.*, pl. 59. 664. *c.* A.D. 120–45. C.G. Sealed beneath road, L 8, Section RR–SS (fig. 50).

3. Form 37. Scrap, probably Antonine. C.G. On Period 3 corridor surface, below L 4, Section P–Q (fig. 6).

4. Form 37. Ovolo of albvcivs (cf. *C.G.P.*, p. 216, fig. 35.1). Antonine, and after A.D. 150. C.G. L 6, Section P–Q (fig. 6).

5. Form 37. Ovolo of ivstvs (cf. *C.G.P.*, p. 201, fig. 31.2, over a wavy line border). *c.* A.D. 150–80. From the filling of Pit A to the south-west of Building C.

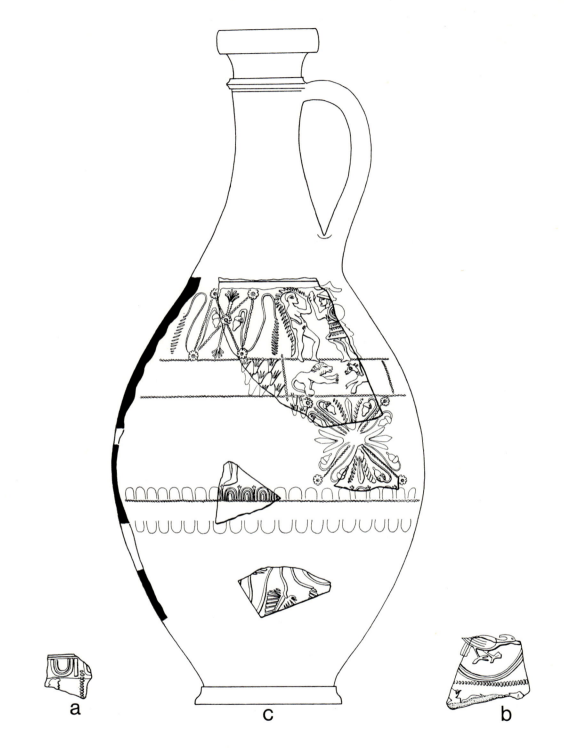

FIG. 93.   Samian ware (scale ½)

6. Form 37. Ovolo of MERCATOR (cf. *C.G.P.*, p. 249, fig. 43.2); the wing tips of the goose O.2316 appear below the coarsely roped border. Late Antonine. C.G. Beneath L 4, Section P–Q (fig. 6).

7. Form 37. ATTIANVS ovolo (cf. *C.G.P.*, p. 167, fig. 23.2). Hadrianic. C.G. From over clay floor in Building B. Equates with L 7, Section S–R (fig. 6).

8. Form 37. GEMINVS style (cf. *C.G.P.*, pl. 66.16 for coarse wavy line border, feet of figure and rosettes). Hadrianic. C.G. In silt pre-dating Building B. Equates with L 8, Section P–Q (fig. 6).

9. Form 37. IVLLINVS ovolo (?) (cf. *C.G.P.*, p. 221, fig. 36.1) but with bead-row border; also the dolphin with the rudimentary pectoral fin close to O.2383 (*C.G.P.*, pl. 125.6) Antonine. C.G. In eaves drip outside eastern corridor wall of Building A. Another fragment was found in rubble equating with the level beneath L 4, Section P–Q (fig. 6).

10(a). Form 37. CINNAMVS ovolo (*C.G.P.*, p. 267, fig. 47.1). The ware, however, does not look like the usual Lezoux production and could be from one of the other sites to which CINNAMVS sent his moulds. *c.* A.D. 145–80. Found in northern conduit gully leading from the well.

11. Form 37. CINNAMVS ovolo (*C.G.P.*, p. 267, fig. 47.3). In eaves drip of Building A.

12(b). Form 30. Large bird in double bordered medallion, all in panel decoration, above an indistinguishable animal running to the right. The bird is O.2198, which Oswald, following Déchelette, attributes to Vichy. Certainly the ware is not a standard C.G. type. See remarks for 10 above. Probably Antonine. From western corridor of Building B. Equates with rubble below L 4, Section P–Q (fig. 6).

13. Form 37. Free-style design, with O.1748 facing a tree. *c.* A.D. 90–110, Banassac. Occupation over eastern corridor of Building B.

14. Form 37. Sea-horse O.33; Antonine. From filling of Pit A to south-west of Building C (fig. 22).

15. Form 37. Scrap, Martres-de-Veyre pottery, Trajanic–Hadrianic. From chalk quarry, Pit V, L 9, Section NN–OO (fig. 48).

16. Form 37. Probably Martres-de-Veyre to judge from the fabric. Hadrianic (?). From eaves drip in inner courtyard Building A. Below L 4, Section N–O (fig. 6).

THE LAGENA
(fig. 93*c*)

This type has been extensively discussed by Stanfield (*J.R.S.*, XXVII (1937), 168–79), and his article is invaluable as a collection of the evidence. In general, the scheme of decoration appears to have provided a wide zone closest to the neck, where figure-types were employed, and then two further zones, separated from each other by the mould junction, which the potter concealed by a plain band fringed with either ovolo, or straight-wreath decoration.

The present vessel, represented by four sherds, enables a reconstruction of the design. Nearest to the neck, a zone 40 mm. high contained panels of St Andrew's cross motif, alternating with figure-type scenes. The cross has a six-lobed leaf as its centre, the tendrils trail acorns and large striated rods. In the remaining panel a *retiarius* faces a figure, O.164A.

P

The next adjacent zone appears to have been about 70 mm. high, and was itself divided into half-panels horizontally, presumably in an alternate scheme. Remains of four half-panels show, to the left a block of inverted barley-ears, which are larger than those flanking the design in the panel below. To the right a lion, O.1417, faces a gryphon, O.882; below this panel is another St Andrew's cross motif, this time with a leaf centre of two striated lobes flanking a sword-shaped centre. It would appear that these panels were unbordered, and there is no division above the small double-bordered ovolo. The tip of the tongue is not clear, but rather looks as if it has a five-pointed end, the two points immediately either side of the stem being very short, so as to look more like the early Flavian trifid tip bent to the left.

The lowest zone, presumably demarcated by a similar ovolo, has a winding scroll with tendrils terminating in large leaves on short striated rods.

Of the figures, the *retiarius* is not shown by Oswald or Déchelette, but it is possible that he is a cut-down poinçon (the net is an addition). O.164A, here used as a gladiator, occurs at La Graufesenque (e.g. Hermet, pl. 79. 12) and also at Rozier (ibid., pl. 126. 3), and it is interesting to note that his right hand is unfilled, unlike the similar poinçon used on the form 30 from Rottweil (Knorr, 1912, Taf. XVI. 3). Obviously his armament was a matter for individual whim. The lion and gryphon, however, appear together on the form 29 (G.H. 1928) shown by Knorr (Knorr, 1952, Taf. 15B). His drawing, and the writer's rubbing show very clearly how the left leg is blurred, but the right has three sharp claws; unfortunately the head is blurred. The bowl is stamped by CELADVS, one of two potters by the same name one suspects, for the vessels stamped OF CELADI are in a very different style to those marked CELADI·MAN. A further examination of his work shows the two types of barley-ear, the small one below the animals on the G.H. form 29 already discussed, the larger ones appearing on a similarly stamped form 29 from London (L.M. 31–72/2). This bowl also has a winding scroll in its lower zone, with leaves and striated rods as in the present lagena. In the lower concavity are a pair of gladiators similar to O.1013A and B. What looks like B's foot appears above the ovolo on the lagena, and the second zone of decoration, *c.* 40 mm. for the lower portion, is just big enough to take him. The upper concavity contains a different gryphon, O.878, which is shown by Hermet (pl. 97. 2), on another unusual form, a gourd, with what may well be the same acorns and small barley-ears as the lagena, and similar leaves to the G.H. 29.

A form 29 from Margidunum (F. Oswald, *The Terra-Sigillata from Margidunum*, pl. VII, 6) shows the beaky-faced gryphon, but the legs this time are blurred, and it is not clear whether the tendrils in the lower zone carry acorns or striated rods. However, the leaf centre of the St Andrew's cross is very similar to that from Cologne (Knorr, 1952, Taf. 15A), where appear the heavy striated rods from the upper zone of the lagena.

While it should be remembered that in South Gaul the interchange of decorative detail makes positive attributions in the absence of stamps (and then only to the producers, not the mould-makers) a chancy affair, the body of evidence above does suggest that CELADVS ii had connections with the mould-maker for the lagena, and this would suggest a date *c.* A.D. 60–80. Found in the gully leading south from the bathing pool, L 9, Section E–F (fig. 40).

POTTERS' STAMPS ON SAMIAN
By B. R. HARTLEY, F.S.A.

1. BVTVRO (II*a*) f. 33 [ ]VRO. ⚒

Buturo of C.G. (Lezoux?). Examples from the Antonine fire at Verulamium and also (burnt) at Wroxeter suggest a date *c.* A.D. 140–65. From occupation material in east corridor of Building B.

2. CETVS (VI*a*) f. 18/31 CËTVS.FE

Cetus is probably to be distinguished from Cettus of Les Martres-de-Veyre and is more likely, judging by his fabrics, to have worked at Lezoux. This stamp is usually on form 18/31 or 18/31 R. Other stamps of Cetus are often on form 27, and two examples are known from the Saalburg, both factors suggesting Hadrianic–Antonine date, *c.* A.D. 130–55. On road-surface to west of Building C. Over L 15, Section GG–HH (fig. 50).

3. CIRIVNA (I*b*) f. 27 CIʁIVNʌF (blurred)

A stamp of Ciriuna of Heiligenberg, though not attested there and only known otherwise as form 33 from Corbridge and London. Late Hadrianic or early Antonine. From corn-drying oven. L 4, Section CC–DD (fig. 26).

4. DAGOMARVS (VII*a*) f. 18/31 [DA]GONʌRʋ S.F]

One of the less common stamps of Dagomarus of Les Martres-de-Veyre, and probably one of his later ones, since it is known from Hadrian's Wall (Chesters Mus. 3263/2101). *c.* A.D. 110–30. L 10, Section S–T (fig. 6).

5. GEMINVS (X*b*) f. 33 GEMINIʌʌ

By a Geminus of Lezoux, possibly though not necessarily by the man who made form 45 commonly. This stamp is certainly Antonine, as it appears at Balmuildy, Bar Hill and Newstead, but closer dating involves subjective factors. Unstratified.

6. PECVLIARIS (VI*a*) f. 80 ᴄECVLARISF

Peculiaris of Lezoux. The stamp occurs with equal frequency on forms 27 and 80 and should, therefore, be early to mid Antonine. Dated sites include Caerleon, Newstead and Rough Castle. *c.* A.D. 145–70. Black occupation on cobbled surface to east of Building A. Over L 10, Section S–T (fig. 6).

7. REBVRRVS (III*b*) f. 33 REBVRRI.OFI

Reburrus of Lezoux worked entirely in the Antonine period. This particular stamp is not common, nor is there much evidence for close dating, though an example of it came from the first destruction of the Wroxeter forum. Probably *c.* A.D. 145–70. On western corridor floor of Building B.

8. SACRILLVS (VII*a*) f. 33 SACRILLI

Sacrillus of Lezoux. This stamp is relatively common in late Antonine contexts at re-occupied sites such as Bainbridge, Catterick and Halton Chesters. *c.* A.D. 155–90. From robber trench of east wall of Room 20.

GADEBRIDGE PARK ROMAN VILLA

MORTARIUM STAMPS

By Mrs K. HARTLEY, F.S.A.

(fig. 94)

(a)   (Slightly burnt.)   The retrograde stamp reads]ARINVS; no complete impression of this stamp exists but it is almost certainly from a die of Marinus who worked in the same potteries as Doinus, perhaps having kilns at Brockley Hill. His work should be dated *c.* A.D. 70–110; the Gadebridge Park rim is probably to be dated later than A.D. 85. Published pottery no. 1. Ditch I.

(b)   Both stamps survive, giving DOINVS (N and S reversed); these are from die D of Doinus. Over a hundred stamps of Doinus have been found at sites throughout England, Wales and Scotland, a typical distribution for the more important potters working in the potteries south of Verulamium in the Flavian period: 48 stamps are from the Brockley Hill pottery, clearly demonstrating some production there (*Arch. J.*, CXXIX (1972), 82–5).

FIG. 94.   Mortarium stamps (scale $\frac{1}{1}$)

The stamps from Flavian forts in Scotland at Loudon Hill, Newstead (2), and Dalswinton II (*Dumfries & Galloway Nat. Hist. and Ant. Soc.*), and the rims used, all attest a date of A.D. 70–110 to cover the whole of his work. The Dalswinton stamp is from die D and judging from its find-spot should have been in use in the last stages of the occupation there. Changes in his rims and stamps tend to support this suggestion that die D was his latest one and would probably be later than A.D. 85. Published pottery no. 140. Ditch I.

(c)   The incomplete stamp reads]LBINV[. Ditch I.

(d)   The broken stamp reads F·LV[. Ditch I.

Stamp (c) is from die D of Albinus and (d) is from the counterstamp always used in conjunction with this die. Stamps from die D are not very common and they could well be from the same vessel.

More than 250 mortaria of Albinus are recorded from Britain, far more than for any other mortarium-maker. These include stamps from Inchtuthil, dated *c*. A.D. 83–7, three from the Neronian–Flavian fort at Baginton and several from Flavian contexts at Verulamium. A date of *c*. A.D. 65–95 is indicated for his work.

The distribution of his mortaria and the forms and fabric used strongly indicate production in potteries situated near Watling Street in the area between Verulamium and London (including Brockley Hill and Radlett). Albinus and a few other potters making closely similar products regularly used these counterstamps (presumably *factum Luguduni*) or some reading F. or FEC LUGD, which show that their workshops were at a place called Lugdunum; its precise location is as yet unknown though it must lie within the above-mentioned area.

(e) No other example of this broken worn stamp is known. Reading doubtful, probably a new potter (DABI[or]EAC [retrograde]. The fabric clearly indicates manufacture in the potteries south of Verulamium, and the rim points to a date in the period A.D. 90–140. The two fragments, both from the same stamp, join, but were found on separate areas of the site. One fragment was found in collapsed wall daub in the eastern corridor, Building B, and the other, published pottery no. 345, from the filling of the water leat north of the pool.

THE COARSE POTTERY
(figs. 95–112)

A very large quantity of pottery was discovered over the site but, with the exception of Ditch I, only relatively small quantities were found in closely dated or sealed groups. For this reason, only pottery from these groups or from within buildings has been published.

It was felt that the pottery from Ditch I, the well, and Room 20 deserved a comprehensive description, since these sources yielded the largest quantities, and in the case of Room 20 a large associated collection of coins. By so doing, a number of forms have been duplicated. It has been possible to use the forms in these groups (not necessarily the fabric) as parallels for sherds found elsewhere on the site. Where pottery groups are associated with a reasonably large quantity of dated coins, no attempt has been made to parallel the sherds with forms from other sites.

The pottery is described as found in individual layers, and is equated with the appropriate published section. The pottery descriptions, therefore, are divided into groups, headed by the relevant section and figure number. The sherds from layers within that section are sub-headed with the layer number. The earliest deposit in a group is described first.

Illustrations are numbered in sequence, the number on the illustration corresponding to the pottery description. Where one form is paralleled with another and needs no separate illustration, it is sub-headed alphabetically. By using the above system it has not been possible to mount the drawings in a strictly dated sequence, although an attempt has been made to describe, where possible, the pottery from the earliest features first in the text.

Bearing in mind that the bulk of the pottery was probably made in the region, it was considered undesirable to stray beyond the borders of Hertfordshire in the search for parallels (although the rule is sometimes broken). Considerable time was saved in the preparation of this pottery report by the loan from Professor S. S. Frere, F.S.A., of the typescript of the pottery section from the report on his Verulamium excavations in 1957–60

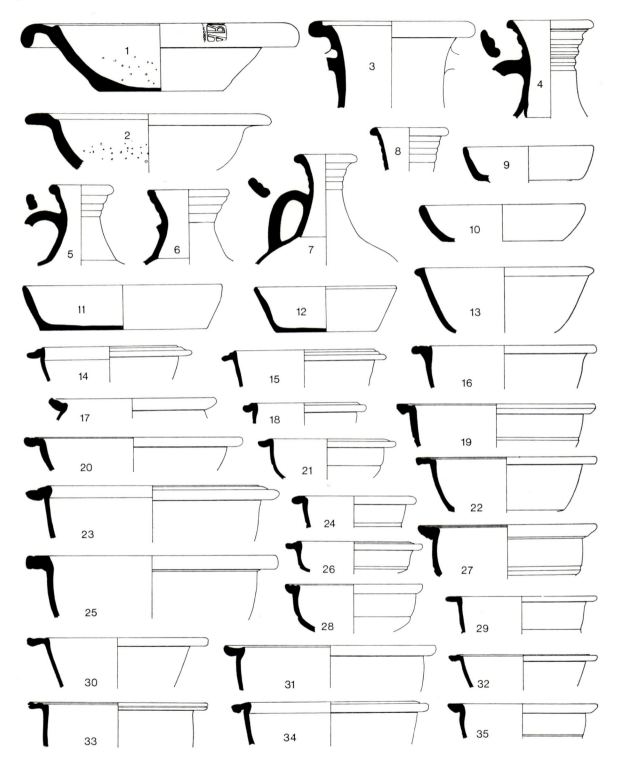

FIG. 95.   Coarse pottery (scale ¼)

(now in print and cited as *Verulamium 1972*) and parallels are quoted from this report extensively (as Ver. followed by a number, e.g. Ver. 566). I am also indebted to Mrs K. Hartley, F.S.A., for commenting on the mortaria (any comments following a description of a vessel are hers), and to Mr H. Sheldon for parallels from the Highgate kilns. Mr C. Henderson and Mr J. Dunkley have also assisted in the preparation of this report.

The following note, kindly supplied by Mrs Hartley, is a general classification of different mortaria fabrics used at kilns near Oxford. Mortaria from these kilns, listed within this report, will be classified accordingly:

Two basic mortarium fabrics were used at kilns near Oxford (Cowley, Sandford, Dorchester, Headington, Littlemore and elsewhere; *Oxon.*, vi (1941), 9–21, *Arch.*, LXXII (1922), 225–42, *Oxon.*, I (1936), 81–102; *Oxon.*, XVII/XVIII (1952–3), 224–5).

A.   A slightly sandy, cream fabric sometimes with a pink core and often with a buff slip; abundant pinkish and whitish translucent, crystalline trituration grits.

B.   Fine-textured reddish brown fabric sometimes with grey core; and with a samian-like red-brown colour-coat; trituration grit as for fabric A.

Bb.   Exactly as fabric B but with a cream or white slip. Fabrics B and Bb would be made from the same clay but Fabric A would require a different clay.

Pottery from Ditch I (figs. 95–9)

1.   Mortarium with stamp of]ARINVS. Hard, sandy, buff fabric. Probably from kiln at Brockley Hill and dated about A.D. 85. For discussion on mortaria stamp see (a), p. 212. Illustration (a), fig. 94. See no. 140.

2.   Mortarium. Hard, sandy, buff fabric. Worn. Place of manufacture unknown, but probably in the south, or in the south midlands. Probably early second century.

3.   Neck from amphora. Hard, sandy, pinkish-buff fabric, with grey core and buff surfaces. (Ver. 819 dated A.D. 155–60.)

4.   Flagon. Fine, sandy, pinkish-buff fabric. The neck has been sharply tooled.

5.   Ring-neck flagon. Same fabric as 4.

6.   Ring-neck flagon. Very soft buff fabric. Similar to above but with no prominent bead rim. (Ver. 563 also with four cordons around neck, and dated A.D. 145–50.) At Verulamium the type does not extend later than the Antonine period.

7.   Ring-neck flagon. Hard, fine, sandy, pinkish-fabric with buff surfaces. A second example is unillustrated. (Ver. 566 dated A.D. 130–50.) At Verulamium similar types with cut ringed necks occur *c.* A.D. 105, but the type does not occur later than *c.* A.D. 160.

8.   Ring-neck flagon. Fine, sandy, buff fabric with light grey slip.

9.   Dish. Hard, pinkish-buff fabric. Dark chocolate slip. Probably an intrusion.

10.   Dish. Orange fabric with grey core. Traces of mica dusting. (Ver. 219–21 dated to A.D. 60–75.) At Verulamium, the form also occurs in deposits dated A.D. 105–30, and occurs in levels dated A.D. 150–5. It is also residual in the fourth century.

11.   Dish. Grey fabric with black surfaces. Internally burnished.

12. Dish. Hard, sandy, orange, buff fabric. Pinkish-orange slip.

13. Bowl. Sandy, dark grey fabric. Exterior burnished. Light grey slip on rim. The basic form occurs at Verulamium in the middle of the second century, and remains in use until the end of the third century.

Reeded-rim bowls

A large number of reeded-rim bowls were found in Ditch I varying in size and form, the latter often with subtle changes. A general selection of these forms is illustrated. The basic type first appears at Verulamium as early as A.D. 49–60 (see Ver. 90) and continues in use until the end of the second century.

14. Hard, sandy, grey fabric.
15. Hard, sandy, grey fabric. Burnt.
16. Hard, sandy, light pinkish fabric.
17. Jar. Hard, sandy, buff fabric. Traces of white slip on rim.
18. Hard, sandy, buff-ochre fabric.
19. Hard, sandy, dark grey fabric with buff surfaces. Burnt.
20. Hard, sandy, pinkish-grey fabric. Burnt.
21. Hard, sandy fabric. Heavily burnt. (Rim form of Ver. 684 similar and dated A.D. 135–45.)
22. Grey fabric, burnished overall. Burnt.
23. Hard, sandy, buff fabric. Burnt.
24. Hard, fine, sandy, grey fabric. Burnt.
25. Hard, sandy, pinkish fabric. Burnt. (Ver. 395 similar but with thinner rim, dated *c.* A.D. 105.)
26. Hard, sandy, pinkish fabric with buff surfaces. (Ver. 673 similar, but wider, dated A.D. 140–50.)
27. Hard, sandy, grey fabric with buff surfaces. Burnt.
28. Hard, sandy fabric. Heavily burnt. (Rim similar to Ver. 669, dated A.D. 130–50 but body less carinated.)
29. Hard, fine, sandy, buff fabric. Burnt. Another slightly smaller example of this form is un-illustrated. (Ver. 90, dated A.D. 49–60.)
30. Grey fabric with brown surfaces. Exterior slightly burnished.
31. Hard, sandy, pinkish fabric and surfaces. Traces of pink-orange slip. Burnt.
32. Hard, sandy, pinkish-buff fabric and surfaces. Traces of off-white slip on rim. (Possibly from dish similar to Ver. 218, dated A.D. 60–75, but residual to A.D. 150–5/60.)
33. Hard, sandy, buff fabric with black surfaces. Burnished internally.
34. Hard, sandy, dark grey fabric. Off-white slip. Burnt.
35. Hard, sandy fabric. Heavily burnt.

Bowls

36. Fine, sandy, dark grey fabric. Burnt. (Ver. 691 dated A.D. 130–40 similar, but without the ridge below the rim.) At Verulamium the type appears to have become obsolete by the late Antonine

period. The latest date the form appears is *c*. A.D. 150. At Gadebridge the type also appears no later than late Antonine.

37. Hard, sandy, pale pinkish fabric.

38. Grey fabric, with traces of grey slip. Burnt and worn.

39. Fine, uniform off-white fabric. (Similar to Ver. 339 dated A.D. 85–105, but also similar to 691 dated A.D. 130–40.)

40. Buff grey fabric with black surfaces. Worn.

41. Orange fabric with pinkish-buff surfaces.

42. Fine, soft, pinkish-orange fabric, with grey core. Slight traces of red colour coat. A second example of this form is unillustrated. At Verulamium the vessel first appears (Ver. 315) A.D. 85–105, but cf. Ver. 945 and 948, dated A.D. 150–5/60, probably from a similar vessel. The form probably derives from Samian form 37.

43. Flanged bowl. Hard, pinkish-buff fabric. Dark chocolate slip.

44. Beaker in soft, brown fabric. Worn, but shows traces of external burnishing. (Ver. 516 in mica-coated reddish ware, dated A.D. 115–30.)

45. Bowl with combed decoration. Grey fabric.

46. Carinated beaker in grey fabric. (Ver. 135 dated A.D. 60–75.) Others residual at Verulamium dated A.D. 105–15 and A.D. 130–50.

47. Dish or bowl. Soft, orange fabric with brown grey core. (Ver. 739 similar, dated *c*. A.D. 150.)

48. Bowl imitating Samian form 29. Red-orange fabric with buff-orange surfaces. Light grey slip. The type does not occur at Gadebridge later than the Antonine period.

Jars and beakers, similar to 49–64 are common in this group, and many are unillustrated. They also occur in the gully beneath Rooms 25 and 26 and also (pot no. 143) in Room 7. (They occur at Verulamium from c. A.D. 60 and continue with minor alterations of form until c. A.D. 175.)

49. Poppyhead beaker with cordon on shoulder and barbotine dot decoration. Grey fabric with light grey slip. The type occurs at Verulamium from early in the second century up until *c*. A.D. 175. (Ver. 379 dated *c*. A.D. 105, Ver. 1047–9 dated A.D. 160–75.) Mr Sheldon considers fabric too gritty for Highgate Ware.

50. Poppyhead beaker with cordon on shoulder and barbotine dot decoration. Grey fabric with light grey slip. Probably from Highgate kiln.

51. Jar. Grey fabric with light grey slip on rim and shoulder. (Ver. 617 dated A.D. 145–50.)

52. Jar with cordon and groove. Soft, red-brown fabric with grey surfaces and traces of grey slip. (Ver. 279 dated A.D. 75–85 similar but has no lower body groove.) The basic type continues in use until the late Antonine period mainly with lattice decoration on the shoulders.

53. Beaker. Grey fabric with grey slip. Undecorated version of 49.

54. Jar with lattice decoration. Smooth, soapy textured fabric with black, slightly burnished external surfaces. Black internal surface with red blotches.

55. Jar with cordon. Sandy, brown-grey fabric. (Ver. 383, dated *c*. A.D. 105.) At Verulamium the type occurs in levels as early as A.D. 60 and in levels dated A.D. 130–50. It also occurs residually A.D. 270–5. At Gadebridge a similar type is found in a late second/early third-century context from the filling of the well. See 201. The form is identical to those produced at Highgate.

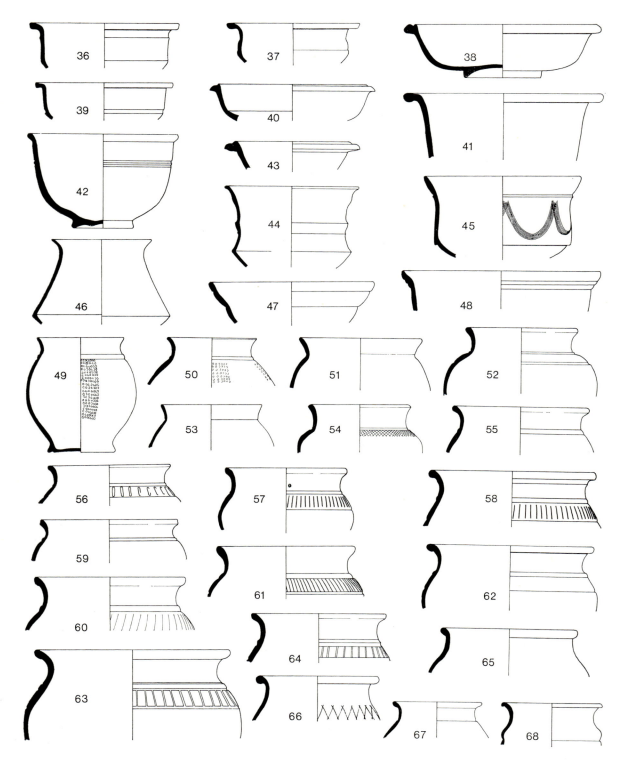

FIG. 96. Coarse pottery (scale ¼)

56. Jar with vertical line decoration between cordon and groove. Brown fabric with grey surfaces and grey slip on rim and shoulder.

57. Jar with vertical line decoration between cordon and groove. Hole drilled in neck. Brown-grey fabric with grey core. (Ver. 440, dated A.D. 115–30.)

58. Jar. Brown fabric and brown-grey surfaces. Burnished vertical line decoration between cordon and groove. Light grey slip on rim and shoulder. Worn.

59. Jar. Brown-grey fabric with traces of grey slip. Worn.

60. Jar in grey fabric and grey slip. Burnished vertical line decoration below cordon.

61. Jar in grey fabric with vertical line decoration between cordon and groove.

62. Jar in brown fabric with grey slip. Cordon and groove on body.

63. Jar. Fairly hard, sandy, grey fabric with some large grits. Burnished decoration of horizontal and vertical lines. Burnt. Possibly manufactured at Highgate.

64. Jar in grey fabric with grey slip on rim and shoulder. Burnished line decoration. (Ver. 611 dated A.D. 130–50.)

65. Jar in grey fabric and grey slip. Traces of burnishing on exterior.

66. Jar in soft, grey fabric and grey slip. Burnished lattice decoration. Burnt.

67. Jar in grey fabric and black surfaces. Burnt.

68. Jar in grey fabric. Worn.

69. Jar. Uniform, fine, sandy, off-white fabric. Base sherd slightly softer so may belong to different vessel.

70. Beaker. Sandy, red-brown fabric with dark grey surfaces. Cordon on shoulder, and vertical comb decoration on the body.

71. Beaker in orange fabric with grey external surfaces. Almost untempered. Another similar form in fine off-white fabric is unillustrated. (Ver. 144 dated A.D. 60–75.) At Verulamium the form has disappeared by c. A.D. 100.

72. Beaker in soft, grey fabric. Worn.

73. Beaker decorated with bosses. Soft, orange fabric sparsely tempered with fine sand. Mica dusted externally. (Rim form identical to Ver. 128 dated A.D. 60–75, and occurring residually up to A.D. 150.)

74. Beaker in light grey fabric with grey surfaces and traces of grey slip. Barbotine dot decoration.

75. Jar with burnished lattice decoration in brown fabric and black surfaces. Highly burnished externally. (Ver. 615 similar, dated A.D. 140–50.) At Verulamium the type also appears in levels dated A.D. 115–30.

76. Jar in sandy, brown-grey fabric with black external and brown internal surfaces.

77. Jar with internal rim. Grey fabric with dark grey exterior; blotches of orange on interior.

78. Jar in grey fabric with light grey slip on rim and shoulder.

Flasks and narrow-necked jars

79. Narrow-necked jar in brown-orange fabric with white slip on exterior.

80. Flask in grey fabric with light grey slip. Burnished lattice decoration below cordon. (Ver. 121, dated A.D. 60–75, similar but undecorated.) Cf. 183, from the well, a later version of the form and probably dated to the late second or early third century.

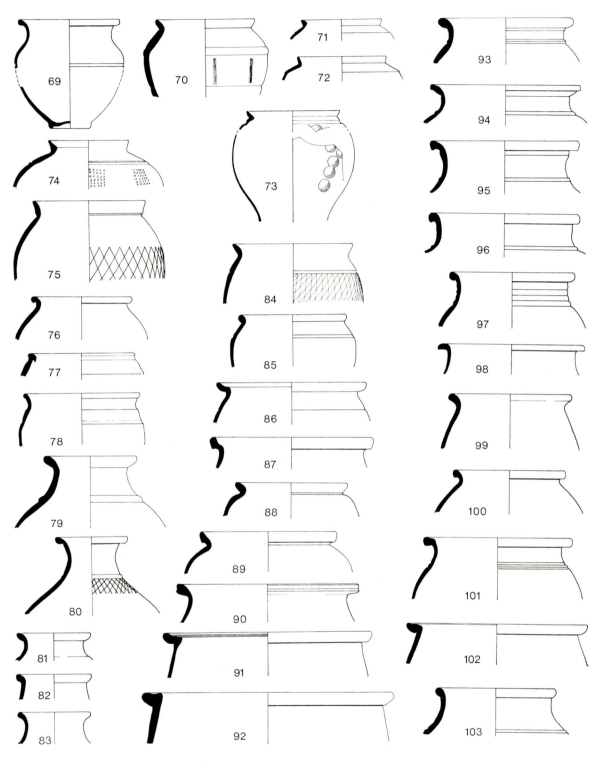

FIG. 97.　Coarse pottery (scale ¼)

81. Sandy, grey fabric with black surfaces. Exterior slightly burnished. (Ver. 831, dated A.D. 155/60.)

82. Soft, orange, shell-tempered fabric with buff surfaces.

83. Sandy, grey fabric with light grey slip on rim and shoulder.

Jars

84. Grey fabric with traces of grey slip. Burnished lattice pattern below groove. Worn.

85. Smooth, soapy textured fabric with black, slightly burnished external surfaces. Groove on shoulder. Burnt. (Ver. 389, dated *c.* A.D. 105.)

86. Hard, sandy, pinkish-grey fabric with pinkish-buff surfaces. Burnt. (Ver. 483, dated A.D. 105–30; for later versions see Ver. 905, dated A.D. 155/160 and Ver. 1062, dated A.D. 200–75.)

87. Hard, sandy, buff fabric. Burnt.

88. Fairly hard, sandy, dark grey fabric with black surfaces. Burnt. (Ver. 194, dated A.D. 60–75. Ver. 857 also a similar type but dated A.D. 150–5/60.)

89. Sandy, red-brown fabric with black surfaces. Burnt.

90. Hard, sandy, buff fabric.

91. Hard, sandy, buff fabric. Burnt. Upturned reeded rim. (Ver. 665, somewhat similar and dated A.D. 130–50. Others occur in levels dated A.D. 115–30, and A.D. 145–50.)

92. Hard, sandy, buff fabric. Burnt.

93. Hard, grey fabric. Slightly burnished externally.

94. Hard, fine, sandy, grey fabric with light grey slip.

95. Fairly hard, sandy, dark grey fabric. Burnt.

96. Hard, sandy fabric. Heavily burnt. (Ver. 69, dated A.D. 49–75, but contaminated.)

97. Jar with three cordons on neck. Soft, grey fabric.

98. Jar. Pale pinkish fabric with traces of orange slip inside rim.

99. Grey fabric with black surfaces. Rim and exterior burnished. (Ver. 288, dated A.D. 85–105.) The type appears not to have extended into the Antonine period.

100. Hard, grey fabric.

101. Hard, sandy, buff fabric. Burnt. (Ver. 648, dated A.D. 140–50.) The form does not appear at Verulamium until the second century.

102. Jar in hard, sandy, pinkish fabric.

103. Jar in grey fabric with light grey slip.

104. Dark grey fabric with burnished lattice decoration between two cordons.

105. Grey fabric with black surfaces. Exterior slightly burnished.

106. Hard, sandy, grey fabric.

107. Hard, grey fabric. Grooves on shoulder.

108. Hard, sandy, pinkish fabric. Burnt.

109. Hard, sandy, pinkish-buff fabric with off-white surfaces. Burnt.

110. Hard, sandy, pinkish fabric with buff surfaces.

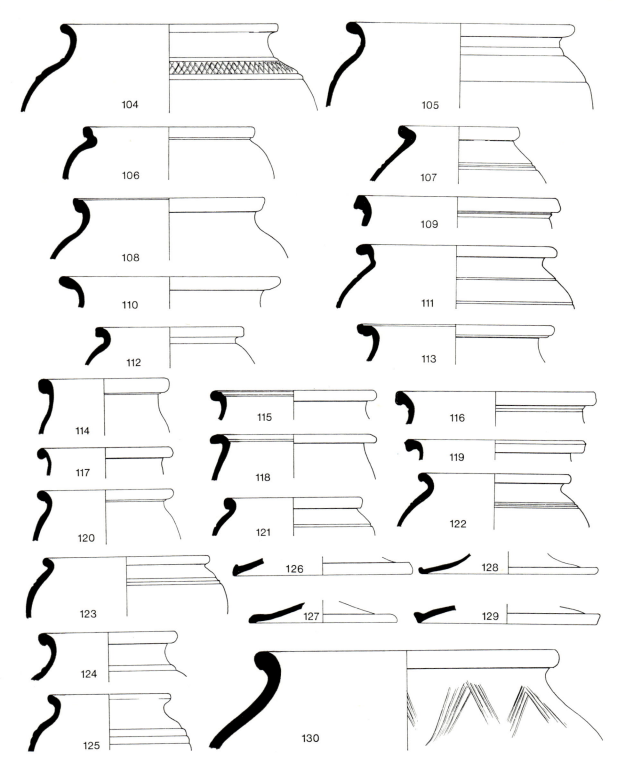

FIG. 98.   Coarse pottery (scale ¼)

111. Hard, grey fabric. Grooves on shoulder.
112. Fine, sandy, light grey fabric.
113. Hard, sandy, pinkish-buff fabric with off-white surfaces.
114. Hard, sandy, pinkish fabric. Burnt (much narrower version of Ver. 877, dated A.D. 155/160).
115. Hard, sandy, buff fabric with orange-ochre internal slip. Burnt.
116. Hard, sandy, buff fabric. Groove on neck. Burnt.
117. Hard, sandy, pinkish-buff fabric. Burnt.
118. Hard, sandy, grey fabric.
119. Hard, sandy, pinkish fabric with buff surfaces. Traces of pink-orange slip on rim.
120. Sandy, brown fabric with grey-brown surfaces. Burnt.
121. Brown fabric with black surfaces. Flint grit tempering.
122. Hard, sandy, buff fabric.
123. Hard, sandy, grey fabric.
124. Hard, sandy, brown-grey fabric with burnished black surfaces.
125. Hard, sandy, brown fabric with grey surfaces.

Lids

126. Hard, sandy, pinkish fabric. Burnt.
127. Hard, fine, sandy, orange fabric. Burnt.
128. Sandy brown-grey fabric. Burnt and worn.
129. Brown fabric with black surfaces.

Storage jars

130. Storage jar with faint burnished decoration. Coarse, grey-orange fabric. (Ver. 86 dated A.D. 49–60.)
131. Storage jar with scored decoration. Coarse, dark grey fabric with black external surfaces and patches of brown on interior. Rim worn, and possibly broken.
132. Coarse grey fabric with black surfaces.
133. Coarse, shell-tempered, grey fabric with blotches of orange on surfaces. Graffito reading ANN cut on to body. See (j) (fig. 113) for illustration. For Mr Wright's description, see p. 255.
134. Cooking pot. Hard, sandy, pinkish fabric with pinkish-buff external surface. Tempered with many ceramic particles.
135. Coarse orange fabric with grey core. Shell and flint-tempered. (Ver. 666, dated A.D. 140–50, a less heavy version.) The form occurs extensively at Verulamium throughout the mid-second century. Smaller versions, 220 and 221, were found in the well.
136. Brown-grey fabric with black surfaces. Rim and exterior burnished.
137. Storage jar. Coarse pinkish-buff fabric with orange external and red internal surfaces. Large flint grits.

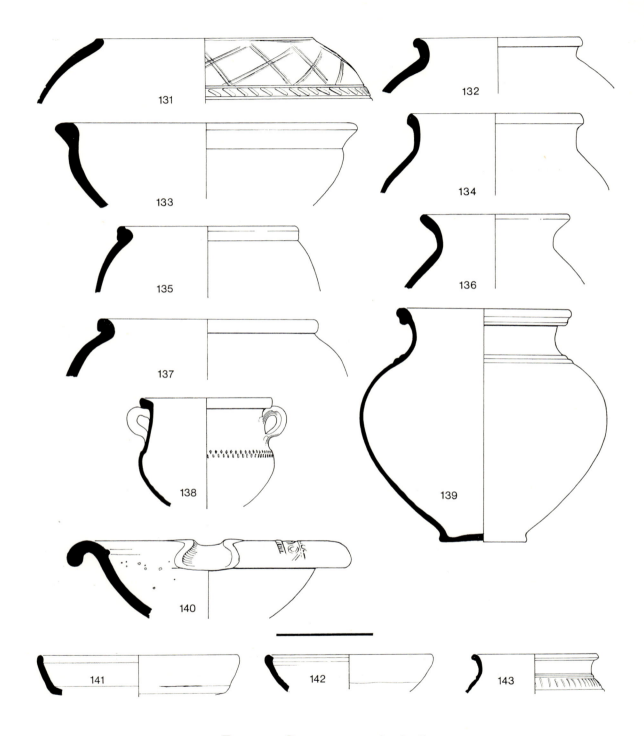

FIG. 99.   Coarse pottery (scale ¼)

138.   Two-handled bowl with rouletted decoration. Hard, sandy, buff fabric.

139.   Jar with cordons on shoulder. Hard, sandy, buff fabric. (Ver. 879, dated A.D. 155/160 very similar.) At Verulamium the type is first represented by Ver. 170, dated A.D. 60–75.

140.   Mortarium. Hard, sandy, buff fabric. Stamps of DOINVS (N and S reversed) from die D of Doinus on either side of spout. Interior surface worn. Brockley Hill pottery. Probably later than A.D. 85. For discussion on mortaria stamp see (*b*), p. 212. Illustration (fig. 94*b*). Two fragments of mortaria stamped]LBINV[and F.LV[in the same fabric as 140 were also found. *c* and *d* consecutively in mortaria report, p. 212 (fig. 94).

Pottery from Room 7, fig. 99 (Section A–B, fig. 11)
Layer 8

141.   Dish in soft pale red fabric. Core a little darker. Traces of mica dusting. (Somewhat similar to Ver. 219 dated A.D. 60–75.) For other Gadebridge examples see 9 and 10 from Ditch I. At Verulamium the form occurs in the mid-second century, and residually into the fourth century.

142.   Dish. Hard, grey, sandy fabric with burnished surfaces. Traces of grey slip on outside rim.

Layer 4

143.   Beaker in hard, grey fabric with pale grey surfaces. Vertical line decoration below cordon. A similar pot was also found in layer 5. Pottery of this type occurred extensively in Ditch I; cf. nos. 55–64. At Verulamium the form occurs in levels as early as *c.* A.D. 60 and remained in use until the Antonine period.

Pottery from gully south of bathing pool, fig. 100 (Section E–F, fig. 40)
Layer 9 — gravel at bottom of leat

144.   Bowl with reeded rim. Hard, sandy, buff fabric. Burnt.

145.   Jar. Smoothed, soapy, dark grey fabric.

146.   Bowl. Fine, soft light grey fabric with grey core. Burnt and worn. (Ver. 945, dated A.D. 150–5/60.)

147.   Jar. Hard, sandy, buff fabric with orange slip inside rim.

Forms similar to 10, 45, 49, 52, 106, and 211, were also found in this layer. The form similar to 211 has a graffito; see (i) (fig. 113). The bulk of the pottery is dated to the late first, mid-second century. The length of survival for the lagena discovered with this group and dated c. A.D. 60–80 is questionable. Such a fine vessel must have been treasured and therefore could well have survived into the second century.

Layer 7 — associated with a coin of Antoninus Pius

148.   Bowl with faint burnished lattice decoration. Hard, sandy, grey fabric with lightly burnished surfaces and light grey slip. At Verulamium the form is first represented by Ver. 715 and 716 dated A.D. 140–50. However the form is residual until the end of the third century.

149.   Lid. Hard, sandy, pinkish-brown fabric with light surfaces.

150.   Bowl with reeded rim. Hard, sandy, grey fabric. Burnt.

151.   Storage jar. Coarse, shell-tempered, pinkish-buff fabric with grey core.

Q

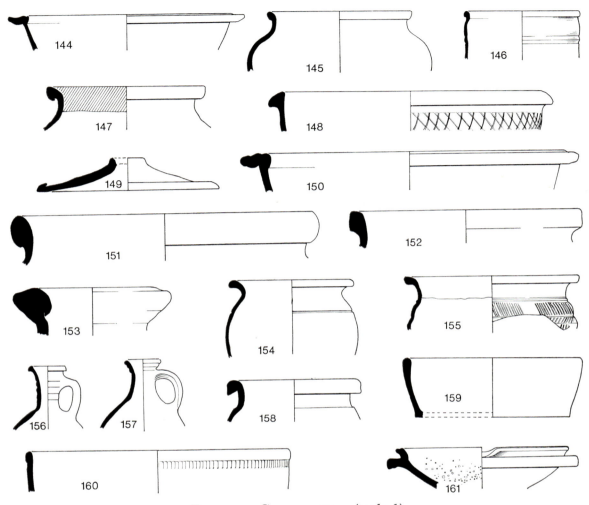

FIG. 100.　Coarse pottery (scale $\frac{1}{4}$)

152.　Cooking pot. Coarse, shell-tempered, buff fabric with grey core.

153.　Amphora neck. Hard, sparsely sandy, brown-buff fabric with grey core.

154.　Jar. Hard, sandy, grey-brown fabric with grey core.

155.　Jar with burnished line decoration between cordon and groove. Black slip on rim and exterior. Burnished externally.

156.　Flagon neck. Hard, sandy, red-brown fabric with slate-grey core and buff external slip. (Ver. 804 dated A.D. 155–60, a similar form, but different fabric.)

157.　Flagon neck. Hard, sandy, pinkish-orange fabric with off-white external slip. (Ver. 560, dated A.D. 130–45, has a thicker body.)

Forms similar to 68, 65 and 91 from Ditch I, and 187, 199, 211 and 214 from the well, also came from this layer. The similarity of pottery forms with those found in the well would suggest that this layer was deposited during the late second/early third centuries.

Layer 4 — associated with three coins, the latest of which is dated A.D. 367–75

158.   Jar. Fine, hard, pinkish-orange fabric with grey core. Surfaces smooth and coated with slip fired dark chocolate externally and reddish-brown internally.

159.   Dish. Coarse, shell-tempered, dark grey fabric. Surfaces smooth, brown-orange internally and black externally.

160.   Wide bowl with band of rouletting. Uniform reddish-orange fabric. Worn, but traces remain of red colour coat. Probably manufactured in the Oxfordshire region.

161.   Mortarium. Fabric A. Made in the Oxford region. Probably late third or fourth century.

Forms similar to 187 and 314 also came from this layer.

Pottery from the well, figs. 101–3, Section X–Y (fig. 17)

Layer 13

162.   Mortarium. Fine textured, brownish-cream fabric with flint trituration grit. Made in south-eastern England (Colchester or Kent), or in Gaul. Probably Flavian.

163.   Flagon neck with horizontal zig-zag decoration. Light grey fabric and internal surface. Black exterior with vertical burnishing.

Layer 12

164.   Ring-neck flagon. Hard, pinkish-orange fabric with orange ochre surfaces.

165.   Bowl. Grey fabric, burnished externally. Traces of light grey slip on rim.

166.   Bowl. Brown fabric with dark grey core and smooth buff-grey surfaces. Traces of black slip. (Ver. 960, dated A.D. 150–5/160 similar, but less straight sided.) At Verulamium the type does not appear until about the second quarter of the second century and continues in use until the late third century (Ver. 1082, dated A.D. 175–275.)

167.   Bowl. Light grey, slightly micaceous fabric with traces of black slip.

168.   Bowl. Sandy, grey, slightly micaceous fabric, smoothed exterior. Grey slip on rim and neck. Dribbles run towards base.

169.   Bowl. Fine, sandy, light grey fabric. (Rim of Ver. 982, dated A.D. 155/60 similar.) Date range as no. 166.

170.   Bowl. Hard, sandy, buff-grey fabric.

171.   Dish with groove below rim and decoration of interlaced arcs. Red-brown fabric with grey core and black burnished surfaces.

172.   Dish. Red-brown fabric with dark grey core. Black exterior burnished.

173.   Beaker. Pinkish-orange fabric with chocolate slip.

174.   Bowl with slight internal rim. Sandy, light grey fabric. Surfaces eroded but traces of grey slip.

175.   Bowl. Fabric similar to 172.

176.   Beaker with barbotine scale-decoration. Hard, pink fabric. Dark chocolate slip. (Ver. 1058, dated A.D. 155/160, is the earliest version illustrated from Verulamium. Others, Ver. 1141 and Ver. 1142, are dated A.D. 310–15.)

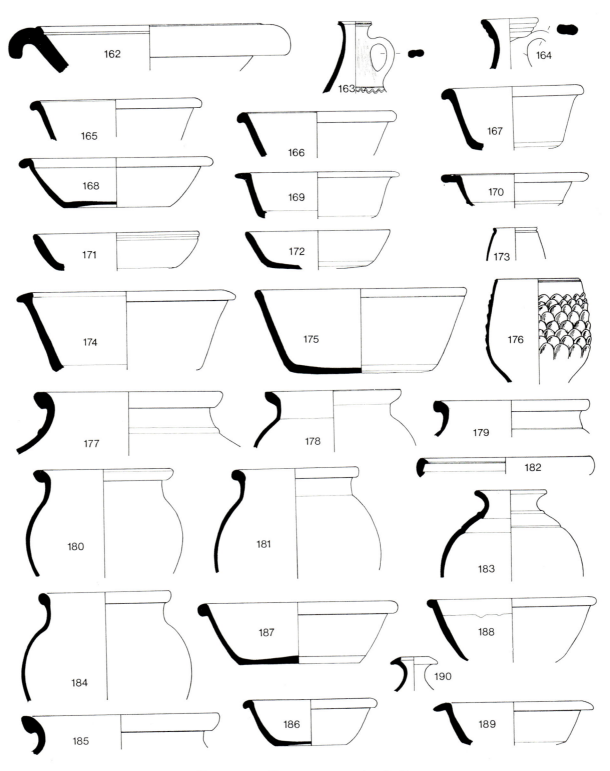

FIG. 101. Coarse pottery (scale ¼)

Jars 177–81

177.   Coarse, grey-brown fabric tempered with large flint grits.
178.   Hard, sandy, buff fabric. Burnt.
179.   Hard, sandy, buff fabric. Burnt.
180.   Hard, pinkish fabric with buff surfaces.
181.   Hard, fine, sandy, pinkish-brown fabric with orange-ochre surfaces. (Ver. 879, dated A.D. 155/60 similar but wider.) Others occur at Verulamium dated A.D. 130–60.
182.   Rim. Fine, off-white fabric with pinkish core.
183.   Flask with cordon and groove on shoulder. Hard, sandy, pinkish-brown fabric. Grey slip on rim and shoulder. Temper contains some large dark brown ceramic particles.

Layer 10

184.   Jar. Hard, pinkish-buff fabric.
185.   Cooking pot. Coarse, buff fabric with grey core. Tempered with large angular grits.
186.   Bowl. Hard, dark grey fabric, burnished externally. Grey slip on rim.

Layer 9

187.   Bowl. Red-brown fabric with grey core and black burnished surfaces.
188.   Bowl. Sandy, dark grey fabric, externally burnished. Grey slip on rim.
189.   Dish. Dark grey fabric with traces of black slip. (Ver. 724, dated A.D. 130–50.) At Verulamium the type first appears *c.* A.D. 130 (see Ver. 711) but occurs residually until *c.* A.D. 280.
190.   Flagon neck with disc rim. Hard, orange fabric.

Layer 8

191.   Bowl. Dark grey fabric with black burnished surfaces. (Ver. 988, dated A.D. 150–5/60.) See 189 for comments on life of type at Verulamium.
192.   Dish. Fabric similar to 191.
193.   Dish. Fabric similar to 191.
194.   Jar. Hard, sandy, pinkish-buff fabric with buff surfaces. Similar to nos. 195, 196 and 225.
195.   Jar. Hard, sandy, grey fabric with buff surfaces.
196–8. Jars. Fabric similar to no. 194. Burnt.
199.   Bowl with reeded rim. Hard, sandy, grey fabric with buff surfaces.
200.   Bowl with reeded rim. Hard, sandy, pink-buff fabric. Surfaces orange-buff.
201.   Jar with girth and neck grooves. Hard, sandy, red-brown fabric. Burnished on shoulder. Overall grey-black slip. Some ceramic temper.
202.   Jar with cordon on shoulder and horizontal burnished lines on body. Hard, fine, sandy, grey fabric. Grey slip on rim and shoulder.

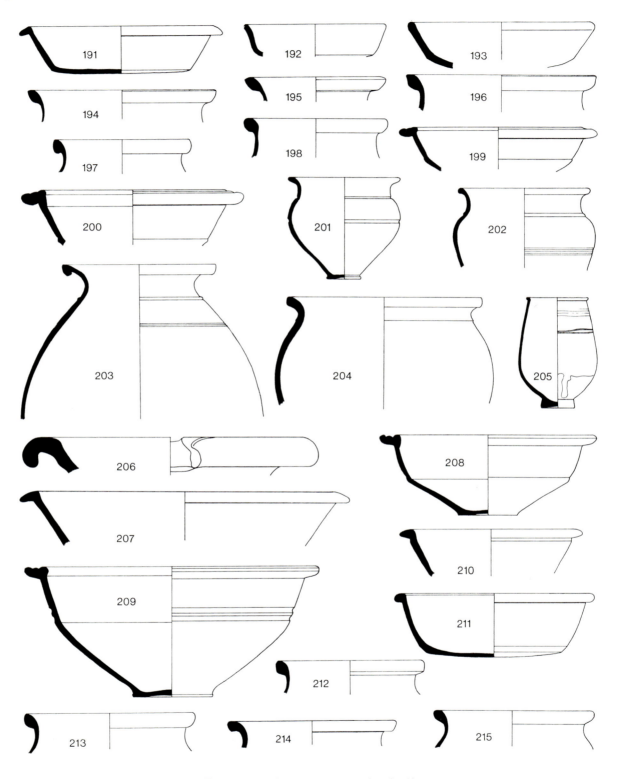

Fig. 102. Coarse pottery (scale $\frac{1}{4}$)

203. Jar with cordon and grooves on neck. Hard, orange-pink fabric. Buff interior and orange-buff exterior surfaces. Some ceramic temper.

204. Cooking pot. Coarse, shell-tempered, grey-buff fabric with buff interior surface.

205. Beaker. Hard red-brown fabric with grey core. Exterior coated in dark grey slip with trail running towards base. Burnished lines on exterior.

206. Mortarium rim. Hard, buff-grey fabric with orange surfaces. Made at kilns in the potteries south of Verulamium, including those at Radlett and Brockley Hill (*B.I.A.*, v (1965), 34). *c.* A.D. 100–40.

Layer 5

207. Flanged bowl. Burnished, light grey fabric. Overall grey-black slip. Larger version of 191.

208. Bowl with reeded rim. Sandy, dark grey fabric. Burnt.

209. Bowl with reeded rim and two body grooves. Hard, sandy, orange-buff fabric.

210. Bowl. Sandy, dark grey fabric. Black slip on rim. Similar rim form to 207, but slightly undercut beneath rim.

211. Bowl. Red-brown fabric with grey core. Grey-black burnished surfaces. (Smaller version of Ver. 1082 dated A.D. 175–275.)

212. Jar. Hard, fine, sandy, pinkish-buff fabric. At Verulamium the type does not occur until the mid-second century (cf. Ver. 878, dated A.D. 155/60). See 213, 225, 226 also in Layer 5 from the well.

213. Jar. Hard, sandy, pink-buff fabric with buff surfaces.

214. Cooking pot. Coarse, brown-grey, shell-tempered fabric. Probably third century. A form, no. 316, of similar type and identical fabric was found in a fourth-century context from Room 20. At Verulamium (Ver. 1283) the type extends into the fifth century.

215. Jar. Brown-grey fabric with light grey core. Black burnished external surface. Traces of grey slip on rim and shoulder.

216. Rhenish beaker. Fine, pink fabric. Lustrous black coating.

217. Amphora with foot-ring. Soft, buff fabric. Large numbers of fragments from these vessels were found at Colchester (*Colchester Kilns*, Form 188, fig. 74, 2). The date range given is A.D. 175–210.

218. Poppyhead jar with rouletted rim, rouletted cordon, and lower body rouletting. Hard, fine, sandy, pink fabric with buff surfaces.

219. Pinch-mouthed flagon. Hard, fine, sandy, orange fabric.

220. Cooking pot. Coarse, grey fabric tempered with large shell and flint grits. See 221.

221. Cooking pot with internal ledge for lid. Coarse, shell-tempered grey-buff fabric. See 135, 220. (Ver. 666, dated A.D. 140–50 similar. Another, Ver. 1050, is dated A.D. 160–75.)

222. Jar with grooves on shoulder. Hard, sandy, grey fabric. Light grey slip on rim and shoulder. Externally burnished.

223. Jar. Grey fabric with traces of light grey slip.

224. Jar. Hard, sandy, buff fabric.

225. Jar. Fabric similar to 224.

226. Jar. Fabric similar to 224.

227. Jar with cordon on shoulder. Grey fabric, externally burnished, with whitish-grey external slip.

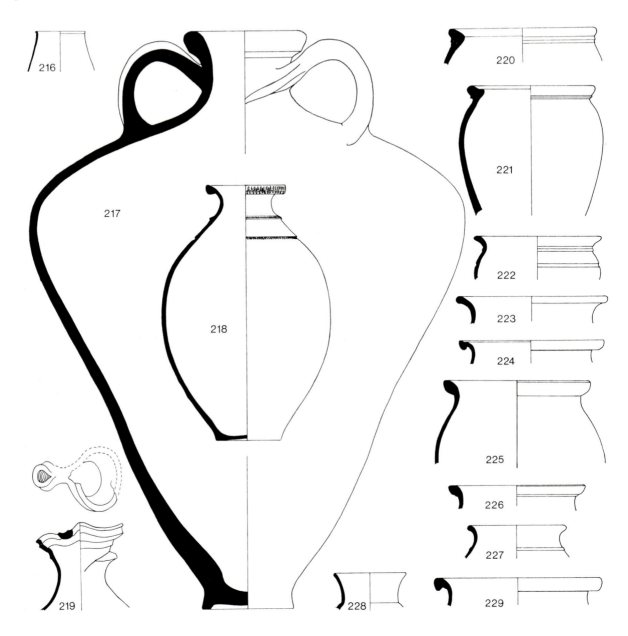

FIG. 103.　Coarse pottery (scale ¼)

Layer 4

228.　Poppyhead beaker. Grey fabric with external grey slip. Beakers of this type occur at Verulamium in the early second century, but the closest forms are Ver. 1049, dated A.D. 160–75 and Ver. 1073, dated A.D. 175–275.

229.　Jar. Grey fabric with grey slip and burnished rim.

Pottery from Southern East–West Ditch 2, fig. 104. Section EE–FF, fig. 7

Layer 3

230. Jar. Buff fabric, burnt.

231. Jar. Hard, sandy, grey fabric. (Ver. 385, dated *c.* A.D. 105.) At Verulamium the type appears to have become obsolete by the middle of the second century.

232. Jar. Hard, sandy, grey-black fabric. Heavily burnt. Similar rim form to 108.

233. Jar. Browny-grey fabric with orange surfaces. (Ver. 284, a similar form dated A.D. 75–85.) The type continues into the Antonine period.

234. Jar. Hard, sandy, grey fabric.

235. Bowl. Grey, fine, sandy fabric. Worn.

236. Jar. Sandy fabric with brown paste and grey surfaces.

237. Cooking pot. Hard, sandy, grey-black fabric. Heavily burnt.

238. Bowl with reeded rim. Soft, orange-red fabric. Temper sparse.

239. Jar. Soapy orange fabric. Surfaces burnished.

Layer 2

240. Narrow-necked jar. Brown fabric with grey core. Surfaces burnished, light grey slip. (Ver. 248, dated A.D. 90–105, and Ver. 828, dated A.D. 150–5/60, similar.)

241. 'Hors-d'œuvre' bowl divided into four compartments by vertical walls. Hard, sandy, red-brown fabric with black soapy burnished surfaces. Some ceramic temper. There is a similar vessel from Colchester (*Colchester Kilns*, fig. 74, nos. 3 and 3A), but with no flange and a circular central compartment dividing the vessel into five units. A late second-century date is probable for this form.

242. Mortarium. Hard, sandy, pink paste with light buff surfaces. Most of the grits inside have been worn off. Made in kilns at the potteries south of Verulamium.

Layer 1

243. Bowl. Hard, sandy, grey fabric. Slightly burnished externally. Traces of white overall slip. (Ver. 720 dated A.D. 130–40 similar.) See also 191 from the well.

244. Bowl. Sandy, browny-grey fabric with black burnished surfaces. (Ver. 715, dated A.D. 140–50 similar, but decorated.) Others from Verulamium residual up to A.D. 270–80. See also 148.

245. Bowl. Grey fabric with grey-black burnished surfaces. Worn. (Ver. 978, dated A.D. 150–5/60.)

246. Cooking pot. Hard, smooth, pink fabric, with buff surfaces. (Ver. 630, dated A.D. 140–50. Ver. 873, dated A.D. 150–5/60.) This form, characterized by its hooked rim, appears to be a mid second-century type.

247. Jar. Hard, sandy, grey fabric.

248. Jar. Hard, sandy, buff-grey fabric. Burnt.

249. Jar. Orange-brown fabric with burnished light grey slip inside and outside rim.

250. Jar. Hard, fine, sandy, brown fabric with black surfaces. Slightly burnished externally. (Ver. 892, dated A.D. 150–5/60.) The form appears at Verulamium during the early second century.

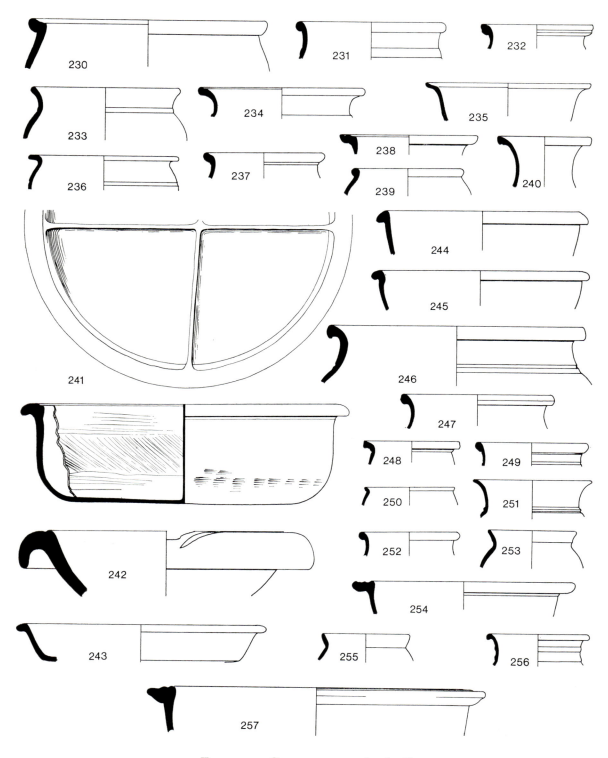

FIG. 104.　Coarse pottery (scale ¼)

251. Jar. Grey fabric. Worn. Rim form similar to Ver. 837, dated A.D. 155/60. Other examples from Verulamium are dated A.D. 200–25/50 and A.D. 270–5.

252. Cooking pot. Soapy-textured orange-brown fabric with smooth burnished surfaces.

253. Jar. Grey fabric. Worn. (Ver. 615 similar, dated A.D. 140–50.)

254. Bowl with reeded rim. Hard, sandy, buff fabric.

255. Jar. Orange-brown fabric with grey core. Burnished slip on exterior, and inside rim.

256. Jar. Hard, fine, sandy, brown fabric with black surfaces. Slightly burnished externally.

257. Bowl with thick reeded rim. Hard, buff, sandy fabric. Another bowl with reeded rim, similar to 91 was also found in this layer.

Pottery from the filling of Room 20, figs. 105–7, Section L–M (fig. 6)

The pottery from Room 20 has been published as a complete group irrespective of whether it came from the rubble filling, L 3, or from the occupation deposit, L 5. Often the pottery forms from both layers were the same type, and in some instances the sherds joined. Also there was no difference between the dates of the coinage in the rubble and the dates of the coinage in the occupation (see Coin Appendix A, page 118). From the numismatic evidence this group of pottery can be assumed to have been in use from about the second quarter of the fourth century up to *c.* A.D. 353, when the room was abandoned. Some of the pottery types from this group continue elsewhere on the site up until the late fourth century. They also continue at Verulamium up to A.D. 410+. Some sherds come from a black squatters' layer in L 3. This was mainly confined to the northern area of the room, and is not shown on Section L–M. However the appropriate sherds will be identified.

258. L 5. Ring-necked flagon. Hard, sandy, grey fabric with grey slip, burnished in places.

Mortaria

259. L 2. Hard off-white fabric with sparse quartz grits in paste. Place of manufacture unknown, but probably from southern England or the south midlands.

260. L 5. Fabric A. Manufactured in the Oxfordshire region. Painted decoration on the flange and bead is very unusual on mortaria made in these potteries. Probably from the same vessel as 399.

261. L 5. Fabric A. Manufactured in the Oxfordshire region. Another rim sherd from the same vessel was also found in L 3.

262. L 5. Hard, sandy, pink fabric with buff surfaces. Made at kilns in the potteries south of Verulamium, including those at Radlett and Brockley Hill (*B.I.A.*, v (1965), 34). A similar form has been noted from a pit of wasters at Radlett (unpublished) and a related form from a pit of wasters at Verulamium (*Antiq. J.*, xxi (1941), 279, fig. 3, k). *c.* A.D. 140–200.

263. L 5. Fabric A. Made in the Oxfordshire region.

264. L 3. Fabric A. Made in the Oxfordshire region. Late third or fourth century.

265. L 3. Fabric A. Made in the Oxfordshire region. This form is usually considered to be fourth-century in date but there is no adequate evidence to prove that they could not have been made in the late third century.

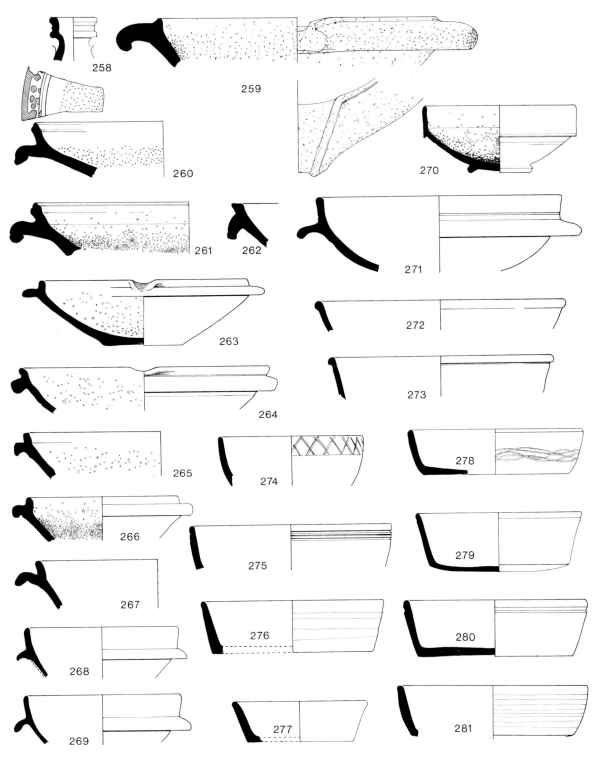

Fig. 105.   Coarse pottery (scale ¼)

266. L 3. Fabric A. Made in the Oxfordshire region.

267. L 5. Fabric A. Made in the Oxfordshire region. Third or fourth century.

268. L 3. Flanged bowl. Pinkish-orange paste with red colour-coat. An identical form was also found in L 5.

269. L 5. Flanged bowl. Orange fabric with red colour-coat. A similar example 11 cm. in diameter is unillustrated.

270. L 5. Mortarium. Fabric B. Manufactured in the Oxfordshire region. Mortaria in imitation of samian form Dr. 45 were commonly imitated at Dorchester, Oxfordshire, and probably elsewhere in the late third, and in the fourth century.

271. L 3. Flanged bowl in pinkish-orange paste, with grey core. Red colour-coat.

272. L 3. Dish in hard orange fabric with red slip.

273. L 3. Bowl in soft brown-orange fabric with red colour-coat.

274. L 3. Pie dish with lattice decoration. Hard, sandy, dark grey fabric. Black burnished surfaces.

275. L 5. Pie dish. Hard, grey fabric with black burnished surfaces. Grooves below rim.

276. L 3. Pie dish. Hard, grey fabric with grey, burnished surfaces. Outer surface below rim left rough.

277. L 3. Pie dish. Hard, sandy, dark grey fabric with burnished black slip internally. An identical form with light grey internal slip was also found in L 5.

278. L 5. Pie dish. Hard, fine, sandy, grey fabric, slightly burnished. Decorated with wave pattern.

279. L 5. Pie dish. Hard, dark, grey fabric with black burnished surfaces.

280. L 5. Pie dish. Hard, dark grey fabric with burnished black surfaces. Groove below rim.

281. L 3. Pie dish. Hard, sandy, dark grey fabric with black burnished surfaces.

282. L 3. Dish. Hard, sandy, dark grey fabric with black, burnished surfaces.

283. From squatter layer in L 3. Dish, Hard, sandy, grey fabric with internal black slip. Burnished.

284. L 5. Deep bowl in hard grey fabric. Lightly burnished.

285. L 5. Bowl. Hard grey fabric with black burnished decoration.

286. L 5. Bowl with burnished arc decoration. Hard grey fabric with black burnished surfaces.

287. L 3. Bowl rim. Hard, sandy, grey fabric with light grey surfaces. Burnished.

288. L 3. Bowl. Hard, fine, sandy, dark grey fabric. Burnished black surfaces.

289. L 3. Bowl. Hard, sandy, grey fabric and burnished black surfaces.

290. L 3. Bowl with burnished interlaced arc decoration. Hard, sandy, dark grey fabric with burnished black surfaces.

291. L 3. Bowl. Hard, sandy, dull grey fabric. Black surfaces, burnished internally.

292. L 5. Bowl. Hard, sandy, buff-grey fabric, with internal white burnished slip.

293. L 5. Bowl with burnished interlaced arc decoration. Hard, dark grey fabric with black burnished surfaces. (Type occurs at Verulamium, Ver. 1250 and 1251, up to A.D. 410+.)

294. L 5. Bowl rim in hard, sandy, dark grey fabric. Black burnished surfaces.

295. L 5. Bowl. Hard, sandy, dark grey fabric with black burnished surfaces.

296. L 3. Bowl. Hard, orange fabric with burnished orange surfaces.

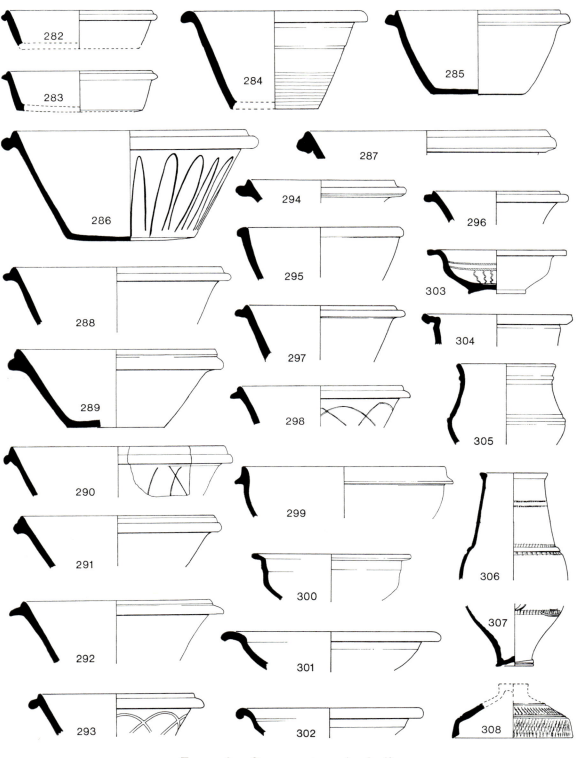

FIG. 106.   Coarse pottery (scale ¼)

297.   L 3.   Bowl. Brown fabric with black burnished surfaces. Burnt. Similar type with interlaced arc decoration also found in L 5.

298.   L 5.   Bowl with burnished interlaced arc decoration. Hard, sandy, dark grey fabric with black burnished surfaces.

299.   From squatter occupation in L 3. Bowl. Coarse, shell-tempered, dark grey fabric. Burnt. (Ver. 1258, a similar form, continues at Verulamium up to A.D. 410+.)

300.   L 3.   Bowl. Hard, sandy, grey fabric with orange surfaces. Burnt.

301.   L 3.   Bowl. Orange fabric with red slip. Traces of white painted decoration on rim.

302.   L 5.   Bowl. Fine, soft, buff-brown fabric with grey core. Red colour-coat. Traces of white tendril decorations on rim. Worn.

303.   L 3.   Bowl. Hard, fine, sandy, red fabric with white painted decoration inside. A similar form, but smaller, and in the same fabric, was also found in L 5.

304.   L 3.   Bowl with reeded rim. Hard, sandy fabric. Heavily burnt. Late second-century form, probably residual.

305.   L 5.   Jar with grooves and cordons. Hard, sandy, grey fabric. Surface black and highly burnished externally from neck down to girth cordon.

306.   L 5.   Beaker. Brown-orange fabric with grey core. Chocolate slip. Rouletting on neck and shoulder.

307.   L 5.   Base with rouletting, and barbotine decoration. Hard, pinkish-orange fabric with dark chocolate lustrous slip.

308.   'Castor ware box' lid. Hard, orange-buff fabric with slip firing dark chocolate externally and reddish-brown internally. Found in silt at bottom of eaves drip to west of room. Another lid, with a diameter of 24 cm., came from L 2.

309.   L 5.   Thumb-indented beaker with rouletted decoration. Dark chocolate slip externally, red-brown internally. Pinkish-orange fabric.

310.   L 2.   Base. Hard, off-white fabric with light brown slip. Same ware as 312.

311.   L 5.   Sherd from flagon. Hard, white fabric. Burnished. Decorated with two brown painted lines.

312.   L 2.   Beaker. Fine, off-white fabric with dark chocolate external, and light brown internal, slip.

313.   L 5.   Cooking pot. Coarse, soapy, shell-tempered fabric with blotches of brown and orange. Burnt.

314.   L 3.   Cooking pot. Hard, grey fabric, lightly burnished.

315.   L 5.   Cooking pot. Coarse, soapy, shell-tempered fabric. Similar to 313. Burnt. Found sitting over remains of oven in south-west corner of room.

316.   From squatter occupation in L 3. Cooking pot. Coarse, brown, shell-tempered fabric. Heavily burnt.

317.   Jar. Hard, grey fabric, lightly burnished. Squatter occupation in L 3.

318.   L 5.   Jar in hard, grey fabric. Notched decoration on rim. Identical form from L 5, Section C–D–E (fig. 38).

319.   L 3.   Jar in hard, fine, sandy, red-brown fabric with external dark grey surfaces. Burnt.

320.   L 3.   Jar in hard, grey fabric, slightly burnished.

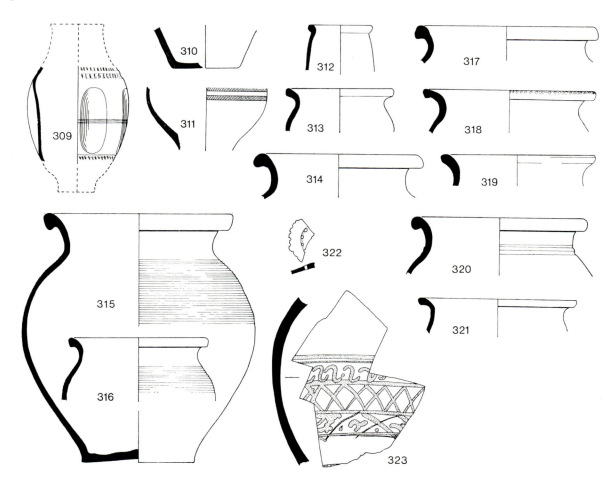

FIG. 107.   Coarse pottery (scale ¼)

321.   From squatter occupation in L 3. Jar in coarse, brown, shell-tempered fabric. Heavily burnt.

322.   L 5.   Colander base. Fine, sandy, grey fabric.

323.   L 3.   Fragment of large storage jar, with orange-ochre fabric, with grey core. Decoration in red-brown paint.

Pottery from the filling of the bathing pool and water leat, figs. 108–9, Section C–D–E (fig. 38)

No differences were observed between the dates of the coinage in layers 8 and 5, although the pottery in these layers has been described separately.

Layer 13 — the pottery in this group is probably associated with the early water leat

324.   Jar. Dark buff, soapy fabric with black surfaces. (Ver. 151 similar, dated A.D. 60–75. Ver. 444, a later example, dated A.D. 105–30.)

325.   Jar. Grey-buff fabric and surfaces. (Ver. 293, dated A.D. 75–85, a similar version.)
326.   Jar. Grey-buff fabric and surfaces.
327.   Jar. Grey, very sandy fabric. Surfaces light grey.

Layer 12

328.   Flanged bowl. Buff-grey fabric and surfaces. A late third/fourth-century type.
329.   Flagon rim in buff fabric and orange surfaces.

Layer 11

330.   Flanged bowl in very dark grey, gritty fabric with black burnished surfaces.
331.   Reeded rim bowl in off-white fabric, grey exterior.

Layer 10

332.   Jar. Coarse, shelly-grey fabric with pinky-orange surfaces.
333.   Jar. Grey fabric with very pale orange surfaces.
334.   Pie dish. Hard, sandy-grey fabric with black surfaces.
335.   Flagon neck. Pale orange fabric with external chocolate slip.
336.   Rim of bowl. Hard, sandy, grey fabric with buff surfaces.
337.   Bowl in pink fabric with traces of red colour-coat. Slightly micaceous.
338.   Bowl with rouletted decoration on exterior. Orange fabric and red colour-coat.

Layer 8 — associated with a deposit of 173 coins, the accumulation of which is dated c. A.D. 340–50

339.   Jar in orange fabric and surfaces. Exterior burnished.
340.   Dish in hard, grey fabric. Traces of light grey slip on surfaces.
341.   Dish in sandy, dark buff fabric. Dark grey surfaces. Swag decoration on exterior.
342.   Deep, straight-sided bowl in orange fabric and surfaces. Tempered with fine ceramic particles.
343.   Jar in hard pale grey fabric, with buff surfaces.
344.   Jar in hard grey fabric, dark grey interior, and dark buff-grey exterior.
345.   Mortarium in hard white fabric and surfaces, probably manufactured in the Verulamium region. Interior sparsely covered with grits. Remains of stamp on rim. Dated A.D. 90–140. For discussion on mortarium stamp (fig. 94) see (e), p. 213.
346.   Jar with everted rim. Grey fabric with pale grey slip on exterior and inside rim.
347.   Flanged bowl in hard buff-grey fabric with black surfaces.

Layer 5

348.   Flanged bowl in hard red-grey fabric with black surfaces.
349.   Bowl in hard grey fabric with black burnished surfaces. Wave pattern decoration below inside rim.
350.   Small bowl in grey fabric. Black burnished outer surface, grey unburnished interior.
351.   Dish in grey, slightly gritty fabric. Traces of black colour-coat on exterior.

R

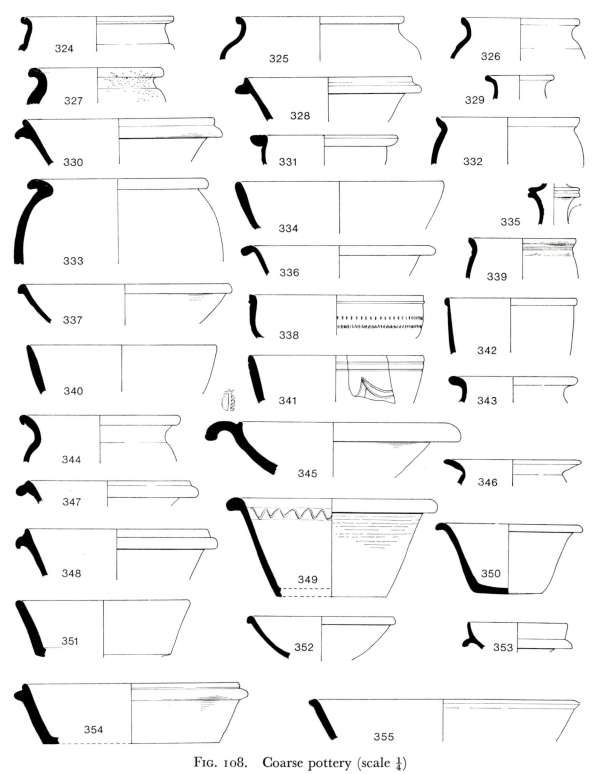

FIG. 108.   Coarse pottery (scale ¼)

352. Bowl in pale orange fabric with red colour coat. Vessel blackened, possibly the result of reducing atmosphere in kiln.

353. Small flanged bowl in very pale orange fabric with dull red colour-coat.

354. Flanged dish in hard, light grey fabric. Light grey exterior surface. Interior and upper flange coated in pale grey slip.

355. Dish in buff-grey fabric with surfaces blotched grey and buff-orange. Traces of black colour-coat on interior.

356. Bowl in fine orange fabric and chocolate surfaces. Rouletted decoration on exterior. (It is possible that this vessel is a lid.)

357. Bowl in pale grey, smooth fabric, with orange surfaces. Red colour-coat. Similar form from L 2.

358. Jar with everted rim. Hard, buff-grey fabric and dark grey inner surface. Exterior burnished very smooth.

359. Jar in hard, grey fabric with grey surfaces.

360. Storage jar in hard, grey fabric with buff surfaces.

361. Jar in fine, pale grey fabric, with pale orange surfaces.

362. Large jar. Coarse, shelly-grey fabric with ochre surfaces.

363. Mortarium. Fabric A. Interior surface pale orange. Made in the Oxfordshire region. Probably fourth century.

364. Mortarium. Fabric A. Made in the Oxfordshire region. Probably late third or fourth century.

365. Jar in fine, orange fabric. Traces of dull red colour-coat. Burnishing on exterior below rim.

366. Pie dish in dark grey fabric and black surfaces. Interior surface burnished.

367. Jar in hard, grey, smooth fabric with dark grey interior and black burnished exterior. Decorated with a boss pushed out from the body, surrounded with a circular burnished outline. The sherd was submitted to Dr J. N. L. Myres, p.s.a., for examination as to whether it was Romano-Saxon and I am grateful to him for the following comment:
      This is certainly typically Romano-Saxon both in form and fabric, as well as the decoration. Slight roundels of this kind with a central depression seem to be a variant of the usual arrangement of alternate round bosses and triangular groups of dimples.

368. Fragment of beaker in grey fabric, fired orange on exterior. Traces of thin chocolate slip over orange body. Horizontal band of rouletting with barbotine decoration — possibly that of an animal, but sherd too small for positive identification.

369. Rim from bowl in orange fabric and red colour-coat. White paint tendril decoration on rim.

370. Mortarium. Fabric A. From pit equated with L 5. Made in the Oxfordshire region. Probably third century.

371. Pie dish in dark grey fabric with 'lug' handle decorated on top with a 'bird's foot' motif. There are also burnish marks on the side of the 'lug'. The underside of the base is decorated with a scribble pattern of no formal design. From pit equated with L 5.
      (a)   Jar identical to 318 from filling of Room 20, L 5, Section L–M (fig. 6).

Pottery from beneath tessellated pavement (L 4) in Room 28 (fig. 110), Section U–V (fig. 37). Associated with two radiates, the latest of which is irregular, dated to c. A.D. 270

      (a)   Mortarium with rim similar to 370, but with wider triangular-shaped flange. Fabric A. Burnt. Made in the Oxfordshire region.

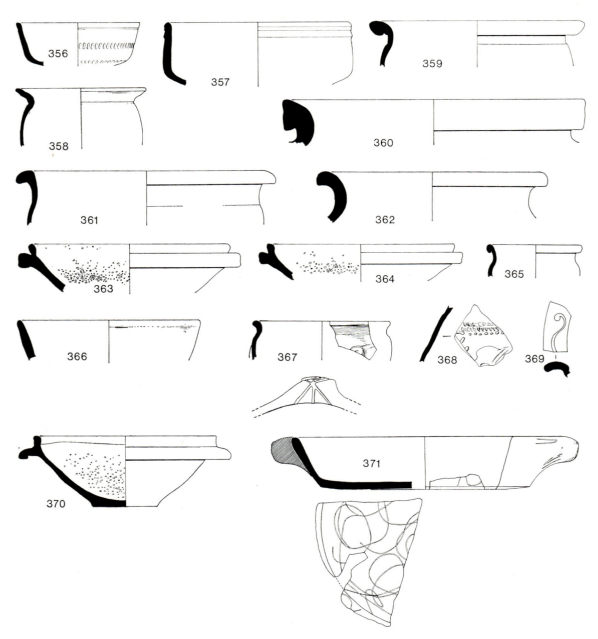

FIG. 109.   Coarse pottery (scale ¼)

(b)   Mortarium in orange-red fabric, grey core. Fabric B. Manufactured in the Oxfordshire region. Similar to 270.

372.   (c)   Fragment of bowl in orange-red fabric, red colour-coat. Decorated with vertical lines of half circles and dots. Probably from lion or bat-headed spout. Imitation of samian form. Dr. 45.
(d)   Pie dish in hard, brown-grey, sandy fabric and surfaces, with burnished inner surface. Form similar to 278.

(e) Pie dish in hard, grey fabric. Burnished internally and externally. Wave decoration on exterior. Form similar to 278.

(f) Pie dish in buff, grey fabric, with deep burnished lines on surfaces. Wave pattern on exterior. Form similar to 278.

373. (g) Shallow dish in hard, light grey fabric with darker grey surfaces. (Ver. 1179 dated A.D. 310–15 similar.) At Verulamium the type continues in use until A.D. 410+.

374. (h) Very small flanged bowl in smooth orange-buff fabric, with dark grey surfaces. (Ver. 1260, a similar form, occurs up to A.D. 410+.)

(i) Flanged bowl, similar, but less heavy than 289. Hard, grey fabric, oxidized orange on flange. Burnished internally and externally.

(j) Flanged bowl similar to 31. Hard, grey, gritty fabric. Burnished internally and externally.

(k) Rim of Castor ware beaker with graffito reading NATV[s on exterior (fig. 113e). See (e), p. 254.

(l) Fragments of scale decorated beaker similar to 176, but in orange-red fabric with pale grey core.

(m) Fragments of thumbed Castor ware beaker, with rouletted decoration on shoulder. Fabric identical to no. 306.

375. (n) Two fragments from beaker with barbotine decoration showing head of stag. Pale grey fabric and interior. Exterior pale orange with chocolate slip.

376. (o) Flagon neck in soft, orange-red fabric. Uniform colouring throughout.

(p) Jar similar to 319, but in hard, orange fabric. Sparsely tempered with red ceramic particles. Burnt.

(q) Jar similar to 320, body thinner. Fine, grey fabric at core, grey-brown exteriors. Horizontal burnishing.

Pottery from Building D, Section II–JJ–KK (fig. 33)

The pottery from this building is generally of similar forms to pottery groups in Room 20 and the filling of the bathing pool. However, whereas grey and black wares predominate in these groups, the pottery from this building has a larger proportion of red colour-coated wares. The greatest bulk was found in the destruction levels, Layers 4, 3 and 2, although a quantity was recovered from the occupation deposit L 5; these forms are described. Unfortunately Pit L beneath the north-east corner of the building yielded only one sherd, this being found in a charcoal layer (not shown on section) between layers 17 and 18. Forms not represented in other groups are illustrated. From the coin evidence none of the pottery is later than c. A.D. 353 though many of the forms continue in use at Verulamium until A.D. 410+.

Pit L (a) Jar in pale grey fabric with orange surfaces. From charcoal layer between layers 17 and 18. Similar to 225.

Layer 5 — associated with 13 coins the earliest of which is dated A.D. 270 and the latest a coin of Magnentius dated A.D. 351–3 (see Coin Appendix B, p. 118)

(a) Flanged bowl in grey fabric and surfaces. Similar to 288.

(b) Deep bowl in soft orange fabric and surfaces. Surfaces now eroded, originally red colour-coated. Form similar to 342.

(c) Bowl in soft orange fabric with red colour-coat. Form similar to 337.

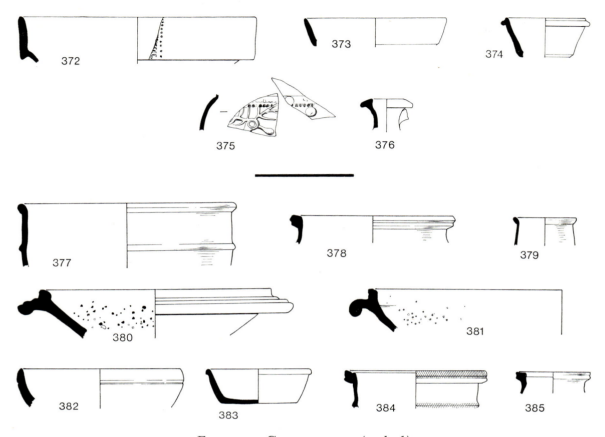

FIG. 110.   Coarse pottery (scale ¼)

377.   (d)   Bowl in soft orange fabric with red colour-coat.
(e)   Bowl in pale grey, sandy fabric with pale orange surfaces. Traces of grey colour-coat.
Form similar to 284.
(f)   Jar in hard, orange fabric and dark grey surfaces. Exterior burnished. Form similar to 225.

378.   (g)   Jar in buff fabric and surfaces.
(h)   Jar in hard grey fabric and orange to brown surfaces. Form similar to 108, but without
indentation on inside rim.

379.   (i)   Beaker in soft, pale orange fabric and surfaces.
(j)   Jar in coarse, soapy, shell-tempered fabric. Burnt. Form similar to 315.

*Layer 4 — associated with 10 coins the earliest of which is of Gallienus dated A.D. 259–68, and the latest a coin
dated A.D. 361–3 (see Coin Appendix B, p. 118)*

380.   (a)   Mortarium in off-white fabric and surfaces. Large black grits on inner surface. Burnt.
Made in kilns in the Castor-Stibbington area of the Nene Valley. Probably late third or early
fourth century.

381. (b) Mortarium. Fabric A. Made in the Oxfordshire region.

(c) Flanged bowl imitation Dr. 38. Grey core, orange surfaces and red colour-coat. Similar form to no. 269.

(d) Bowl in red fabric and surfaces. Red colour-coat. Form similar to no. 337 and another form from L 5.

(e) Bowl in slightly sandy, orange-red fabric, with red colour coat. Similar form to 357 but thinner body. Fragment from same vessel also in L 3.

382. (f) Bowl in hard, pale grey fabric, grey burnished interior, buff exterior.

383. (g) Small pie dish in grey fabric and dark grey surfaces.

384. (h) Jar in pink fabric and off-white surfaces. Red-brown painted decoration on rim and cordon. (Ver. 1245 similar and dated A.D. 370–410+ but type occurs in an earlier context dated A.D. 275–300.)

(i) Jar in coarse, soapy, shell-tempered fabric. Form and fabric similar to 315, but rim more rounded.

(j) Fabric as above, but form more similar to 316.

385. (k) Small jar in soft, pale grey fabric, with dark grey surfaces.

Layer 3

(a) Bowl in orange fabric, red colour-coat. Form as 352, but larger.

(b) Cooking pot in dark, coarse, soapy, shell-tempered fabric. Form the same as 316 but larger.

(c) Flanged bowl in hard, grey fabric with dark grey surfaces. Rim form similar to 354.

Pottery from Building E. A total of 20 coins were associated with this building. The earliest is dated c. A.D. 270 and the latest A.D. 388–402 (see Coin Appendix C, p. 119)

The pottery from this building either came from an occupation layer over the floor, or was found in the destruction material: there were no other layers. The layer in which the pot was found is indicated. The coins in the occupation would suggest that the pottery was in use up until the late fourth century.

386. Mortarium. Fabric A. Manufactured in the Oxfordshire region. Sealed by ash from oven in south-east corner of room.

387. Mortarium. Fabric A. Destruction material in western room. Manufactured in the Oxfordshire region.

388. Mortarium. Fabric A. Manufactured in the Oxfordshire region. In deposit of ash sealed by destruction material.

389. Bowl in grey fabric. Destruction material.

390. Flagon. Hard, orange-red fabric with external slip. Filling of gully to east of building.

391. Bowl with impressed decoration on reeded rim. Orange fabric with light grey core. Destruction material.

392. Base of jar in pale buff-orange fabric with brown slip overall. Set into clay floor in eastern room.

393. Jar. Fine, orange fabric and surfaces. Occupation deposit.

394. Bowl with stamped decoration. Pinkish-orange fabric with traces of orange slip. Occupation deposit.

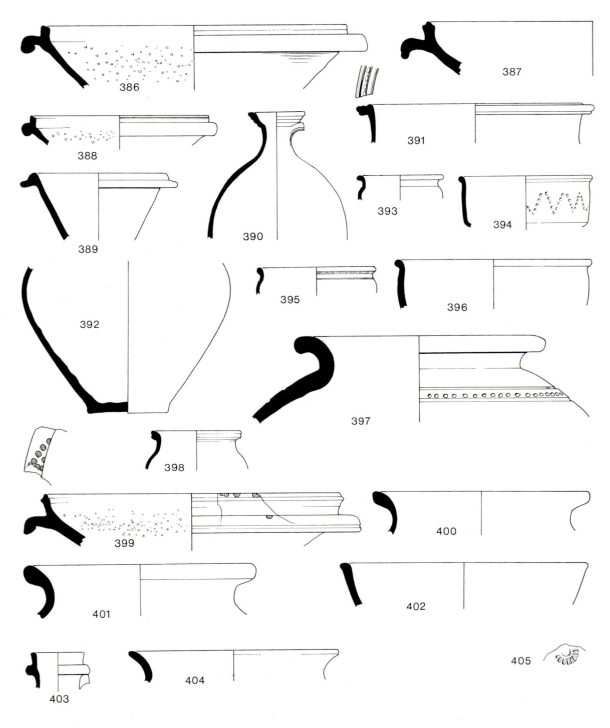

FIG. 111.   Coarse pottery (scale $\frac{1}{4}$, except 405, $\frac{1}{2}$)

395. Bowl with rouletted decoration under rim. Orange fabric with red slip. Destruction material.

396. Bowl with beaded rim. Sandy, dark grey fabric with black, slightly burnished surfaces. Destruction material.

397. Storage jar with indented decoration between horizontal grooves. Fairly hard, grey fabric with pinkish-buff surfaces. Temper of fine sand and flint grits. Destruction material.

398. Small jar in buff fabric and surfaces. Destruction material.

In addition to the above, three sherds were similar to types from other groups, and there was one medieval sherd

    (a) Jar in hard, grey fabric and surfaces. Form similar to 232. Destruction material.

    (b) Jar in fine, grey fabric and surfaces. Form similar to 320. Destruction material.

    (c) Flanged bowl in buff-grey fabric with dark grey surfaces. Traces of pale grey slip on interior surface. Form identical to 290. Destruction material.

    (d) Medieval sherd (Pot no. 423) from upper destruction material. Described in an appendix to this report, p. 253.

Pottery from Pit M, Section II–JJ–KK (fig. 33)

Layer 3 — this layer yielded four coins, the latest of which is dated A.D. 341–6

399. Mortarium decorated with brown spots. Fabric A. Manufactured in the Oxfordshire region. Similar form and possibly from the same vessel as 260. See 260.

400. Cooking pot. Coarse, shelly, dark grey fabric with buff exterior and black interior surfaces. Similar form also found in L 2.

401. Large jar. Coarse, shelly, dark grey fabric with brownish surfaces.

402. Dish. Coarse, dark grey fabric with burnished buff surfaces.

403. Flagon neck. Hard, orange-buff fabric with traces of orange slip.

Layer 2

404. Jar. Hard, sandy, grey fabric. Grey slip.

405. Body sherd with impressed wheel decoration: twice the scale of other drawings. Pale orange fabric with pale grey core. (Similar stamps on Ver. 1229 and 1290 dated A.D. 350–410+ and A.D. 370–410+ respectively.)

Pottery from chalk quarry, Pit U, Section PP–QQ (fig. 47)
Layer 6

406.   (a) Deep flanged bowl in hard, pale grey fabric with darker grey surfaces.

    (b) Jar in pale grey fabric, with pale orange surfaces. Rim form similar to 313.

Layer 5 — associated with two coins of Allectus (A.D. 293–6)

407. Neck of flask in hard, dark grey fabric and surfaces. Shoulder burnished.

408. Storage jar in hard, grey, sandy fabric with grey surfaces. Decorated on body with impressed chevrons.

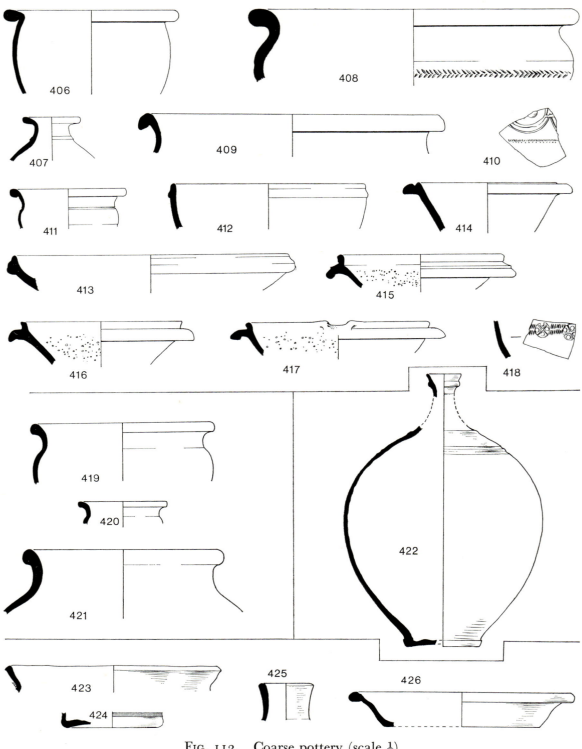

FIG. 112.　Coarse pottery (scale ¼)

Layer 4

  (a) Cup in pale orange fabric and surfaces. Form similar to 312.

409. (b) Jar in soft, pale grey fabric with pale orange surfaces.

410. (c) Fragment of beaker in pale grey fabric with pale orange surfaces. Chocolate slip on exterior. Barbotine decoration.

Layer 3 — associated with 19 coins, the latest of which is dated A.D. 341–8

  (a) Jar in grey-brown fabric with dark gray surfaces. Form similar to 358, but rim somewhat thicker.

411. (b) Jar in fine, hard, reddish-grey fabric with pale grey surfaces. The fabric of this vessel is very similar to many of the second-century vessels from the filling of Ditch I, e.g. form 51.

  (c) Storage jar in coarse, dark grey fabric with pale reddish surfaces. Form similar to 397 from Building E.

  (d) Bowl in pale orange-red fabric with traces of red colour coat. Form similar to 337.

412. (e) Bowl in pale grey fabric with pale red surfaces. Red colour-coat.

413. (f) Bowl in pale grey fabric with pale red-orange surfaces. Red colour-coat.

  (g) Flanged bowl imitating samian form Dr. 38. Pale grey fabric with orange surfaces. Dark red colour-coat, possibly overfired. Form similar to 269.

414. (h) Bowl in soft, white fabric with reddish-brown colour-coat.

  (i) Base from a beaker in fabric similar to the above, but with orange colour-coat.

  (j) Jar in pale grey fabric with surfaces fired pale orange. Red colour-coat. Form similar to 365.

415. (k) Mortarium. Fabric B. Manufactured in the Oxfordshire region. Red colour-coat.

416. (l) Mortarium. Fabric B. Manufactured in the Oxfordshire region.

  (m) Mortarium imitating samian form Dr. 45. Pale grey fabric with orange surfaces. Very dark red colour-coat, probably overfired. Form similar to 270, but has thicker rim.

417. (n) Mortarium. Fabric Bb. Manufactured in the Oxfordshire region.

418. (o) Sherd in pale grey fabric with pale orange surfaces. Dull red colour-coat. Circular stamp decoration over rouletting.

Pottery similar to nos. 278, 282, 288 and a smaller version of 373, was also found.

Pottery from chalk quarry, Pit V, Section NN–OO, fig. 48

Layer 8

  (a) Jar in very pale red fabric with ochre surfaces. Grey slip on outside body and on inside rim. Form similar to 125, but with no cordons.

  (b) Bowl in hard, pale grey fabric and surfaces. Burnished. Form similar to 289.

  (c) Bowl in orange-red fabric and surfaces. Red colour-coat with white painted scroll decoration on rim. Imitation of samian form Dr. 36. Similar to 301. This bowl was subsequently used as a mortarium and the inside surface is extremely worn.

Layer 7

  (a) Mortarium in soft grey fabric, with orange surfaces. Red colour-coat. Form the same as 270, but wider.

Layer 6

      (a)   Pie dish in hard, grey fabric with dark grey surfaces. Form similar to 281, but thicker.

      (b)   Cooking pot in coarse, grey, shell-tempered fabric. Form the same as 316.

419.   (c)   Jar in orange fabric and surfaces. Traces of red colour-coat on exterior.

420.   (d)   Small jar in orange fabric and surfaces. Traces of brown slip on outer rim.

Layer 3 — associated with a single coin dated A.D. *335–41*

421.   (a)   Large jar in hard, grey fabric with dark grey surfaces. Fragment rather eroded, possibly residual.

      (b)   Pie dish in brown-grey fabric with grey surfaces. Burnished. Form similar to 281.

      (c)   Bowl in orange fabric and surfaces. Dark red colour-coat. Form imitating samian form Dr. 38. Similar to 269.

Layer 2

      (a)   Jar in coarse, shelly, grey fabric with orange surfaces. Form the same as 135.

Pottery from chalk quarry, Pit X, Section RR–SS (fig. 50)

Pit X

With the exception of (d) in Group L 9 the sherds would appear to be similar to pottery from Ditch A and the well. A second- or early third-century date would therefore be reasonable. The colour-coated sherd (d) may be later, since this type of fabric is very common in the fourth-century groups. However it should be noted that the sherd was of a slightly harder fabric than the fourth-century types so it is possible that it too is dated to the late second or early third century.

Layer 9

      (a)   Pie dish in hard, dark grey fabric. Form similar to 166.

      (b)   Jar in pale buff fabric and surfaces. Form similar to 213, but with slight carination on inside rim.

      (c)   Jar in brown-grey fabric and surfaces. Rim form similar to 93.

      (d)   Base sherd with footring in pale grey fabric with orange surfaces. Red colour-coat firing darker red on interior than exterior. Rouletted decoration on interior.

Layer 7

      (a)   Bowl in hard, dark grey fabric with orange surfaces. Lustrous red colour-coat. Form similar to 352.

Layer 4

      (a)   Pie dish in hard, sandy, dark grey fabric with dark grey burnished surfaces. Wave decoration on exterior. Form similar to 281.

      (b)   Squat pie dish in hard, fine, sandy, light grey fabric with dark grey surfaces. Form similar to 277, but with an outward curved external profile.

(c)   Bowl in hard, sandy, grey fabric with black burnished surfaces. Form similar to 293, but body thicker.

(d)   Bowl in pale grey fabric with dull red-orange surfaces. Traces of red colour-coat. Rim sherd only — form similar to 270.

(e)   Sherd from lid of Castor ware box. Off-white, creamy fabric with dark chocolate slip. Rouletted.

(f)   Jar in hard, grey fabric with brown-orange surfaces. Form similar to 220, but not so heavy.

(g)   Mortarium in pinkish-white fabric with off-white surfaces. Form similar to 259, but rim slimmer. Very worn.

Pottery from the corn drying oven, Section CC–DD (fig. 26)

The sherds from the stoke-hole of the corn drying oven were in some cases from the same vessels as sherds in the upper levels. This was probably due to the collapse of the structure over pottery thrown into the flue, the latter being used as a rubbish dump. The pottery was mainly of late second-century forms. The only pot not represented in pottery groups from elsewhere was a flagon in orange sandy fabric (described below, no. 422). Sherds from this vessel were found in layers L 4 and L 3. From the pottery evidence the oven was probably in use during the second half of the second century.

Layer 4 — black charcoal layer in stoke-hole and eastern extent of flue

(a)   Jar in hard, pale grey fabric and surfaces, burnished externally. Vertical scored lines on body. Form similar to 62.

(b)   Jar in brown-grey fabric with dark grey slip on exterior. Form similar to 68.

(c)   Jar in pale buff fabric and surfaces. Burnt on exterior. Form similar to 226.

(d)   Pie dish in hard, fine, grey, sandy fabric with black surfaces. Burnished interior. Form similar to 172.

(e)   Small pie dish in fine, dark grey fabric with paler grey surfaces. Traces of pale grey colour coat on exterior. Form similar to 186.

(f)   Fragment from shoulder of a Castor ware beaker. Whitish fabric with chocolate slip. Rouletted.

422.   (g)   Flagon in fine, orange, sandy fabric. Drawing mainly reconstruction, vessel very fragmented. It probably had a handle.

UNASSOCIATED POST-VILLA POTTERY
By Stephen Moorhouse
(fig. 112)

423.   Rim from a cooking pot with slightly thickened everted neck in a hard-fired, fine, sandy, grey-brown fabric with evidence of an applied strip below the rim. This vessel belongs to the class of pottery defined by Dunning as Early Medieval Ware[1] and expanded by Hurst,[2] who demonstrated that the type dates to the period *c.* A.D. 1050 – *c.* 1150 and has a wide distribution in

[1] G. C. Dunning in 'Anglo-Saxon Pottery: A Symposium', *Med. Arch.*, III (1959), 44.

[2] J. G. Hurst, 'The kitchen area of Northolt manor, Middlesex', *Med. Arch.*, V (1961), 259–61.

southern England. Biddle[1] has shown that the type went out of use by *c.* A.D. 1100 at Therfield, Hertfordshire; the present sherd can be best paralleled by the examples of this type at Therfield[2] and a date in the second half of the eleventh and possibly extending into the twelfth century could be suggested.

424.   Base from a Westerwald vessel, the form of which is difficult to determine on the size of the sherd. Fine, hard fired, buff stoneware with a lustrous deep cobalt blue band in the groove above the base, under an all-over light grey glaze. Difficult to date but the quality of the sherd would suggest a nineteenth- rather than an eighteenth-century date.

425.   Neck in a hard, fine grey stoneware with an all-over dull brown glaze. The rim comes from a common type of 'ink' bottle with a flat base, cylindrical sides varying in height and a flared rim as in the present example. Probably first half of the nineteenth century.

426.   Large sherd incorporating rim to base, from a platter or shallow plate, in a fine, smooth, sandy, pinkish fabric with internal deep yellow ochre to brown glaze. The plate has been fired in an inverted position in the kiln for glaze has gathered on the top of the rim. Probably seventeenth century.

THE GRAFFITI

By R. P. WRIGHT, F.S.A.

(fig. 113)

(a)   Base of pie-dish in dark grey fabric. The graffito reads . . .]ithous. The name Peirithous would fit, and probably belonged to a Greek slave: for an example about A.D. 200 see *Inscriptiones Graecae*, III, 1169. The other examples of this name and any others with this termination seem to have been used only in mythological contexts. From soot filling in Room 10 (cf. *J.R.S.*, LIV (1964), 185, no. 48).

(b)   Flanged bowl in grey fabric. On two fragments (which do not join) a reversed N has been cut below the rim. From soot filling in Room 10 (cf. *Brit.*, II (1971), 296, no. 47).

(c)   Grey bowl. Graffito reads TARE[NTINVS. No trace of the crossbar of T remains, but the vertical may have been taller. Found in hypocaust channel of Room 35.

(d)   Sherd from the shoulder of a flagon in orange fabric. I read this as . . .]MM[. . . The four apexes are so close that it is not likely to be . . .]AMA[. . . From occupation level associated with Period 6, to south of western wing, Building A.

(e)   Rim from a Castor ware beaker. NATV[. . . The V has been cut twice. Sealed beneath tessellated pavement in Room 28 (cf. *Brit.*, II (1971), 296 no. 46).

(f)   Fragment from the wall of a Drag. 18/31. . . .]MV[. . . Filling of southern stoke-hole, Room 35.

[1] Martin Biddle 'The Excavation of a Motte and Bailey Castle at Therfield, Hertfordshire' *J.B.A.A.*, XXVII (1964), 70–1.   [2] Ibid., 75, fig. 20, nos. 3 and 4.

(g)   Fragment from the wall of a Drag. 33 cup with . . .]MV[. . . incised on the outside. It may be the same name as that which occurs on f. Found on east side of Building A, but in earlier context than f.

(h)   Sherd from the shoulder of a jar in hard off-white fabric with VINB[. . . incised on the outside. From filling of Ditch I (*Brit.*, I (1970), 315, no. 47).

(i)   On a fragment from the rim of a flanged dish . . .]VIN[. . . has been incised. It may be the same name as that which occurs on jar h. Filling of water leat (*Brit.*, I (1970), 314, no. 51).

(j)   Part of the rim and wall of a bowl. A graffito cut on the exterior when the vessel was inverted reads ΛNN, an abbreviation of one of several *nomina* or *cognomina*. The cutter added three vertical strokes to the second letter and two cross-strokes to the third letter. No more than three letters were incised. Published pottery no. 133. From Ditch I (*Brit.*, I (1970), 314, no. 42).

(k)   On part of the rim and wall of flanged bowl ꓱN[has been cut. Upper filling of water leat.

(l)   Base sherd of bowl. The graffito reads]INGENTI. From chalk quarry, Pit V (*Brit.*, II (1971), 296, no. 45).

(m)   For an additional item with a graffito reading N̄II see bronze fragment SF 41 (fig. 55).

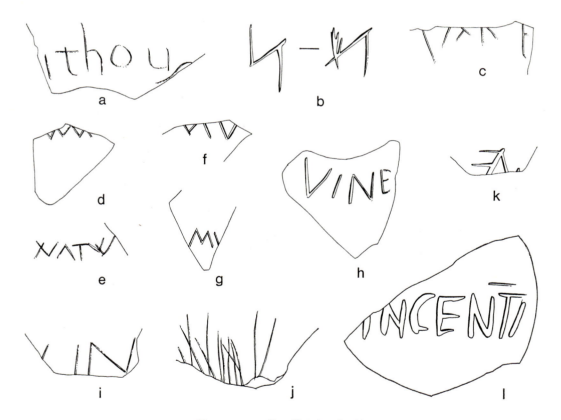

FIG. 113.   Graffiti (scale ½)

ANIMAL BONES

By R. A. Harcourt

Introduction

The bones from this site were dated to the first, second and fourth centuries A.D. There was no clear-cut division between those of the first and second century so these were amalgamated and the fourth-century material studied separately. The only detectable difference between the two groups, which may anyway be due to chance, was that in the earlier group more different species were represented.

Description of Material

All measurements are in millimetres and those of extremities of long bones are taken across the articular surfaces. In all the farm animals all parts of the skeleton were present. The species represented from the first and second centuries were cattle, sheep, pig, horse, cat, dog, and the three species of deer. All these, except the cat and fallow deer, were also present in the fourth-century material. Bird bones were found in both groups.

TABLE I

Minimum Numbers of each Species (domestic)

Century	No. Frags.	Cattle	Sheep	Pig	Horse	Cat	Dog
First and second	666	8	15	9	2	2	4
Fourth	575	12	7	5	2	–	3

Cattle

Size.   The bones from this site do not reflect any change in the size of the cattle throughout the period of occupation of the villa.

The metapodial measurements shown in Table II indicate animals of 45–53 in. (115–36 cm.) in height at the shoulder. The ratio of metatarsal: metacarpal in cattle is approximately 1 : 0.87. From this the metacarpal corresponding to the steer metatarsal (254 mm.) would be 220 mm. This is considerably (17 mm.) more than the longest metacarpal from the Roman period quoted by Jewell[1] and both it and the metatarsal on which it is based are also bigger than any known to the writer from that period. The animal represented may just have been an unusually large individual and not necessarily typical of the local cattle population.

[1] P. A. Jewell, 'Cattle from British Archaeological Sites' in C. A. Mourant and F. E. Zeuner (eds.), *Man and Cattle* (British Anthrop. Inst. Occasional Paper no. 18, 1964), p. 80.

TABLE II
Measurements of Cattle Bones

	t.l.	p.w.	m.s.d.	d.w.
Humerus*	281	—	45	62
	—	—	—	68–83 (7)
Radius	288	—	42	64
	—	70–8 (6)	—	53–63 (2)
Tibia	348	82	41	55
	—	—	—	44–60 (12)
1st Phalanx	—	25–35 (12)	—	—

Astragalus   64–70 (6) lateral length

Horn Cores†   110–221 (11) basal circumference

* To head only.

† Only three were unbroken and their lengths (outer curvature with basal circumference in brackets) were 240 (185); 150 (180); 95 (110)

t.l. = total length   p.w. = proximal width
m.s.d. = mid shaft diameter   d.w. = distal width

Figures in brackets refer to numbers of specimens.

TABLE III
Measurements of Cattle Metapodials

	t.l.	p.w.	m.s.d.	d.w.	m.s.d. %	Sex	Height cms.	in.
Metacarpals	192	60	39	67	20.3	Bull	120	47
	193	56	33	60	17.1	Cow	116	45
	204	65	40	66	19.6	Bull	130	51
	—	50–68 (8)	—	52–72 (9)	—	—	—	—
Metatarsals	208	—	30	60	14.4	Bull	115	45
	220	53	27	58	12.3	Cow	118	46
	254	56	35	68	13.8	Steer	136	53

m.s.d. % = m.s.d. as % of total length.

Sex determinations are based on metapodial indices and a graph of these indices against total length.[1]

The heights have been calculated by the method of Fock.[2]

[1] Margaret M. Howard in Mourant and Zeuner, op. cit., p. 91.

[2] J. Fock, *Metrische Untersuchungen an Metapodien einiger europäischer Rinderrassen* (Diss. Munich, 1966).

s

Age

The long bone epiphyses were grouped into early and late fusing moieties and the number of unfused epiphyses in the early fusing group, indicating juvenile animals, and fused epiphyses in the late fusing group, indicating fully mature animals, were each counted and expressed as a percentage of the total of its group. Although the sample from this collection was small, the results, using this method, indicate that 54% of the cattle represented were at least fully mature at death and that only 11% were juvenile. The intermediate young adult group comprised, by subtraction, the remaining 35%.

The eruption and state of wear of the teeth provided similar evidence. There were 31 mandibles and of these one (3%) had only the first molar erupted, in two (6%) the second was erupted, and in the remaining 28 (91%) the third molar was fully erupted. In seventeen (55%) all three pillars were well worn and in six (19%) they were very heavily worn, so much so that the pits had completely disappeared and the teeth had lost the high crowned appearance characteristic of cattle. It is at least possible that the beasts from which these came were ten to fifteen years old. Cattle of this age are a commonplace in parts of Scotland and in Cornwall at the present day.[1]

Two mandibles from two different animals had only five cheek teeth instead of the usual six.

Sheep

In spite of the number of animals represented (Table I) the actual number of specimens from sheep was too small for analysis of the age structure.

TABLE IV

Measurements of Sheep Bones

	t.l.	p.w.	m.s.d.	d.w.	m.s.d. %
Humerus	—	—	—	25–8 (5)	—
Tibia	—	—	—	21–3 (9)	—
Metacarpal	126	20	13	—	10.3
	133	21	14	24	10.5
	133	22	14	24	10.5
Metatarsal	128	18	11	21	8.6
	128	20	11	—	8.6
	131	17	10	—	7.65
	135	18	10	21	7.4
	144	20	12	23	8.35
	144	21	12	23	8.35

[1] Personal communications from W. W. Robertson (1967) and G. B. Taylor (1968).

The bone dimensions of sheep seem to remain almost unaltered throughout the archaeological record and indicate small slender animals. Some specimens, rather bigger than those from other periods, are however found on Roman sites, including this one.

Horse

The measurements (Table V) indicate ponies of about 13–14 hands (132–45 cm.). There were also numerous teeth and a few vertebrae.

TABLE V

Measurements of Horse Bones

	t.l.	p.w.	m.s.d.	d.w.
Humerus	—	—	—	65–70 (3)
Radius	—	—	—	63
Tibia	320	87	37	49
Phalanx 1	80	48	31	42
	82	51	32	44
Metatarsal	252	48	29	47
	280	54	34	53

Pig

This animal was very poorly represented in spite of the minimum numbers as shown in Table I. Those from the early group were all immature, probably not more than six months old, and in the later group the only specimens of note were two from a large boar.

Dog

In the early group there was a nearly complete skeleton from an animal of about 18 in. (47 cm.) shoulder height. Three other individuals were represented only by mandibles and their measurements indicate an approximately similar size. A single small humerus suggests a shoulder height of about 13 in. (34 cm.).

Also from this group there came two specimens, a femur and tibia, both, unfortunately, with their distal ends missing, but of a unique slenderness. The writer has examined dog bones from some seventy sites, thirty-four of these being of the Romano-British period but has so far encountered no bone of less than 8 mm. midshaft diameter. These two were respectively 5.7 mm. and 5.8 mm. in diameter and closely matched those of a Maltese Terrier in the Osteology Department of the British Museum and of a Pomeranian in the writer's own collection.

Two animals are represented in the fourth-century group, one of about 22 in. (56 cm.) in height and the other, with a mandibular tooth row length of only 50 mm., much smaller.

A wide range of size is a marked feature of dogs from the Roman period.

TABLE VI

Measurements of Dog Bones

FIRST/SECOND CENTURY

(a)   *Complete skeleton*

Humerus	146–11	Dorsum of axis	41
Radius	144–11	Greatest length of mandible	130
Femur	153–11	*Mandibular tooth row	67
Ulna	167.	Lower carnassial	21

(b)   *Others*

Humerus	101–8	Mandibular tooth row	55 : 69 : 69 : 71
Femur	†80–5.7		
Tibia	†82–5.8		

FOURTH CENTURY

Femur	188–14	Mandibular tooth row	50
		Lower carnassial	15.5

* Molars and premolars only.

† Total lengths estimated.

The total length and midshaft diameter of the long bones is given.

Cat

As indicated in Table I the remains of this animal were found only in the early material and comprised an almost complete skeleton from the well together with various other fragments. The lengths and midshaft diameters of the long bones were: humerus, 112–18; radius, 110–17.2; ulna, 128; femur, 124–8.4; tibia, 133–7.5. The mandible measured 56 mm. and the lower carnassial 7.9 mm. These long bone dimensions indicate a large animal but the carnassial is relatively small. There is so much variability in the size of domestic and feral cats[1] and so much overlap between domestic and wild cats[2] that differentiation by size alone is probably not valid. It seems reasonable to assume that in the Roman period and thereafter any cat remains, whether bone or footprints, found near buildings are those of the domestic cat.

Red deer

Not more than one animal could be identified from the earlier period but from the later there were three or more. None of the material was of particular note with the exception of various portions of antler which showed very distinct saw marks. Similar marks were found

---

[1] R. A. Harcourt in N. Smedley and Elizabeth J. Owles, 'A Romano-British Bath-House at Stonham Aspal', *P.S.I.A.*, xx, 3 (1966), 221 (animal bones, p. 248).

[2] K. Branigan and Judith E. King, 'A Roman Cat from Latimer Villa, Chesham', *Annals and Mag. Nat. Hist.*, Ser. 13, VIII (1965), 461.

on an antler from the Stonham Aspal bath house[1] and also on some from the deep Roman well at Findon which is still being excavated.[2]

Fallow deer

The only specimens were a right humerus and radius, both broken off short and very probably from the same elbow joint. The fallow deer is always said to have been introduced to Britain by the Romans and it certainly does not appear on earlier sites. Indeed, it does not seem particularly common even in the Roman period.

Roe deer provided only a few specimens, mostly fragmentary.

Birds

The species present were common buzzard, raven, crow or rook, duck of about mallard size and domestic fowl. This collection is typical of those from Roman sites.

Discussion

The range of bone sizes of cattle in the Roman period has been shown to be wide[3] and if the large specimens already referred to from this site together with the humerus (83 mm. distal width) shown in Table II are included then the range becomes even greater.

The importation of improved stock is traditionally ascribed to the Romans, without, it would seem, much in the way of evidence to support this belief. It seems more likely that improved methods of stock rearing and nutrition may have been introduced, as a consequence of which bigger animals began to appear. Animals as small as those of the earlier Iron Age persisted but this can be explained by the assumption that, in Roman times, some farmers and stockowners tried out new ideas, others, ignoring the manifest advantages, did not. The situation is no different today.

On only two sites known to the writer have sheep bones bigger than those from this collection been found in any period up to medieval times and they were both of the Roman period. At the East Malling villa there was a metacarpal of 137 mm.[4] and in the Findon well[5] a metatarsal of 149 mm.

Acknowledgements

The identity of the two very slender dog specimens was confirmed by Dr Juliet Clutton-Brock and Mr D. Bramwell examined and reported on the bird remains.

---

[1] See p. 260, n. 1, above.
[2] H. Pearman, 'The Excavation of a Roman Well at Findon in Sussex', *Kent Arch. Rev.*, no. 13 (1968), 16.
[3] Page 256, n. 1.

[4] R. A. Harcourt in A. Wacher, *The Roman Villa at East Malling* (in preparation).
[5] See n. 2.

THE MOLLUSC SHELLS

(This report is based on information kindly supplied by Professor A. J. Cain and A. Featherstone)

Snails from Pit O, Room 7 (A very large number of snails were found in the pit, and about 100 were sent for examination).

These all belong to the species *Avianta arbustorum* (L) which is a close relation of the two British species of *Cepaea* and closely resembles them in its ecology. The principal difference is that *A. arbustorum* prefers damper habitats, lush vegetation in ditches or along streams, dense herbage in regions of high rainfall, or notably damp woods. It can occur in almost marshy ground. The eggs are rather gelatinous and laid under light cover on the surface of the ground, like those of slugs, not like those of *Cepaea* which are hard-shelled and nearly always buried — not suitable in this respect for marshy ground.

Over 600 of this species, together with about 300 *C. nemoralis* occurred as whole, unbroken shells in a small pit with midden refuse at Rainsborough Camp[1] and were probably collected for food and boiled. They were in far too high a density to occur naturally, and were all, or very nearly all, whole.[2]

Snails from the floor of the bathing pool

These were identified as belonging to the species *Planorbis planorbis* (Linné) by A. Featherstone who obtained further confirmation from Dr M. P. Kerney.

Planorbis planorbis is described as preferring hard, weedy waters, mainly ditches and small ponds. It still occurs in the River Gade near to the site, and further upstream at Great Gaddesden.

---

[1] *P.P.S.*, XXXIII (1967), 207.

[2] Although the snail shells in Pit O were also of a high density, and were also mainly whole, there was no other midden material, only a uniform chalky brown soil (D.S.N.).

CHARCOAL AND WOOD SAMPLES
By G. C. MORGAN

Species		Location of Find	Estimated minimum diameter
Oak (*Quercus* sp.)			
	1	Filling of leat N. of bathing pool	40 mm.
	2	Filling of leat N. of bathing pool	50 mm.
Brushwood preserved in waterlogged conditions	3	Floor of bathing pool	
	4		
	5	Filling of Ditch 2	200 mm.
	6	Filling of Ditch 2	150 mm.+
	7	Filling of Ditch 2	90 mm.
	8	Ditch 1 beneath Building A	100 mm.+
	9	Ditch 1 beneath Building A	100 mm.+
	10	E. of Building A	15 mm.
	11	E. of Building A	20 mm.
	12	E. of Building A	80 mm.
	13	Inner courtyard, Building A	150 mm.
	14	Water conduit S. of Building A	150 mm.+
	15	S. of Building A	15 mm.
	16	R.–B. turf level of S. outer courtyard	40 mm.
	17	Post destruction level over kitchen area, Building C	35 mm.
	18	Upper filling of chalk quarry, Pit V	
Hazel (*Corylus avellana*)			
	19	Filling of leat N. of bathing pool	100 mm.
	20	Floor of bathing pool	10 mm.
	21	Northern courtyard	25 mm.
	22	Ash probably originating from stoke-hole in Room 10	25 mm.
	23	N. stoke-hole, Room 35	35 mm.
	24	Pit L beneath N.E. corner of Building D	55 mm.
	25	Pit L beneath N.E. corner of Building D	35 mm.
	26	Ploughsoil over Pit A, southern courtyard	30 mm.
	27	Destruction material over Building C	15 mm.
	28	Upper filling of well	35 mm.
Crataegus sp. (probably Hawthorn)			
	29	Destruction rubble over Room 35	40 mm.
	30	Ash probably originating from stoke-hole in Room 10	30 mm.
	31	E. of Building A	20 mm.
	32	Ditch I beneath inner courtyard, Building A	30 mm.
	33	E. of Building D	50 mm.

Species		Location of Find	Estimated minimum diameter
Field Maple (*Acer campestre*)			
	34	Filling of Room 20	12 mm.
	35	Ditch I beneath inner courtyard	60 mm.
Ash (*Fraxinus excelsior*)	36	Ditch I beneath inner courtyard	100 mm.
Poplar (*Populus* sp.)			
	37	Stoke-hole of corn-drying oven	50 mm.

REPORT ON THE SLAG

By G. C. MORGAN

Sample No.	Description and report	Location of find
1	Base of pot with vesicular iron slag attached. Iron present in quantity, copper present. Traces of tin and lead. The presence of copper inside the pot may indicate melting or smelting activity.	Early occupation W. of Building A.
2	Fragment of pot with vesicular iron slag attached. Bronze globule inclusions. Iron present in quantity, copper present. Traces of tin and lead. Similar to sample no. 1.	West side of Building A in upper filling of Ditch I.
3	Iron slag: Ferrite showing heavy twinning and traces of subsequent annealing. Probably part of a bloom.	Cobbled surface of N. courtyard.
4	Vitrified tile and slag.	Occupation in Room 20.

Sample No.	Description and report	Location of find
5–34	*Vesicular iron slag of fayalite type.*	
5–12	1 sample dumped whilst almost molten.	Early levels east of Building A.
13–16	Dumped whilst almost molten. No. 13 contains spheroidal iron. Completely unworked as would be produced in furnace before the bloom-making stage.	Filling of water leat N. of bathing pool.
17–19		Early levels south of Building A.
20	Smelting residue. Dumped whilst almost molten.	Filling of Ditch I to west of Building A.
21–2		Fouth-century destruction west of Building A.
23–4	1 sample dumped whilst almost molten.	Destruction material over Building A.
25	Iron concretion.	Ditch I, beneath Room 35.
26		Robber trench E. wall of Room 20.
27	Nail inclusion.	Occupation, Room 20.
28–9		Early levels in N. courtyard.
30		Fourth-century occupation in N. courtyard.
31	Smelting residue. Dumped whilst almost molten.	Clay pit W of Building B.
32	Smelting residue. Dumped whilst almost molten.	Post-destruction material over Building C.
33		Drain from Room 13.
34		Associated with timber building beneath Building E.
35–59	*Vesicular iron slag.*	
35–9	Dumped whilst almost molten.	Early occupation E. of Building A.
40–1	Dumped whilst almost molten.	Eastern corridor, Building A.
42		Fourth-century material E. of Building A.
43–4		Destruction material over Building A.
45	Traces of wood.	Occupation, Room 20.
46		Stoke-hole, Room 35.
47		Beneath tessellated pavement, Room 28.

Sample No.	Description and report	Location of find
48–50	1 sample with high iron content, partly smelted (see also sample no. 3).	Fourth-century occupation, N. courtyard.
51	Vitrified material with slag.	Rubble W. of Room 11.
52	Conglomerate, with iron nails. Dumped whilst almost molten.	Water leat N. of bathing pool.
53	Traces of wood (Hazel).	Filling of bathing pool.
54		Ditch I beneath Building A.
55		Early levels S. of Building A.
56	Traces of iron.	Building E.
57	Traces of wood residues.	Fourth-century occupation E. of Building D.
58–9		Fourth-century filling of chalk quarry, Pit V.

Distribution of slag

A distribution of the samples submitted for identification was made. The samples were divided into 8 groups (findspots), subdivided into 2, one from levels probably pre-dating the construction of Building A, and the other from levels post-dating its construction. The percentage of samples is given.

Groups	% of samples in early deposits	% of samples in later deposits
Under or over Building A	6.7	11.8
Room 20	—	5.08
Northern Courtyard	3.3	10.1
E. of Building A	22.03	1.6
S. of Building A	6.7	—
W. of Building A	5.08	3.3
Water leat	—	8.4
Miscellaneous	10.1	5.08
	53.91	45.36

The majority of the fragments submitted for identification are smelting residues showing that ironworking was being practised in the vicinity. It appears from the distribution that this practise was mainly confined to the earlier phases of occupation, but the discovery of slag in Room 20 associated with hearths, and the discovery of slag in the northern courtyard and in the water leat, would also suggest that ironworking was still being practised in the fourth century.   [D.S.N.]

INDEX

PLATE I

General view of site looking east

PLATE II

a. Period 1 structure (Room 17) with associated chalk floor, quern and oven.
View north

b. Southern view of the Period 1 *caldarium* and *tepidarium* (Rooms 1 and 2).
The niches in the division wall were cut later

PLATE III

a. Period 3 western extension to the bath house (Room 9). A variety of re-used tiles can be seen in the southern apse. View west

b. View south of the Period 3 extension (Room 8) to Room 7. A later pit (Pit O) can be seen cutting the corner of the room

PLATE IV

b. Decorated flue-tile from drain shown on Pl. IV*a*

a. Drain of re-used flue-tiles running beneath the Period 3 floor over earlier Room 1. View north

c. Drain emerging from east wall of Room 1. The 'dog-leg' in this wall is also visible. In the foreground is a flint foundation associated with the water leat. View west

a. Stoke-hole in Room 10, cut by Period 7 post- and stake-holes. View east

b. Imitation ashlar rendering on Period 3 division wall between Rooms 23 and 24. View west

PLATE VI

a. View north of Room 20 showing earlier Ditch I, bases of piers, and beam slots for raised floor. The southern wall of the room (demolished in Period 5) can be seen in the foreground

b. Detail of base of pier in Room 20. View east

PLATE VII

a. View north of Ovens A and B, Room 28

b. View south of Ovens C, D and E in Room 28. Oven E is cut by a
Period 5 wall

PLATE VIII

a. Water cistern beneath later gatehouse. The line of a water conduit from the well can be seen on the left. View west

b. Post-holes blocking north-west corridor of Building B. A water conduit with an iron pipe collar cuts the floor. View north

PLATE IX

b. Northern extent of hypocaust in Room 35. The original outer corridor wall of Building A runs beneath the western wall of the main flue. The Period 4 divisions in the corridor are also visible. View north

a. Ovens in northern corridor of Building B. View west

PLATE X

a. North-west corner of plunge-bath (Room 13). View north

b. Plunge-bath (Room 13). Floors of Periods 4, 5 and 6, with drain beneath.
View north

PLATE XI

b. Settlement of northern wall of Room 12.
View east

a. Sleeper beam and collapsed wall-plaster over eastern corridor wall.
View east

PLATE XII

a. View south of Building C. The post-holes of the Period 7 stockade
are on the left

b. View west of corn-drying oven

PLATE XIII

a. Period 5 rebuilding over narrower Period 3 corridor wall. The channel on the left is the hypocaust flue in Room 29. View east

b. Period 5 extension to Room 20. The door into the room is in the far wall. View west

PLATE XIV

a. View east of door into Room 20 and charred timber drain

b. Oven in south-west corner of Room 20. Collapsed voussoirs in foreground.
View south

PLATE XV

a. Y-shaped hypocaust in Room 27. View south

b. General view north of west side of Building A. Room 27 is in the distance

PLATE XVI

DAVID S. NEAL 1967 FT GADEBRIDGE PARK 1966

Reconstruction drawing of mosaic in Room 27

PLATE XVII

View south of Building D

PLATE XVIII

a. Receptacle for ash from hypocaust furnace in Room 26. View south

b. Oven in Building D. View east

PLATE XIX

b. Oven in Building E. View south

c. Slate-lined cist in Building E. View south

a. View east of Building E

PLATE XX

a. Swastika-shaped hypocaust in Room 18. A double Y-shaped hypocaust is in the foreground. View west

b. Swastika-shaped hypocaust cutting earlier tessellated pavement. View north

PLATE XXI

a. Overall view of Room 20 as visible in Period 6. View west

b. North wall of Room 20 with lattice decoration on wall-plaster

PLATE XXII

a. View south of hypocaust in Room 35, and Y-shaped hypocaust in Room 29. The northern end of the large hypocaust is shown on Pl. IX*b*

b. South-west wing of Building A. The lower level of the courtyard is in the foreground. View west

PLATE XXIII

a. Detail of hypocaust flues in Room 35. The earlier Ditch I runs beneath the room. View west

b. Stoke-hole in north-west wall of Room 35. View east

PLATE XXIV

a. View west of the bathing pool steps

b. Bathing pool. View north

PLATE XXV

b. Holes in seat along north wall of the bathing pool. View north

c. Tile-mortar sill of overflow in south wall of the bathing pool. View south

a. Water inlet leading into the north-west corner of the bathing pool. View north

PLATE XXVI

Post-holes and drain cutting cobbled surface of the northern courtyard.
View south

PLATE XXVII

b. Bronze head of Medusa

a. Reconstruction of the ceiling-plaster fragments found in the well